The Modernist Cult of Ugliness ∾

The Modernist Cult of Ugliness ∿

Aesthetic and Gender Politics

Lesley Higgins

palgrave
macmillan

First published 2002 by PALGRAVE MACMILLAN™
175 Fifth Avenue, New York, N.Y. 10010 and
Houndmills, Basingstoke, Hampshire, England RG21 6XS.
Companies and representatives throughout the world.

PALGRAVE MACMILLAN is the global academic imprint of the Palgrave
Macmillan division of St. Martin's Press, LLC and of Palgrave Macmillan
Ltd. Macmillan® is a registered trademark in the United States, United
Kingdom and other countries. Palgrave is a registered trademark in the
European Union and other countries.

ISBN 0–312–24037–6 hardback

Library of Congress Cataloging-in-Publication Data
available at the Library of Congress.

A catalogue record for this book is available from the British Library.

Design by Letra Libre, Inc.

First edition: August 2002
10 9 8 7 6 5 4 3 2 1

Printed in the United States of America

for
Olga Higgins

Contents

For I am homesick after mine own kind
And ordinary people touch me not.
And I am homesick
After mine own kind that know, and feel
And have some breath for beauty and the arts.

—Ezra Pound, "In Durance"

I have been reading some of your work lately. I enjoyed the article on the Vortex (please tell me who Kandinsky is). I distrust and detest Aesthetics, when it cuts loose from the Object, and vapours in the void, but you have not done that. The closer one keeps to the Artist's discussion of his technique the better, I think, and the only kind of art worth talking about is the art one happens to like. There can be no contemplative or easychair aesthetics, I think; only the aesthetics of the person who is about to do something.

—T. S. Eliot to Ezra Pound, February 1915

[L]iterature becomes progressively more differentiated from the discourse of ideas, and encloses itself within a radical intransitivity; it becomes detached from all values that were able to keep it in general circulation during the Classical age (taste, pleasure, naturalness, truth), and creates within its own space everything that will ensure a ludic denial of them (the scandalous, the ugly, the impossible). . . . [S]o there is nothing for it to do but to curve back in a perpetual return upon itself [.]

—*Michel Foucault,* The Order of Things

The forms of artistic production available to the artist play an active part in constructing the work of art. In this sense, the ideas and values of the artist, themselves socially formed, are mediated by literary and cultural conventions of style, language, genre and aesthetic vocabulary. Just as the artist works with the technical materials of artistic production, so he or she also works with the available materials of aesthetic convention. This means that in reading cultural products, we need to understand their logic of construction and the particular aesthetic codes involved in their formation.

—*Janet Wolff,* The Social Production of Art

Acknowledgments

I have been fortunate to receive unwavering support from those closest to me and timely assistance from complete strangers who have made my research possible. Funding for various stages of this project has been provided by the Social Sciences and Humanities Research Council of Canada and the Office of Research Administration, York University.

Institutions that have opened their doors and archives include the Berg Collection, New York Public Library; Bodleian Library, University of Oxford; British Library, London; Centre for Whistler Studies and the Hunterian Art Gallery, University of Glasgow; King's College Library and Archives, Cambridge University; National Library of Scotland, Edinburgh; Scott and Frost Libraries, York University.

Long before I began thinking about the "Cult of Ugliness," I learned how to think critically about Ruskin and Pater from Dr. Stella Slade. Since the early 1980s, Dr. Norman MacKenzie's insights and scholarly example have been inestimable.

Kristi Long has supported the book since she first read about it. Enormous thanks are owing to her and her staff, especially Roee Paz and Meg Weaver, to an insightful Anonymous Reviewer, and to Karin Bolender.

Sylvia Vance's discerning editorial advice and influence have been crucial. Elicia Clements has been an exemplary research assistant for several years, always resourceful and accommodating. Jennifer Orme also deserves thanks, as well as Stephanie Hart and Kerry Doyle.

How do I thank the following? For encouragement beyond words, and the example of her intellectual élan and personal commitment to others, Marie-Christine Leps. For everything from travel arrangements and timely jokes to knowing when I needed care the most, Michael Suarez, S. J. For friendship that sustains, always, Mary Gelinas. For scholarly advice and kindness, Laurel Brake, John Conlon, Billie Inman, Leslie Sanders, and Carolyn Williams. I have also depended on Beryl Batts, Bryan Bonnah, Cathy Farbiak, Graham Pugin, and Liam Richardson.

Even before I had words, my parents were encouraging me to express myself, and teaching me to define and pursue what's most challenging. This book is dedicated to them: to the exceptional Olga Higgins, and the sweetest dad, Laurence Higgins (1923–1997).

≈ ≈ ≈

ILLUSTRATIONS. Wyndham Lewis, *Two Missionaries*, 1917, © V & A Picture Library, Victoria and Albert Museum, London. James McNeill Abbott Whistler, *Nocturne in Black and Gold: The Falling Rocket*, c. 1875 © Detroit Institute of Arts (Gift of Dexter M. Ferry Jr.), Detroit, Michigan (photograph © 2001 The Detroit Institute of Arts). Whistler, *Symphony in Flesh Colour and Pink: Portrait of Mrs Frances Leyland*, c. 1871–1874 © The Frick Collection, New York. Whistler, *Symphony in White, No.1: The White Girl*, 1862 © National Gallery of Art (Harris Whittemore Collection), Washington, D. C.; photograph © 2002 Board of Trustees, National Gallery of Art. Whistler, *Symphony in White, No. 2: The Little White Girl*, 1864 © Tate, London 2001. Whistler, *Variations in Flesh Colour and Green: The Balcony* © Freer Gallery of Art, Smithsonian Institution, Washington, D. C. (Gift of Charles Lang Freer).

Abbreviations

P/EP	Ezra Pound, *Collected Early Poems*
Per	Ezra Pound, *Personae*
P/L	Timothy Materer, ed., *Pound/Lewis: The Letters of Ezra Pound and Wyndham Lewis*
PP	Walter Pater, *Plato and Platonism*
P/Q	Timothy Materer, ed., *The Selected Letters of Ezra Pound to John Quinn, 1915–1924*
P/SP	William Cookson, ed., *Ezra Pound: Selected Prose 1909–1965*
P/SPo	Ezra Pound, *Selected Poetry*
SofC	Garland Greever and Joseph Bachelor, eds., *The Soul of the City: An Urban Anthology*
SE	T. S. Eliot, *Selected Essays*
SW	T. S. Eliot, *The Sacred Wood*
Tarr	Wyndham Lewis, *Tarr*
TAS	Henry James, *The American Scene*
TCC	T. S. Eliot, *To Criticize the Critic and Other Writings*
TR	Walter Pater, *The Renaissance*
UPUC	T. S. Eliot, *The Use of Poetry and the Use of Criticism*
VMP	T. S. Eliot, *The Varieties of Metaphysical Poetry*
WJR	E. T. Cook and Alexander Wedderburn, eds., *The Works of John Ruskin*, 39 Vols.
WLA	Wyndham Lewis, *Wyndham Lewis the Artist*

List of Illustrations

Introduction

In 1922, the same modernist annus mirabilis in which *Ulysses, The Waste Land,* and *Jacob's Room* were published, the following conversation was featured in Alice Herbert's now-forgotten novel *Heaven and Charing Cross:*

> "Honesty is fine [observed Rev. Browne]. One grants [the new generation] that; but one can't agree that it's the only beauty. It seems to me that artists—everybody—think it is."
>
> "Beauty is truth—truth beauty," murmured Martin [Burke].
>
> "Yes, of course. But there are lovely aspects of things to be truthful about. You moderns despise them, and only care to be truthful about the ugly ones. You are always 'facing facts,' but they are invariably ugly facts. Why doesn't one of you face a symmetrical fact in his picture or a melodious one in his music or a musical one in his poetry? Surely the *only* truthful beauty doesn't lie in thin green women with crooked noses, and music that takes care not to come within a mile of a sweet tune, and poetry that takes you all you know to scan, and is all about the Tube lifts and things?" (Herbert 118–119)

Rev. Browne's sentiments were echoed, vehemently and often, in the very real letters that John B. Yeats sent to his son, William. In March 1913, for example, he issued a general warning about the imperilled condition of beauty: "Do you notice how busy people always like ugliness. It has for them the actuality of a stench. It takes prolonged effort, and prolonged leisure to begin to enjoy beauty. The modern doctrine of strenuousness so popular with democracies is fatal to Beauty" (J. B. Yeats 157). In March 1918, the elder Yeats was much more specific in his admonitions:

> The poets loved of Ezra Pound are tired of Beauty, since they have met it so often in plays and poems and novels and in ordinary life. . . . [T]hey know its tricks, or think they do. It has ceased to be unintelligible, so very naturally and inevitably they turn to the ugly, celebrating it in every form of imitation. And they will continue to imitate it until they have found the trick. I am tired of Beauty my wife, says the poet, but here is that enchanting mistress Ugliness.

With her I will live, and what a riot we shall have—not a day shall pass without a fresh horror. . . . Ezra's poets are like the dogs that licked the sores of
Lazarus. (244–245)[1]

Why were the fictional Browne and the fatherly Yeats so convinced that traditional aesthetic *values* had been egregiously overturned, so much so that
the modern aesthetic was devoted to a repugnant ugliness? How could a celebration of ugliness compromise the intelligibility of the new works of
painting, literature, and music? In all three passages, it is assumed that a particular group of moderns is responsible for the artistic horrors being produced. Was this an example of generational paranoia, or was John Yeats
correct in specifying Pound and "the poets loved of Ezra Pound"? Should
one wonder that the concrete embodiment of this new ugliness, for both
Herbert and Yeats, is a distorted or dangerous female body? Should one be
surprised that an allegory of modern art features a fearless, godlike male hero
and a nonhuman female menace?

Questions such as these animate *The Modernist Cult of Ugliness*. Deliberately, however, I am not offering a seamless history of aesthetic theories, an
exhaustive catalogue of artistic strategies and practices, nor even a revisionary
account of the Anglo-American modernist canon. Instead, the ways in which
selected literary texts, lectures, paintings, pronouncements, manifestoes, and
essays articulate a historically determined, culturally-encoded aesthetic ideology are examined from a feminist perspective. Furthermore, my analysis of
what Ezra Pound so aptly termed the "cult of ugliness" identifies both how
and why aesthetic theorizations and artistic practices in the late nineteenth
century and early decades of the twentieth century were the product of, and
contributed to, the social construction of gender differentiation.

The questions that one can ask when embarking on a traditional history
of aesthetics are somewhat limited: what is art, what constitutes aesthetic
pleasure, and are the viewer's responses to the work of art objectively or sub-
jectively constituted? One requires different resources, however, to identify
who becomes an artist; who is presumed to be *naturally* imaginative and creative; what are the barriers to practicing one's art and presenting it to various audiences? Why is the ability to control the *objects* to be represented
(primarily, female bodies) concomitantly such an effective, historically
proven means of controlling the ranks of publicly recognized artists? To
begin these interrogations, one must look to the lessons of Michel Foucault's
analyses of power-knowledge relations. As Marie-Christine Leps elegantly
summarizes, one must consider that

the exercise of power and the production of hegemonic or "true" knowledge are
inextricably linked in discourse. In this sense, the truth of a period corresponds

not to the closest perception of a primary reality, but rather to the sets of information which, having been legitimized by institutions, organize the mode of being, the social arrangement, the historic reality of people and products. Thus, power is not a thing one can acquire or maintain by force, or at least, not by force alone; rather, power is both the result and the support of a complex system of production and distribution of knowledge which, once in circulation, acquires a truth value placing it in a position of domination. (3–4)

By examining the aesthetic discourse of John Ruskin, Ezra Pound, or Wyndham Lewis as it inscribes and reproduces social power structures, one can identify their profoundly gendered constitutions. Furthermore, by insisting upon the interconnectedness of then-contemporary definitions of aesthetic principles and gender-inflected definitions of human nature, one can determine why a new and, to borrow T. S. Eliot's term, "importunate" regime of truth concerning aesthetic priorities and practices could publicize and accomplish its goals under the banner of a "cult of ugliness."

Some readers may wonder why this book is preoccupied with canonical male writers and artists. Three reasons can be readily cited. Firstly, as Linda Nochlin has so persuasively argued, it is vital to explore "what happens when you look at a canonical figure against the grain, from a position outside the usual ones offered by [literary or] art history, revisionist or otherwise" (1991:xvi). Secondly, in addition to providing a notably *à rebours* perspective, this study attempts to disrupt traditional narratives of literary history that present modernism as being both aesthetic apotheosis and "natural" development. To borrow from Carol Duncan's work in art history,

According to the established narrative, the history of art is made up of a progression of styles and unfolds along certain irreversible lines: from style to style, it gradually emancipates itself from the imperative to represent convincingly or coherently a natural, presumably objective world. Integral to this narrative is a model of moral action, exemplified by individual artists. As they become liberated from traditional representation, they achieve greater subjectivity and hence greater artistic freedom and autonomy of spirit. (190)

This study demonstrates that the "emancipation" of male modernists was made possible, initially, by textual and sometimes personal discrimination practices, and subsequently by historical narratives complicit in these preferences and prejudices.

As explained above, two of three informing strategies can be characterized as contributing to the "paradigm shift" that feminist reappraisals of art and literary history are currently effecting. Insisting upon the centrality of gender issues in historical analyses, this shift destabilizes the "dominant mode of investigation and explanation" known familiarly as "modernist"

(Pollock 1988:2). As Griselda Pollock has argued, "it is not so much that [the dominant paradigm] is defective but that it can be shown to work ideologically to constrain what can and cannot be discussed in relation to the creation and reception of art" (1988:2). To learn about art "through the canonical discourse," she insists, "is to know masculinity as power and meaning, and all three as identical with Truth and Beauty. So long as feminism also tries to be a discourse about art, truth, and beauty, it can only confirm the structure of the canon, and by doing so corroborate masculine mastery and power" (Pollock 1999:9). Accordingly, the present study offers unauthorized, noncanonical connections among male culture workers; networks of power and influence are revisited, interrogated, and renamed.

The third reason for this particular grouping of writers and artists is more covert, yet nonetheless important. Again, I have taken a cue from Pollock, who considers canons to be "the retrospectively legitimating backbone of a cultural and political identity; a consolidated narrative of origin, conferring authority on the texts selected to naturalise this function" (1999:3). Some of the most fascinating and productive feminist archival research in the past two decades has been devoted to recovering the texts and reviving the reputations of twentieth-century writers such as Djuna Barnes, H. D., May Sinclair, Gertrude Stein, and Rebecca West.[2] At some level, however, the project of expanding the canon as a whole should not be confused with enlarging the canon of modernism. The latter term, within the Anglo-American tradition, actually refers to a "selective tradition which normalizes, as the *only* modernism, a particular and gendered set of practices" (Pollock 1988:50). Consequently, this study hopes to further the argument that it is inappropriate to assume that the modernism of Eliot, Pound, Joyce—and their legions of dedicated critics and scholars—is simply a recipe to which we add "women writers," stir, and voilà, produce a new and improved canonical soup. If one agrees that the writings of Eliot, Pound, and others is informed by, and represents, structures of sexual difference that are implicitly and explicitly antifeminist, then one could also conclude that such a masculinist paradigm can never accommodate the work of women writers and artists.[3] Therefore, rather than pursuing *correctional* projects that try to adjust the existing canon of modernist culture, one should concentrate on alternative, *confirmative* efforts to generate revised and multifaceted narratives of late-nineteenth- and twentieth-century literary and art history. Correctional studies assume that a shared aesthetic both identifies and guarantees a place for the work of women artists within the existing (male) canon; they provide guidelines for annexation and accommodation. But if the texts by women were and are deliberately *un*accommodating—created in response to, to voice a protest against, the regime of sexual difference encoded within the dominant aesthetic ideology and practices—then their value as cultural productions must be confirmed in and with expansive new terms. By exploring fully the "cult of ugliness" and the aesthetic discourse that produced and empowered it, one can appreciate how extremely and deliberately exclusionary toward its Others masculinist modernism really was. Before launching into specific studies, however, a fuller exposition of my governing problematic is in order—as informed by discourse analysis, feminist explications of the social production of art, and a reevaluation of the Platonic aesthetic tradition that was challenged, in the early twentieth century, by an aesthetics of denial and defilement.

Aesthetic Discourse

Aesthetic theorists such as Lukács, Benjamin, Adorno, and Bürger offer compelling arguments for establishing "the only possible authentic expression of the contemporary state of the world" (Bürger 85). Feminist scholars, on the other hand, insist that *any* expression of the historical or contemporary state of the world depends entirely on one's place in that world—"place" being a function of "intertextual ideological maxims on race, sex, class, and morality" (Leps 47), the discourses and power relations that constitute and inevitably constrain one and all.

Michel Foucault has challenged some of our most fundamental notions about the existence of objective, absolute truths and the pursuit of knowledge in the "human sciences"—and does so in order "to tear away from them their virtual self-evidence, and to free the problems that they pose" (1972:26). Feminist and cultural studies have benefitted from three specific aspects of Foucault's work: the investigation of fundamental shifts in epistemological paradigms; the possibilities of discourse analysis (including the need to study general sociocultural conditions of knowledge production and distribution, and the correlations of truth and power in discourse); and the production of "Man" as "the difficult object and sovereign subject of all possible knowledge" (Foucault 1973:310). In general terms, Foucault's work has had such a tremendous impact because of the way in which it teaches readers to reexamine the exercise of power in human society. As Pollock summarizes, "power is not just a matter of coercive force but a network of relationships, of inclusions and exclusions, of domination and subordination" (1988:33).

Rather than accept a quasi-Hegelian model of progressive historical development, or a theory of the "natural" growth and eventual dissolution of epochs, Foucault organizes his analyses in terms of *epistemes:* "the epistemological field, the *episteme* in which knowledge, envisaged apart from all criteria having reference to its rational value or to its objective forms, grounds its positivity and thereby manifests a history which is not that of its growing perfection, but rather that of its conditions of possibility" (1973:xxii). Within the terms of his "archaeological inquiries," Foucault perceives "two great discontinuities in the *episteme* of Western culture: the first inaugurates the Classical age (roughly half-way through the seventeenth century) and the second, at the beginning of the nineteenth century, marks the beginning of the modern age" (1973:xxii). In the chapters that follow, I shall be arguing that the aesthetic discourse to which Ruskin, Whistler, Pound, and Eliot all contributed was very much the product of the modern *episteme.*

Knowledge and power are fundamentally intertwined in Western culture—as Adam and Eve proved all too quickly. Foucault's work is more than just post-lapsarian, however: it radically reorients our notions about the production, distribution, and consumption of knowledge within society. If one accepts that discourse produces its subjects and its objects—that meaning, consciousness, even the objects of thought are constructed in discourse—then one must also study how the producing subject affects or mediates the knowledge being circulated. Power-knowledge relations are both intentional and nonsubjective, as Leps explains: "[intentional] as they are actively sought by individuals with immediate goals and objectives in mind. . . . [But] nonsubjective in that the individuals involved have interiorized their positions of enunciation and their objects of knowledge, and have come to recognize as their own the topics, modes of argumentation, and rules of validation imposed by the discursive practices in which they participate" (13).

Foucault's theory of discursive formations concentrates one's attention on the systematic interconnections of "statements" that define a field of knowledge, the "profound historicity" of those fields, and the "institutional sites" of their enunciation. Consider the possibilities in terms of the present study: instead of offering yet another "objective" account of the history of modernist aesthetics and literature, with the occasional excursion into the history of art for comparative purposes, these chapters probe the very discursive formations—literary history, art history, aesthetics—that invented or constructed the disciplines. Discourse analysis also encourages one to interrogate the "institutional *sites* from which . . . this discourse derives its legitimate source and point of application (its specific objects and instruments of verification)" (Foucault 1972:51). A reexamination of the London workshops and cliques, the "little" magazines and their timely reviews, the manifestoes, public lectures, gallery shows, and the groups of writers organizing themselves around marketable, distinctive "-isms" (Symbolism, Imagism, Vorticism, Futurism) will enable one to reconsider the ways in which they all contributed to and tried to control the production of modernist aesthetic discourse.

Attuned to "the different *spaces of dissension,*" discourse analysis reveals the "distribution of gaps, voids, absences, limits, divisions" in discursive formations and disciplines (Foucault 1972:152, 119). As I demonstrate, many of the limits, voids, and silences in modernist aesthetic discourse are actively produced by gender discriminations operating within Anglo-American society; what appear on the surface to be discipline-specific concerns are fundamentally connected to a public forum of values.[4]

When Foucault speaks of "the emergence of man" in the modern *episteme,* he is referring to "man" in his "ambiguous position as an object of knowledge and as a subject that knows":

> man, as a primary reality with his own density, as the difficult object and sovereign subject of all possible knowledge. . . . [a]n individual who lives, speaks, and works in accordance with the laws of an economics, a philology, and a biology, but who also, by a sort of internal torsion and overlapping, has acquired the right, through the interplay of those very laws, to know them and to subject them to total clarification. (1973:312, 310)

Feminist theorists and critics have taught us to reread statements such as this with thoroughly enunciated gender inflections. The modern *episteme* not only placed Man-as-generic-and-universal-human-being at the origin of meaning, and installed Him as the arbiter of all meanings, it also placed Males-as-Man within that privileged position of power and oppression.

As outlined by Foucault in *The Archaeology of Knowledge,* one of the first questions in discourse analysis is "who is speaking?": "Who, among the totality of speaking individuals, is accorded the right to use this sort of language? Who is qualified to do so? Who derives from it his own special quality, his prestige, and from whom, in return, does he receive if not the assurance, at least the presumption that what he says is true?" (1972:50). Modernist aesthetic discourse, I argue, was dedicated to creating and policing exclusive groups of individuals who alone were qualified to participate in the production and criticism of literature and the visual arts. What so enraged Whistler about Ruskin's negative barbs? The fact that a mere critic, and not a fellow artist, had made them. Both Eliot and Lewis cherished their privileged roles as artists and cultural commentators; Yeats and Pound disagreed about many things over the years but held firm the belief that only a few were qualified, in each age, to be the "sages" and "singing-masters" (1966:408). For these figures, who became "not only the privileged, but also virtually the exclusive, enunciator[s] of this discourse" (Foucault 1972:164), preserving male coteries of art production (the "*Men* of 1914"[5]) was crucial. Only they could confirm and protect the "autonomy of the artist and . . . the artwork as a complete, self-sufficient world" (Boone 6).

Throughout this study, I shall pose new questions about the *function* of aesthetic theory in the late nineteenth and early twentieth centuries. What were its aims, objectives, and silences? Which were the major problems in circulation concerning the vexed issues of judgment, taste, and theories of creativity? How do discussions organized around aesthetic values, especially the Beautiful, reveal fundamentally ingrained assumptions concerning gender and creativity, cultural production, and cultural value? The extent to which discursive formations are both intertextual and interdiscursive will be particularly notable as the argument unfolds.

In addition to learning from the works of Foucault directly, I have had the great benefit of consulting the exciting and resourceful work of Foucault-indebted feminist art historians and critics such as Duncan, Nochlin, and Pollock. Duncan, for example, has argued for more than two decades that "art objects" become "more intelligible when considered in historical context" (xi); Pollock's studies of modern art and avant-gardism are particularly insightful. All three scholars have considerably enriched our understanding of art as it reproduces and further constructs ideologically-imbedded social structures and strictures. As Pollock cogently asserts,

> The sexual divisions embedded in concepts of art and the artist are part of the cultural myths and ideologies peculiar to art history. But they contribute to the wider context of social definitions of masculinity and femininity and thus participate at the ideological level in reproducing the hierarchy between the sexes. (1988:21–22)

An analysis of aesthetic discourse produced from the 1850s to the 1930s identifies both sexual divisions and the cultural and political forces brought to bear in order to reinforce them.

Ideological Implications and Formulations

Discussions of ideology have become such a commonplace of literary studies that one hesitates between two noxious alternatives: remaining silent as to fundamental definitions, and thereby running the risk of seeming to be insufficiently grounded, or rehearsing theoretical and critical materials already rendered mundane by overexposure. Yet, at the outset of this critique of the cult of ugliness, it is very important to reassert the comparatively recent argument that *all* aesthetic theories are ideologically encoded. As Jameson notes, because of the work of Althusser, Macherey, and many others, "we can observe . . . the process by which the work of art can be said to 'produce' the ideological as an object for our aesthetic contemplation and our political judgment" (1981:22). Pollock has amplified this crucial tenet:

> Not only do we have to grasp that art is part of social production, but we also have to realize that it is itself productive, that is, it actively produces mean-

ings. Art is constitutive of ideology; it is not merely an illustration of it. It is one of the social practices through which particular views of the world, definitions and identities for us to live are constructed, reproduced, and even redefined. . . . For artists do not passively reproduce dominant ideology; they participate in its construction and alteration. Artists work in but also on ideology. (1988:30, 46–47)

Two scholars who have also extended our understanding of art "in that ideological reading of it known as the aesthetic" (Eagleton 1990a:64) are Terry Eagleton and Janet Wolff. Both have helped to expose "the extra-aesthetic elements involved in aesthetic judgment—the values of class, or the influence of political or moral ideals, for example" (Wolff 1981:7).

In *The Ideology of the Aesthetic*, Eagleton provides a challenging historical survey of the ways in which both art objects and theories of art constitute a "production" of ideology, drawing particular attention to the intersections of aesthetic theorizing and the increasing commodification of cultural productions since the eighteenth century. Eagleton begins by noting "the curiously high priority assigned by [European philosophy since the Enlightenment] to aesthetic questions," and the extent to which the "category of the aesthetic" represents "a supreme form of value" in post-Enlightenment culture (1). Foucauldian studies would suggest that there is nothing "curious" at all about the timely emergence of aesthetic discourse as an autonomous, systematic discipline—it complements, and informs, the "emergence of man" in the modern *episteme*. Nevertheless, Eagleton's Marxist perspective is particularly helpful in highlighting the class-related investments of aesthetic ideology; in "speaking of art," he reminds us, the bourgeoisie allude to matters "which are at the heart of the middle class's struggle for political hegemony" (3).

Eagleton astutely locates the discursive need for aesthetics in the Enlightenment's assumption that "the world of perception and experience cannot simply be derived from abstract universal laws" (16). Consequently, aesthetics "emerges as a theoretical discourse . . . a kind of prosthesis to reason, extending a reified Enlightenment rationality into vital regions which are otherwise beyond its reach" (Eagleton 16). By insisting upon the political dimensions and motives of aesthetic criteria, Eagleton also refreshes our understanding of the strategic importance of this all-too versatile theoretical category. "Few ideas," as he suggests, "can have served so many disparate functions" (Eagleton 3). Why was Edmund Burke, for example, so insistent that beauty is both absolute and objective? Because "if beauty is merely relative," as Eagleton reminds us, "then the bonds which leash society together are in danger of loosening. . . . If aesthetic judgment is unstable, then so must be the social sympathies founded on it, and with them the whole fabric of political life" (52). My examination of the cult of ugliness demonstrates how specific writers and artists capitalized on the instability of aesthetic and political values in the first two decades of the twentieth century in order to install an alternative regime of aesthetic truths, one which paradoxically enabled them to enact the "masculine reclamation of a feminized literature" (Chinitz 1997:328) and to reiterate conventional, previously stable gender norms. Additionally, I provide a new reading of the strategies by which writers such as Pound and Lewis tried to correlate aesthetic stratagems with the actual, material conditions of existence as they understood them. At a time when Thomas Bailey Aldrich, editor of the *Atlantic Monthly*, was declaring that, "'Art should create nothing but what is beautiful and leave real life to the rest'" (qtd F. Cox 215), the cultists insisted on a new discursive relationship with "real life," new modes of representation to express what Pound terms "frankness as never before" (*P/SPo* 64).

Previously, aesthetic theorists and critics mastered a ubiquitous lexicon that enabled them to talk in wholly abstracted terms of *judgment, taste,* and *standards of excellence.* More revealingly, I would argue, aesthetic discourse is preoccupied with a fundamental, pervasive, and contentious dimension of human life: pleasure. As Eagleton strikingly observes, aesthetics is "a discourse of the body. . . . That territory is nothing less than the whole of our sensate life together—the business of affections and aversions, of how the world strikes the body on its sensory surfaces, of that which takes root in the gaze and the guts and all that arises from our most banal, biological insertion into the world" (13). Despite its critical insights, however, a passage such as this reminds us that one must continually dismantle gender-neutral and therefore gender-denying generalizations such as "the body" or "our . . . biological insertion into the world." In order to do so, one must turn from Eagleton to the work of Wolff and her excellent summaries of current studies within the sociology of art.

The question "what is art," Wolff reminds us, "is centrally a question about what is taken to be art by society, or by certain of its key members" (1981:12). If one accepts that art is both social product and social knowledge, then the historically located social relations that control the conditions of production and reception for that commodity demand special attention. Sociological critiques of issues that have been traditionally reserved for aesthetics have a great deal to offer, especially in terms of their efforts to collapse barriers between disciplines such as literary studies, art history, sociology, and philosophy. "It may be threatening to an absolute aesthetics," as Wolff acknowledges,

> to have to realise that criticism and its evaluations are ideological. It is probably even worse to learn that values change. . . . [Works of art] are not closed, self-contained and transcendent entities, but are the product of specific his-

torical practices on the part of identifiable social groups in given conditions, and therefore bear the imprint of the ideas, values, and conditions of existence of those groups, and their representatives in particular artists. (1981:18, 49)

Sociological inquiries (which include investigations of the social history of art) cogently challenge the "supra-historical status" of works of art and the philosophy of art. Nevertheless, as Wolff cautions us, "the experience and evaluation of art are socially and ideologically situated and constructed, and at the same time irreducible to the social or the ideological" (1981:84).

A brief outline of some of the post–World War II publications in the sociology of art school will clarify its intellectual parameters. (Many of these studies actively foreground the burden of the discipline's nineteenth-century positivistic heritage.) Three works by Arnold Hauser have been particularly influential: *The Social History of Art* (1951), *Mannerism: The Crisis of the Renaissance and the Origin of Modern Art* (1965), and *The Sociology of Art* (1974). James H. Barnett's 1959 essay "The Sociology of Art" has had a major impact on North American audiences in particular. European contexts were profitably explored in several studies by Lucien Goldmann, including *The Hidden God: A Study of the Tragic Vision in the "Pensées" of Pascal and the Tragedies of Racine* (1955; English translation, 1964), *The Human Sciences and Philosophy* (1966; 1969), and *Towards a Sociology of the Novel* (1964; 1975). In 1978, Nicos Hadjinicolaou published *Art History and Class Struggle.* Pierre Bourdieu's *Distinction,* "a social critique of the judgment of taste," first appeared in 1979 (it became available to English-speaking readers in 1984). Nothing less than a critique of Kantian aesthetics, especially the notion that judgment is characterized by profound disinterestedness, Bourdieu's work relies upon the concept of "cultural capital" to identify "in the structure of the social classes the basis of the systems of classification which structure perception of the social world and designate the objects of aesthetic enjoyment" (1984:xiii-xiv). Most importantly, he has since insisted, "specifically aesthetic conflicts about the legitimate vision of the world, . . . about what deserves to be represented and the right way to represent it, are political conflicts (appearing in their most euphemized form) for the power to impose the dominant definitions of reality, and social reality in particular" (Bourdieu 1986:154–155). Also in 1979, John Hall's *The Sociology of Literature,* and a collection of essays prepared by Michèle Barrett and several others, *Ideology and Cultural Production,* summarized the contributions being made by British scholars. (In the late 1970s, investigations underway at, or organized by, the universities of Birmingham and Essex were especially fruitful.) Two works by Terry Eagleton should also be cited in this survey: *Criticism and Ideology* (1976), and *The Ideology of the Aesthetic.* Wolff has contributed two invaluably synthetic studies, *The Social Production of Art* (1981) and *Aesthetics*

and the Sociology of Art (1983). More recently, her book of essays entitled
Feminine Sentences (1990) has signalled the potential for feminist interventions within this burgeoning discursive field.

' Work such as Wolff's, then, provides a collateral perspective, an additional lens with which to view the social construction of art and culture; it enables "[a] critique of the ideology of timelessness and value-freedom which characterises art theory and art history in the modern world. It enables us to see that art always encodes values and ideology, and that art criticism itself, though operating within a relatively autonomous discourse, is never innocent of . . . political and ideological processes" (Wolff 1981:143). One crucial aspect of Wolff's approach that assails conventional training in literary studies is the rigorous displacement or removal of the individual artist from the "centre of the activity of artistic production" (1981:67). Such a devaluation of the "idea of the artist-as-creator" (Wolff 1981:25), the independent genius, usefully refocuses our attention on social and ideological factors that shape cultural productions and highlights the active, determining roles of institutions and audiences (readers, viewers, critics) in creating the meaning and significance of artifacts. Nonetheless, as the organization of the present study attests, literary and cultural histories often depend upon the specific works of individuals to demonstrate socially and discursively determined practices. Moreover, the ways in which aesthetic codes and social relations—particularly those dedicated to the definition and regulation of femininity—are mediated by a particular writer or visual artist are often most revealing. The role of the individual, therefore, is both creative and at the same time socially and historically situated; the artifact expresses the "cultural unconscious," if one prefers Bourdieu's terms, but it is a site in which the play of subjectivities is crucial.

The "Radically Historical" Categories
of Aesthetic Discourse

One foundational anomaly of aesthetic theory is that it has separated itself so rigorously from art history and art criticism. The discipline that emerged in the eighteenth century—as practised by Baumgarten, Kant, and Schiller—cloaked itself in philosophical garb, borrowing the robes of epistemology and ontology to conduct its search for the nature of aesthetic experience and judgment, the source of beauty, and the true character of that which links the external world of nature and the internal world of self-consciousness. Yet as early as Baumgarten's *Aesthetica* (Part 1, 1750; Part 2, 1758), problems inherent in trying to explicate the individual's sensuous response to created artifacts, and the function of aesthetic pleasure as it defines the communion between the phenomenal and noumenal, have been readily apparent.

Six crucial problems that traditional aesthetic discourse has tried to elucidate and at the same time monitor can be isolated: What is art? What is the nature of aesthetic experience? What is beauty? What are the criteria for aesthetic judgment? What is aesthetic value? What is aesthetic merit? (Wolff 1983:68). As this introduction suggests, each of these questions begs a host of others. "What" is art, for example, depends entirely on "who" controls the cultural significance of art at a specific historical juncture. Boundaries between what is considered high art and popular or domestic handiwork are regulated by, among other forces, the investments of class, gender, and race. Aesthetic evaluation and merit are illuminating categories, but highly unstable and wholly unreliable.

Rather than inquire, what is beauty? and assume that the answer will provide general laws of "metahistorical validity" (Bürger 92), the chapters that follow address two interrelated issues: by whom, when, and according to what criteria were particular works of art considered accomplished; and, how and why was "the beautiful" deployed as the only appropriate category to define and reward that accomplishment, even when the representation of "ugliness" was deemed more topical. To some extent, I take my cue from Walter Pater's *The Renaissance: Studies in Art and Poetry* (1873), the preface to which daringly eschews the received wisdom of Kant, Burke, and Ruskin:

> Many attempts [Pater begins] have been made by writers on art and poetry to define beauty in the abstract, to express it in the most general terms, to find some universal formula for it. . . . Beauty, like all other qualities presented to human experience, is relative; and the definition of it becomes unmeaning and useless in proportion to its abstractness. To define beauty, not in the most abstract but in the most concrete terms possible, to find, not its universal formula, but the formula which expresses most adequately this or that special manifestation of it, is the aim of the true student of aesthetics. (*TR* xix)

Paterian "relativity," I would suggest, creatively anticipates a contemporary commitment to elucidating the cultural codes, subject positions, and the "radically historical" (Bürger 15) networks of power and knowledge that construct and corroborate social and personal identity. For aesthetics, the "most concrete terms" now available are articulated by feminist discourse analysis that concentrates on the social production of art and the cultural production of sexual difference.

Discarding a Kantian guise of disinterestedness and impartiality, Pater replaces traditional considerations of objective beauty with a more (im)pertinent challenge: "What is this song or picture . . . to *me*? What effect does it really produce on me? Does it give me pleasure? and if so, what sort or degree of pleasure? How is my nature modified by its presence, and under its influence?" (*TR* xix-xx). Such a foregrounding of subjectivity, and intimations that one's nature or identity is neither stable nor monolithic but contingent, an ongoing process of "modification"—all within the framework of a discussion concerning aesthetic pleasure—clearly encourages readers to challenge long-cherished disciplinary categories. At the same time, Pater's text clearly reminds us of the primary currency of *value* in aesthetic discourse.

"Surely this is the nub of the matter," as Hayden White argues:

> For it is the value of art as one activity among many in culture and the value of one or more artworks among all of the artifacts claiming title to being artworks that ultimately interests critics and theorists, and even practising artists. Truthfulness we can give up, along with referentiality; meaning we can problematize, along with the very notion of culture. . . . But value is another matter. If artistic activity does not possess a value different from and superior to other kinds of cultural activity, and if some artworks do not possess a value superior to that of others, then what is aesthetics to deal with, much less the art market trade in? (51)

The writings and artistic productions of Ruskin, Whistler, Eliot, Pound, and Lewis highlight the urgency with which the intersecting problems of artistic and aesthetic values were debated from the 1850s onward, complicated as they were by notions of emotional response, spiritual compensation, and cultural ascendancy. Rather than accept the debates on their own terms, however, one must probe the investments of gender and class as they predetermined any considerations of "worth, desirability, and utility." The latter triad constitutes the *Oxford English Dictionary*'s definition of "value." As the *OED* reminds us, *value,* a word that entered the English lexicon in the Middle Ages, is derived from the Old French word *valoir,* to be worth, which in turn stemmed from the Latin *valere,* to be strong. However abstract they may seem on the surface, considerations of value in patriarchal culture can inevitably be traced to physical and hence gendered phenomena such as strength. Aesthetic values are no different, as this study will confirm.

To complete this preliminary argument that aesthetic values are part of a "coded vocabulary" (Foucault 1972:73) of specialized meanings and at the same time signifiers of sexual difference within our culture, I must briefly consider how a regime of absolute values organized around notions of the True, the Beautiful, and the Good was installed and secured in Western culture. It was this "already valorized context of meanings" (Pollock 1992:15) that framed and determined the most seemingly radical utterances and artifacts of masculinist modernism.

"Beauty is Certainly a Soft, Smooth, Slippery Thing"

In institutions such as Oxford, Harvard, Cambridge, and the Slade School of Art, Ruskin, Pater, and the Men of 1914 were schooled[6] to understand and appreciate an ideal, triadic correlation of aesthetics, ethics, and epistemology known familiarly as the Beautiful, the Good, and the True. These may seem like basic words, yet they embody what Eagleton terms "the three great questions of philosophy": What do we find attractive? What are we to do? and What can we know? (1990a:366). One of the most fascinating aspects of aesthetic history is its unchallenged assumption that the field of statements in aesthetic discourse has not appreciably changed since Plato. It might be more accurate to say that although the boundaries of enunciative possibilities have not been significantly altered, the interdependence of the concepts in circulation has altered considerably.

From Plato to Hegel, Hegel to Worringer, each system of thought to which Ruskin or Lewis and his co-"outlaws"[7] were exposed not only interrogated the special interrelatedness of goodness, truth, and beauty, but speculated as to whether the latter was a "form" synonymous with excellence and perfection, a quality inherent in the object, or a subjective response to that which gives one pleasure. Crucially, there emerged in the nineteenth century a new hierarchy of statements within the traditional paradigm. The present study suggests that the modernists' cult of ugliness marks a particular, culminating moment in Western culture's gradual dismantling or fracturing of the Platonic triad.[8] At the outset, however, I would like to suggest that even in the Platonic texts the ideal of a unified knowledge is threatened by beauty—a troubling capacity to elude the powers of reason and truth that is often expressed in gendered terms.

Although the Platonic texts are never wholly systematic, they consistently articulate a commitment to the Beautiful that is constructed within, and always answerable to, a closely circumscribed ethical and political formation. Aesthetic discourse, as such, is limited, and extremely focused—functioning always as a correlative of the broader social discourse. A commitment to the Beautiful, in other words, should not be confused with a fully developed aesthetic (ideologically-encoded, historically-located theories of art, artistic practices, and the production and consumption of art within society). Certainly the hallmarks of classical aesthetic discourse—"the principles of order, proportion, balance, of economy of means, and of rationalism and naturalism in the rendering of reality" (Hauser 1986:3)—are enunciated in Plato's dialogues. But the temporal, corporeal embodiments of the ideal are not unproblematic. Hence, a seemingly conflictive array of positive and negative statements concerning beauty can be discerned throughout the dialogues. In Book 10 of the *Republic,* for example, Socrates instructs Glaucon as to "the excellence or beauty or truth of each structure" (*Republic* X, 601/Jowett 2:432).[9] He who "utters the beautiful," Socrates promises Theaetetus, "is himself beautiful and good" (*Theaetetus* 185/Jowett 3:389). Yet in other dialogues, when attention shifts from the excellence of absolute, eternal beauty to actual artistic production, dissenting comments predominate. Poets can create mere "images of beauty"; the philosopher, on the other hand, "beholding beauty with the eye of the mind," brings forth "not images of beauty, but realities; for he has hold not of an image but of a reality" (*Symposium* 212a/Jowett 1:503).

Why are circumstantial or physical beauty, and "absolute beauty" or the Beautiful, affiliated so uneasily? Throughout the dialogues—and especially in the *Apology, Laws* IV, *Ion, Symposium,* and the *Republic*—aesthetic discourse is inscribed within a "strange empirico-transcendental doublet" (Foucault 1973:318). Transcendence and immanence, one could almost say, represent the twin horns of an idealized dilemma. In the Platonic schema, one can only begin to apprehend the Beautiful through or because of physical objects (including human bodies) that exhibit beauty. Yet each such manifestation is rife with dangerous possibilities. Art objects are suspect because they can mislead or distract—and thereby distort the reality that lies behind the literal and the physical. Consider the power-knowledge relations operating within this model. The "beauty of earthly things" is supposed to lead one to "the perfect beauty of eternal knowledge" (Jowett 1:463), but the process must be zealously guarded and policed (even to the extent of expelling poets from the Commonwealth). Art is inherently amoral, according to Socrates; poets lack knowledge, and visual artists can only provide the semblance of reality as they copy appearances and surfaces. Given these convictions, Socrates's sympathies towards art are necessarily limited, hesitant, his views ranging from reluctant admiration to condemnation.

The problems articulated around beauty in the aesthetic discourse of Ruskin or Pound, I am suggesting, can be traced back to these power-inflected Platonic paradoxes in which beauty is a wayward, sometimes hazardous signifier, and absolute truth is the only secure form of knowledge. The Beautiful is intrinsic and pure, according to the *Philebus;* a "form" or mode of goodness that is synonymous with excellence and perfection. That is why the apprehension of the beautiful produces "true pleasures"—"those which are," according to Socrates, "given by beauty of colour and form, and most of those which arise from smells; those of sound, again, and in general those of which the want is painless and unconscious, and the gratification afforded by them palpable to sense, and pleasant and unalloyed with pain" (*Philebus* 51/ Jowett 3:191). Throughout the dialogues, however, Socrates must rigorously assert that absolute beauty and its pleasures are not to be confused with "beautiful things" (see *Euthydemus* 300–301). In the *Repub-*

lic, he distinguishes forcefully between "the sight-loving, art-loving, practical class . . . and [those] who are alone worthy of the name of philosophers" (*Republic* V, 476 / Jowett 2:304). "The lovers of sounds and sights," Socrates replied, "are, as I conceive them, fond of fine tones and colours and forms, and all the artificial products that are made out of them, but their mind is incapable of seeing or loving absolute beauty. . . . Few are they who are able to attain the sight of absolute beauty" (*Republic* V, 476 / Jowett 2:304). Significantly, the name of the few is "philosopher/guardian," not "artist." Only the philosopher who is disciplined (in both the physical and intellectual senses of the term) has access to a vision of idealized beauty and truth. The latter, as Partee observes, can "be legitimately linked [for Plato] only in the realm of the dialectic, not in the verbal creations of man" (54).

One should not be surprised, therefore, to find Socrates admitting to Menexenus, "my head is dizzy with thinking of the argument, and therefore I hazard the conjecture, that the beautiful is the friend, as the old proverb says. Beauty is certainly a soft, smooth, slippery thing, and therefore of a nature which easily slips in and permeates our souls" (*Lysis* 216/Jowett 1:56). A soul can be enlightened *or* jeopardized by the insinuating presence of beauty.

The complexities of Plato's aesthetic discourse result from the pressures of interdiscursive imperatives; ethical and epistemological needs are always paramount. Three other complications should also be kept in mind. Firstly, the relationship between the physical and the metaphysical, the phenomenal and noumenal realms, is not always harmonious. Secondly, there are the enigmatic and perplexing operations of desire and pleasure. The emotional coloring of the aesthetic debates and the artistic productions cited by Socrates is considerable, and always troublesome to the Athenian. Obviously connected to the notion of desire is the third and undoubtedly the most complex factor: the gender distinctions of Plato's culturally-sanctioned sexual-aesthetic discourse. The beauty analyzed, appreciated, and sometimes deprecated in the Platonic texts was grounded in the homoerotic—a matrix that included and was sustained by male-male sexual relations, the primacy of male beauty, and the civic and cultural supremacy of males in ancient Greek society. (A woman, therefore, was typically a sign of powerlessness; the "predicament of femininity" was firmly entrenched [Pollock 1999:33].)

Given the near-invisibility of women in the culture of the Greek *polis,* the gender dynamics of the most critical scene of aesthetic instruction in the *Symposium* may surprise one. For it is Diotima, the sibyl or "wise woman" of Mantinea, who teaches Socrates to comprehend the ways in which "the beauties of the earth" can lead one to "absolute beauty" (*Symposium* 211/ Jowett 1:503). Jowett certainly took great pains to explain this exceptional circumstance to readers of his late-nineteenth-century translation: Diotima's "sacred and superhuman character raises her above the ordinary proprieties of women" (Jowett 1:463). (The latter statement not only highlights the regime of gender inequities that Jowett thoroughly endorsed, but reminds us of the extent to which *propriety* and *protocol* functioned as the iron fist within the velvet glove of Victorian antifeminism.) The conditions of possibility for Diotima's pivotal role, however, are clearly enunciated earlier in the *Symposium*—it is all a matter of genealogy and patrilineage.

The men attending the banquet at Agathon's—the "occasion" for the *Symposium*—are congenially debating the subject of Love. Phaedrus begins by affirming the personal and cultural value of *eros*. Although initially he extols the salutary effects of male homosexual relationships only, he expands his examples to include famous heterosexual couples and their demonstrations of virtue inspired by love. Pausanias, however, does not think that Phaedrus has been sufficiently discriminating. "If there were only one Love," he observes,

> then what he [Phaedrus] said would be well enough, but since there are more Loves than one, he should have begun by determining which of them was to be the theme of our praises. . . . For we all know that Love is inseparable from Aphrodite, and if there were only one Aphrodite there would be only one Love; but as there are two goddesses there must be two Loves. For am I not right in asserting that there are two goddesses? The elder one, having no mother, who is called the heavenly Aphrodite—she is the daughter of Uranus; the younger, who is the daughter of Zeus and Dione, whom we call common. . . . [T]he Love who is the son of the common Aphrodite is essentially common, and has no discrimination, being such as the meaner sort of men feel, and is apt to be of women as well as of youths, and is of the body rather than of the soul. . . . The goddess who is his mother is far younger, and she was born of the union of the male and female, and partakes of both sexes. But the son of the heavenly Aphrodite is sprung from a mother in whose birth the female has no part, but she is from the male only[.] (*Symposium* 180–181/ Jowett 1:474)

One should be grateful to Pausanias for explaining the matter so lucidly and emphatically. Long before the Christian fathers enshrined their essentialist paradigm of womanhood (the virgin/whore antinomy), Plato's dialogue codified the tradition of two Aphrodites. The elder, "heavenly" Aphrodite, metaphorically delivered from the stain of femaleness as she was "foamborn," fully grown, sanctions a tradition of associating love—and beauty— with wisdom, law, and good conduct. Liberated from the contaminating mediation of female parturition, this Aphrodite can embody, for the male imagination, the possibilities of female exceptionality.

When Socrates eventually joins in the debate, he does not correct or amend Pausanias's genealogical lesson. Instead, he refocuses the group's attention in order to expound on the relationship between the beautiful and the good, and the process by which desire for physical beauty can lead to a vision of "true beauty—the divine beauty, . . . pure and clear and unalloyed, not clogged with the pollutions of mortality, and all the colours and vanities of human life" (*Symposium* 211/ Jowett 1:503). The lessons of Diotima are then described at length (*Symposium* 201–212).

The sibyl's ability to instruct Socrates, I am suggesting, has been rationalized—for the guests of Agathon, and the readers of Plato—by the previous lesson of the two Aphrodites. Diotima, one should conclude, is related to the elder or "heavenly" Aphrodite, and therefore is as male-identified as possible. Socrates does not explain her lineage; his account concentrates on the instruction that will lead the individual from the pursuit of physical beauty to become "a lover of all beautiful forms," a wise person who considers "that the beauty of the mind is more honourable than the beauty of the outward form" (*Symposium* 210/Jowett 1:502). Nevertheless, "the beauty of the mind" that Diotima promises, a union of beauty, truth, and goodness, has as its dramatic emblem the spectacle of Aphrodite emerging from the foamy Cytherean waves, the direct offspring of Uranus's severed genitals. This unnatural female figure thus becomes part of the essential and unified knowledge, the higher truths, which make possible the hegemonic values of masculinist Western culture. The Mantinean sibyl not only initiates Socrates into a new appreciation of love, she provides a remarkable pedagogical exercise in constructing power-knowledge relations. By codifying a transcendental truth to which all human truths must surrender and answer, Plato's sibyl provides a model for producing seemingly unassailable and authentic codes of knowledge and behavior. Furthermore, although endorsing the Beautiful as being the equivalent of the True and the Good, the sibyl introduces a hierarchical taxonomy, one which begins with sensuous beauty and ranges through beautiful deeds and moral beauty to the most exalted and desirable idealization, absolute beauty. In the aesthetic discourse of late nineteenth- and early-twentieth- century writers and artists, the substantial, absolute value of the artifact is wholly separated from any accidents of physical appearance. Consequently, the production of ugliness is not only accommodated but justified.

The Platonic aesthetic both privileges and deprecates beauty. As an approximation of the Beautiful (*to kalon*), sensuous beauty (*kallos*) can serve as a catalyst toward the ideal and as a pedagogical tool. Unlike the Beautiful, however, mere beauty can fetter one to the physical and its manifestations (language itself, poetry, or the human form). As Partee observes, "Plato admits that beauty in all its forms has a profound effect on the soul. He stresses, however, that only the beauty of virtue and of knowledge does not lead to the impure enjoyment of pleasure" (26).

"Aesthetic theories may strenuously strive for metahistorical knowledge," Bürger reminds us, "but that they bear the clear stamp of the period of their origin can usually be seen afterward, and with relative ease" (15). Plato's aesthetic utterances are no exception. References to human forms of beauty, for example, participate in a code of gender discriminations that must be carefully assessed. The "dominative pleasures" of the "visual field" (Pollock 1988:15) endorsed by the dialogues are homoerotic; the male body is valorized as the site of inspiration and the possible catalyst for higher realms of understanding. Centuries of indoctrination within a Christian and heterosexist patriarchal system will be required before "the cult of beauty" is "imposed upon the sign of woman" (Pollock 1988:153). Nonetheless, it is impossible for Plato's dramatis personae to discuss pleasure, love, and human aspiration without mentioning females. In the *Symposium,* Pausanias summarizes the most blatantly antifemale position; to be fully operative, the categories of "love" and "beauty" must be disassociated from a "natural" woman. The tradition of the "two Aphrodites" naturalizes and at the same time aggrandizes a disavowal and denigration of maternity, offering instead the reification of a male-identified female.

Interestingly, only when referring to human procreation and parturition—when the necessity of the female body is unavoidable—does Plato mention the antithesis of physical beauty, foulness and deformation. Yet even then the lesson is displaced from its male source onto a female enunciator, Diotima. According to the sibyl,

> the deformed is always inharmonical with the divine, and the beautiful harmonious. Beauty, then, is the destiny or goddess of parturition who presides at birth, and therefore when approaching beauty the conceiving power is propitious, and diffuse, and benign, and begets and bears fruit: on the appearance of foulness she frowns and contracts in pain, and is averted and morose, and shrinks up, and not without a pang refrains from conception. (*Symposium* 206/Jowett 1:499)

The Men of 1914 will completely rescript the scenes of artistic conception and birth to argue for the *necessary* "appearance of foulness" and the multivalent possibilities of the inharmonious. What they learned from Plato, I am suggesting, is that aesthetic discourse has a privileged yet covert relation to issues of sexual difference. Although ostensibly a revered domain of philosophy, aesthetic discourse is a regime of knowledge, one that has as its chief preoccupation the definition and management of visual pleasures.

Repositioning the Beautiful

According to the Mantinean sibyl, "foulness" is denied birth by the presiding deity of parturition. Subsequent to Plato, however, aesthetic commentators were unable to define and control beauty without situating it within an oppositional framework. Beauty thereby became a category of norm and counternorm, another product of a dialectical or dualistic definitional code rooted in the self-same/Other binary. As Bowie suggests, "aesthetics is not simply to be equated with Plato's view of beauty as the symbol of the good, because it is bound up with the emergence of subjectivity as the central issue of modern philosophy" (2).

If one were embarked upon a history of the function of "ugliness" within aesthetic discourse, there would be many touchstones to consider. Within the classical *episteme*, for example, it was invoked as a necessary and negative definitional field by Aquinas to categorize the integrity of perfection. Within the modern *episteme*, the ugly came into its own: in projects such as Schlegel's 1797 "theory of ugliness" and Hegel's suggestion that ugliness is a "species" of beauty. Under the guise of truth-telling, therefore, the beautiful has been gradually repositioned: not simply negated or rejected, but supplanted by an enthusiasm for a complex, seemingly new and dynamic category. As I shall consider more fully in the discussion of Ruskin, supplemental categories such as the sublime and the grotesque also expose the limitations of the beautiful in aesthetic discourse, allowing male commentators to express strong emotions that exceed existing aesthetic lexicons and parameters, but reinforce gendered behavioral codes.

A casual inventory of European and North American painting in the nineteenth century would seem to suggest that the celebration of physical, human beauty had reached its apogee. Upon closer examination, however, one discovers that expressions of the beautiful had become narrow and fixated, confined within aesthetic conventions and socially prescribed codes that demanded the almost obsessive commodification of female bodies by male artists. Women were little more than ciphers for and within the male fantasy of womanhood, sequestered within a "cult of art as a compensatory, self-sufficient, formalized real, of aesthetic beauty in which the beauty of the woman-object and the beauty of the painting-object become conflated, fetishized" (Pollock 1988:153). At the same time that art production became dedicated to male phantasms of female beauty, and reaffirmed "the stability of sexual categories and gendered identities" (Elliott and Wallace 61), the art criticism of writers such as Baudelaire and Ruskin became more and more preoccupied with social critique. That is to say, rather than overtly contesting traditional categories of aesthetic judgment and practice, the writers devoted themselves to exposing the social, economic, and political conditions that threatened the reification of conventional values, including the possibilities of coherence and order. By the time that Eliot, Pound, and Lewis began publishing, in the years just preceding World War I, a commitment to the artistic production of ugliness was believed to foreground—thematically and technically—the disorder, instability, and lack of regulation and control perceived in the world at large.

As such, the terms of their discourse were not only historically determined but enslaved, to borrow Plato's term, to the contemporary.

Dedicated to a new "order of meaning,"[10] I am suggesting, modernist aesthetic discourse and production had as a fundamental precondition of its emergence a traumatic response, by those most implicated in bourgeois culture, to an urbanized, industrialized, rapidly changing "social world being remade by capitalism, and its predominant forms, the cities of production and consumption" (Pollock 1992:52–53). The trauma or wound to the body politic, and the artistic sensibility, was created by what Nochlin terms "the experience of living in the society of the spectacle, of making a living in a market economy in which exchange value took the place of use value and mass production that of artisinal production" (1991:171–172). The cult of ugliness, as I demonstrate, simultaneously offered an indictment of contemporary cultural conditions and a celebration of artistic achievement in spite of *and* because of those very conditions. As such, it constituted the fundamental antimodernity of masculinist modernism, a supposedly nonsentimental and nonillusionist engagement with the present as well as a "ludic denial" (Foucault 1973:300) of past "traditions" no longer viable for writers and artists. Representations of physical beauty had been the quintessential feature of an ideological system that privileged nature, the organic work of art, taste, and mimesis—a system that the modern writer and artist believed to be wholly "exhausted" (Jameson 1981:64). Conventional commitments to the reproduction of "earthly beauties" were therefore sacrificed in order to preserve the fiction that the meaning of art, secure in its autonomy, is capable of transcending the material conditions of its production. Transcendence was no longer a means toward an absolute end, as Diotima had promised Socrates, but a fragile compensation unto itself.

Relieving the "Ache of Modernism"

The trenchant phrase "ache of modernism" did not come from the pen of Ezra Pound or T. S. Eliot: it was formulated in the early 1890s by Thomas Hardy to describe the dislocation and deracination experienced by Tess Durbeyfield and her contemporaries. Nevertheless, the almost proverbial expression addresses both the nostalgic sense of loss and the burden of contemporary conditions that animate texts by the Men of 1914. As several critics point out, these were artists "sharply conscious of their historical entanglements" (Levenson 1999:2); their works signalled "a portentous, confused, yet curiously heightened self-consciousness of [the] ... historical moment, at once self-doubting and self-congratulatory, anxious and triumphalistic" (Eagleton 1988:139). By representing a response to the cultural zeitgeist in terms of a physical trauma, an *ache,* Hardy's phrase personalizes the experience and the expression of modernity. If one recalls the saga of rape, betrayal, ritualistic sacrifice, and execution enacted in *Tess of the d'Urbervilles,* one finds another precedent for the infliction of suffering and degradation onto female bodies that male artists found so apt for dramatizing the "ache of modernism."

As Levenson has recently stated, "a coarsely understood Modernism is at once an historical scandal and a contemporary disability" (1999:1).[11] Delineating the development of a cult of ugliness is only one among many possibilities for exploring the interplay of aesthetic and gender ideology in the culture of the early twentieth century. Yet it offers, as I hope to show, a particularly acute means of reevaluating male modernists' attempts at aesthetic innovation—theoretical and stylistic—as they were constructed in a specific sociohistorical matrix, and clarifies exactly how they were able to claim "the central aesthetic ground" (Scholes 1:3) for their efforts. The contributions that have been made, and can be made, by feminist art and literary histories are considerable. Working from the "vantage point of Otherness," to borrow Nochlin's phrase (1991:xv), feminist spectators/critics can produce both "different positions" and different insights "within this sexual politics of looking" (Pollock 1988:85). No longer "enthralled to a masculine viewing position" (Pollock 1988:85) or enunciating sites for literary and cultural studies, one can develop new paradigms for cultural studies and aesthetic practices. Looking back, one learns much from asking who spoke for the "new" and inquiring, not "who's new" in 1890 or 1920 but *whose* definition, practice, and dissemination of "new" literary and visual art work predominated.

Invoking a cult may seem an outrageous or inappropriate notion for modernist studies, but the chapters that follow demonstrate how and why it aptly summarizes the strategies of "differentness" (Randall Jarrell's term), of self and group "consolidation" (Lyon 1992:109), deemed necessary in late and post-Victorian culture. Chapter 1, organized around the figures of John Ruskin and James McNeill Whistler, concentrates on the problems inherent in modern legitimizations of idealized beauty, and identifies the underlying coherence of the misogyny shaping their seemingly different articulations.[12] Each in his own way argued that "truth and beauty are entirely distinct" (*WJR* 5:55); each extended the traditions of gendered sphere ideology in his representations of femininity and masculinity. Chapter 2 offers a reformulation of modernism's "aesthetic said and . . . sexual unsaid" (Pollock 1999:53) by exposing the homophobic energies with which male modernists made an "enemy" of Walter Pater and the innovative aestheticism his writings promoted. The reification of ugliness enabled Lewis and "brethren" to disguise homophobic responses under the cloak of aesthetic impartiality. Chapter 3 concentrates on the self-styled "cult" of "us moderns," including Pound, Hulme, Eliot, and Lewis, analyzing how their innovative discursive strategems to expose the ugliness of modernity produced, in turn, what Lewis called the "attractive terror" of works now pivotal in the modernist canon. Also considered are the ways in which Eurocentric high modernism was defined against Italian Futurism. The final chapter examines the intersections of gender and race in American poetry in the representation of urban and nonurban topographies. Alternatives to masculinist modernism are located in works by H. D., Langston Hughes, and several others. Each chapter pursues the argument that aesthetic ideology within a Western patriarchal system produces a sexual-aesthetic discourse privileging masculinist, heterosexual, class-inflected values—a dominant discourse wholly dependent on its constructed Others (women, homosexuals, nonwhites).

It is the impossible task of aesthetic discourse to try and surmount the actually unbridgeable gap between the realm of sensory and sensuous experiences and the domain of philosophical concepts and propositions. In the chapters that follow, the reader moves beyond a consideration of aesthetics in terms of theories of art and beauty to investigate the aesthetic as a specific, privileged type of perception. By approaching art—literary and visual—as social knowledge, one can scrutinize the ways in which it challenges or endorses normative gender and ethical systems. The cult of ugliness is one of the most fascinating stories in modern Anglo-American art and literature. By exposing and exploring the power-knowledge relations of modernist aesthetic discourse, one can discern that the self-proclaimed or socially-endorsed prerogative to promote "ugliness" or pronounce an object "beautiful" is one of the basic and most effective privileges of patriarchal culture. It is, indeed, an aesthetic power play, a confirmation of masculinist judgment. The cult of ugliness afforded an exclusive, almost exclusively male, group of writers and artists new opportunities to impose aesthetic sanctions and verdicts, and to police standards of sexual differentiation at a time when women were ardently advocating the demolition of gender barriers to education, political activity, vocational and cultural opportunities, and social recognition. It is a complicated story, and rarely pretty.

Chapter 1 ∾

The Trials of Beauty:
Ruskin, Whistler, and
a "New Series of Truths"

A few words well chosen, and distinguished, will do work that a thousand cannot, when every one is acting, equivocally, in the function of another. Yes; and words, if they are not watched, will do deadly work sometimes. . . . [T]here are masked words abroad, I say, which nobody understands, but which everybody uses, and most people will also fight for, live for, or even die for, fancying they mean this or that, or the other, of things dear to them: for such words wear chameleon cloaks[.]

—Ruskin, *Works* 18:66

A brilliant artist praised for "inaugurating a revolution, leading intransigent youth against the strongholds of tradition and academic complacence" (Fry 1903:345) but also known for his irascible temperament and timely barbs lashes out at an eminent critic (once, the chief proponent and defender of "new" art) who has trashed the artist's work, in writing, as a deliberate and very public affront. Is this Ezra Pound defending "us moderns" from the likes of J. Middleton Murry or F. R. Leavis? Or Wyndham Lewis engineering another confrontation with Roger Fry or T. S. Eliot? Both scenarios are probable, but not factual: the adversarial artist and critic to which I refer are James Abbott McNeill Whistler (1834–1903) and John Ruskin (1819–1900). One must return to these gifted polemicists' bitter dispute in the late 1870s in order to understand fully the combative spirit of the cult of ugliness and the cultists' commitment to difficult new "truths."

Yet this is not the same thing as claiming Ruskin, Whistler, or the infamous trial for which both were responsible, as some indisputable, "distant ideality of the origin" of modernism (Foucault 1984:80).[1] Both contributed significantly, and singularly, to aestheticism and cultural development for more than 40 years; the works of both taught Victorians, Edwardians, and self-proclaimed modernists why and how the fundamentals of artistic expression and critical discourse should and could be renovated. Tirelessly, sometimes flamboyantly, they worked to prove that art *matters*.

Making Enemies

James Whistler sued John Ruskin for libel because, on July 2, 1877, Ruskin published caustic remarks about *Nocturne in Black and Gold: The Falling Rocket* (Figure 1) in his monthly letter for *Fors Clavigera*[2]:

> For Mr. Whistler's own sake, no less than for the protection of the purchaser, Sir Coutts Lindsay ought not to have admitted works into the [Grosvenor] gallery in which the ill-educated conceit of the artist so nearly approached the aspect of wilful imposture. I have seen, and heard, much of Cockney impudence before now; but never expected to hear a coxcomb ask two hundred guineas for flinging a pot of paint in the public's face. (*WJR* 29:160)[3]

The ensuing trial, deferred and delayed until November 1878, produced a seemingly Pyrrhic victory for Whistler: he won the case, but was only awarded a farthing in damages *and* was required to pay court costs. In the *Punch* caricature of the decision (Figure 2), a bewigged justice has pulled an enlarged coin from a box marked "DAMAGES." "THE LAW ALLOWS IT[;] THE COURT AWARDS IT" declares the judge; above the jury one reads, "NO SYMPATHY WITH THE DEFENDANT." The bill of the modest Ruskin-bird is inscribed, "OLD PELICAN IN THE ART WILDERNESS." Although personally vindicated, Whistler was financially ruined. The farthing, which he wore on his watch chain as an emblem of victory, was a poor substitute for the new home and studio on London's Tite Street he had to surrender to creditors, along with cherished personal possessions. Ruskin's legal costs, on the other hand, approximately £400, were paid through a public subscription organized by Marcus Huish of the Fine Art Society (Hilton 399).

In 1877, Ruskin had been "eager for the courtroom, perhaps not realizing the nature of legal proceedings. 'It's mere nuts and nectar to me,' he told Burne-Jones, 'the notion of having to answer for myself in court, and the whole thing will enable me to assert some principles of art economy which I've never got into the public's head, but . . . may get sent all over the world vividly in a newspaper report or two'" (Hilton 357). In November 1878, however, he was confined at home, recovering from an acute breakdown that had occurred in late February. In January 1879, Ruskin decided he had to resign his chair at Oxford. "It was not at all an obligation," as Hilton explains, "but Ruskin always felt that his writing in *Fors Clavigera* had the especial authority of his position at Oxford" (399). As Ruskin informed a friend, "'the result of the Whistler trial leaves me no further option. I cannot hold a chair from which I have no power of expressing judgment without being taxed for it by British Law'" (Hilton 399). Paradoxically, the financial and social disaster of the trial prompted Whistler to organize a trip to Venice, where he embarked on what proved to be an exceptional new venture in etching.

Not surprisingly, the trial has assumed very different roles in Ruskin and Whistler studies. Even Linda Merrill's excellent 1992 book, *A Pot of Paint: Aesthetics on Trial in "Whistler v Ruskin,"* takes a somewhat David-and-Goliath view of the conflict—Whistler, iconoclastic American expatriate, takes on the giant of British art criticism and sycophantic artist friends (especially Edward Burne-Jones) and successfully defends both what he paints and his right to creative independence. In the context of the present discussion, one could say that Whistler attempted, through the courts, to prove Ruskin guilty of unlawful utterance of aesthetic discourse, to defend his own innovative mode of representation, and to protect the lexicon he was devising to champion his project.[4]

Whistler was impugning both Ruskin's right and ability to offer himself publicly as a moderator of aesthetic opinion. By extension, Whistler was also challenging some of the predominant institutional sites that Ruskin represented: the review columns of newspapers and journals, the academies (the Grosvenor Gallery was opened in the spring of 1877 to enable artists to exhibit their works for sale *outside* the Royal Academy's rigid purview),[5] and the universities (Ruskin was Slade Professor of Fine Art at Oxford). As Whistler later observed in "Whistler v. Ruskin: Art and Art Critics" (December 1878),[6] "a life passed among pictures makes not a painter, else the policeman in the National Gallery might assert himself.... Let not Mr. Ruskin flatter himself that more education makes the difference between himself and the policeman when both stand gazing in the Gallery" (*GA* 26–27). Unquestionably, the professor's reference to an "ill-educated conceit" continued to rankle. According to Whistler, the production of aesthetic discourse should be the province of practicing artists *only.* Anyone else—especially the critic—lacks sufficient knowledge to judge the work of art fairly or intelligently. To make this argument, Whistler refused to acknowledge Ruskin's considerable talents as a watercolorist and sketch artist, or his work as art instructor.[7]

After three decades of "significant toil" and prolific publication, Ruskin had established himself as an informed arbiter of aesthetic taste and judgment; accusing Whistler of "wilful imposture" was an assertion of Ruskin's right to police the ranks of socially-acceptable artists. Although famous for declaring "all great Art is Praise" (*WJR* 15:351), Ruskin did not believe that all great art critics must be devoted to praise. Ruskin's lawyers[8] not only challenged the value of Whistler's paintings, aesthetic and monetary, they tried to ridicule the new discursive strategies he had devised to signal his works' distinctiveness. A prominent critic, Thomas Taylor of the London *Times,* and two painters, William Powell Frith (*Derby Day, The Railway Station*) and Edward Burne-Jones, were called upon to decry Whistler's compositional skills and the comparative formlessness of his works. (Burne-Jones was especially willing to echo Ruskin's charges that the paintings did not meet accepted standards of "finished" art.) Much was made of Whistler's titles for his paintings—his penchant for calling them "nocturnes," "symphonies," and "arrangements." Belittling Whistler in front of the jury was not the only motive, I would suggest; mocking the unusual names was another way of denying the fact that Whistler was engaged upon an alternative "discursive practice that is embodied in techniques and effects" (Foucault 1972: 194). Not surprisingly, Whistler was asked by his counsel, William Petheram, to clarify his terminology:

> PETHERAM: Will you tell us the meaning of the word "nocturne" as applied to your pictures?
> WHISTLER: By using the word "nocturne" I wished to indicate an artistic interest alone, divesting the picture of any outside anecdotal interest which might have been otherwise attached to it. A nocturne is an arrangement of line, form, and colour first. The picture is throughout a problem that I attempted to solve. . . .
> PETHERAM: What do you mean by "arrangement"?
> WHISTLER: I mean an arrangement of line and form and colour. Among my works are some night pieces, and I have chosen the word "nocturne" because it generalizes and simplifies the whole set of them; it is an accident that I happened upon terms used in music. (qtd Merrill 1992:144)

Eschewing support from any other quarter, Whistler insists on the supposedly "accidental" attempt to enfold (and thereby legitimate) his alternative aesthetics within musical discourse. (The contentious role of "color" in his works is discussed below.) Today one realizes that the effort to divest painting of narrative meaning begins with the assumption that art is innocent of ideology. Yet this was one of several crucial lessons that poets such as Pound took from Whistler—to simplify, strip the work of nonessential "anecdote" or "rhetoric," then call attention to the technical or compositional feat (with a label such as "Arrangement," "Nocturne," or *Imagisme*).[9]

The barely-breathed class inflections of Ruskin's written diatribe—denigrating Whistler's work as being nothing more than "Cockney impudence"[10]—remind us that Ruskin's privileged role as adviser to the British public depended upon the willingness of largely middle-class readers to be educated in art appreciation and aesthetic betterment. Ruskin's insistence that art answer to, and reflect, nationalistic purposes—a notion particularly palatable to his audience—was diametrically opposed to Whistler's insistence on the autonomy of artistic production and product. "False again," Whistler later proclaimed in his *Ten O'Clock Lecture:* the "fabled link between the grandeur of Art and the glories and virtues of the State, for Art feeds not upon nations, and peoples may be wiped from the face of the earth, but Art *is*" (*GA* 155). Whistler was the first of many expatriate Americans who assumed that his personal, relatively detached and marginalized status in European society was somehow a universalized sine qua non for all serious artists.

Beneath all the bluster and public posturing, Whistler *v* Ruskin vividly reveals the vexed nature of power relations within late-nineteenth century British art circles. In two sentences, Ruskin not only names all of the figures participating in the circulation of aesthetic discourse—the artist, the critic, the gallery owner, the purchaser, and the public—but alludes to the economic dimensions of these discursive practices. For what offends Ruskin the most: the painting itself, or the fact that Whistler was charging two hundred quid for it? Implicitly, Ruskin's ill-natured critique translates discursive power into guineas (or pounds); he challenges Whistler's right to assign a monetary value to his works, especially such a high price, and lambastes Sir Coutts Lindsay for establishing an independent gallery that circumvents the Academy's (and the reviewer's) control of artistic production, valuation, and profit-making. Yet Ruskin's willingness to assail Whistler's art as a bad investment should not obscure his campaign to improve the economic situation of art and cultural workers alike. Ezra Pound is among several modernists whose "economic theories of art are profoundly influenced by Ruskin" (Birch 1999b:187).

Whistler's legal entanglements with Ruskin also remind us of the extent to which beauty and truth became polarized in later Victorian aesthetic discourse.[11] Ruskin defended his *Fors Clavigera* article as being a frank exercise in truth-telling; Whistler contested the critic's right to do so, and the entire validity of the Ruskinian regime. Specifically, he challenged Ruskin's insistence that truth in art is synonymous with fidelity to nature, and dependent upon the conventional representational codes of mimetic realism. In a pretrial appeal to the jury of public opinion, Whistler informed the readers of *The World* (May 1878) that, "The imitator is a poor kind of creature. If the man who paints only the tree, or flower, or other surface he sees before him were an artist, the king of artists would be the photographer. It is for the artist to do something beyond this . . . to treat a flower as his key, not as his model" (*GA* 128).

The truth-claims of Ruskin's criticism were not stressed by his lawyers, however. During the trial, Sir John Holker attempted to deflect attention from the factual elements of the case—whether or not Ruskin had published a libellous statement about Whistler—by appealing to the more intangible realms of beauty and good taste *and* to public discomfiture with Whistler's extremely distinctive style of painting. The following is an excerpt from Holker's cross-examination of Whistler:

> HOLKER: You have made the study of art your study of a lifetime. What is the peculiar beauty of that picture [*Nocturne in Black and Gold*]?
> WHISTLER: I daresay I could make it clear to any sympathetic painter, but I do not think I could to you, any more than a musician could explain the beauty of a harmony to a person who has no ear.
> HOLKER: Do you not think that anybody looking at that picture might fairly come to the conclusion that it has no peculiar beauty?
> WHISTLER: I think there is distinct evidence that Mr. Ruskin did come to that conclusion.
> HOLKER: Do you think it fair that Mr. Ruskin should come to that conclusion?
> WHISTLER: What might be fair to Mr. Ruskin I can't answer. No artist of culture would come to that conclusion. (qtd Merrill 1992:153–154)

In Holker's lexicon, beauty is a coded term for established canons of publicly-accepted art. And it was as Defender of Beauty that Holker tried to present the absent Ruskin during his opening statement to the jury. "Mr Ruskin is a man of the keenest appreciation of that which is beautiful," Holker insisted; "He has a great love and reverence for art and a special admiration for highly finished pictures. His love for art amounts almost to idolatry; and to the examination of the beautiful in art, he has devoted his life" (qtd Merrill 1992:163). As this chapter demonstrates, however, the devotion of critic and artist alike should not be confused with submission. What Ruskin and Whistler have most in common is a masculinist need to exercise control over a category of value that is for them wholly, disturbingly feminized.

Time and again Holker stressed the asking price of the *Nocturne in Black and Gold* as if it were proof positive that Whistler was an artistic poseur and charlatan. He *must* say that his hastily-executed, carelessly finished works are beautiful, Holker implied, because it would be unprofitable for him to do otherwise. Ruskin, on the other hand, was represented as being an unimpeachable source of aesthetic opinion, beyond any taint of profit-motive (his private, inherited income was never mentioned):

Mr. Ruskin has lived a long life without being attacked. No one has been able to say that he purchased Mr. Ruskin's praise, and no one has attempted to control Mr. Ruskin's pen through the medium of a jury. The defendant requested me to say that he does not retract one syllable of what he said in the criticism: he believes he is right. . . . I ask the jury not to paralyse his hand now. . . . It would be an evil day for the art of this country if he were prevented from indulging in proper and legitimate criticism, and from pointing out what is beautiful and what is not[.] (qtd Merrill 1992:171)

Ruskin had been transformed into a national monument, the British bulldog metamorphosed into a devoted watchdog of and for the Beautiful. By finding for the plaintiff but awarding him only a farthing, the coin of least value, the jury tried, as much as possible, to legitimate Ruskin's aesthetic discourse—both the iconographic traditions he had taught the public to admire, and his role as their privileged enunciator. The latter was consolidated at a time when the expert, in a commodity-driven economy, began to take on the specialized function of guiding "the reading [or art-appreciating and acquiring] market to appropriate works" (Leps 138). In a European context, Ruskin was furthering the "normative practice of art criticism, which introduced a new class of professional writers to the regular operations of determining quality and taste" (Jensen 27).

I am not presenting Ruskin, however, as the first official Enemy of the Cult of Ugliness; far from it. In the discussion that follows his self-appointed role as cultural critic, the devaluation of beauty in his works and insistence that "great" art "will not deny the facts of ugliness or decrepitude" (*WJR* 3:32), the coherent manner in which gender differentiation and prejudice informs aesthetic *and* sociological writings alike, and his paradoxical need to speak *about* the modern but *against* "the social spaces and relations" of modernity (Pollock 1992:53) will be surveyed to suggest how Ruskin functioned as "one of the writers who made the evolution[s] of modernism possible" (Birch 1999b:187). Attention will then turn to Whistler, who denied Ruskin's right to pronounce his works beautiful, ugly, or otherwise, but whose aesthetic theories and practices depended upon the same entrenched demarcations of gender. *Japonisme*, I shall explain, enabled Whistler to "master" beauty on canvas specifically because of the complex cultural power relations it endorsed. The final section of the chapter summarizes the indelible lessons of each man regarding the aggressive advancement of his works.

Sacrifices for Truth

> I takes and paints
> Hear no complaints
> And sells before I'm dry;

Till savage Ruskin
He sticks his tusk in
Then nobody will buy.
                —"Poem by a Perfectly Furious Academician" (Conner v)

So prolific are Ruskin's writings, and so diverse in subject matter, that it is common to work with them in discrete categories: the art theory and criticism, the architectural studies, the social and economic analyses. This study insists upon the interconnectedness and ideological coherence of these works, at the very least in terms of a gender-specific view of the world that buttresses Ruskin's theories of artistic creativity and social productivity. As he states evocatively at the conclusion of *Praeterita,* "How things bind and blend themselves together" (*WJR* 35:561).[12] This is not to accuse Ruskin of excessive or excessively formal thinking, however. To quote Hunt, "Ruskin was not a philosopher nor, though he pretended on occasions to be more systematic and logical than his opponents, did he depend much upon the rigours and consistencies of formal thinking" (1986:51). My argument, which stresses exemplarity rather than singularity, eschews any interest in Ruskin as a "unique aesthetic visionary" (Bloom 1986:2). Also avoided is any attempt to produce a psycho-biographical study of Ruskin's gender-inflected discourse. Rather than identify Ruskin as a sadly dysfunctional individual with complex sexual "issues," I would like to stress that his writings participate in the circulation of gender-based truths that were constructed within and conditioned by a historically-specific cultural moment. That is to say, the opinions expressed in "Of Queen's Gardens" (1865) are not solely the product of Ruskin's feelings for Rose La Touche, 31 years his junior.[13] Instead, they reveal "the degree to which he internalized the conflicts of his culture, including the Victorian male's ambivalence toward female authority" (Sawyer 1990:131), and reaffirm then-contemporary gender typologies and sphere ideologies. Just as importantly, the cultural and sociological writings continue the prejudicial gender work established in his art theory and criticism.[14]

Ruskin's reputation was initially forged through the success of *Modern Painters, The Elements of Drawing, The Stones of Venice,* and *The Seven Lamps of Architecture;* "in the 1850s [he] came to be regarded as an authority to whom all should defer in matters relating to the arts" (Newall 111). When the art educator and theorist broadened his interests in the late 1850s and 1860s to address the social factors inhibiting or promoting the production of "great" art—when he honed his skills as "active and visible controversialist" (Maidment 159)—he was extending a self-sanctioned ability to distinguish between what is "right" and what is not, what is "good" and "bad" in art, society, and human conduct. The 1871 preface to *Sesame and Lilies* neatly summarizes this discursive certainty: "Being now fifty-one years old, and little likely to change my mind hereafter on any important subject of thought (unless through weakness of age), I wish to publish a connected series of such parts of my works as now seem to be right, and likely to be of permanent use" (*WJR* 18:31). Ruskin's texts promised, even reassured, readers that "there *is* such a thing as essential good, and as essential evil, in books, in art, and in character;—that this essential goodness and badness are independent of epochs, fashions, opinions, or revolutions" (*WJR* 18:50). It is this position as arbiter of truths that one should consider carefully.

Although not all critics then or now would agree with John Wise's 1865 disclaimer, "'Mr. Ruskin's nonsense is sometimes more valuable than his critics' sense'" (Bradley 301), they would have to acknowledge the "extraordinary influence which Ruskin wielded in his lifetime" (Fellows 1981:xvii). In Kemp's trenchant phrase, Ruskin was "the Luther of the Arts" (205), a self-styled prophet and reformer absolutely convinced of the rightness of his opinions. As one of Whistler's lawyers acknowledged in his opening statement of the trial (the paraphrase is Whistler's): "'Mr. Ruskin, as would be probably known to the gentlemen of the jury, held perhaps the highest position in Europe and America as an art critic, and some of his works were, he might say, destined to immortality'" (qtd *GA* 2).

Few could have guessed that Ruskin would "immortalize" the demise of beauty as art's apotheosis. Without question, Ruskin's works are informed by an urgent, Platonic sense that aesthetics, ethics, and civic responsibilities are inextricably connected. Responsibility thus emerges as a major leitmotif in Ruskin's writings, incorporating the artist's obligations to nature, artistic medium, and community; the art critic's accountability to a diverse audience, including the producers of art; and the duties of a society toward its members (particularly its educational and economic obligations). Close examination of the aesthetic writings, however, reveals a particular, culminating moment in Western culture's fracturing or dismantling of the Platonic triad. *Modern Painters* has as its epigraph lines from Wordsworth's *The Excursion* in which the speaker walks "with Nature" and offers "My heart a daily sacrifice to Truth" (Wordsworth 140)[15]—not beauty or art. The writings anticipate and make possible a cult of ugliness because beauty is supplanted in a hierarchical discourse that privileges truth; it is indelibly identified with a feminine "mask" (*WJR* 8:161) that could mislead; and it is supplemented by the Grotesque. Furthermore, Ruskin's works helped to intensify the "cult of art as expressive genius" (Pollock 1988:97) that Pound, Eliot, and so many others gladly inherited.

Once one realizes the ways in which paradigmatic distinctions between truth and beauty first enunciated in *Modern Painters* are played out— extended and reinscribed—in Ruskin's sociological discourse (especially

Sesame and Lilies), the regime of gender difference that he consistently advances becomes explicit. In all discursive fields, truth is equated with masculinity, authority, and the mind, and beauty is (uneasily) equated with femininity, passivity, and the body. Whenever an institution, value, or personified idea becomes an object of scrutiny about which knowledge can be produced and commodified, it is feminized. The ground of Ruskin's gender-expressiveness is cloaked in patriarchal moral terms: everything and everyone is answerable, ultimately, "to Him who is the origin of virtue" (*WJR* 8:24). Several trenchant examples should demonstrate the basic patterns of his discourse. A description of Italy, initially written for an unfinished novel and then incorporated into *The Poetry of Architecture,* establishes connections between death and the "female city and nation-state" that will resonate throughout Ruskin's canon: "[T]he cypress befits the landscape of Italy, because she is a land of tombs, the air is full of death—it is the past in which she lives, the past in which she is glorious—she is beautiful in death, and her people, her nation, are the dead" (*WJR* 1:542). Artists are advised not to "ape the execution of masters" but to go the source of all good art: "go to Nature in all singleness of heart, and walk with her labouriously and trustingly, having no other thoughts but how best *to penetrate* her meaning, and remember her instruction" (*WJR* 3:624; emphasis added). This phallic discourse is intensified in subsequent volumes of *Modern Painters;* Ruskin's drama of creativity becomes increasingly sexualized. The "Imagination Penetrative" never "stops at crusts or ashes, or outward images of any kind; it ploughs them all aside, and plunges into the very central fiery heart; nothing else will content its spirituality. . . . [I]t gets within all fences, cuts down to the root, and drinks the very vital sap of that it deals with" (*WJR* 4:250–251). Several pages later, however, when Ruskin (in a very Coleridgian gesture) wants to compare the stability of the imagination with the fluctuations and limitations of the fancy, the latter becomes, in his fantastic allegorization, a skittish and vivid young woman:

> [T]he imagination being at the heart of things [he observes], poises herself there, and is still, quiet and brooding, comprehending all around her with her fixed look; but the fancy staying at the outside of things cannot see them all at once; but runs hither and thither, and round and about to see more and more, bounding merrily from point to point, and glittering here and there, but necessarily always settling, if she settle at all, on a point only, never embracing the whole. And from these single points she can strike out analogies and catch resemblances. Which, so far as the point she looks at is concerned, are true, but would be false, if she could see through to the other side. This, however, she cares not to do; the point of contact is enough for her, and even if there be a gap left between the two things and they do not quite touch, she will spring from one to the other like an electric spark, and be seen brightest in her leaping. (*WJR* 4:258)

Bright and energizing as fancy may be, it is unreliable and shallow. Imagination, on the other hand, is wisely schooled in womanly ways; implicitly, it serves the male artist as constant helpmate.

One of the ostensible purposes of *Modern Painters* is to celebrate the idealized figure of the creative genius. "He stands upon an eminence," Ruskin intones, "from which he looks back over the universe of God and forward over the generations of men" (*WJR* 3:630–31). But another figure emerges in equally eminent tones and responsibilities: the art critic, part expert interpreter of the natural world, part sensitive explicator of aesthetic practices, and entirely discerning arbitrator of natural, artistic, and cultural "laws." Ruskin did not invent art criticism, but he almost single-handedly invented the position of critic as crucial and innovative cultural worker. By blending legal, moral, and aesthetic discourses, he presented himself as unimpeachable truth-teller and truth-*controller*—not the producer of art, but judge, jury, and promoter. In effect, he taught people to accept the critic as the person most capable of disciplining artists and their works; he preconditioned subsequent generations to accept the critical word of Eliot, I. A. Richards, or F. R. Leavis. Holloway coined the phrase "Victorian sage" to describe this exceptional discursive enterprise; subsequently, Landow, Morgan, Sawyer, and others have tried to explain Ruskin's success in establishing himself "as a virtuoso interpreter of the real" (Landow 1993:56).[16] Only Sawyer, however, fully acknowledges that "the figure of the Victorian sage as a prophet underscores the notion of discursive authority itself as patriarchal—which was perhaps the chief reason for the figure in the first place. . . . [W]hat was generally at stake for the men known as Victorian sages was less the status quo than the question of who should control the necessary changes" (1990:129, 140). To borrow terms from the chivalric ethos Ruskin prized, he was embarked on a crusade of legitimation: legitimizing the social necessity of art, and at the same time sanctioning the critic's role.

A typical passage from *Modern Painters* vividly demonstrates the way in which Ruskin's texts construct their "truth-effects" (Foucault 1979b:36) and thereby cement the reader's faith in the critic:

> Often as I have paused before these noble works, I never felt on returning to them as if I had ever seen them before; for their abundance is so deep and various, that the mind, according to its own temper at the time of seeing, *perceives some new series of truths* rendered in them, just as it would on revisiting a natural scene; and detects *new relations and associations of these truths* which set the whole picture in a different light at every return to it. (*WJR* 3:492; emphasis added)

Truth is produced and confirmed through a series of statements that accumulate significance and intensity; the text readily reveals its procedures for the production, circulation, and regulation of those statements, a process that the discriminating reader can emulate.

Ruskin preferred to describe his methods with a folksy agricultural metaphor: "the labour of a critic who sincerely desires to be just, extends into more fields than it is possible for any single hand to furrow straightly" (*WJR* 5:6). I would suggest that he attempted to elevate his truth claims by securing them in disciplines both intellectually well-established (ethics and law) and newly emerging (science). Recurrent recourse to justice and "the law" also enabled Ruskin access to other, specific effects of discursive power (Foucault 1979b:46) unavailable to aesthetics alone. Claims for and to juridical wisdom established him as Patriarchal Law-Giver and Legal Interpreter (a "lawyer without a wig," to quote *Fors Clavigera* [*WJR* 27:386; Birch 1998:149]). The latter role might seem innocuous enough when a drawing lesson is involved, and "*three* laws that all good drawing of landscape" obeys are identified (nature's organic unity, liberty, and mystery; *WJR* 15:115–116). But Ruskin went on to dictate "the laws of beauty" in demeanor and conduct that should control the behavior of women in "the present extremely active and ingenious generation of young people" (1882 preface to *Sesame and Lilies; WJR* 18:50). And who would think to challenge the Moses of British culture? Interlacing his aesthetic discourse with the scientifism pervading mid-Victorian culture—arguing for a new *kunstwissenschaft,* or the sciences of art—not only inspired the taxonomical structure of Ruskin's writings, it predetermined the elevation of truth over beauty. Long associated with emotions, pleasure, and other categories of value that defy instrumental knowledge, beauty is demoted in favor of truths that can be generated, in Ruskin's "science of aspects," by "an empirical science constructed on the basis of careful observation" (Foucault 1973:376).[17]

"Attending to the Sum and Harmony of His Truths"

The position taken *against* beauty in *Modern Painters* is a crucial step toward a cult of ugliness. Chapter IV of Volume 2[18] confronts four "current" and "False Opinions Held Concerning Beauty": "Those erring or inconsistent positions which I would at once dismiss are: the first, that the Beautiful is the True; the second, that the Beautiful is the Useful; the third, that it is dependent on Custom; and the fourth, that it is dependent on the Association of Ideas" (*WJR* 4:66). Asserting that the Beautiful "is the True" is a "strange position," Ruskin insists,

> instantly contradicted by each and every conclusion of experience. A stone looks as truly a stone as a rose looks a rose, and yet is not so beautiful. . . . I am at a loss to know how any so untenable a position could ever have been

advanced; but it may, perhaps, have arisen from some confusion of the beauty of art with the beauty of nature, and from an illogical expansion of the very certain truth, that nothing is beautiful in art, which, professing to be an imitation, or a statement, is not as such in some sort true. (*WJR* 4:66–67)

The need to dismantle "so untenable a position" is not easily satisfied. At the outset of Volume 3, a discussion of "the love of beauty" is interrupted by the following extended footnote:[19]

As here [Section 12], for the first time, I am obliged to use the terms Truth and Beauty in a kind of opposition, I must therefore stop for a moment to state clearly the relation of these two qualities of art; and to protest against the vulgar and foolish habit of confusing truth and beauty with each other. People with shallow powers of thought . . . are continually doing the most serious mischief by introducing confusion into plain matters. . . . Nothing is more common than to hear people who desire to be thought philosophical, declare that "beauty is truth," and "truth is beauty." I would most earnestly beg every sensible person who hears such an assertion made, to nip the germinating philosopher in his ambiguous bud; and beg him, if he really believes his own assertion, never henceforward to use two words for the same thing. The fact is, truth and beauty are entirely distinct, though often related, things. One is a property of statements, the other of objects. The statement that 'two and two make four' is true, but it is neither beautiful nor ugly, for it is invisible; a rose is lovely, but it is neither true nor false, for it is silent. That which shows nothing cannot be fair, and that which asserts nothing cannot be false. Even the ordinary use of the words false and true, as applied to artificial and real things, is inaccurate. An artificial rose is not a "false" rose, it is not a rose at all. The falseness is in the person who states, or induces the belief, that it *is* a rose.

Now, therefore, in things concerning art, the words true and false are only to be rightly used while the picture is considered as a statement of facts. The painter asserts that this which he has painted is the form of a dog, a man, or a tree. If it be *not* the form of a dog, a man, or a tree, the painter's statement is false; and, therefore, we justly speak of a false line, or false colour; not that any lines or colours can in themselves be false, but they become so when they convey a statement that they resemble something which they do *not* resemble. But the beauty of the lines or colours is wholly independent of any such statement. . . . If this were not so, it would be impossible to sacrifice truth to beauty; for to attain the one would always be to attain the other. But, unfortunately, this sacrifice is exceedingly possible, and it is chiefly this which characterizes the false schools of high art, so far as high art consists in the pursuit of beauty. For although truth and beauty are independent of each other, it does not follow that we are at liberty to pursue whichever we please. They are indeed separable, but it is wrong to separate them; they are to be sought together in the order of their worthiness; that is to say, truth first, and beauty afterwards. High art differs from low art in possessing an excess of beauty in addition to its truth, not in possessing excess of beauty inconsistent with truth. (*WJR* 5:55–56)

The most radical truth-claim of Ruskin's complex and monumental project is therefore the assertion that "truth and beauty are entirely distinct." Close scrutiny of the first two volumes of *Modern Painters* reveals that this "opposition" has actually been operative from the outset. The analysis "Of Truth of Skies" in Volume 1, for example, suggests that beauty can interfere with one's ability to apprehend the "infinity of truth": "[I]f we wish, without reference to beauty of composition, or any other interfering circumstances, to form a judgment of the truth of painting, perhaps the very first thing we should look for, whether in one thing or another . . . should be the expression of *infinity* always and everywhere, in all parts and divisions of parts" (*WJR* 3:387). Beauty is circumstantial, not substantive or absolute—and so the divisive distinctions proliferate.

Two particular elements of Ruskin's argument regarding the truth/beauty schism should be noted. The first concerns the hierarchical mind set that controls all of his pronouncements. Although the famous footnote from Volume 3 initially declares that "truth and beauty are entirely distinct" and "independent," difference is not left unpoliced. Or, in Ruskin's terms, truth cannot be in any way "sacrificed" to beauty. To defend against any such discursive manoeuvre, Ruskin borrows a basic twofold strategy from the scientific discourse he so admires: classify, and rank. Consequently, we are told to consider truth and beauty in the "order of their worthiness"—"that is to say, truth first, and beauty afterwards" (*WJR* 5:56).

The second element concerns the gender inflections of Ruskin's dichotomous propositions. Truth and beauty can be dissevered because "[o]ne is a property of statements, the other of objects" (Ruskin 5:55). One is therefore an attribute of mental activity, supported by the acquisition of knowledge; the other is a condition of concreteness or physicality—of bodies, in other words. Western culture's most cherished dualism has been invoked to correct an overly zealous "love of beauty," a love (or "strange position") that apparently threatens the "natural" preeminence of truth. The "order of worthiness" Ruskin freely installs answers to a culturally-proscribed system of gendered "worth" that places men first and women "afterwards." Anything else is "inconsistent with [the] truth" as Ruskin perceives and promulgates it, in aesthetic texts and social treatises alike.

Some of the most eloquent sections in *Modern Painters* are occasioned by "the contemplation of truth." In a reversal of the New Testament trope,[20] the best artistic mind is compared to a glass, clearly:

And thus, though we want the thoughts and feelings of the artist as well as the truth, yet they must be thoughts arising out of the knowledge of truth, and feelings arising out of the contemplation of truth. We do not want [the artist's] mind to be like a badly blown glass, that distorts what we see through it, but like a glass of sweet and strange colour, that gives new tones to what we see through it; and a glass of rare strength and clearness too, to let us see more than we could ourselves, and bring nature up to us and near to us. (*WJR* 3:137)

One needs to remember that, throughout the nineteenth century, strength was *the* criterion of sexual difference, in physical, moral, and emotional terms. (After Darwin, the argument was given a particular biological spin.) A masculinist code that emphasizes strength and physical power pervades Ruskin's major aesthetic treatise, as an excerpt from Volume 3 of *Modern Painters* attests:

[A]s the great painter is always attending to the sum and harmony of his truths rather than to one or the other of any group, a quality of Grasp is visible in his work, like the power of a great reasoner over his subject, or a great poet over his conception, manifesting itself very often in missing out certain details or less truths (which, though good in themselves, he finds are in the way of others), and in a sweeping manner of getting the beginnings and ends of things shown at once. (*WJR* 5:61)

This gendered discourse of aesthetic appreciation is only intensified, two decades later, when Ruskin analyzes "The Mystery of Life and Its Arts." Because of "all that skill and strength" entailed, the "Art of Building" is deemed "the strongest—proudest—most orderly—most enduring of the arts of man; that of which the produce is in the surest manner accumulative, and need not perish, or be replaced" (*WJR* 18:177). Furthermore, it is the "art which is associated with all civic pride and sacred principle; with which men record their power—satisfy their enthusiasm—make sure their defence—define and make dear their habitation" (*WJR* 18:177).

Critics such as Wihl have praised the "quest for truth" underlining Ruskin's works without considering that the "mosaic of 'truth'" (1985:xi) and its terms "of universal application" (*WJR* 3:104) are derived from and reinforce exploitive, demeaning gender distinctions. In a Donne-like moment *The Seven Lamps of Architecture* insists that truth is "the very equator and girdle of them all . . . of which there are no degrees" (*WJR* 8:54). Encircling and enveloping Ruskin's aesthetic discourse is a cloud of gender prejudice, the full effects of which are not discernible until applied to cultural criticism.

"Helpfully Beautiful"

Ideas of beauty both animate Ruskin's writings and confound them. More precisely, a singular nervousness informs and frames the pursuit of beauty conducted in his aesthetic texts, resulting in the manufacture of a plethora of distinctions and definitional categories. At every turn, the hazards of falseness, or accuracy and inaccuracy, are both anticipated and staged, to the point that beauty almost imperils truth through its association with "degrading and dangerous supposition[s]" (*WJR* 4:67). Unlike truth, which is associated with abstracted fact and information and the "grasp" of reason, beauty necessarily involves the senses, instincts, and physical embodiments. For this reason, I would suggest, Ruskin takes great pains to distinguish between "the instinctive, or aesthetic, and the real or theoretic perception of Beauty" (*WJR* 4:69), a discursive strategy that attempts to elevate beauty to some quasi-rationative or truth-full state. His suggestion that there exists a theoretic faculty not only reveals an interest in the study of physiognomy so popular in his day, but is another means of separating the study of beauty from the sensuous realm of *aesthesis.* Similarly, beauty is further defined (and controlled) through the distinctions made between vital and typical beauty. The former refers to a "felicitous fulfilment of function" (*WJR* 4:64); the latter, as Landow observes, is "concerned not with form but with expression—with the expression of the happiness and energy of life, and, in a different manner, with the representation of moral truths by living things" (1971:148). Again, according to Ruskin, beauty is best deployed when serving truth.

I have already observed that the tone of Ruskin's opposition to beauty intensifies in Volume 3 of *Modern Painters.* To understand the vivid polarities that seem suddenly to have entered his argument, one must turn, as Ruskin did in the late 1840s, from studies of painting to studies of architecture. The second volume of *Modern Painters* was published in 1846; the third, in 1856. The intervening years were devoted to architectural projects, as represented in *The Seven Lamps of Architecture* (1849),[21] *Examples of the Architecture of Venice* (1851), and *The Stones of Venice* Volumes 1 (1851) and 2 and 3 (1853). It is in these books that Ruskin fully encounters—in his own mind, that is—the incompleteness of beauty, its inadequacies and limitations. Put another way, beauty becomes a very circumscribed part of the whole aesthetic truth that Ruskin is trying to construct.

Throughout *Seven Lamps,* beauty is represented in terms of compromising situations or potential perturbation and deception. It may be "sought for" in "every-day life," but only if one enquires "in places where it can be calmly seen; but not if you use the beautiful form only as a mask and covering of the proper conditions and uses of things, nor if you thrust it into the places set apart for toil" (*WJR* 8:161). Most importantly, however, even the "purer beauty" cannot be equated with "more spiritual power" (*WJR* 8:101). Two distinct "orders of building" are posited by Ruskin—"classes" that decidedly articulate prevailing gender stereotypes. One "order" is

characterised by an exceeding preciousness and delicacy, to which we recur with a sense of affectionate admiration; and the other by a severe, and, in many cases, mysterious, majesty, which we remember with an undiminished awe, like that felt at the presence and operation of some great Spiritual Power. . . . Now, the difference between these two orders of building is not merely that which there is in nature between things beautiful and sublime. It is, also, the difference between what is derivative and original in man's work; for whatever is in architecture fair or beautiful, is imitated from natural forms. (*WJR* 8:100–101)

Beauty is now associated with "affection," and things that are "fair"; it is imitative and lacking in power. The latter, reaffirmed through and because of its connections with the sublime,[22] originality, and "severe" majesty, provides Ruskin's aesthetic discourse with its fundamental *auctoritas*.

Schooled in these architectural truths, Ruskin's devaluation of beauty only escalates in the texts subsequent to *Seven Lamps*. In *The Stones of Venice*, the grotesque is seized upon as a supplementary category of aesthetic expression and truth (an issue to be discussed in detail below). *Modern Painters* resumes, in Volume 3, to explain that "'What is beautiful, and what is good?'" are "not the main, at least not the first questions" requiring or deserving one's attention (*WJR* 5:44). As section three of the chapter so succinctly states, "That a thing should be beautiful is not enough" (*WJR* 5:46). Wyndham Lewis or T. E. Hulme would only concur.

Supplementing Beauty

Architectural studies in the early 1850s led John Ruskin to Venice, the city that inspired not only remarkable texts and drawings but a newly emphatic gendered discourse. Venice became, for Ruskin, a decrepit femme fatale in stone, boastful of her previous glory yet inescapably enmeshed in decay and death. (These experiences in and with Venice also provided an impetus for the critique of modern built environments.) Newly impressed with the inadequacies of beauty as category and aesthetic imperative—and, one could add, convinced of the inextricable relationship between the beautiful and the beauty of females—Ruskin turned his attention to the revivification of two aesthetic properties that would profitably supplement beauty and its limitations: the picturesque, and the grotesque. This work constitutes Ruskin's major contributions to ongoing intellectual attempts—under the banner of the supra-aesthetical sublime—to rationalize and systematize emotional responses to nature and to art. Of the two, it is the grotesque that most inspires the reformulation of aesthetic priorities in Volumes 3, 4, and 5 of *Modern Painters*.

Commentators such as Hunt, Harpham, and Helsinger have capably explained the ways in which Ruskin seized upon the picturesque and the grotesque as a means of answering to and for the sublime. "More than any other Victorian," as Helsinger notes,

> Ruskin retained a romantic taste for sublimity. Yet the "beholding imagina-
> tion" he described is not well suited to cope with the romantic or Burkean
> sublime. His beholders have the picturesque traveller's limitations: they must
> gather and compare many partial views before they can comprehend or fully
> respond to what they see. . . . The noble picturesque uses excursive explo-
> ration to explore strong feelings, while the grotesque, though it is a response
> to a single impression, consists of fragmented images like those acquired by
> excursive feeling. . . . Both the fantasy or fearful symbolism of the grotesque
> and the active sympathy of the noble picturesque are equal in emotional force
> to the experience of the [sublime]. (1986:117)

Helsinger further suggests that "first grotesque and then picturesque art become a cooperative effort between artist and spectator to comprehend greatness and enlarge sympathies" (1986:129). But one can also ascertain that the
grotesque, especially, becomes the critic's strategic means of deflecting interest away from beauty and toward an alternative "true ideal." Sanitized of any
association with the ludic, the bestial, or the satanic, this new (and not false)
grotesque is offered to readers as a visual embodiment of exceptional truths.
The grotesque, one might say, performs the truth in arresting new ways.
Demonstrably, the more that the grotesque becomes, for Ruskin, "the only
one of art's modes that can serve as an emblem of the entire field of art, from
the depths to the heights" (Harpham 184–185), the less important the beautiful can be and is. The latter ceases to govern any of the major aesthetic
statements Ruskin wishes to make; increasingly, it occupies a sociological
zone or sphere of influence associated with women (their bodies, motives,
and behaviors). As well, the emphasis on the grotesque brings a new gesture
to aesthetic writing in English: what one can call, to borrow Proust's term
for Baudelaire, the *grimaçant*. The distance between a favored *grimaçant* and
a cult of ugliness is comparatively small indeed.

"Ugliness" is not unknown in Ruskin's discursive enterprise, but is reserved to express the antithesis of beauty. It is featured, for example, in the
extended footnote to Volume 3, Chapter 3 of *Modern Painters:* beautiful
"lines" in a painting may be "inaccurate," and "ugly lines" may be "quite
faithful" to the object being represented; a "picture may be frightfully ugly,
which represents with fidelity some base circumstance of daily life" (*WJR*
5:55–56). The tone is much more subdued than one finds in *The Seven
Lamps of Architecture,* which associates "every element of ugliness" (*WJR*
8:154) with that which is unnatural or deformed. Traditionalist enough to
decry the "monstrification" of architecture and the visual arts, Ruskin is

nonetheless enthralled by the possibilities of producing "new" truths through the idealization of the grotesque.

"All the Influence I Now Desire"

Ruskin scholars almost unanimously suggest that, throughout the late 1850s and 1860s, crucial changes in his attitudes, projects, and pronouncements became apparent. (Somewhat ironically, this was the same decade in which Whistler's artistic productions underwent radical rethinking, resulting in new aesthetic purposes and practices.) Before the fifth and final volume of *Modern Painters* appeared in 1860, Ruskin had, in Hunt's words, "announced fresh territories for his mind in *The Political Economy of Art* in 1857" (1982a:3). Ruskin says as much in "The Mystery of Life and Its Arts":

> [W]hereas in earlier life, what little influence I obtained was due perhaps chiefly to the enthusiasm with which I was able to dwell on the beauty of the physical clouds, and of their colours in the sky; so all the influence I now desire to retain must be due to the earnestness with which I am endeavouring to trace the form and beauty of another kind of cloud than those; the bright cloud of which it is written—"What is your life? It is even as a vapour that appeareth for a little time, and then vanisheth away." (*WJR* 18:146)

A decade earlier, he had informed a Cambridge audience that some "may occasionally have heard it stated of me that I am rather apt to contradict myself. I hope I am exceedingly apt to do so. . . . Mostly, matters of any consequence are three-sided, or four-sided, or polygonal; and the trotting round a polygon is severe work for people any way stiff in their opinions" (*WJR* 16:187). Despite his boasts, Ruskin's texts demonstrate time and again that, regarding issues of sexual difference, contradictions never emerge. However much Ruskin refashions himself as the purveyor of social, political, and economic truths rather than the promoter of beauty, the gender presumptions of his discursive interventions remain fixed, and the consequences for the countless women and men taught to follow Ruskin's example were stiff.

Ruskin's essentialist vision accommodates only highly restrictive taxonomies of gendered types. Men, it would seem, can expend their "whole masculine energy" (*WJR* 18:97) in ways that are either true or false, but their subjectivity is unified and stable. Women, on the other hand, are ultimately as strange, arbitrary, and mysterious as Nature. For that reason, Ruskin attempts to control females through a carefully proscribed program of "women's work." The latter is outlined, "once for all" in Letter 34 of *Fors Clavigera:* "Women's work is,—I. To please people. II. To feed them in dainty ways. III. To clothe them. IV. To keep them orderly. V. To teach them" (*WJR* 27:645). Idealized, women play the role of "angel in the house" to perfection. Increasingly, Ruskin becomes obsessed with the disconcerting truth about women's negative qualities and capabilities. This "intense fascination with the processes by which young girls transform into true daughters of Eve" (Walsh 32) frames *Sesame and Lilies,* figuratively and literally.[23] Both the 1871 preface to the book and the conclusion of "Of Queen's Gardens" speak to Ruskin's uncanny ability "to see the utmost evil that is in women" (*WJR* 18:47). As Sawyer suggests, "The Ruskinian woman seems capable of radically unsettling the balance of forces she supposedly also contains" (1990:138). The following passage, from the final section addressed to "Queens," is perhaps the most remarkable in *Sesame and Lilies*—remarkable in terms of its venom and inverted logic:

> There is not a war in the world [Ruskin insists], no, nor an injustice, but you women are answerable for it; not in that you have provoked, but in that you have not hindered. Men, by their nature, are prone to fight; they will fight for any cause, or for none. It is for you to choose their cause for them, and to forbid them when there is no cause. There is no suffering, no injustice, no misery, in the earth, but the guilt of it lies with you. (*WJR* 18:140)[24]

By demonizing women to some extent, Ruskin hopes to blame them for the woes of the world and exculpate the men actually responsible. Having worked more than 20 years to achieve "the status of those who are charged with saying what counts as true" (Foucault 1979b:46), Ruskin utilizes his position to disseminate gender oppression and enmity.

And what of women and the beautiful? Ruskin is always very careful to distinguish between the apotheosis of aesthetic values and the human approximation of the ideal. A "womanly beauty" (*WJR* 18:124) is the most that any individual female can hope to embody. As such she can aspire to be, both "within her gates" and "without," not just the "centre of order" but "the mirror of beauty" (*WJR* 18:137). Not surprisingly, a woman's education should be directed toward the perfection of such beauty as she is capable. Her program of instruction should consist of "such physical training and exercise as may confirm her health, and perfect her beauty; the highest refinement of that beauty being unattainable without splendour of activity and of delicate strength. . . . [O]nly remember that all physical freedom is vain to produce beauty without a corresponding freedom of heart" (*WJR* 18:123–24). Women are not only literally and figuratively confined within the domestic sphere, their subjectivity begins and ends with their bodies. Generally speaking, they *are* the body politic in Ruskin's "commonwealth," just as men are the minds.

The production of beauty in Ruskin's sociological discourse is fraught with difficulties. Women can be associated with beauty, but he does not want to overwork the designation "beautiful," nor undermine values established in reference to Nature and reserved for aesthetic enterprises. Consequently, to distinguish the merely female he invokes the same slighting terms that modernists such as Lewis and Pound will come to prefer: *pretty* and *prettiness.* The latter are used primarily for satirical purposes: to insist that "girls" should avoid religious issues and stick to their "pretty dresses" (*WJR* 18:36); to comment on the "pretty" drawings they make to amuse themselves and others; to castigate middle-class complacency and indifference to the poor. "You belong to the middle or upper classes," Ruskin surmises of his "queenly" auditors; "[y]ou have, then, I suppose, good food, pretty rooms to live in, pretty dresses to wear, power of obtaining every rational and wholesome pleasure" (*WJR* 18:43). His solution to such economic disparity? "[L]et a certain part of your day . . . be set apart for making strong and pretty dresses for the poor" (*WJR* 18:39–40).

Modernity's "Mischief"

In Lewis's 1937 novel *The Revenge for Love,* the supportive and always self-sacrificing Margot Stamp (a "frail contraption") reads *Sesame and Lilies* and worries that heroic literary women are responsible for men's belittlement (V. Parker 220). A first-time reader of Ezra Pound's "Hugh Selwyn Mauberley" might be surprised to find the names of Ruskin and "Of King's Treasuries" mentioned, with approbation, in the "*Yeux Glauques*" section of the poem. Whether attracted by Ruskin's fervent medievalism or his once-commanding discursive presence, Pound was undoubtedly keen to identify a kindred spirit who appreciated that civilization should be more than "an old bitch gone in the teeth" (*P/SPo* 64). Ruskin's attempts to separate truth and beauty in aesthetic discourse and cultural critique, and his insistence on elevating the truth to new levels of artistic and social responsibility, represent a significant "jolt" in the history of aesthetic theorizing, one of those gestures that "mark[] a pause between the laying aside of one great ruling principle, and the taking up of another. . . . It was the great watershed" (*WJR* 8:89). Several other ways in which Ruskin's writings anticipate and even frame the "watershed" agendae of modernist critics and writers should be considered. These include an intense commitment to championing new art, however selectively; a belief in the critic as king-maker; the notion that the best art is *impersonal;* a paradoxical and vehement antimodernity, including a denunciation of urbanization; and a disparaging attitude toward "the mob."

Ruskin was just 24 when the first volume of *Modern Painters* was published in May 1842; he had only recently achieved the status of "A Graduate of Oxford" that the title page simply (and anonymously) acknowledged. His task was nothing less than to rebuke established art institutions (including the Royal Academicians, art reviewers, and gallery owners) for their inability to appreciate the works of J. W. W. Turner. The original subtitle of his project, *Modern Painters: Their Superiority in the Art of Landscape Painting to All the Ancient Masters,* reminds us that he was reanimating the ancients vs. moderns debate in order to argue for the excellencies of radical, contemporary works of art.[25] At the same time, he was asserting his right to occupy a self-created position as arbiter of the new.

Both Arrowsmith and Wihl have identified a link between Ruskin's admonitions that the artist conceal himself in his works and the impersonality of art cited by writers such as Pound, Lewis, and Eliot. "The power of the masters is shown by their self-annihilation," *Modern Painters* insists,

> It is commensurate with the degree in which they themselves appear not in their work. . . . Every great writer may be at once known by his guiding the mind far from himself, to the beauty which is not of his own creation, and the knowledge which is past his finding out. . . . If we stand for a little time before any of the more celebrated works of landscape, listening to the comments of the passers-by. . . . [m]ultitudes will laud the composition, and depart with the praise of Claude on their lips . . . [without realizing that the] skill of the artist, and the perfection of his art, are never proved until both are forgotten. The artist has done nothing till he has concealed himself; the art is imperfect which is visible. (*WJR* 3:23, 22)

As Arrowsmith points out, Ruskin's theory of artistic "self-annihilation" very "vividly anticipates, and perhaps influenced, Eliot's doctrine of poetic 'impersonality'" (90).

Ruskin reproached Whistler for working too quickly; for "flinging" paint rather than carefully applying it, brushstroke by painstaking brushstroke. Intriguingly, by lamenting that "precious things," especially works of art, are no longer valued as they should be in these "modern times, which desires to produce the largest results at the least cost" (*WJR* 8:30, 31), Ruskin forecasts some of the arguments put forward by Walter Benjamin seven decades later. As Helsinger notes, "Benjamin's work is, like Ruskin's, permeated with a profound nostalgia for a lost way of seeing—what he calls the 'aura' of a work of art and what Ruskin called 'awe.' Both men accept what they see as an irreversible historical change, but the reforms they urge within this new mode of seeing are conceived in terms of a displaced romantic art" (1986:132). It is his determination to don the mantle of displaced respecter of the "beautiful past" and its cultural coherence and vitality *and* to be the critic of "the frightful and monotonous present" (*WJR* 5:369) that underscores Ruskin's ties with the modernists' complex sensibility. Citing then-contemporary life as being "more than terrible," Ruskin frequently launches into a Jeremiad against "this awful globe of ours as it is indeed, one pallid charnel house,—a ball strewed bright with human ashes, glaring in its poised sway to and fro beneath the sun that warms it, all blinding white with death from pole to pole" (*WJR* 4:376). A passage such as this could easily function as prefatory guide to *The Waste Land*. More specifically, Ruskin sounds an anguished cry against the "Unreal City"—the "reckless luxury, the deforming mechanism, and the squalid misery of modern cities" (*WJR* 18:150)—with increasing regularity.

Venice was the site of Ruskin's first lessons in the historical and cultural decay of built environments, and the moral to be derived from this devolutionary spectacle. A description of Venice as a half-livid corpse, dead in the suburbs and vaguely alive in the city centre, is particularly memorable:

> In the centre of the city there are still some places where some evidence of vitality remains, and where, with kind closing of the eyes to signs, too manifest even there, of distress and declining fortune, the stranger may succeed in imagining, for a little while what must have been the aspect of Venice in her prime. But this lingering pulsation has not force enough any more to penetrate into the suburbs and outskirts of the city; the frost of death has there seized upon it irrevocably, and the grasp of mortal disease is marked daily by the increasing breadth of its belt of ruin. (*WJR* 10:36)[26]

In later years, Ruskin insisted upon the special moral "diseases" to which men would be exposed in the city, thus interchanging the city and a woman's body as sites of contamination. The Bishop of Manchester, of all people, is rebuked for underestimating "urban influences" of this sort; reminding readers that any city can be a latter-day Babylon, Ruskin bemoans "the special influence of cities over a vicious, that is to say, a declining, people. They are the foci of its fornication" (*WJR* 34:414–415).

Other infection motifs can be traced in Ruskin's comments about city life in *Time and Tide, Queen of the Air,* and *On the Old Road.* As a "punishment" for the "reckless crowding in cities" (*WJR* 34:276), Ruskin predicts "the hot fermentation and unwholesome secrecy of the population crowded into large cities": "each mote in the misery lighter, as an individual soul, than a dead leaf, but becoming oppressive and infectious each to his neighbour, in the smoking mass of decay. The resulting modes of mental ruin and distress are continually new; and in a certain sense, worth study in their monstrosity" (*WJR* 34:268). In addition to citing, presciently, "the mere trampling pressure and electric friction of town life" that brings "every law of healthy existence into question" (*WJR* 34:269), Ruskin identifies the ennui that pervades urban life. One passage in particular deserves citation:

The monotony of life in the central streets of any great modern city . . . where every emotion intended to be derived by men from the sight of nature, or the sense of art, is forbidden for ever, leaves the craving of the heart for a sincere, yet changeful, interest. . . . [But] there is no interest of occupation for any of the inhabitants but the routine of counter or desk within doors, and the effort to pass each other without collision outside; so that from morning to evening the only possible variation of the monotony of the hours, and lightening of the penalty of existence, must be some kind of mischief[.] (*WJR* 34:270–271)

Fears of the mischief-making capabilities of urbanites, described by Ruskin in Bosch-like terms as a "fermenting mass of unhappy human beings,—news-mongers, novel-mongers, picture-mongers, poison-drink-mongers, lust and death-mongers; the whole smoking mass of it one vast dead-marine storeshop" (*WJR* 28:137), prompts him to focus on "the mob" as emblem of an energized and somewhat demonized crowd. Even true kings among men cannot rule without disquiet, Ruskin laments; the mob is always "pretty sure to make *its* 'gran rifiúto' of *them*" (*WJR* 18:101). Just as he scoffs at the notion that "a division of the land of the world among the mob of the world would immediately elevate the said mob into sacred personages" (*WJR* 18:106), he mocks the fact that such a mass of people can maintain an intelligent opinion for more than "an hour." The mob "thinks by infection," he harshly insists, "catching an opinion like a cold, and there is nothing so little that it will not roar itself wild about, when the fit is on" (*WJR* 18:81–82). Small wonder that he warned, time and again, "No nation can last, which has made a mob itself" (*WJR* 18:84). When the views expressed by Lewis, Eliot, and Pound are highlighted in Chapters 3 and 4, Ruskin's pronouncements should resound all over again.

Making Alternative "Arrangements"

> There is a young artist called Whistler,
> Who in every respect is a bristler;
>   A tube of white lead
>   Or a punch to the head
> Come equally handy to Whistler.
>
> —Dante Gabriel Rossetti[27]

The Whistler paintings that suffered the greatest scrutiny and ridicule during the trial included *Nocturne in Black and Gold: The Falling Rocket,* both works entitled *Nocturne in Blue and Silver,*[28] and *Nocturne in Blue and Gold.*[29] All were begun and completed by Whistler in the early to middle 1870s, an intensely productive phase of his career during which he furthered his experiments in color tonalities, comparatively abstract and austere compositional structures, and resolutely nonnarrative subject matter. But I would like to turn to his work of the previous decade—projects in which the convergence of gender ideology and aesthetic discourse is more discernible. It should be clear, though, that Whistler would have loathed this analysis—for two reasons, at least. Firstly, because it presumes to offer a critique of his paintings. Whistler despised criticism in any form, from any type of critic, whether in the guise of exhibition organizers and judges (the "gentlemen of the hanging committee," as he liked to call them [*GA* 190]), newspaper art critics, or (especially) academics. (After the trial, Whistler summarized his views about that "creature," the "art critic" thus: "'Je n'en vois pas la nécessité'" [*GA* 25].) The second reason he would have rejected this inquiry: I do not discuss his paintings in the terms he preferred, such as the pursuit of Beauty, the superiority of Art over Nature, or the privileged role of the Artist as Nature's master and Art's lover-genius. Rather, I am challenging Whistler's claims that he created ideologically-free paintings in the service of "art for art's sake," demonstrating instead that his wonderfully evocative, evanescent works are informed by intersecting masculinist and imperialist codes. And this is especially true of the portraits and groupings of women he created in the 1860s. Yet I am also arguing for the singular importance of *The Gentle Art of Making Enemies* as a proto-modernist manifesto and performance piece—which Whistler would have expected, if not appreciated.

Furthermore, I suggest how the person who painted *Battersea Reach, Wapping,* and *Symphony in White No.1: The White Girl* thoroughly reeducated himself in order to create *Nocturne in Black and Gold: The Falling Rocket.* (As Pound later observed of T. S. Eliot, "He has actually trained *and* modernized himself" [*LEP* 40]). The necessary bridge between these radically dissimilar systems of modelling and representation—one realistic and mimetic, the other stylized and much more abstract—is the double lesson of *Japonisme* and Japanese art. The international aesthetic Whistler developed, the genuine cross-fertilization of American, European, and Asian approaches and techniques that his canvases realized, not only made it possible for him to paint differently, but established a precedent for painters and writers alike to follow.

Japonisme should be read as a particular, nineteenth-century subfield of Orientalism, a "style of thought based upon an ontological and epistemological distinction made between 'the Orient' and . . . 'the Occident'" (Said 1978:2). Orientalism is that "enormously systematic discipline by which European culture was able to manage—and even produce—the Orient," as Said has determined, a "mode of discourse with supporting institutions, vocabulary, scholarship, imagery, doctrines" (1978:3, 1–2). Just as importantly, "it is a method for transforming a distant and often threatening Otherness

into a highly artificial mythic formation to serve a network of interests"
(Board 371). *Japonisme* was coined in 1872 by the art collector Philippe
Burty; others, like Van Gogh, preferred the term *Japonaiserie*. Both French
words[30] remind us that Whistler was adapting and promoting a European
reconstruction of Oriental culture as well as learning firsthand from porce-
lains, prints, paintings, and handicrafts. Nevertheless, *Japonisme* is a mis-
nomer insofar as it seems to distinguish between Japanese and other Asian
cultural productions. As Sandberg comments, "Though Chinese porcelain is
quite distinct from Japanese prints, Whistler seems to have discovered both
at the same time. Indeed, few artists in the 1860's made any aesthetic distinction between the art products of the various Oriental countries"
(1964:503). Spencer concurs that Whistler made "little distinction between
Japan and China. There are Chinese pots and Japanese items as well in his
picture [*The Lange Leizen*]. Whistler's mother referred to it as a 'Japanese
study,' and in 1864 Whistler called it his 'Chinese picture'" (1980: 60).

Said has convincingly argued that "Orientalism was ultimately a political
vision of reality whose structure promoted the difference between the familiar (Europe, the West, 'us') and the strange (the Orient, the East, 'them')"
(1978:43). Always underscoring the us/them confrontation is an unshake-
able belief in Western superiority and Oriental inferiority, as Nochlin stresses
in "The Imaginary Orient" (1991). Such chauvinistic attitudes certainly in-
terlace the comments of Whistler's contemporaries. George Moore, for example, confidently boasts that Whistler's superior intelligence enables him
to surpass his mentors: "It was Japan that counselled the strange grace of the
silhouette," and inspired the "subtly sweet and magical passages" of color in
Harmony and Green and Grey: Miss Cicely Alexander, but "a higher intelligence massed and impelled those chords of green and grey than ever mani-
fested itself in Japanese fan or screen; the means are simpler, the effect is
greater, and by the side of this picture the best Japanese work seems only
facile, superficial improvisation" (24). Whistler is presumed to have absorbed the lessons of Japanese art and then to have overmastered them.
Moore is not simply flattering his peer—he is reasserting the dominant position of Western cultural practices.

For Whistler himself, the rejection of Western traditions of representationalism *necessitated* a process of defamiliarization and denaturalization—thus effecting an estrangement that would free him from the bonds of a visually
mimetic, narrative, and often times moralistic tradition. An immersion in
Japonisme made that project possible; it provided a "syntax for an otherness, an
unfamiliarity, a distance, which is too casually called the exotic in tourist literature and 'synthesist' in art historical literature" (Pollock 1992:31).[31]

Diverse factors and resources contributed to Whistler's "orientalism." In
1841 his father, an American army engineer, went to Russia to supervise the

construction of the St. Petersburg-Moscow railway. The family followed in 1842, when James was eight. This extraordinary adventure enabled the young Jimmy Whistler to visit the Chinese Room of Catherine the Great's Tsarkoe Selo Palace, an Orientalist's dream. Subsequently, Major Whistler died; the family returned to New England. James Whistler graduated from West Point in 1854, the same year that American Commodore Matthew C. Perry and his fleet of "Black Ships" arrived at Japan and, "with a show of force, convinced Japan to sign diplomatic agreements with the United States. With the opening of Yokohama in 1859, Japan, its art, and its culture became more readily accessible . . . to the West for the first time in almost two hundred and fifty years" (Cate 7).[32] From 1855 onwards Whistler devoted himself to gaining access to the art circles and bohemian centers of Paris and London. Both cities became intensely caught up in a "'collective day-dream of the Orient'" (Said 52) in the next two decades; Whistler was instrumental in spreading the Parisian gospel of *Japonisme* in London through his ties with the Rossettis.[33] The European passion for woodblock, *ukiyo-e* prints began with Félix Bracquemond's 1856 discovery of Hokusai's "sketchbook" series, *Manga*. Six years later, Madame de Soye and her husband "opened a shop in the Rue de Rivoli ["La Porte Chinoise"] to sell Oriental wares. Manet, Tissot, Fantin[-Latour], the Goncourts . . . were good customers, as was Whistler when in Paris" (Young 16).[34] Whistler's collection was installed in a series of houses in London's Chelsea district, in which, according to then-contemporary visitors, "he filled his rooms with screens and lacquer, arranged his blue-and-white on shelves, hung prints, fans, kakemonos and plates on his walls" (Pennell 1941:300).

For decades, some Whistler scholars have argued that just as he *decorated* his home, so he decorated his paintings.[35] A cursory examination of canvases such as *Symphony in White No.2: The Little White Girl* (Figure 4) and *Caprice in Purple and Gold No.2: The Gold Screen* would seem to support this view— that the kimonos, screens, fans, and flowers are incidental features, examples of what Said calls the "domestication of the exotic" (1978:60). To translate the argument into textual terms, this would be equivalent to asserting that the Japanese properties and motifs are "accidental" rather than "substantive" elements of the composition. Yet, just as recent textual theorists have argued that *nothing* in a text is accidental, that even seemingly minor components such as punctuation contribute to the processes of textual signification, I would contend that the *Japonisme* at work in these paintings is crucial to their processes of visual signification.[36]

In his letters, Whistler often spoke of the need to gain better control over his brushwork and compositional techniques; in his *Ten O'Clock Lecture,* he referred to the artist as the "master" of Nature who answers only to Art. One of the chief thematics of his personal and creative activities was thus a need for power: over his models, his patrons, and his artistic materials and media. As a painter, he was struggling with the entire system of representation that he, as a Western, post-Renaissance painter, had inherited.

The first stage in effecting control was a tactic similar to that of countless male artists: Whistler chose female subjects for many of his noncommissioned paintings in the 1860s, thus intensifying in his creative field the gendered patterns of dominance and submission underlying everyday social experience. As Charles Harrison suggests, "a problem-ridden involvement with the representation of women may be connected at some level to those changes in the conceptualization of the painted surface that we have learned to identify with modernism" (1997:2). Unlike many continental counterparts, however, Whistler's Orientalist gaze was not preoccupied with sexualized pleasures—an erotics of engagement that concentrated on the female nude and the possibilities of sexual experiences "unobtainable in Europe" (Said 1978:190). In the work of Ingres, Gérôme, and others, the nude "was given new life by the orientalist movement, a Western myth . . . which colonizing Europeans refashioned through literature and imagery as a timeless mise-en-scène for erotic fantasies of captive, sexually subservient women" (Pollock 1992:23). Whistler's completed oil paintings of the 1860s and 1870s evince little interest in the "Orientalist assertions of masculine power over feminine nakedness" that "were popular, and appeared frequently in the Salons" (Nochlin 1991:44). (*Three Figures: Pink and Grey,* in the early 1860s, is one exception, as is the 1892 pastel on brown paper, *The Arabian.*) Whistler seemed less interested in faces and erogenous zones than in the overall domination of bodies in space. Generally speaking, nudes were too conventional, too "academic" for Whistler; as he condemned the efforts of his peers, "'They are all tarred . . . with the same brush; they are of the schools'" (qtd Starr 529). Some art historians contend that Whistler's lack of draftmanship was responsible—poor training resulting in poor execution. But one could also suggest that the female body was too volative, too undisciplined if naked—the spectator's erotic engagement with the canvas would make him the "principal protagonist" of the aesthetic encounter (J. Berger 54), not the artist. Whistler was much more successful in commandeering his subjects through an expansive Orientalist imaginary.[37]

If female figures seem more than usually subjugated in Whistler's aesthetic realm, it could be an exaggerated response to the painter's disturbing fears that the artist occupies a feminized position within society. The following is Whistler's account of the genesis of art in the *Lecture:*

In the beginning, man went forth each day—some to do battle, some to the chase; others, again, to dig and to delve in the field. . . . Until there was found among them one, differing from the rest, whose pursuits attracted him not, and so he stayed by the tents with the women, and traced strange devices with a burnt stick upon a gourd.

    This man, who took no joy in the ways of his brethren—who cared not for conquest, and fretted in the field—this designer of quaint patterns—this deviser of the beautiful—who perceived in Nature about him curious carvings, as faces are seen in the fire—this dreamer apart, was the first artist. (*GA* 139)

To counteract this sense of difference and marginalization, Whistler not only depends upon the regular operations of the male artistic gaze to discipline his female subjects, but lends to their poses an extra dimension of stillness and muteness—physical and mental passivity almost to the point of paralysis. Degas, Van Gogh, and Gauguin learned from Hokusai new methods of representing human movement; Whistler, on the other hand, perfected female immobility.

    The second stage in disciplining and mastering his subjects was made possible by adopting or temporarily inhabiting the gaze of a male Japanese artist, one whose culture endorsed the physical repression of women as well as social, legal, and educational oppression. The postures of female figures so prominent in Japanese paintings and prints, and borrowed in Whistler's paintings—the sloping line of the back and slightly forward inclination of the body—were the result of the short-stepped walk necessitated by the confining robes and the clogs they wore. The carriage of Chinese women, of course, was even more marked because of their bound feet. (Like bonsai trees, women were physically maimed and their growth distorted in order to achieve particular cultural and aesthetic effects.[38]) I am suggesting that Whistler adapted from the wood-block prints of Kiyonaga, Hokusai, and Hiroshige cultural standards and artistic practices that greatly objectify women. This enhanced freedom to consider a woman as commodity and surface was a crucial step toward exerting an unprecedented authority over the representational systems at his disposal—an authority that took Whistler into a new dimension of impressionistic, nonmimetic stylization.

    The two "symphonies in white" that brought Whistler immediate public notice in the 1860s not only demonstrate the compositional simplicity he was striving to achieve but the consequent reliance upon compliant female figures.[39] When scrutinizing *Symphony in White, No. 1* (Figure 3), the strikingly stationary "white girl" may lead us to overlook the rug on which she stands. Once noticed, however, connections between the woman enclosed by the champagne-colored wall-coverings and patterned carpet, and the animal, long since captured, killed, and skinned for decorative purposes, seem inevitable. Both have been rendered powerless; the dead wolf's face actually seems more animated than the living model's.[40] *Symphony in White, No.2* thoroughly reinscribes the patriarchal stereotype of woman as a vain and thoughtless vessel. George Moore's assessment of the painting is particularly telling: "The woman stands idly dreaming by her mirror. She is what is her image in the glass, an appearance that has come, and that will go leaving no more trace than her reflection on the glass when she herself has moved away" (20). Put another way, the mirror seems to preclude any interiority. Hiffernan has been transformed into a depersonalized everywoman who leaves no cultural trace, an image—or chimera—of femininity only to be realized by the double energies of masculinist painter and viewer/critic. Evidently, a woman and a vase can be assigned the same value within a male economy of desire. Both canvases are paradigmatic of almost all Whistler projects involving female figures: he is not interested in them as psychological subjects; any concern for "a historically constituted and culturally specific feminine subjectivity . . . falls under his erasure" (Pollock 1992:71). There is only room for one subjectivity in the canvas: Whistler's. *His* aesthetic vision and practices are being expressed and displayed. As Varnadoe states, "the modern artist is the giver . . . of identity. The artist assigns . . . a particular expressiveness and significance that originates in his own work . . . [and the sitter is] completely remade in terms of a system of artistic invention" (xiv-xv).[41] In other words, a beautiful woman's image "represents the triumph of art, functioning . . . 'as a synecdoche for the beauty of painting itself'" (Simons 68).

Many Whistler paintings feature immobile, solitary female figures. As Sickert notes with some asperity, "The great portrait painters, Velasquez, Vandyck, Reynolds, Gainsborough, achieved splendid 'arrangements' without thereby immolating the person depicted, as Whistler too often did. . . . One feels he was not interested in the personalities of the sitters, who were to him mere patterns made to fit into his scheme like the dresses or the backgrounds or the sprays of foliage" (19, 434). In the Japanese prints he so assiduously studied, however, even the female figures are imagined to be active and productive within their own separate, domestic spheres. Whether women of the court or courtesans, officiating at a tea ceremony or sharing communal activities, the figures one finds in Kiyonaga's *Early Summer at Mukejima* and *Laundry Scene,* Eishi's *The Courtesan Nakagawa and Two Maids,* or Harunobu's *Young Woman Attended by a Maid,* are presented within a framework of quotidian purpose and industry. They are not, as they become in Whistler's paintings, isolated rather forlornly or backed into a corner, powerless amid the cherry blossoms, a "kind of human still life" (Nochlin 1992:238).

In the stunning *Symphony in Flesh Colour and Pink: Mrs F.R. Leyland*[42] (Figure 5), all but the solemn face of Frances Leyland addresses the wall; only her profile is returned to the viewer's (or public) domain. Her arms are flattened against her back, hands clasped in the lower spinal region. The positioning of arms and hands is accentuated by the ribboning that appears to entwine the sleeves—and suggests, to this viewer at least, the extent to which she is ideologically bound within a cultural system that recognizes her as someone's "Mrs," the "patron's wife as a particularized material possession" (Simons 67). Appliqué flowers on the gossamer fabric of the dress complement both the exquisite blossoms framing the lefthand spatial field of the canvas and the cluster of gracefully elongated leaves on the right (the leaves intersect with and highlight Whistler's, "signature" butterfly emblem). Deftly, the female figure is not only relegated to a private, interior sphere but also associated with the natural world, perpetuating the patriarchal equation that male is to culture as female is to nature.[43] (To understand the "restraining control of the profile format" featured in *Symphony in Flesh Colour and Pink*, one turns to quattrocentro Florentine paintings, for which "the profile, presenting an averted eye and a face available to scrutiny," was developed for female sitters, because it "suited the representation of an ordered, chaste, and decorous piece of property," a "passionless object of passion" [Simons 41, 50]. A male figure, contrarily, was "shown in three-quarter length and view," a "spatial occupation and bodily assertion" forbidden to females [Simons 41].)

Three of Whistler's most famous paintings in the *Japonisme* mode, *Rose and Silver: La Princesse du Pays de la Porcelaine, Caprice in Purple and Gold, No.2: The Gold Screen,* and *Purple and Rose: The Lange Leizen of the Six Marks* (1863–1864), are also his most luxurious in terms of vivid textures and colors. They should be regarded, however, as much more than fanciful exercises in dressing Western women in Eastern garb and surrounding them with decorative Oriental *bibelot.* Strategically, *Japonisme* has displaced and subsumed the women, metaphorically dramatizing their noncentral status within their own (or Japanese) culture. Two different semiotic systems are skillfully conflated in each painting, with a net result of estranging the women from viewer and painter, highlighting their essential status as foreign Other, commodities to be treasured, posed, and exploited as much as the robes, fans, and vases.

Gray has discerned that the sitter's pose in *La Princesse du Pays de la Porcelaine,* an "exaggerated curve of the tall girl with the small head," derives from the work of Utamaro, closely parallel to "a well- known print from his series *Twelve Hours of the Clock,* the Hour of the Cock" (324). Finding a precedent for the model's stance, however, does not obviate the fact that her body has been manipulated into an unnatural position. The latter is further intensified by the way in which the figure is so closely cropped within its frame. Christine Spartali, daughter of the Greek Consul General in London, has been rendered as anonymously as possible, her subjectivity suppressed. She is distinguished only by the elaborate robes that represent the painter's creative "vision"—apparel that reminds us that, as Pollock suggests, "femininity [is] a masquerade, a veiling, a body literally re-*fashioned*" (1992: 39).

The carefully enunciated horizontal plane of *La Princesse*—one of the central features of Whistler's *Japoniste* discourse—is achieved through the placement of the folded screen dominating the visual field behind the female figure. Because the woman is taller than the screen, however, she does not seem as claustrophobically sequestered as the seated figure in *Caprice in Purple and Gold, No. 2.* The latter is segregated within a gorgeously burnished space that restricts and almost obliterates her. Seemingly confined to the rug on which she sits, the woman is so enveloped by the kimono that only one hand is free to hold up a wood-block print for examination.

Both *The Golden Screen* and *The Lange Leizen of the Six Marks* reinforce the notion that a woman is an "object for art rather than producer of it" (Pollock 1988:45). In the former painting, the seated figure, however resplendent, can aspire to nothing more than the role of consumer. *The Lange Leizen of the Six Marks*[44] presents a parody—or travesty—of creativity. This is not a potter's studio or any other such workplace; the woman is as ornately finished and functionless as the porcelain pieces that surround her. Not even the artist's mother assumed that the female figure represents an actual artist. In a letter of February 1864 she remarks, "'A girl seated *as if* intent upon painting a beautiful Jar which she rests on her lap, a quiet & easy attitude, she sits beside a shelf which is covered with Chinese matting a buff colour, upon which several pieces of China & a pretty fan are arranged *as if* for purchasers. . . . [B]y her side is a large Jar & all those are fac-similes of those around me in this room'" (qtd Spencer ed. 72; emphasis added).[45] One learns from this painting that an occidental woman has a greater chance of becoming Asian than she does of becoming a seriously engaged artist; in either role, she is little more than a "fac-simile."

Duncan's studies of later-nineteenth-century French painting have revealed that, "Far from contesting the established social order, the male-female relationship that these paintings imply—the drastic reduction of women to objects of specialized male interests—embodies on a sexual level the basic class relationships of capitalist society" (105). Examining the representation of bodies and their socially-assigned gender performances in Whistler's (nonportrait) canvases, one discovers that the males are dedicated to productive labor, and the females to purposeless posing or perambulation. To borrow John Berger's succinct generalization, "men act and women appear" (7). In two of Whistler's earliest—and non-*Japonisme*—works, *At the Piano* (1858–1859) and *Harmony in Green and Rose: The Music Room* (1860), the possibilities of limited female accomplishment, albeit within a wholly domestic sphere, are acknowledged. In *Wapping,* on the other hand, begun in 1861 and only finished (although *not* to Whistler's satisfaction) in 1864, the woman is literally and figuratively separate: distinguished from the men by the backward slant of her body, the coloration of flesh in face and neck, and the halo effect created by the watery background and the ships' prows. The mast behind her also effectively divides the woman from the bustling Thames-side activities—what Mrs. Whistler called "'The Thames and so much of its life, shipping, buildings, steamers, coal heavers, passengers going ashore, all so true to the peculiar tone of London & its river scenes'" (qtd Spencer ed. 73). In the midst of all that, the woman is decorative and inexpressive, a silent and silenced figure.

Throughout his career, Whistler addressed the challenges of painting water at various times of day and night. From *Thames in Ice* (1860) and *Last of Old Westminster* (1862) to *Brown and Silver: Old Battersea Bridge* (1865) and *Nocturne in Blue and Gold: Old Battersea Bridge* (1873), male industriousness is a commonplace feature of the waterscapes, whether necessitated by the subject-matter (bridge engineering) or simply presented to suggest the scale of representation. Just as effectively, water replaces the screen as boundary for the "spaces of femininity" in *Variations in Flesh Colour and Green: The Balcony* (1864–1870; Figure 6). One of Whistler's most overtly intertextual efforts, *The Balcony* cites Harunobu's *Ladies on a Balcony* and several "arrangements" from Kiyonaga's *Twelve Months in the South,* especially *The Fourth Month* and *The Sixth Month.* It may also echo Shunmann's *On A Balcony,* in which one female figure faces indoors, one leans over the railing, and another kneels to gaze at a contemporary riverside scene featuring a bridge, the masts of ships, and industrial activity.[46] Kiyonaga's prints depict life in a geisha house; the women on the balcony frame the very visible ships in the harbor (presumably bearing new customers). In the Harunobu, a strong vertical axis is established by the long handle of a musical instrument; the two seated women are poised in the midst of a tea ceremony. However stylized, the recreational energies of the Asian women differ markedly from the idleness and torpor of the four in Whistler's painting. According to Spencer's research, "the figures were eventually painted, not from living models, but from Japanese toy dolls which Whistler bought in a London shop" (1980:64). Three of the women trapped in the doll-like life of middle-class "comfort" listlessly return the gaze of the viewer in *The Balcony;* only one looks out to the world at large. Pollock's comments about a Berthe Morisot painting are very apposite: "What Morisot's balustrades demarcate is not the boundary between public and private but between the spaces of masculinity and of femininity inscribed at the level of both what spaces are open to men and women and what relation a man or woman has to that space and its occupants" (1988:62). Unlike other Whistler exercises in female-centered *Japonisme, The Balcony* actually represents the spaces of masculinity: the places of work and enterprise symbolized by the smokestacks and industrial buildings on the far side of Battersea Reach.[47] (Visual coordinates are provided by *Grey and Silver: Old Battersea Reach,* 1863.) The incongruity of juxtaposing Western female subjects garbed in seemingly old-fashioned Japanese costumes with the landscape of industrialization and encroaching urbanization only heightens the viewer's sense that the women are not *of* their own time; femininity is somehow transcultural, transhistorical, and temporally irrelevant. In a gesture similar to the portrait of Frances Leyland, only beautiful blossoms share the feminine realm of *The Balcony;* the contrast between the flowers and the production of industrial waste across the Thames reinforces the gender dynamics of the composition, intensifying the women's isolation.

Many Whistler commentators refer slightingly to the period between the mid-1860s and the early 1870s as unsuccessful "years of uncertainty" (Spaulding 44), the "deepest trough in Whistler's life" (Walden 20), or an "interlude of crisis" (Gray 507) that was more frustrating than it was fruitful. My rereading of his oeuvre suggests that *Japonisme* empowered Whistler to challenge established painterly conventions, especially the authority of realism. Having discovered how best to dominate his sitters and topoi, Whistler then began to extend his experiments to pictorial construction and nonmimetic representationalism. *Japonisme,* one could say, led him to the traditions of Japanese design: innovative compositional theories and practices that enabled him to rethink perspective, pictorial structure, framing, coloration, and tonal values, resulting in new formats (both elongated and intensively horizontal), planar simplicity, a daring fluidity of style and line, and a remarkable "compositional severity" (Sandberg 1964:503). In the late 1860s, he tried to accomplish all of this and still retain the female figure as a focus. But as the unfinished oil sketches of the *Six Projects* indicate, the enterprise was defeated by intransigent flesh. Small wonder, then, that Whistler turned his attention in the 1870s and 1880s to landscapes and seascapes, the play of mist on water at twilight, or the sudden burst of fireworks.

Whistler's notion of beauty depended upon the construction of female subjects who were rare, passive, frail, and domestically confined—figuratively bound by patriarchy rather than literally bound in the feet. Furthermore, *Japonisme* was a means of containing the female within a static, ahistorical frame of reference—"not so much Utopia," to quote Nochlin's observations about Ingres and Gauguin, "as U-chronia" (1991:174).[48] Ironically, but not coincidentally, Whistler's *Japonisme* paintings re-enshrined conventional codes of femininity at the same time that American and European women were organizing and agitating for political and social independence. The thousands of people who flocked to see the paintings during Whistler's lifetime, or during one of several memorial exhibitions in 1904, 1905, and 1912, were exposed to female figures imprisoned within an imposed exoticism—"de-realized," their features and circumstances "evacuated" of any contemporary referents (Pollock 1992:56, 57). This "absence of history" not only confirmed Western assumptions that the "Oriental world is a world without change, . . . untouched by the historical processes that were 'afflicting' or 'improving' . . . [or] drastically altering Western societies at the time" (Nochlin 1991: 35–36), but effectively re-endorsed the notion that women have no proper or crucial place in human history or contemporary events.

Whistler often referred to himself as a butterfly, the motif that became his canvas signature. Yet beneath the apparently gossamer surfaces of Whistler's representations of women one finds the tensile, iron-clad strength of patriarchal ideology and a masculinist symbolic code enhanced and intensified by Orientalism. Paradoxically, however, it was Orientalism that provided access to a genuine and genuinely innovative engagement with Japanese art.

"Poor Art! What a Sad State the Slut Is In"

I would like to return, briefly, to the allegory of Art with which Whistler entertained the audiences of his *Ten O'Clock Lecture*.[49] When one considers the gender inflections of his discourse—the ways in which "it mediates and represents social relations" (Parker and Pollock 119)—and then compares Whistler's remarks with those expressed by the defense counsel during the legal action against Ruskin, one can observe the sometimes conflicting means by which patriarchal ideology is reproduced. (The gender exclusivity of the discourse also reminds us why, in Whistler's society and for decades afterward, female artists were virtually unimaginable.)

In *Whistler v Ruskin,* a rant against critics produces these offhand remarks: "yes, they all do good to Art. Poor Art! what a sad state the slut is in, an [*sic*] these gentlemen shall help her" (*GA* 29).[50] Art is not only eroticized but debased—she will, after all, share her favors.[51] Whistler's extended allegory in the *Ten O'Clock Lecture* has a titular protagonist—his "whimsical goddess"—and an actual, favored hero—the Artist, master of Nature and Art's perfect lover. In a fascinating revision of the Platonic myth, it is Art who seeks out the Artist—and beauty is their progeny.

> Art, the cruel jade, cares not, and hardens her heart, and hies her off to the East, to find . . . a favourite with whom she lingers fondly—caressing his blue porcelain, and painting his coy maidens, and marking his plates with her six marks of choice—indifferent in her companionship with him, to all save the virtue of his refinement!
>
> He it is who calls her—he who holds her!
>
> And again to the West, that her next lover may bring together the Gallery at Madrid, and show to the world how the Master towers above all; and in their intimacy they revel, he and she, in this knowledge;. . . . She is proud of

her comrade, and promises that in after-years, others shall pass that way, and understand.

So in all time does this superb one cast about for the man worthy her love—and Art seeks the Artist alone.

Where he is, there she appears, and remains with him—loving and fruitful—turning never aside in moments of hope deferred—of insult—and of ribald mis-understanding; and when he dies she sadly takes her flight, though loitering yet in the land . . . refusing to be consoled.

With the man, then, and not the multitude, are her intimacies; and in the book of her life the names inscribed are few—scant, indeed, the list of those who have helped to write her story of love and beauty. (*GA* 156–57)

Artistic production, one is supposed to believe, is all a matter of Art (inspiration) and her congress with "great men" (one wonders if Whistler recognized the Ruskinian note) and lesser men—some honor her, some abuse her.

According to the gender ideology inscribed in this fable—which only seems fanciful and mock-serious on the surface—Art symbolizes Victorian womanhood: both the passive Virgin and the aggressive Whore. At times, she is "a goddess of dainty thought—reticent of habit, abjuring all obtrusiveness" whose sole and "selfish" preoccupation is "her own perfection only" (*GA* 136). More often, however, she behaves like any other highly (and thus abnormally) sexualized Victorian woman—indiscriminately and fatalistically, exercising little volition and an almost rapacious appetite. "Art is upon the Town!" Whistler announces at the outset of his *Lecture:* "to be chucked under the chin by the passing gallant—to be enticed within the gates of the householder—to be coaxed into company, as a proof of culture and refinement" (*GA* 135). If not carefully monitored, Art could become involved in sordid relationships—the "lowest stage of intimacy" (*GA* 136)—with critics and sham artists. Fortunately, a great man and perfect partner will eventually become available.

The same power relations are replicated in Whistler's theory of the artist's relationship with the natural world. Creativity, he stresses, is entirely a matter of control and domination: operating with or under "the power of creation," the male artist goes "beyond" feminized Nature (*GA* 140). (Clearly, Ruskin is the negative interlocutor for such remarks.) Always cooperative, Nature reveals its "secrets" and offers invaluable "lessons" to the "great man": "In all that is dainty and lovable he finds hints for his own combinations, and *thus* is Nature ever his resource and always *at his service,* and to him is naught refused" (*GA* 145; emphasis added). The artist's production always surpasses servile nature; the *master*piece is thus a triumph of male ingenuity over mere female essence. Nature "contains all the elements," Whistler reminds his auditors (and subsequent readers), but "the artist is born to pick, and choose, and group with science, these elements, that the result may be beautiful. . . . To say to the painter, that Nature is to be taken as she is, is to say to the player, that he may sit on the piano" (*GA* 142–143). Small wonder that, in the evening, "Nature, who for once, has sung in tune, sings her exquisite song to the artist alone, her son and master—her son in that he loves her, her master in that he knows her" (*GA* 144). Once again carnal knowledge is the male artist's best metaphor for the privileges of his aesthetic enterprise.

As was suggested in the previous section, the aggressively eroticized and heterosexual tones of Whistler allegory betray a great deal of gender anxiety regarding the role of the artist in society. Whistler's problem is rudimentary and all-consuming: how can the artist—the potential "master"—be both *different* from ordinary men yet at the same time distinguishable from the established sign of difference, woman? Unwilling to "do battle" or "to dig and delve in the field," the artist "stayed by the tents with the women, and traced strange devices with a burnt stick upon a gourd" (*GA* 139). Artistic industry immediately distinguishes him, however, and his innate originality. Fortunately, too, he is protected in this act of "differing" (*GA* 139) by the normalizing agency of homosociality:

> This man, who took no joy in the ways of his brethren . . . this deviser of the beautiful . . . this dreamer apart, was the first artist. . . . And presently there came to this man another—and, in time, others—of like nature, chosen by the Gods—and so they worked together; and soon they fashioned, from the moistened earth, forms resembling the gourd. And with the power of creation, the heirloom of the artist, presently they went beyond the slovenly suggestion of Nature, and the first vase was born, in beautiful proportion. (*GA* 140)

Whistler's account reminds one of the extent to which, and how readily, metaphors of conception have been usurped in patriarchal aesthetic discourse. And one also notes, somewhat sadly, that even in the small gestures Whistler cannot enhance male creative potency without degrading that which is female: nature provides only "slovenly" suggestions that the artist transforms into a thing of "beautiful proportion." Beauty, therefore, is not an innate characteristic: it is a function of male artistic production.

Not surprisingly, Whistler's critics also invoked codes of sexual difference and gender distinction—to denigrate his work. One of the most glaring examples of this can be found in the transcripts of *Whistler v Ruskin*. To distinguish between the negative response of Ruskin, the established and *bona fide* critic, and those people wrong-headed enough to regard Whistler's paintings approvingly, Sir John Holker describes a hypothetical visit to the Grosvenor Gallery. "'Yesterday,'" he reminds the court, "'I was asking you to accompany me thither in the imagination'":

> [After lunch], we would get into the gallery and be attracted by Mr. Whistler's pictures. . . . We would find "nocturnes," "arrangements," and "symphonies" surrounded by groups of artistic ladies—beautiful ladies who endeavour to disguise their attractions in medieval millinery . . . and I daresay we would hear those ladies admiring the pictures and commenting upon them.
>
> For instance: A lady, gazing on the moonlight scene representing Battersea Bridge, would turn round and say to another, "How beautiful! It is a 'nocturne in blue and silver.' Do you know what a 'nocturne' means?" And the other would say, "No, but it is an exquisite idea. How I should like to see Mr. Whistler, to know what it means!" Well, having seen Mr. Whistler and heard him give his explanation of a nocturne in the witness box, I doubt whether the young lady would be any the wiser. . . . And the ladies would admire and adore, and after they had all poured incense upon the altar of Mr. Whistler, other people would be able to get near the pictures. (qtd Merrill 1992:165–166)

Unthinking, untutored appreciation or hero-worship is the risible domain of pretentious women ("In the room, the women come and go/ Talking of Michelangelo" [*CPP* 13]); informed art criticism is the sole province of serious men—Ruskin, his attorneys, the gentlemen of the jury—to be carried out "after the ladies had dispersed." Ironically, Holker's narrative relegates the painter to the same womanly sphere that Whistler himself impugns in the *Lecture.* Both invoke an antifemale regime of gender differentiation to speak negatively *and* to try to reestablish control over the tenor and content of public aesthetic discourse. Subsequent critics who judged Whistler's work very favorably nonetheless also hinted at a personal subtext of effeminization: some, because the painter seemed an "exquisite" man for all that he was "insolent, charming" (Macfall 9); others, because of his mercurial temperament: "That he was volatile—in his way, almost feminine—counts for a part of his charm. He had Watteau's sensitiveness, and a lighter wit. Not his—it never could have been his—the soul of Holbein—the unshaken soul of Dürer" (Wedmore 5–6). Manliness and volatilty, it would appear, constitute an unimaginable combination. Hence the remark that Whistler was "a man of nerves rather than a man of muscle" and his *Nocturnes,* "clearly the outcome of a highly-strung, bloodless nature whetted on the whetstone of its own weakness to an exasperated sense of volatile colour and evanescent light" (G. Moore 4, 6).

Moore's remarks about "volatile" color deserve comment. Throughout the trial, Holker and Bowen focused negatively on three aspects of Whistler's artistic production: lack of "finish," the apparent formlessness of his compositions, and the extent to which he had eschewed the principles and practices of modeling in order to concentrate on experiments in coloration. Neither the second nor the third category is exempt from gender bias. As Summers points out,

In Western philosophy the distinction between "form" and "matter" has always been a deeply and simply gendered one, and this durable and pervasive opposition, rooted in equally durable and pervasive patriarchal social institutions, has had the deepest formative consequences for our notions of artistic making, of imagination ("conception"), and in its latter-day form, of "creation." According to this view, form has always been an active "male" principle opposed to passive, "female" matter, which was of course considered necessary (or a necessary evil) but was also considered lower than form and relatively nonexistent. (397)

The unease critics experienced in the face of *Nocturne in Black and Gold: The Falling Rocket* or *Nocturne in Blue and Gold: Old Battersea Bridge* is directly related to the ways in which the paintings transgress the conventions that Summers outlines.

Whistler's trademark emphasis on coloration—the privileging of "harmonious" arrangements as signalled in his elaborate titles—also defied aesthetic codes that meticulously reinscribed culturally-embedded gender distinctions. "The association of color with 'accident,'" Summers explains, "and with the superficial and feminine is an important habit of Western thought with all kinds of ramifications . . . from Plato through the critical reaction to impressionism and beyond" (403). For Renaissance theorists, "color's materiality was the source of both its attraction and repulsion" (Reilly 90). Armenini and Alberti, for example, insisted upon the "ornamental and supplementary role" played by *colore;* unlike "*disegno,* which brought the human form nearer to perfection, *colore* brought it nearer to reality" (Reilly 93). Through their "figures of femininity, theorists characterized color as beautiful but dangerous, engaged in a complex and antagonistic relationship with a masculinized *disegno*" (Reilly 87). As Herbert has discerned in his studies of Whistler's contemporary, Georges Seurat (1859–1891), most nineteenth-century painting instructors and theorists also despaired when an individual artist devoted himself to coloring rather than drawing.:

> [Charles] Blanc taught that color itself was unstable, too much a creature of the moment; it needed a strong hand, manifest in "dessin," that male conception of form based on black and white. Seurat's modernity resides in part in his belief that the assessment of color was not mere instinct, not mere spontaneity, as the Impressionists appeared to profess; it had been brought into the realm of science [which also "bore the connotations of masculine authority"] by men he admired[.] (5)

Ruskin always instructed his art students, "begin by *getting command* of line, that is to say, by learning to draw a steady line, limited with absolute correctness the form or space you intend to limit; to proceed by *getting command* over flat tints . . . and finally to *obtain the power* of adding such fineness of gradation within the masses" (*WJR* 20:128–129; emphasis added).[52] Clearly Whistler had other ideas and aesthetic priorities. To the pupils of the "short-lived Académie-Whistler" in Paris, he explained his "practice of colour arrangement": selected colors were ranged on the palette's outer rim; on the lower part, a palette knife was used to mix them, in sequence from light to dark. "'You must see your picture on the palette,' he used to say. . . . 'Here, not on your canvas, is your field of experiment, the place where you make your choices'" (Mulliken 237).[53] Holker not only complained that *Nocturne in Blue and Gold* had "'a good deal of color,'" but directly linked this overemphasis on pigment and hue to the production of "'fantasies and exaggerated conceits'" (Merrill 1992:166, 168). In other words, he was chastising Whistler (on Ruskin's behalf) for failing to conform to the masculinist dictates of aesthetic tradition. Small wonder that, according to Holker, only "the ladies" would and could find the paintings "exquisite."

Throughout the *Ten O'Clock Lecture,* Whistler not only castigates "the false prophets, who have brought the very name of the beautiful into disrepute" (136), but positions himself as a self-styled defender of beauty against an encroaching "*culte*" of the "unlovely." To play his role successfully, he denies the validity of Hegelian-cum-Ruskinian histories of art, and rejects the notion that "the ugly" is somehow preferred in contemporary culture.

> A favourite faith, dear to those who teach, is that certain periods were especially artistic, and that nations, readily named, were notably lovers of Art.
>
> So we are told that the Greeks were, as a people, worshippers of the beautiful, and that in the fifteenth century Art was engrained in the multitude. . . .
>
> That we, of to-day, in gross contrast to this Arcadian purity, call for the ungainly and obtain the ugly. . . . [This is "false,"] built upon fable, and all because "a wise man has uttered a vain thing and filled his belly with the East wind." (*GA* 138–139)

Interestingly, it was this beauty / ugliness antinomy that Oscar Wilde seized upon in his review of the lecture for the *Pall Mall Gazette,* comments Whistler reprinted, highly excerpted, in *The Gentle Art of Making Enemies.*[54] "That an artist will find beauty in ugliness," Wilde playfully commented,

> *le beau dans l'horrible,* is now a commonplace of the schools, the argot of atelier, but I strongly deny that charming people should be condemned to live with magenta ottomans and Albert blue curtains in their rooms in order that some painter may observe the side lights on the one and the values of the other. (*GA* 229)

Never commonplace in his views or artistic practices, Whistler refused to embrace "*l'horrible*" as much as he declined to promote aesthetic beauty as the only possible compensation for contemporary life. He would not agree with Wilde, nor with the view of Sidney Colvin that "beauty is precisely the element wanting in the ordinary aspect of modern London streets and London skies" (Olmstead 3:526). Whatever "sad state" the institutions of Art might be, however deplorable the creative productions or critical practices of some contemporaries, Whistler always firmly believed that he was uniquely qualified to add another significant chapter to "the story of the beautiful" (*GA* 159).

Making Confederates

There is a moment in the *Lecture* when Whistler strikingly anticipates Pound's pronouncements on the cult of ugliness. During a tirade against the critic as "amateur" and "meddler" Whistler announces, "And there are curious converts to a weird *culte,* in which all instinct for attractiveness—all freshness and sparkle—all woman's winsomeness—is to give way to a strange vocation for the unlovely—and this desecration in the name of the Graces!" (*GA* 152). The rather paradoxical ways in which the late-nineteenth-century champion of artistic beauty himself became a cult or heroic figure among the modernists most dedicated to "[t]he contemplation of the horrid or sordid or disgusting" (*SW* 169) deserve close attention—not to prove *if* or *why* Whistler's works were modern or modernist productions,[55] but to retrace the steps by which Whistler was installed as a crucial precursor to the modernists' own projects and self-championing efforts. One quickly discovers that people were responding to his paintings, his writings, *and* to his reputation as a flamboyant, truculent antiestablishment figure.

The trial's notoriety had "marked the galvanizing of Whistler's protracted and often stormy dialogue with media that became the basis of his strategy for retaining a privileged place in the limelight of late nineteenth-century publicity" (Burns 30). Brilliantly manipulating "the ever more popular press, Whistler attracted and held the spotlight of celebrity just when celebrity—a public, consumable image—was in the process of becoming a cultural commodity" (Burns 30). Whether one was turning the pages of *Harper's, Dial, The Critic, The Saturday Evening Post,* or *Ladies' Home Journal,* Whistler was on display. His death in 1903 only intensified the media and public scrutiny; his works reached an apogee of attention in the years just prior to World War I. Roger Fry's "influential obituary" in the *Athenaeum* set the tone for British approbation (Merrill 1998:329). 1904 saw the first memorial exhibition in Copley Hall, Boston. The 1905 Whistler Memorial Exhibition at London's New Gallery, Regent Street had a tremendous impact. "By the end of the third week of February 1905," Spencer reports, "25,000 people, including King Edward VII and Queen Alexandra," had visited the exhibition that Rodin had officially opened (Spencer 1989:25).[56] In Paris, "similar numbers were drawn to the Memorial Exhibition at the École des Beaux Arts in the same year" (Spencer 1989:25). One of the most important art events of 1912 was the Whistler exhibition at the Tate Gallery, London. In a banquet speech celebrating the New Gallery Show, Sir Walter Raleigh praised Whistler for being a "a wit, and a warrior, and the most versatile of craftsmen" (7). The tribute, which as subsequently published, shares tenor and tripartite focus (Whistler's intelligence, rebelliousness, and artistry) with countless other pan- egyric books, pamphlets, and articles put into circulation in that posthumous decade.[57] Publisher T. N. Foulis, for example, launched his "Spirit of the Age" series with Haldane Macfall's *Whistler: Butterly, Wasp, Wit, Master of the Arts, Enigma;* Mortimer Menpes's *Whistler as I Knew Him* was available in three formats (deluxe, regular, popular) by 1905. So prolific did the Whistler in- dustry become that Wedmore could lament, "And everybody who had known Whistler a little, and had an anecdote or two about him, was trans- formed, in imagination, into his chosen friend. . . . Over a closed grave, was there ever before such effusive pushing or pressure?" (15).[58] From beyond that same grave, one could read several different editions of *Ten O'Clock Lec- ture* and *The Gentle Art of Making Enemies* (see Seitz 19–23), and either a German translation or Stéphane Mallarmé's French version.[59] Selected letters by Whistler were published in the *Gazette des Beaux-Arts,* Paris, in the May, June, August, and September 1905 issues. Seitz's "hefty" bibliography in 1910 "devoted 181 pages to canvassing some 772 entries on writings by and about the famous American expatriate" (Burns 281). As Sidney Starr told the readers of *Atlantic Monthly,* "No artist of our time, leaving us, has been the subject of so much writing, so many recollections" (528).

Interestingly, in 1908, the same year that Pound arrived in London, *Burlington Magazine* (then codirected by Roger Fry) featured a review of the Pennells's *Life of James McNeill Whistler,* which praised the painter as "a man of science in an age of sentimentality; a courageous, uncompromising talent in an age of cowardly, petty concession; an irrepressible wit in a society which left wit to its inferiors. . . . His words and his precepts are perhaps the most important contributions to European art knowledge that any one man has made since the time of Reynolds" (1908b:172). The following year, C. J. Holmes, newly-appointed director of the National Portrait Gallery, ex- plained to *Burlington Magazine*'s readers that Whistler, one of the rare "in- novators" in art, "brought a new element of vitality, and a new technical method corresponding with it, into the art" of his time (204). Although each of "these novelties was attacked as ugliness and affectation," Holmes observed, "each is now accepted as beauty"; "all remarkable art movements have seemed over-emphatic, mannered, ugly, until their secret has been slowly discovered, and the new qualities which they introduce have been recognized as part of the world's inheritance of beauty" (204, 205).[60]

Whistler was the most famous "outsider" of the day, the artist whose self-selected position as subversive "dissenter" (Durét 92, 99) was as important as the cultural hybridity or "cosmopolitanism in art" his work symbolized (G. Moore 3). Whether considering the response of Ernest Fenellosa or Roger Fry, Pound or Lewis, one finds that four aspects of Whistler's aesthetic practices and public persona are confirmed appreciatively: his *Japonisme;* his insistence upon the exclusivity of art and the need to restrict access to the institutional sites of enunciation; his campaign for nonanecdotal or nonnarrative art, "independent of all clap-trap" (*GA* 128); and his willingness, as self-styled combative "rebel," to name and confront the "enemies" of art. A fifth (and paradoxical) factor, the work of his etchings to capture everyday urban life, is also noteworthy.

Whistler's elitism, his readiness to discriminate between "the many" and "the few," the "excellent army of mediocrity" and the exceptional "great" artists (*GA* 172), struck a particular chord with several modernists. As he had announced to *The World* in February 1883, and reprinted in *The Gentle Art of Making Enemies*, "There are those, they tell me, who have the approval of the people—and live! For them the *succès d'estime;* for me . . . the *succès d'exécration*—the only tribute possible from the Mob to the Master! This I have now nobly achieved" (*GA* 107). The rhetorical flourishes are almost indistinguishable from Pound's. Whistler was also the person who concluded his *Lecture* by boasting that the artist—always and only a male figure, of course—is he "with the mark of the Gods upon him," one of "the chosen" who "shall continue what has gone before" (*GA* 159). A predilection for referring to "'the many'" as "the mob" (*GA* 152) also seemed prescient. Whistler's refusal to admit critics to the ranks of specially "initiated" aesthetic supporters has already been discussed. But one should also recall his adamant insistence that only art practitioners can be "competent" critics. When asked during the libel trial if he "approved" of criticism, Whistler replied in these pre-Eliotic terms: "It is not for me to criticize the critics. I should not disapprove in any way of technical criticism by a man whose life is passed in the practice of the science that he criticizes; but for the opinion of a man whose life is not so passed I would have as little respect as you would have if he expressed an opinion on the law. I hold that none but an artist can be a competent critic" (qtd Merrill 1992:148; see *GA* 5–6). This ardent disrespect for critics and academics not withstanding, it was the praise his oeuvre received from an American art scholar and Sinologist that helped to institutionalize Whistler's reputation posthumously.

Ernest Fenellosa's interest in Whistler is actually the story of the Patron and the Academic. The patron was Charles Lang Freer (1854–1919), a Detroit multimillionaire who manufactured railway cars and other rolling-stock. Freer purchased his first of many Whistler compositions (etchings of Venice) in 1887; three years later, the two men met and began a mutually-appreciative friendship. As Spencer has noted, "it was Whistler's passion for Oriental art which encouraged . . . Freer in the 1890s to form his collection of Chinese and Japanese art. Freer visited Japan and sent Whistler photographs of the works he brought back" (1980:74). For suggestions as to subsequent purchases of Asian art, and advice when first negotiating with the U.S. federal government to bequeath his collections to the Smithsonian Institute,[61] Freer turned to Ernest Fenellosa (1853–1908). Harvard graduate, student of painting and philosophy, Fenellosa initially visited Japan in 1878 when he took up a post as philosophy instructor at Tokyo University. From 1890 to 1895, Fenellosa was prominent in American art circles as the first curator of the Japanese department in the Boston Museum of Fine Arts; in 1894, he organized a major exhibition of Japanese prints at the museum. At the same time, Fenellosa promoted the economic advantages of collecting Asian artifacts through public lectures, a 1901 monograph entitled *An Outline of the History of Ukiyo-e,* and his involvement with a "good friend and business partner, Kobayashi Bunshichi. . . . [a] wealthy young print dealer and vendor of old books [who] opened a shop in the Asakusa district of Tokyo around 1887" (Meech 1971a:49). Over the years, Fenellosa sold several Japanese screens to Freer (Chisholm 4), and recommended other purchases. Freer, in turn, introduced Fenellosa to the cross-cultural art productions of Whistler.

Recognition for Whistler's accomplishments as an independent artist, and as a bridge between Eastern and Western cultures, was carefully orchestrated by the two men—the connoisseur and the expert—after the painter's death. As Chisolm explains, "Freer managed to persuade the Copley Society of Boston to present a memorial exhibition in February 1904. For the occasion *Lotus,* a new magazine published in Boston by a friend of Freer's [Bunkio Matsuki], issued a special Whistler memorial number in which Fenellosa assessed 'The Place in History of Mr. Whistler's Art'" (172–173). In the latter article, Fenellosa praises Whistler for being chief among the "pioneers" who learned invaluable, entirely new lessons from Japanese and "Asiatic" art and "blended" Eastern and Western aesthetic discourse (1903:17). This response to an "Oriental influence," Fenellosa declared, "was no accident, no ephemeral ripple on the world's art stream, but a second main current of human achievement sweeping into the ancient European channel" (1903:15). Consequently, Whistler cannot be accused of "vain eccentricity" in his deliberately yielding himself for a time to the Japanese spirit. Rather was he throwing himself into the universal current, in making his individual feeling the sole test of his constructive schemes. The simple truth is that he is the first great master who comes after the union of the East and West, the first who creates naturally and without affectation in their mingled terms. (Fenellosa 1903:16)

Whistler thus emerges as the perfect transnational progeny, the true artist of "the future." It was an argument Fenellosa would reiterate in subsequent essays, exhibition catalogues, and in his posthumously published study of *Epochs of Chinese and Japanese Art* (1912). Volume 2 of *Epochs* features ten pointed comparisons between Whistler and Asian artists in terms of coloring, modernity, tonal qualities, austerity, and nocturnal "impressions" or "special atmospheric effects" (Fenellosa 1912 2:204).

Most importantly, Fenellosa praised the way in which Japanese art taught Whistler to locate new kinds of beauty in the natural world: "Nature became to him infinitely richer in pictorial suggestions, because a thousand settings of subjects, before tabooed, flashed upon his freed eye as beautiful. . . . It is this chiefly that sets Whistler apart from Western art, without making him a mere copier of Eastern" (1907:366).[62] Because of "the wide play of his experimenting with absolute beauty," and his ability to synthesize "the characteristic beauties" of Western and Eastern art, Fenellosa declared Whistler to be not only a *"central"* artist, but an artist of *"modern centrality"* (1907:367). It is not difficult to understand why Fenellosa would identify so thoroughly with a man who "stands forever at the meeting-point of the two great continental streams; he is the nodule, the universalizer, the interpreter of East to West, and of West to East" (1907:366). After Fenellosa's death, the man who tried to assume the coveted role of interpreter—to occupy the Whistler/Fenellosa position as indisputable, universal "nodule"—was Ezra Pound.

As a university student and fledgling poet in Pennsylvania,[63] Pound was drawn to the public persona of Whistler as vocally independent artist and *American* who made a name for himself in Europe. "It was at this time [circa 1905]," H. D. later recalled, that Pound "brought me Whistler's *Ten O'-Clock.* He scratched a gadfly, in imitation of Whistler's butterfly, as a sort of signature in his books at that time. He was a composite James McNeill Whistler, Peer Gynt and the victorious and defeated heroes of the William Morris poems and stories" (1979:23). As Humphrey Carpenter summarizes, "Whistler seemed a sort of modern troubadour, an outcast for Art's sake, a Bohemian dandy whose clothes Ezra began to copy—the best model he could think of at present" (63). Fortunately, too, Whistler was a painter and not a poet (a noncompetitive role model). In 1908, Pound went to London to become known, as had Henry James and Whistler before him.[64] There, as he had no doubt planned and hoped, his Whistler-like affectations were not overlooked. Frederic Manning, for example, remarked in 1909 that "Ezra was becoming 'more like Kh-r-ist and the late James McNeill Whistler every year'" (Carpenter 130).[65] The following description of Whistler best sums up the mask that Pound had assumed: "Theatrical, eccentric, and quarrelsome according to the common view, he had . . . a nice idea of the requirements of advertising, and quite upset the ethics of his profession by his assiduity in keeping himself before the public until his merits as an artist were so clearly recognized as no longer to need what might be called the 'playing up' of his personality" (Seitz 2). All in all, the painter proved to be an excellent role model of the artist as promoter, agent provocateur.

Pound's efforts to secure for Whistler a place in the canons of modern art and the greatest art of all time began in essays such as "I Gather the Limbs of Osiris" and "Vorticism," his contributions to *New Age* and *BLAST* 1, and *Gaudier-Brzeska*. Not surprisingly, remarks about Whistler proliferated at the time that Pound was working on the Fenellosa papers.[66] Some months after Pound first saw the Whistler exhibition at the Tate Gallery, Harriet Monroe wrote to him on behalf of the new *Poetry* magazine and asked for contributions. Pound replied on August 18, 1912:

> I send you all that I have on my desk—an over-elaborate post-Browning "Imagiste" affair and a note on the Whistler exhibit. I count him our only great artist, and this informal salute, drastic as it is, may not be out of place at the threshold of what I hope is an endeavour to carry into our American poetry the same sort of life and intensity which he infused into modern painting. (*LEP* 10; Zinnes ed. 272)

The poem, "To Whistler, American,"[67] is anything but a nonnarrative, haiku-like Imagist text:

> You also, our first great,
> Had tried all ways;
> Tested and pried and worked in many fashions,
> And this much gives me heart to play the game. . . .
>
> You had your searches, your uncertainties,
> And this is good to know—for us, I mean
> Who bear the brunt of our America
> And try to wrench her impulse into art.
>
> You were not always sure, not always set
> To hiding night or tuning "symphonies";

Had not one style from birth, but tried and pried
And stretched and tampered with the media.

You and Abe Lincoln from that mass of dolts
Show us there's a chance at least of winning through.

(Zinnes ed. 217–218)

The accumulation of verbs in the poem—tried, tested, pried, worked, play, bear, wrench, stretched, tampered–reminds us of Pound's newly-emerging devotion to a vortex-like dynamism in the arts. Several months later he again declared to his editor: "Dear Harriet Monroe:—/—Whistler and Whitman—I abide by their judgment" (Zinnes ed. 287). The Fenellosa-inspired *Cathay* volume, 1915, was even designed to match Whistler's distinctive publications: short, squarish, brown paper cover, the names of the publication and author discretely announced on the bottom half of the front cover. More than several poems have Whistlerian undertones; "The Beautiful Toilet" in particular owes as much to the painter as it does to Mei Sheng (who composed the original in 140 B. C.).

Poetry magazine was only one of several fora for preaching the "gospel" of Whistler's greatness and exemplary status (Zinnes ed. 305). For Orage's *New Age*, Pound contributed notes on the American arts scene (later reprinted in *Patria Mia*, 1950). Whistler "had spared himself nothing," Pound states admiringly; "he had struggled in one direction until he had either achieved or found it inadequate for his expression. After he had achieved a thing, he never repeated" (Zinnes ed. 1). The October 1912 column celebrates the accomplishments of Whistler for their own sake, but most especially because he was a Europeanized or noncolonial[68] American who took London and Paris by storm—yet remained tenaciously independent, a controversial figure who never succumbed to the dictates of his critics. "But what Whistler has proved once and for all," Pound proclaimed, "is that being born an American does not eternally damn a man or prevent him from the ultimate and highest achievement in the arts" (1912:368; Zinnes ed. 2). Whistler also figured favorably in *New Age* essays and reviews signed with the alias B. H. Dias in 1912, 1917, and 1918. The "masterwork" of the Whistler paintings at the Tate provided Pound with "courage for living" (1912:367).[69] The manifesto-like *Lecture* encouraged Pound to publish and proselytize as part of the "struggle" necessary to achieve a "revolution" in the arts (*P/SP* 388). To praise Lewis's *The Caliph's Design* (1919), Pound observed that, "Since Whistler's 'Ten O'Clock' no man actually a painter has been able to present thought about painting; and treatises from the actual workman have always an interest unattainable by aesthetes and men who analyze from the outside" (Zinnes ed. 128).

For all of these reasons, Whistler is allocated a place of privilege in Pound's genealogy of Vorticism for *BLAST* 1, and is cited throughout *Gaudier-Brzeska* as another example of the artist-martyr. "Our battle began with Whistler," Pound announces,

> the delicate, classical "Master." . . . Whistler was the only man working in England in the "Eighties" who would have known what we are at and would have backed us against the mob. . . .
>
> Whistler was the great grammarian of the arts and one should not confuse the particular form of his expression, *i.e.,* the peculiarity or the individuality of his expression of himself and his temperament, with the principles he uttered. . . .
>
> There is another phase of "the revolt" as they call it, which is also traceable to Whistler. I mean to say "art for the intelligent."
>
> We are, I think, getting sick of the glorification of energetic stupidity. . . . The art of the stupid, by the stupid, for the stupid is not all-sufficient. Whistler was almost the first man, at least the first painter of the last century to suggest that intelligent and not wholly ignorant and uncultivated men had a right to art. (1916:122–124)

For the *Lecture* Pound reserves an exclusive place in the canons of aesthetic revolution: "Any action of intelligence is of course a 'revolt' against the dough-like properties and propensies of the race. There would be no need of 'revolt' if things said were also things thought by hearers. So one is destined to reiterations, and turns again to the 'Ten O'Clock'" (1916:125).[70] Whether explaining the "Possibilities of Civilization" to a periodical audience, or advising Lewis about his painting, Pound readily cited the American iconoclast.[71] So ingrained was Pound's sense of indebtedness to Whistler that references to the painter even punctuate the rambling rant of World War II radio broadcasts. Not surprisingly, in the extremity of his physical and mental isolation in Italy Pound cited Whistler (on October 26, 1941) as the great prototype of the American artist in exile. "Jimmy Whistler's remarks about Hokusai" are also praised for what they taught Pound about "Japanese civilization" (Doob 10). Nine months later, Pound's "Disbursement of Wisdom" broadcast (July 2, 1942) included references to Whistler's "very great talent" and his "limitations"; to the last, Pound utilized Whistler to argue for the necessary elitism of the arts. "[C]ertainly some of his work will give joy to the elite," Pound observed in a paraphrase of his 1912 *New Age* essay, "as long as the canvas or paper remains" (Doob 187).[72] Whether one happens across Pound's August 1914 essay for the *Egoist* or *The Guide to Kulchur* (1952), "Jimmy Whistler," his *Japonisme,* and the "real wisdom" of his oeuvre are praised unstintingly (Zinnes ed. 192, 258).

Pound was not the only contributor to *BLAST* who was willing to claim Whistler as a special predecessor. It would not be an exaggeration to say that Wyndham Lewis absorbed, better and more fiercely than anyone else, the Whistlerian "art" of "making enemies"—*making,* that is, in the sense of discursively constructing an opposition, enunciating the sites of confrontation so indispensable for the promulgation of one's own aesthetic ideology.[73] Whistler taught Lewis how to antagonize, productively, and how to profit from the discomfiture of one's critics. ("He has a genius for war," Macfall's comment about Whistler, applies equally to Lewis [16].) Additionally, Whistler's publications proved the necessity, for a painter, of committing one's aesthetic opinions to writing. As Lewis acknowledged in his preface to *The Diabolical Principle and The Dithyrambic Spectator* (1931), "Whistler's pen was never at rest—every creative art of the butterfly-brush was accompanied by a critical or militant operation of the pen" (1931:viii). *The Gentle Art of Making Enemies* and *BLAST* 1 and 2 have a great deal in common as examples of manifesto writing; the hybrid, collage textuality of the former undoubtedly provided an incitement to experiment graphically and typographically, and to write subversively, in the latter.[74] As Lewis first commented in *BLAST* 1 ("Vortices and Notes") and reorganized into the retrospective essay "The Skeleton in the Cupboard Speaks," the "immense weight of opposition" in Great Britain that "is mobilized against any innovation" necessitates "a defensive verbal barrage"; "[a]lmost, I have become a professional writer in the process of defending my paintings. Mr Shaw's 'Prefaces' tell the same story; Whistler's admirable pamphleteering was a phenomenon of the same kind" (1969:334).

Lewis's interest in Whistler was first expressed in the early stages of his career. In February 1905, Lewis wrote to his mother from Paris asking her to "tell me about the 'Whistler' show and the French impressionists . . . I dont [*sic*] want to miss them if possible" (*LWL* 17). (The Whistler Memorial Exhibition opened on February 22, 1905; in January 1905 London's Grafton Gallery launched a major show of Impressionist art). Some time later, he informed his mother that, "The Whistler show is coming on here [Paris], so that if by any chance I am here on the 1st May, I shall see it" (*LWL* 19).[75] Almost three decades later, Lewis's critics were noting striking similarities. In May 1932, an article appeared in the *Daily Herald* by M. Maurice Dekobra, entitled "The Art of Making Enemies." The column was illustrated with pictures of Lewis, Edith Sitwell, and Whistler. Lewis responded, ten days later, with his essay "What It Feels Like to Be an Enemy." After denominating "good enemies" such as Dickens and Dante, Lewis remarks, "What worries an 'Enemy' most? Well, I should put first on the list *the poor quality* of his enemies. The breed leaves much to be desired, it must be at once conceded" (1969:266). In his art reviews of the late 1940s and early 1950s Lewis invoked the example of

Whistler as one of the "inveterate professional opponents of the Academy" and as a painter of "perfectionist exquisiteness" (1969:442).

In terms of his own artistic production, Lewis was emboldened by Whistler's attempts to abjure codes of mimetic representation, to contest a Ruskinian or slavish devotion to "nature."[76] As Lewis observes in *BLAST* 2, nature is unimportant, insignificant in and of itself; the artist's job is to rearrange nature, to "ENRICH abstraction." Whistler was also cited as one of the best "examples of *universalizing artists*," a transnational figure whose work fruitfully "transgresses national and racial frontiers" (Lewis 1969:386). Throughout Lewis's writings, however, one discerns the careful way in which Whistler is positioned "at [a] distance"; Lewis might consider Whistler a "revolutionary" of his "day," but the latter occurred several aesthetic revolutions ago.

A similar arm's-length approach can be found in Roger Fry's assessment of Whistler. In a July 1903 essay for the *Athenaeum,* Fry applauds Whistler's "attitude of pugnacious antagonism" but places it in the immediate past:

> He seemed to be always inaugurating a revolution, leading intransigent youth against the strongholds of tradition and academic complacence. And all the time, without our noticing it, he was becoming an old man, and now, too soon, he is an Old Master. For, whatever may be thought of his theories, his rankling and sometimes cruel witticisms, whatever may be thought of him as a friend and as an enemy, his work will remain even more interesting to posterity than his interesting and whimsical personality. . . . Himself the most serious of artists, he injured himself by his Quixotic tilt against the dull-witted cunning of the "serious" charlatan. (1903:345)

In addition to demarcating the boundaries between his own time and Whistler's, Fry attempts to separate Whistler's artistic productions from his writings. Neither Pound nor Lewis ever expressed the idea that Whistler might have injured himself in his battles against various institutions of the art establishment.

Fry does not acknowledge Whistler as one of the first to insist that British audiences should become familiar with nineteenth-century French painting. And for all that he admires "the now classic Whistler" (1908a:375), Fry faults the American for being too individualistic, altogether insufficient as a mentor for contemporaries and subsequent generations. Furthermore, Fry will not endorse the "cult of genius" that Whistler inspired and cultivated. To quote the Introduction Fry penned for a 1905 edition of Reynolds's *Discourses,*

> [Since the second half of the nineteenth century] the subsequent history of art has been the story, not of a gradual process of construction, but of successive revolutions, each illuminated by one or more heroic figures, and each ending without establishing more than a provisional government. The greatest art of

the period has been an art of revolt, and it bears the trace of its origins in its extravagant individualism, its feverish and quickly exhausted energy. . . . Ten years ago the revolutionary forces were still strong; it still seemed worth while to destroy and to liberate; . . . [but] we are tired of a too self-assertive individualism; the cult of genius has passed its climax with the death of Whistler[.] (1905:xx-xxi)

Such comments not only explain Fry's attitude toward Whistler, but help us to understand why the leader of the Omega Workshop was so much at odds with Lewis, that other great revolutionary only too willing to destroy and liberate.

Fry's memorial essay of 1903 attempts to solidify—and fix—Whistler's reputation as Protester par excellence and Defender of the beautiful. "In the achievements of his prime," Fry acknowledges, "he will, we think, live as a great painter—above all, as a great protest and an amazing exception" (1903:347). Most importantly, Whistler can be hailed as someone who came "under the spell" of his contemporaries—arch-Victorians such as Rossetti—then rejected their aesthetic theories and practices. From Japanese art, Fry agrees, Whistler learned "the most congenial expression of that purely pictorial, that non-plastic view of things" (1903:347), an almost clinical detachment ("as of a great surgeon") from his subject matter that ultimately enabled him to resist the ugliness of the world around him. "But, indeed," Fry contends,

> [Whistler] reaped to the full the benefit of his detachment, for in an age when the works of man's hand were becoming daily uglier, less noble, and less dignified in themselves, he found a way to disregard the squalid utilitarianism which they expressed. If to him nothing was in itself noble or distinguished, neither was anything in itself common or unclean. Mean Chelsea slums, ignoble factories by the Thames, the scaffolding and *débris* of riverside activity, all might afford to his alert perception at a given moment the requisite felicitous concatenation of silhouettes and tones. (1903:346)

For the "great men" of modernism who followed Whistler, no such "felicitous concatenation" was desired.

Ten and 20 years after his death, Whistler was cited by art critics and literary writers alike to register an anti-Victorian point of view and legitimate innovative theories and practices. Whether one turns to Clive Bell (*Art*),[77] T. E. Hulme (especially the "Lecture on Modern Poetry"), W. B. Yeats ("A Symbolic Artist and the Coming of Symbolic Art," *The Trembling of the Veil*), or others contributing to the construction of the modern in the twentieth century, Whistler is a substantial discursive presence. Somewhat surprisingly, however, neither the Bloomsbury critics nor the Men of 1914 distinguished between Whistler canvases that presented ahistorical harmonies and those paintings and (especially) etchings that wholly embraced quotidian faces, places, and lives. Whereas Fry insisted that Whistler "found a way to disregard the squalid utilitarianism" of his day (1903:346), immediate contemporaries such as Sickert, Moore, Durét, and Wedmore praised Whistler because he could take "for his theme the most commonplace subject which any of us could see for himself—the ugly warehouses, the prosaic bridges, the lumbering barges of our own river, and [transform] them . . . by sheer observation" (Sickert 31–32). As McMullen observes, Whistler "fell in love, not with the rural Thames favored by artists like Seymour Haden, but with the presumably unlovable Thames of working London, the stretch where, in T. S. Eliot's often Whistlerian account of the city, 'The river sweats/ Oil and tar / The barges drift/ With the turning tide'" (86). George Moore is most eloquent regarding Whistler's gifts as "interpreter of the night. Until he came the night of the painter was as ugly and insignificant as any pitch barrel. . . . [N]ot the unhabited night of lonely plain . . . but the difficult populous city night" (22). Wedmore concurs that "more to Whistler than to anyone who has worked with brush or [engraver's] needle" one owes "that complete acceptance of Modern Life, of the modern world, of all that is miscalled its ugliness. . . . [He] accepted the very things that seem most commonplace to commonplace people, and showed us their interest" (28; see also Cary 107). Perhaps those dedicated to the difficult work of promulgating a cult of ugliness could only deal with Whistler's urban interests by underplaying them—otherwise, their work would be too closely associated with that of a nineteenth-century artist, a gesture that would undermine an unflinching and seemingly original pursuit of the new.

Taking Up the Cudgels

What did Ruskin and Whistler, and *Whistler v Ruskin,* teach the modernists? Fundamentally, they learned to walk noisily among the aesthetically and culturally impaired, and to carry as many cudgel-like publications as possible. The July 1877 issue of *Fors Clavigera* (Nail-Bearing Fate[78]) injured both the plaintiff and the defendant, yet also strengthened their belligerent resolve concerning the different truths they had to tell about art. Ruskin had determined that beauty could serve truth splendidly, but truth-telling was ultimately more important for artist, critic, and viewer alike; his writings had the effect of legalizing the attack on beauty that the cult of ugliness would fully exploit. Whistler staunchly defended beauty, and produced wonderfully evocative paintings that embodied his commitment, but just as clearly he asserted his rights as beauty's master. Working at arm's length from both, one realizes that the gender "truths" informing and reiterated by their works are identical; whether expressing powerlessness, otherness, lack of status or quality, or that which is unstable or degenerate, a female figure is mandatory and always at hand.

Yet repackaging patriarchy's favorite gender myths just in time for a new century was only part of it. Fending off the reduction of art "to commodity status" (Eagleton 1988:140) was crucial to both. Separately and because of their fateful entanglement, Ruskin and Whistler developed modes of "combative satire" (Birch 1999b:185) that would set the standard for Pound, Lewis, and many others. "Making enemies" to advance an aesthetic or personal agenda was an art at which both excelled. Ruskin's scope as a commentator, the interdisciplinary thinking that he insisted upon, was as impressive as his insistence upon national and international perspectives. Whistler not only radically reconstructed "the picture space" for Western art (Lochnan 85), he insisted upon the significance of Eastern art to effect the changes—a public endorsement of cross-cultural enterprise, and appropriation, that the modernists would intensify.

Ruskin's career was an object lesson in the power to be gained by a critic, and its limits. He labored tirelessly in various genres, using books, pamphlets, letters to editors, lectures, essay collections, and a prestigious university position to disseminate his views as widely as possible. Crucially, he understood that there was more than one "public" to be reached with his message, whether aesthetic or economic; he worked within and beyond the confines of existing class and education systems to prophesy the possibilities of new socio-economic relations. Thriving on controversy, Ruskin savored the role as agent provocateur as much as Whistler did.

Welcoming "notoriety" (Crane 270), even cultivating it, was Whistler's specialty. Taking a page from Ruskin's book, and also heightening the offensive actions, Whistler promoted his aesthetic vision and tried his "enemies" in the court of public opinion by means of newspaper items, publishing private correspondence, holding a press conference in the Leyland home to showcase the Peacock Room, delivering the *Ten O'Clock Lecture* in three cities, and in every way possible managing the design and dissemination of his publications. As Burns summarizes,

> In a large degree, he became one of the "greatest" artists of his time *because* he presented himself as the most original, and was also the most ruthlessly competitive, the most successful self-advertiser, the one who had fashioned the most attention-getting and enduringly interesting brand name (complete with the butterfly, and other trademark symbols) for himself and his art products. His personality gave visibility to his art. Conversely, . . . his art by its perceived quality gave sanction to his eccentricities. (39)[79]

(Lewis and Pound would continue the tradition of artist and critic as Mr. High Visibility; Eliot, their Possum friend, would cultivate the art of deceptive invisibility.) There was nothing eccentric, however, about Whistler's decisive acts to seize control of the art adjudication/exhibition/sales system. Inspired by the *Salons des Réfusés* to which he contributed in the 1860s and 1870s, he set about to reconfigure the intersections of artist and audience. Instead of "large mixed public exhibitions" (Lambourne 95) with their "bazaar" look and atmosphere (Koval 104), Whistler created the illusion of withdrawing from the marketplace by staging exceptional one-man shows for which he designed everything from the invitations, advertisements, and catalogues to the gallery interiors, staff members' uniforms, and the method and style of hanging the paintings. The exhibition itself became the manifesto. As Bendix summarizes, "Whistler tried to make each show a *cause célèbre,* a perfect moment of high drama, conflict, intrigue, and beauty" (212). Subsequently, his "exhibition reforms constituted the most advanced articulation of the idealized space of the gallery" (Jensen 47).[80] Whistlerian installations and the publicity they garnered increased gallery attendance and public awareness of "the new" even as, paradoxically, they reinforced the elitism of the artist's endeavors. Ruskin taught the Men of 1914 how to function as a latter-day Jeremiah; Whistler, how to relish the role as Exhibitionist.[81]

James McNeill Whistler, *Nocturne in Black and Gold: The Falling Rocket.* ca. 1874.

By Permission of Punch.

No. 198

above Linley Sambourne, "*WHISTLER VERSUS RUSKIN—An Appeal to the Law.*" 1878.

left James McNeill Whistler, *Symphony in White, No. 1: The White Girl.* 1862.

above　James McNeill Whistler, *Symphony in White, No. 2: The Little White Girl.* 1864.

left　James McNeill Whistler, *Symphony in Flesh Colour and Pink: Portrait of Mrs Frances Leyland.* 1871–74.

J. A. M. WHISTLER

James McNeill Whistler, *Variations in Flesh Colour and Green: The Balcony.* 1865.

Chapter 2 ～

No Time for Pater:
Breaking the Homophobic Silence

If he died "leaving great" prose "unto a little clan" of appreciators, "a little clan" sure of increase and of successors, *satis est,* for him as for them.

—Lionel Johnson, "Mr. Pater and his Public"

Forms of intellectual and spiritual culture often exercise their subtlest . . . charm when life is already passing from them. . . . Then comes the spectacle of the reserve of the elder generation exquisitely refined by the antagonism of the new. That current of new life chastens them while they contend against it.

—Pater, "Coleridge's Writings"

There were many accolades from Oscar Wilde, including the 1890 declaration, "Mr Pater's essays became to me 'the golden book of spirit and sense, the holy writ of beauty.' They are still this" (*CWW* 9:539). There was his digressive admission from the witness box in 1895: "the only critic of the century whose opinion I set high, [is] Mr. Walter Pater" (Ellmann ed. 437).[1] Memorably, there was the typically outlandish Wildean witticism, best preserved for subsequent generations in W. B. Yeats's memoirs:

"I never travel anywhere without Pater's essay on the Renaissance, that is my golden book, but the last trumpet should have sounded the moment it was written—it is the very flower of the Decadence." "But," said somebody, "would you not have given us time, Mr. Wilde, to read it?" "Oh no, plenty of time afterwards in either world." (1972:22–23)

Unwittingly, Wilde's unstinting praise for Pater, his efforts to canonize the writings in the discourse of decadence, helped to ensure that, in the afterwards of masculinist high modernist culture, in the after-words of T. S. Eliot, T. E. Hulme, and Wyndham Lewis, there was never any time for positive assessments of beauty or beauty's most radical champion. Wilde's professional enthusiasm and personal misfortunes also guaranteed that, posthumously, Pater and his writings could not be read separately from Wilde, or, more accurately, the Scandal that dared to speak its name. Instead, the two men were often deliberately conflated, two disparate lives and canons distilled into one repugnant figure for personal and cultural "sin and infection" ("Manifesto" 11) from which the greatest possible distance must be secured. The substance of modernity permeates Pater's writings—a theory of relativism and contingent subjectivity; historical consciousness; an effort to revivify the present through cultural appropriation; a preoccupation with "the conditions of modern life" (*TR* 184)—but he was not only disowned as a fellow "modern" but largely denied recognition as an important precursor.[2] As this chapter argues, exclusion of Pater was produced by strategic gestures of avoidance, derision, and erasure. For the Men of 1914, it was not simply a matter of distancing their innovative critical arguments from a nineteenth-century critic's lavish praise for "aesthetic beauty" (*TR* 102), and constructing a new object of study—ugliness—more in keeping with contemporary life. Reorienting aesthetic ideology was also necessary to protect modernist discourse (and most especially, its enunciators) from the doubly-tainted undertones of effeminacy and homosexuality so often associated with Pater and Wilde.[3]

If, to quote Terry Eagleton, the "current left triptych of concerns" is "class, race, and gender" (1990a:5), the male modernists' triptych of phobic concern and abhorrence was women, Jews, and homosexuals. The misogyny and anti-Semitism of modernist culture have been thoroughly analyzed by several critics, among them Gilbert and Gubar, and Gilman.[4] My purpose is to redress a dominant critical silence concerning the modernists' homophobia—and to demonstrate the extent to which a reification of ugliness enabled Lewis and "brethren" to disguise homophobic responses under the cloak of aesthetic impartiality.[5] McGrath's excellent study is too discrete regarding the modernists' motives for creating such a critical distance: after Wilde's trial, he states, "and the scandal associated with it, Pater's aesthetic philosophy was linked to the misfortune of Wilde and other writers who never survived the nineties" (161). My argument also refuses the psychologizing approach of Bloom and his followers, who insist that one must "place Pater in his Oedipal context" in order to "apprehend his influence not only on Stevens and Yeats, but on Joyce, Eliot, Pound, and many other writers" (1974:ix).[6] Rather than suggesting that modernists were trying to achieve "autonomy" by killing off the "father," I am contending that their various distancing or silencing strategies in relation to Pater and his writings were catalyzed by what Sedgwick terms "homosexual panic." Yeats's memoirs astutely suggest that the spreading stain of Wilde's "condemnation" cost many "novelists and essayists and artists" the approving "ear of the great public" (1972:89). This contradicts Moliterno's hasty generalization that "Pater's fame and notoriety . . . must have been an attraction for most young writers at the turn of the century" (6).

Parts one and two of this chapter survey the antipathy to sexual difference and gender destabilization, the virulent reaction against an emerging homosexual discourse, which circulated in Lewis's writings, and links these preoccupations with a critical devaluation of beauty. Part three presents a brief overview of Pater's contributions to the modernist "paradigm" (McGrath 4). In the fourth section, a close reading of Pater's place as acknowledged, negative interlocutor in Eliot's criticism yet unacknowledged textual presence in Eliot's poetry confirms Pater as one of modernism's silenced Others.

The "Vicious Circle"

Once again it is Wyndham Lewis who states publicly, stridently, what others would only suggest *sotto voce:*

> There is a great deal of the intellectual snob about the invert: but since he converts what he borrows from the intellect to the purposes of *sex,* he is a great enemy of the intellect. As a feminine facsimile, further, he takes over the traditional idiosyncracies of the feminine rôle; and certainly one of them has always been to be the "enemy of the Absolute." The natural feminine hostility to the intellect, and a desire to belittle the purely masculine and abstract type of success, he takes over. . . . Even so late as the famous 'nineties the english courts made a martyr of that description of Oscar Wilde. (*Art* 244, 209)

Had the members of the cult of ugliness drawn up rules of affiliation, the first regulation would have stated, emphatically: none of those "nancies" or "homos." The latter, disparaging terms were Lewis's, but the sentiments where shared by Pound, Eliot, and Hulme. In their revisioning of aesthetic history, beauty had been seized and irrevocably contaminated not once but twice in the late nineteenth century: first by Pater, and subsequently by his appreciators, the Aesthetes of the 1880s and 1890s—chief among them, to quote Lewis, "Oscar Wilde, the arch-aesthete of England" (*CH* 34). The first, 1914 issue of *BLAST* shrilly exposes the "effeminate lout within" England as one of its greatest "SINS AND INFECTIONS" ("Manifesto" 11);[7] Lewis's favorite euphemism, "DIABOLICS," is defined as "raptures and roses | of the erotic bookshelves" ("Manifesto" 18).[8] Blending discourses of morality and diagnosis, the purveyors of the new pledged themselves and their works as antidotes to such social and civil contamination, the deplorable and "'willed sickness of modern man'" (Lewis qtd Normand 124). As Boone suggests in another context, Pater and Wilde were "scapegoat[s] sacrificed to the anxieties of masculinity and femininity that beset" the modernist men (30).[9]

In an era in which "traditional models of male bourgeois identity" (Felski 1094) were variously threatened and destabilized—by aesthetes, New Women, suffragettes, the spectacle of shell-shocked, hysterical veterans,[10] sexologists who hypothesized the existence of an "intermediate sex" or "womanly men" born "on the dividing line between the sexes" (E. Carpenter 123), and the public and discursive emergence of self-avowed lesbians and homosexuals—it is small wonder that astute yet reactionary men such as Pound or Lewis would give voice to their multifaceted anxieties. After all, the writings of Pater and Wilde disrupted the culturally-sanctioned fiction of sexuality *as* heterosexuality. Given the "quintessentially modern formulation of sex as the wellspring of human subjectivity" (Boone 69), suggestions of sexual difference could only threaten. Rather than producing straightforward misogynistic or homophobic rants, however, they displaced their fears and loathings, transmuted them into "rich and strange" aesthetic and cultural critiques. To mock the Omega Workshop—participants and cultural products alike—Lewis insisted that he had been invited to join the London group because they "were compelled to call in as much modern talent as they could find, to do the rough and masculine work without which they knew their efforts would not rise above the level of a pleasant tea-party, or command attention" (*LWL* 49). Pound, who preferred to condemn "sodomy" as Dante had taught him to do,[11] was only following a trend, and extending its authority, when he dismissed the Bloomsbury circle of intellectuals and artists as "the bloomsbuggahs" (*P/L* 172). When the Men of 1914 called for art that was *hard*, their phallic criterion was partially a response to what Pound disingenuously termed the "softness of the 'nineties'" (*LEEP* 362).[12] In "Redondillas, or Something of that sort," a poem later withdrawn from *Canzoni*, Pound's speaker satirically sings "of the diverse moods / of effete modern civilization" (*P/EP* 218). What would be the best "world prescription" to cure the ills of a culture too preoccupied with "delicate hues" and "perceptions scarce heeded"?

> A little less Paul Verlaine,
> > A good sound stave of Spinoza,
> A little less of our nerves
> > A little more will toward vision.

> > > > > > > (*P/EP* 218–219)

One has Lewis to thank for a gloss on Verlaine as emblematic invert: "The 'Nineties' movement in England . . . was the Seventies in Paris, reproduced upon our miniature island stage, in a romantic and self-conscious form. Verlaine was an Oscar Wilde—was advertising that particular vice—even went to jail, and recorded the fact in tragic verse" (1939b:70). Among the *Personae* of 1909 one finds a Pound speaker in high "Revolt" against "the lethargy of this our time," which is characterized by a lack of "strong men, / Hearts hot, thoughts mighty" (*P/EP* 96). If people "dream pale flowers" or live as "dabblers," the speaker fearfully acknowledges, they (assuming a gendered audience) cease to be "men." The final verse paragraph is both prayer and warning:

> Great God, if these thy sons are grown such thin ephemera,
> I bid thee grapple chaos and beget
> Some new titanic spawn to pile the hills and stir
> This earth again.
>
> (*P/EP* 97)

Pound and Lewis, presumably, are among the new titans of culture; their works constitute a corrective for several decades of decadence and unmanliness, providing new "definitional boundaries" between "normative and non-normative behaviours" and values (Boone 276). When Pater referred, more than four decades earlier, to "the antagonism of the new," he could not have imagined the discursive venom of the "chastening" they would undertake.

Although Lewis's promulgation of official fascist discourse was comparatively short-lived, his praise for Hitler repudiated in the late 1930s, and his anti-Semitism publically renounced,[13] his efforts to root out "every variety of Perversion" (*Hit* 26) only intensified with each new decade, each new tract for his times. As Hewitt perceptively suggests about the "politics of anality" that Lewis blasted, "Lewis's analysis of modernity—his critique of contemporary politics, and his original enthusiasm for Nazism—is structured taxonomically in terms of an analysis of homosexuality" (528, 527).[14] Readers of *Tarr* (1918) encounter Alan Hobson, a Clive Bell-esque figure who is derided for belonging to a particularly heinous "set": "'The Cambridge set that you represent,'" Tarr remarks, "'is, as observed in the average specimen, a hybrid of the Quaker, the homosexual and the Chelsea artist. You represent, my good Hobson, the *dregs* of anglo-saxon civilisation. . . . Your flabby potion is a mixture of the lees of Liberalism, the poor froth blown off the decadent Nineties, the wardrobe-leavings of a vulgar bohemianism'" (*Tarr* 23). The 1920–21 painting of *Tyros: A Reading of Ovid* features "a satire on womanly men. They fawn, in sensual delight, at the presence of the observer, their entire demeanour signals their instinctive responses to life" (Normand 123–124). But it is *The Art of Being Ruled* (1926) that fully explicates a geneaology of the "sex-invert," outlines his "material physiognomy" (*Art* 212), lambastes him as a great enemy of manliness—a "turncoat, or 'turn-sex' male, feminizing invert" (*Art* 244)—and provides a taxonomy of his kind (the "male-pole type of invert" as opposed to "the female of the genus" [*Art* 213]).[15]

Foucault suggests that self-identified homosexuality emerged and "began to speak in its own behalf" in resistance to the burgeoning "appearance in nineteenth-century psychiatry, jurisprudence, and literature of a whole series of discourses on the species and subspecies of homosexuality, inversion, [and] pederasty" (1978:101). Lewis provides his readers with an alternative theory: in the aftermath of the "feminist revolution," at a time when "post-war life" is dominated by "a *bourgeois* revolution," a new and "gigantic phase of the sex war" is responsible for producing "'homo,'" the "legitimate child of the 'suffragette'" (*Art* 209, 237, 218).[16] Noticeably, this malignant progeny is not given a father, thus intimating that the "sex- transformation" involves an antithetical virgin birth engendering a kind of anti-Christ. Yet the main discursive field in which Lewis situates his argument is political rather than biological. Like the suffragette before him, the "joy-boy" is an "equally *political*" phenomenon, Lewis insists: "Is it not the same old hag that in a 'morality' would be labelled Power, and for whom pleasure, in the simplest sense, means very little, who has pupped this batch of related fashions" (*Art* 215)? The satirical remarks are laced with a Swiftian zest for dehumanizing the opposition; the misogynistic spin of "old hag" and "pupped" could be considered rhetorical bonuses. Inversion, according to Lewis,

> is much more [than] an instinctive capitulation of the will on the part of the ruling male sex. It is much more a political phenomenon than anything else, too: its sensual character, although it is from that angle that it is popularly viewed, of course, is insignificant. Shamanization, and the affecting of inversion by a great number of people not physiologically abnormal, is a social device to gain freedom[.] (*Art* 239)

In the vacuum created by the absence of dominant, heterosexual men, the inverts begin to assert themselves.

Despite casual references to the "*natural* superiority" of males, it is the idiosyncratically constructionist bent of the argument that complicates Lewis's analyses. At times the discussion seems strangely to anticipate de Beauvoir: "A man, then, is made, not born," Lewis declares, "and he is made, of course, with very great difficulty. . . . Men were only made into 'men' with great difficulty even in primitive society: the male is not naturally 'a man' any more than the woman. He has to be propped up into that position with some ingenuity, and is always like to collapse. . . . It is not until he is about thirty

years old that the present European becomes resigned to an erect position"
(*Art* 247, 248). Penile puns aside, Lewis seems to understand that citations of
gender norms are learned habits, not the expression of innate characteristics.
There is actually more gender peril in his scenario: what can be made can also
quickly be unmade in "the contemporary social atmosphere" (*Art* 216).
Hence the need to force men to confront and work with ugliness—sociological, urban, psychological, or aesthetic—in an effort to toughen their responses and stiffen their metaphorical backbones. Lewis further insists that
the discerning eye can read the physiological signs appropriated for, inscribed
upon, the body of an "invert." The "human norm" is repelled by the "material physiognomy," the "'Nancyism' of the joy-boy or joy-man," Lewis insists;
"the over-mannered personality, the queer insistence on 'delicate nurture,'
that air of assuring those met that he is a 'real lady,' like the traditional music-
hall 'tart' who is always a 'clergyman's daughter,' the grating or falsetto lisp, or
the rather cross hauteur of the democratic teashop waitress" (*Art* 212, 210).

The man who readily identifies the various "sets, cells, or cliques" of modernist culture also indicts (or "outs") a "'vicious' circle" of inverts operating
throughout the "anglo-saxon countries and beyond" (*DPDS* vii; *Art* 212), a
"snobbery or cult . . . [featuring] a dozen sentimental fashionable addicts to
one physiological pervert" (*ChM* 391).[17] At the heart of their "great numbers" he perceives "the small nucleus of 'pukka' material" (*Art* 213) who have
been "till very recently living in the shadow of the Oscar Wilde case" (*Art*
213). Elsewhere in *The Art of Being Ruled,* however, Lewis maintains that "the
present widespread invert fashion is not an Oscar-Wildeism, or the excres-
cence of a dilettante sex-snobbery only, . . . although such elements are to be
found in it and are part of its conspicuous advertisement" (*Art* 239). Even
among the inverts he is reluctant to ascribe to Wilde any lasting power.[18]

So convinced was Lewis of his argument's merits that he quotes from *The
Art of Being Ruled* in several works of the 1930s, most notably *Doom of
Youth.* In the latter, however, he implicates the "homo" in the "*Child-Cult,*
artistic and otherwise" (*DY* 207) currently polluting European culture. His
rationale: "the homosexual is, of course, an imitation-woman—or at least
the pathic is that. As such, he is subject to the same unkind sexual law as
women—namely, that to be desired he must be young" (*DY* 206). Homosexuals need to "be eternally 'children'—never to enter the category of 'Fathers,'" never to be conscripted within the heterosexual marriage and
procreation plots, never to assume their roles as "sternly, adultly, masculine"
men (*DY* 218, 219). Most worrisome, according to Lewis, is the fact that
"*the 'Pretty-Boy' state of mind* is not confined to homosexuals":

> There is no occasion for a man to be actively homosexual for him to possess some
> of the eternal characteristics of the "pathic." All you men now at universities and

elsewhere are in contact with active and practising "Fairies": it is unavoidable that at least some of the mannerisms and points of view of the homosexual should pass over into them. . . . So it is not unusual to find what is a homosexual frame of mind or outlook flourishing in a body that is in practice "normal." (*DY* 218)

A wholly essentialist paradigm might have comforted Lewis, reassured him that an inherent homosexuality resides in the bodies and souls of a cursed few. Instead, he can detect "the homosexual habit of mind" (an insidious "master-fashion") almost anywhere (*DY* 218, 256), in any one, a talent that produces both paranoia and new publications decrying "the homosexual cult" (*DPDS* 146).

Before focusing on "Adolf Hitler—The Man and the Party" in Part II of *Hitler* (1931), Lewis devotes significant attention to the enemies within Germany whom Hitler is destined to rout, among them communists and homosexuals. But Lewis does so cautioning that neither he nor "the Nazi" is a narrow-minded "moralist" on some "arch-farce" of a witchhunt (*Hit* 23). This investigation is to be conducted on political and sociological grounds, not ethical. Chapter 3 of Part I is devoted to an evening at the "Eldorado," a Berlin nightclub "within cat's call of [the] Reichstag" in which "everything is absolutely as it should be in the best of all possible Hollywood cabarets. There is the true appropriate glitter and nigger-hubbub—super-sex and pink champagne" (*Hit* 23).[19] Lewis begins by introducing us to the "western Babylon" that is Berlin, particularly the "*quartier-général* of dogmatic Perversity—the Perverts' Paradise, the Mecca of both Lesb and So," yet quickly asserts that, because the Nazis "have something better to think about," they do not bother with sex workers, homosexuals, or peddlars of "obscene publications": "This seems to me of very great importance in estimating the Nazis. Pink-clothed backsides are not their political quarry. That is good. . . . You cannot make war upon an Orbe-Rose, a Rose-Bottom, without making yourself ridiculous" (*Hit* 21–22). (How little Lewis knew.) The reader is then engaged as "sightseer," a "sceptical tourist" and *flâneur,* led to the "'Eldorado of the Motzestrasse" (*Hit* 23, 24)[20] to gaze at the transvestites and inverts who caricature both the feminine and the masculine (as "the super-masculine" [Hewitt 538]). At this textual remove, however, one can look but not be contaminated: for "the dispassionate eye of the 'restless analyst,' these 'strange women' and 'strange men' are very interestin'" but their "expensive traps and tricks" are ineffective (*Hit* 27, 26).[21] Nonetheless, what is seen and learned? Once again any belief in gender-sex essentialism is undermined: the transvestite's successful impersonation means that "the 'feminine' will never be quite the same . . . again. Who can say if this will be for his [the sightseer's] good or no? The sex-absolute will to some extent have been disintegrated for him by this brief encounter—it will have caused him to regard, with a certain sceptical squint, all specifically feminine personal-ity" (*Hit* 25–26). With deadpan irony, Lewis acknowledges that, in Hewitt's terms, the "transvestite lifts femininity out of the realm of biology and into the realm of politics in a way which . . . the woman cannot. The feminine—estranged from the body of the woman—reveals itself as a categorical and political construction" (*Hit* 530). The text, however, cannot bear to perform the same gender-sex separation upon a man's body (even if a Rose-Bottom is involved). Instead, the narrator imagines and enjoys vicariously the violent way in which a "young german politician" would want to destroy the Eldo-rado and all its patrons by rolling this "luxury-spot up like a verminous car-pet, and drop it into the Spree—with a heartfelt *Pfui!* at its big sodden splash" (*Hit* 28). The "young Nationalsocialist" would forebear, of course—because of the "asceticism not without its nobility" that guides his thoughts and actions (*Hit* 22, 28). Undoubtedly the reader is encouraged to ascribe to the narrator a similar asceticism and nobility of purpose, to appreciate that *Hitler* decries democracy ("merely the Punch and Judy show of Tory and of Whig" [*Hit* 194]) and endorses instead Nazism in order to purge West-ern culture of its Babylon-like ways.

For all that he criticizes scientists and scientific discourse, Lewis's approach to cultural and political change is unabashedly that of a disenchanted social Darwinist: we have the ability to evolve, he argues, but everywhere there are signs of a repulsive devolution. The "child-cult" he deplores is identified as "a phenomenon of 'revolutionary' *anti-authority*," a rejection of "responsibility" and the "*natural* superiority" of Fathers (*Art* 240). Similarly, threateningly, "male sex-inversion can be regarded . . . as the prognostication of a deep rev-olution in the european character" (*Art* 240), a revolution that could make the Western race unfit for life (after its decline or extinction, another creature more like the "Asiatic" may emerge). Lewis's solution is to write, cajole, and bully men into becoming (heterosexual) Men. "CALL YOURSELF A *MAN!*" bellows forth from the pages of *The Art of Being Ruled* as the wake-up call for the male's "*instinct of self- preservation*" (*Art* 249). The alternative is almost too grim for words: "he collapses and becomes to all intents and purposes a woman"—or worse, a womanly man (*Art* 250).

Violently Disowned, Scarcely Respectable

Wilde once suggested that Pater "has no rival in his own sphere, and he has escaped disciples" (*CWW* 9:545; Ellmann ed. 234). Contrarily, I am argu-ing that "Pater" was anathema to the Men of 1914 partially *because of* his disciples. The writings were always doubly refracted: generally, through a culturally-ingrained homophobia such as Lewis reiterates; specifically, through the lens of the Wilde spectacle—his theatrical life and writings, the conviction and imprisonment for homosexual acts (praised by Lewis as "the grand finale of the 'naughty' decade" [*MWA* 148]), and his subsequent life (and afterlife) as social and artistic pariah. Lewis once again provides the best example of these personal and discursive predilections. By 1931, he had fully explored and expressed his antipathy to the "verminous" "homos" who had infiltrated popular culture and high art alike, and had made occasional, slighting references to Pater. Three years later, when comparing "the serious work of art" against the current crop of *Men Without Art* nonetheless flourishing as writers and critics, he was fully prepared to excoriate whatever reputation Pater might have had left.[22]

Men Without Art is announced from the outset as a work of "satire," that privileged weapon in the cultist's discursive arsenal. As Lewis explains in his "Introduction," "This book has, in fact, been written, to put it shortly, to defend Satire. But to 'Satire' I have given a meaning so wide as to confound it with 'Art.' So this book may be said to be nothing short of a defence of art" (*MWA* 13). In order to "define it anew," Lewis's satirical exercise is fabricated from terms with scientific, medical, legal, and ethical resonances. In "reality," the reader is assured, satire "is nothing else but *the truth*—the truth, in fact, of Natural Science. The objective, nonemotional truth of the scientific intelligence sometimes takes on the exuberant sensuous quality of creative art: then it is very apt to be called 'Satire,' for it has been bent not so much upon pleasing as upon being true" (*MWA* 99).[23] Switching discursive gears, Lewis insists that, "It is with man, and not with manners, that . . . 'satire' is called upon to deal. It is a *chronic* ailment (manifesting itself, it is true, in a variety of ways) not an *epidemic* state, depending upon 'period,' or upon the 'wicked ways' of the particular smart-set of the time" (*MWA* 101–102). If the reader is not fully impressed with a medical practitioner of words, however, there is always the astute advocate:

> Indeed, for the satirist to acquire the right to hold up to contempt a fellow-mortal, he is supposed, first, to arm himself with the insignia of a sheriff or special constable. No age, for many centuries, has been so lawless as ours—nothing to compare with Capone, it is said, for instance, has ever been known in America. And perhaps for this reason an unnatural sensitiveness to law and order is noticeably in all of us: and in the field of the ethical judgment, as much as in that of the civil law, is this the case. Perhaps that is the reason why, in this defence of the art of satire, I give the place of honour to the moral law, and settle accounts with that source of interference first. (*MWA* 87)

Throughout the text, Lewis maintains that, "I am not a moralist"; *Men Without Art* is devoted to a defense of "non-ethical satire" (*MWA* 87, 88). One could also position it as a brief on behalf of ugliness: satire "can only exist *in contrast* to something else," Lewis argues, "it is a shadow, and an ugly shadow at that, of some perfection. And it is so disagreeable, and so painful (at least in the austere sense in which we appear to be defining it here) that no one would pursue it *for its own sake,* or take up the occupation of a satirist unless compelled to do so, out of indignation at the spectacle of the neglect of beauty and virtue" (*MWA* 89).

The prosecution of Pater builds slowly in *Men Without Art,* beginning with introductory charges of critical malfeasance:

> [H]eaven defend us from the *beaux yeux* of the *beaux arts!* Art is not here defended for its own sake: *art-for-art's-sake,* of Walter Pater, is nothing to do with art—it is a spectator's doctrine, not an artist's: it teaches how to enjoy, not how to perform. I am a performer. It is as a performer that I shall speak. (*MWA* 13)[24]

Then, in a move that was sure to needle Eliot (who had already published his negative views of Pater's work; see below[25]), Lewis insists that his peer (not a "humbug," we are told, but now a "*pseudo* everything . . . [who] has found his theorist to explain and justify him, namely Mr. I. A. Richards") is following in Pater's dubious critical footsteps:

> But meanwhile we have got here, in this Eliot-Richards combination, a new aesthetic of *art pur.* . . . The *Disbelief Theory* we could label it for convenience. It is, I dare say, the most important literary theory, upon the English scene, since that of Walter Pater, and deserves all our attention. I will attempt therefore to outline this new *art-for-art's-sake*—or stylists' evangel—universal and "catholic" in the popular sense—for, *however disguised,* that is what I believe it is. (*MWA* 64)

In the latter comments, guilt by association is deemed aesthetic only, rather than a matter of "pathic" sympathies. This is not the case when Proust, "archetype of the internal traveller," is cited only to be "disowned": "Pater and Marcel Proust are patently of kindred intelligence. Joyce is far more robust and spacious, at his best. . . . For 'aestheticism,' though in truth rampant and ubiquitous, is on all hands violently disowned . . . although the manner of Pater is today constantly imitated, on the sly, and his teaching absorbed along with his style, he is scarcely *respectable,* in the intellectual sense" (*MWA* 120). Contradictions abound in Lewis's argument: aestheticism is "disowned" yet rampant; Pater is *passé,* yet his prose is "constantly imitated."

The brunt of the satirist's critical and personal animus is reserved for those who function as the un-men of *Men Without Art,* writers who must be indicted for offenses against Lewis's repressive sex-gender code. With seeming subtlety, the discussion begins with a diatribe against Virginia Woolf and

her "feminine mind" then shifts to those whose minds are "deeply feminized," namely Pater and all of the other "cissies" and "distinguished dia-
bolists" (*MWA* 140, 142, 143). *Mrs Dalloway* is dismissed as "a sort of
undergraduate imitation of" Joyce's *Ulysses;* Woolf's narrative experiments in
"tunnelling" among, interconnecting, various characters' consciousnesses are
referred to as explorations in "the half-lighted places of the mind—in which,
quivering with a timid excitement, this sort of intelligence shrinks. . . . A little old-maidish, are the Prousts and the sub-Prousts" (*MWA* 138–139).[26]
This "manner" or narrative stance of "standing, half-concealed, but alone—
it was the way of life of Marcel Proust," Lewis observes,

> But it has also, in one degree or another, been the way of life of many a recent
> figure in our literature—as in the case of [Pater's] Marius the Epicurean,
> "made easy by his natural Epicureanism. . . . prompting him to conceive of
> himself as but the passive spectator of the world around him." Some, not con-
> tent with retreating into the ambulatories of their inner consciousness, will in-
> stal [*sic*] there a sort of private oratory. From this fate "the fleshly school" of
> the last century was saved, not much to its credit certainly, by the pagan im-
> pulses which still lingered in Europe. And it became ultimately the "art-for-
> art's-sake" cult of the Naughty Nineties. Walter Pater was, of course, the
> fountain-head of that cult. . . . the non-religious, un-theosophic, pleasure-
> cult, of which—in that ninetyish pocket at the end of the nineteenth century,
> in full . . . reaction against Victorian manners—Oscar Wilde was the high-
> priest. (*MWA* 139)

Just as Robert Buchanan tried to punish Pre-Raphaelite poets for failing to
meet his literary and personal standards,[27] so Lewis hopes to devastate the
reputation of Pater, Wilde, Woolf, and any other contemporary writers "of
the essentially feminine sensibility" (*MWA* 145) who have made postwar
culture a latter-day and "peculiar Slough of Despond" (*MWA* 141). (Interestingly, Lewis resorts to an essentialist argument as it suits his purposes to
unman his enemies.) What is the worst thing that can be said about such
poisonous figures? "[I]ndeed, how *girlish* are all these intellectual leaders"
(*MWA* 143). Wilde may have been the most outlandish figure, but Lewis
identifies Pater as the intellectual "fountainhead." (In retrospect, the cultural
potential of Pater's writings can be adduced inversely according to Lewis's vehement denunciation of them.)

Westermarck's *The Origin and Development of Moral Ideas* was pressed into
service as chief intertextual resource for *The Art of Being Ruled;* Mario Praz's
The Romantic Agony[28] is commandeered as the ultimate, authoritative
weapon in *Men Without Art.* Whenever the argument might seem idiosyncratic or vituperative, "Prof. Praz" is cited for his collaborative assessments. At
no point does Lewis acknowledge (or realize) that, long before Praz or Eliot,

Hulme or Babbitt recognized a classical-romantic antinomy in cultural movements, Pater was responding to the work of Sainte-Beuve and Stendhal to
theorize these "two real tendencies in the history of art and literature," suggesting that "however falsely" they "may be opposed by critics, or exaggerated
by artists themselves, they are tendencies really at work at all times in art" (*Ap*
253, 259).[29] Nor does Lewis recognize that "Pater's rhetoric" is "thoroughly
and ardently anti-Romantic" (McGrath 21). Instead, Lewis installs Pater as
the "girlish" patriarch of a deviant House of Decay:

> The exquisite palsies or langours of decay are . . . present in this mid-Victo-
> rian moralist aesthete. The fisticuffs of Lord Queensberry are already mobi-
> lized in the wings: and to come down to the present time, the droopings and
> wiltings of [Eliot's] Mr. Prufrock, or, better, the androgynous permutations of
> [Woolf's] *Orlando,* might already have been foreseen. Next, as a mate for
> Pater, we can take André Gide—for as Pater stands to Oscar Wilde, so Wilde
> stands to Gide. So we shall have three consecutive generations of moralists—
> of moralists-gone-wrong. (*MWA* 145)

Again the text lashes out at the creator of "Prufrock" by making his works
sound guilty by association; this second link between Eliot and Pater is more
deliberately damaging because of the sexual differentiation implied.
Prufrock's dandyism has been recontextualized by association, and damned
for its inversionist sympathies. The self-proclaimed goal of Lewis's work is
purgative: by exposing those responsible for "the stale and sickly airs which
have been hanging over Europe for a century" (*MWA* 143), the satirist hopes
to return art to men, and vice versa.

The "Spirit of Rebellion and Revolt"

Texts such as *Time and Western Man* remind us that Lewis could exercise
considerable critical acumen; illustrations and paintings such as *A Battery
Shelled* (1919), *Red and Black Principle* (1936), and the *Portrait of T. S. Eliot*
(1938) attest to his uncommon artistic vision and technical skills. Had his
assessment of Pater not been filtered through a toxic homophobia—had he
read in the canon widely, as Pound and Eliot did, and appreciated its intellectual diversity and discursive breadth, as they did not—he would have encountered "one of the major formulat[ion]s" of modernist culture (McGrath
5), texts that not only laud the "spirit of rebellion and revolt" that emerged
in previous eras but address the "needs" of individuals coping with "modern
life" (*TR* 184). As McGrath vividly demonstrates, although "Pater's own
writings could not be classified as Modernist, except marginally, in their
techniques and methods, his theoretical articulation of the paradigm is one

of the earliest and most comprehensive available" (4). Among the "cardinal principles and constellations of corollaries" developed in Pater's brilliant synthesis of "British, German, and French thought" are "the subjectivity and relativity of knowledge, epistemological skepticism, the primacy of sensory experience, an observance of the Kantian limits on knowledge, aesthetic and historical idealism, a functionalist attitude toward all the products of imagination and intellect, the notion of a unified sensibility of mind, body, and feeling, an expressive orientation toward the creative process, and an ascetic devotion to aesthetic craftsmanship" (McGrath 6).[30] For this resolutely nonsystematic critic with a pronounced "taste for avant-garde thinking" (McGrath 1), established certainties of self and others were among the most highly contested notions. When compared with Pater's radical suppositions, the underlying conservatism of Hulme's early essays and Eliot's critical corpus is very apparent. In his first publication, a manifesto-like article that positions itself against "Coleridge's Writings" (1866), Pater makes the following, provocative assertions:

> Modern thought is distinguished from ancient by its cultivation of the "relative" spirit in place of the "absolute." Ancient philosophy sought to arrest every object in an eternal outline, to fix thought in a necessary formula. . . . To the modern spirit nothing is or can be rightly known except relatively under conditions. . . . The moral world is ever in contact with the physical; the relative spirit has invaded moral philosophy from the ground of inductive sciences. (*CW* 49)[31]

For almost 30 years, Pater continued to weigh the individual, aesthetic, and cultural ramifications of these seismic discursive shifts. Yet defining the modern conditions of existence—"the transitory, the fugitive, the contingent" (*GDL* 57)—did not mean the same thing as acquiescing to a paralyzing pessimism about the present or future. Provisional subjectivity does not have to reduce "the individual mind" to "a solitary prisoner in its own dream of a world" (*TR* 187–188); the "strange, perpetual, weaving and unweaving of ourselves" could yield the "fruit of a quickened, multiplied consciousness" (*TR* 188, 190).

To quote Bucknell, subject-object relations "remain mobile" in Pater's theorizations; they take place "upon the site of a subject that cannot form itself without the 'world,' and a world continually remade by the mobile subject" (603). Pater's imaginative reformulations of Hume and Kant were first articulated in literary and philosophical discursive fields, but by the late 1860s he fastened upon the possibilities of aesthetics and art criticism (inaugurating, as it happens, a new standard of interdisciplinarity in cultural analyses). The "Preface" to *The Renaissance*[32] unhesitatingly expresses the implications of ontological and epistemological mobility for the study of the beautiful, and at the same time takes aim at two shibboleths of Victorian and Oxonian aesthetic commentary, Ruskin and Arnold:

> Many attempts have been made by writers on art and poetry to define beauty in the abstract, to express it in the most general terms, to find some universal formula for it. The value of these attempts has most often been in the suggestive and penetrating things said by the way. Such discussions help us very little . . . to use words like beauty, excellence, art, poetry, with a more precise meaning than they would otherwise have. Beauty, like all other qualities presented to human experience, is relative; and the definition of it becomes unmeaning and useless in proportion to its abstractness. To define beauty, not in the most abstract but in the most concrete terms possible, to find, not its universal formula, but the formula which expresses most adequately this or that special manifestation of it, is the aim of the true student of aesthetics.
>
> "To see the object as in itself it really is," has been justly said to be the aim of all true criticism whatever; and in aesthetic criticism the first step towards seeing one's object as it really is, is to know one's own impression as it really is, to discriminate it, to realise it distinctly. . . . What is this song or . . . book, to *me?* What effect does it really produce on me? Does it give me pleasure? and if so, what sort or degree of pleasure? How is my nature modified by its presence, and under its influence? (*TR* xix-xx)

Beauty is vehemently defended in these paragraphs and the book as a whole, but subversively so. Gone are any promises of absolute values and "great" objects that inherently embody them; instantiations of the beautiful are deemed to be "like all other qualities presented to human experience, . . . relative." Contingency prevails: Paterian aestheticism consists of impressions, fine discriminations, and concrete, time-bound experiences. Appreciation is identified as a significant source of *pleasure,* but the process begins and ends with the subjective responses of the perceiver.

Pater's efforts to establish a new mode of "true criticism" in *The Renaissance* prompted subsequent animadversions on truth and its relation to beauty. The essay on "Style" (1888) argues that "there can be no merit, no craft at all, without" truth (the "essence" of "artistic quality"), insisting that "all beauty is in the long run only *fineness* of truth, or what we call expression, the finer accommodation of speech to that vision within" (*Ap* 6). This may sound vaguely Platonic, an assertion of "the immutable and absolute character of truth" (*PP* 192), but *Plato and Platonism* eschews any such possibility. All that the argument allows is the "truth of a particular time and place, for one and not for another" (*PP* 192); truth is just as multiple in its possibilities and local in its manifestations as beauty. Gone is the secure Keatsian romanticism of "'Beauty is truth, truth beauty'"; Pater's discourse is decidedly postromantic, perhaps even postmodern, in its acceptance that "truly the last, the infallible word, after all, never gets spoken" (*PP* 192).

Celebrating the possibilities of beauty in a world in which "Πάντα ῥεῖ, all things fleet away" (*PP* 6) made Pater all the more sensitive to "the group of conditions, intellectual, social, material, amid which it was actually produced" (*PP* 9). Anticipating cultural-materialist criticism by almost a century, he maintains that "in every age there is a peculiar *ensemble* of conditions which determines a common character in every product of that age, in business and art, in fashion and speculation, in religion and manners, in men's very faces" (*PP* 9–10). It was he who demanded, in the "Winckelmann" essay of 1867, that writers "deal" effectively "with the conditions of modern life. What modern art has to do in the service of culture is so to rearrange the details of modern life, so to reflect it, that it may satisfy the spirit" (*TR* 184). Had the Men of 1914—and subsequently, their critics and apologists—considered Paterian texts such as these rather than dwelt on the salacious notoriety that enveloped Pater's name and canon, then the "vast heterogeneous inheritance" of modernism would have been written very differently.

"Who is That Third Who Always Walks Behind You?"

If one has heard a recording of Eliot intoning *The Waste Land,* one can imagine the aloof, stentorious voice declaring, "I do not believe that Pater . . . has influenced a single first-rate mind of a later generation" (*SE* 442). Yet these final words of a 1930 essay are not as conclusive as they may seem. The dismissive remarks are directed at Pater's *Marius the Epicurean;* the complete phrase is, "I do not believe that Pater, in this book, has influenced . . ."[33] Is one to assume that other books *have been* influential, books that "'ring all through our modern literature'" (*SE* 443)? Is it fair to say that Pater's "modern" moment is connected with Eliot's? The answer is yes, to both questions, but Eliot would have it otherwise, and would like his readers to concur.

Pound referred to Eliot as the Possum, but another apt moniker would be the Politician.[34] Eliot was the one most concerned with reputations, and rhetoric; his were the most careful and carefully-orchestrated efforts to legislate and police the canon; he cultivated the right friends and acquaintances, and acquired strategic financial support for his publishing campaigns. As politically astute and subtle as Lewis was brash or Pound outspoken, Eliot's homophobic response to Pater (the historical figure, his writings, and his reputation) was muted, barely expressed. But its discursive traces are indelible. Lewis's caustic remark that "as a mate for Pater, we can take André Gide—for as Pater stands to Oscar Wilde, so Wilde stands to Gide. So we shall have three consecutive generations of moralists—of moralists-gone-wrong" (*MWA* 145) is actually a response to Eliot's insinuating observation that, "Pater is always primarily the moralist. . . . [A] writer may be none the less classified as a moralist, if his moralizing is suspect or perverse. We have to-day a witness in the person of M. André Gide" (*SE* 438–439).[35] Rather than denounce Pater outright as a homosexual, Eliot merely names another, and allows the guilt by association to resonate. In the 1933 Turnball Lectures, Eliot's censure is also oblique yet succinct: Remy de Gourmont, the audience is told, was a "brilliant literary critic, [but] he was no philosopher; and being no philosopher, he was filled with all sorts of philosophical prejudices—about sex, for instance—after all, he lived in the time of Walter Pater" (*VMP* 97).

In taking pains to make Pater's writings seem "merely eccentric and, in any event, outside the main English tradition" (Poirier 169), Eliot was also following in the discursive footsteps of mentors Paul Elmer More and Irving Babbitt. More castigated Pater the Romantic at length in an April 1911 essay for the *Nation,* comments he repeated in his *Shelburne Essays* of 1913. "Of the critical mind," More opined, Pater "had little, being at once something more and something less than this" (Seiler ed. 415). Most damningly, he accused Pater of not being a "true critic," of falsifying "the reality" of Platonic culture, Aurelian Rome, and the Renaissance ("subtly perversive of the truth"), and making "truth the servant of beauty" (Seiler ed. 419, 420). Babbitt, on the other hand, who held Pater responsible for setting readers "afloat on a boundless sea of relativity" (174), preferred slighting, comparative asides in works such as *Masters of Modern French Criticism* (1912).[36] For all three, Pater was the vampiric figure who, in the early twentieth century, "ruled from the grave"; theirs would be the silver bullets of criticism that would silence him forever.[37]

Although Eliot's writings rarely mention a particular Pater text—as if denying him such tangible recognition—it is possible to ascertain how steadily the criticism is aimed at central works in the Pater canon, and how widely the poetry is engaged. (Most commentators refer generally to Eliot's reading of Pater, and claim various intertextual gestures, but do not or cannot confirm the texts in question.) Of the ten volumes in Macmillan's Library Edition of Pater's works, Eliot admits familiarity with the contents of seven: *Appreciations* (which includes "Coleridge," "Style," and the "Postscript" on the classic-romantic antinomy), *Imaginary Portraits, Marius the Epicurean* (two volumes), *Miscellaneous Studies* ("Pascal"), *Plato and Platonism,* and *The Renaissance.*[38] Before moving to Europe in the mid-1910s, Eliot owned four volumes, which were among the books sent to him in London by his mother, Charlotte Eliot, in 1920 (*LE* 1:399). The Hayward Bequest in the archives of King's College, Cambridge includes Eliot's annotated copy of *The Renaissance* (first edition, 1873), purchased secondhand ("for 10 cents") by Mrs. Eliot as a gift.[39] Eliot also refers to two biographies of Pater: the now-discredited *Life of Walter Pater* by Thomas Wright (1907), and A. C. Benson's *Walter Pater* (1906). One must also remember that he was reading Pater's art criticism knowledgeably. In 1907–1908, as a Harvard student, he studied Fine Arts 3, "History of Ancient Art"; in 1909–1910, Fine Arts 20b: "Florentine Painting." Lessons from both courses were applied during Eliot's tour of Italy in the summer of 1911 and his visits to the galleries and museums of London from 1914 onward, Baedecker in hand to guide him, "meditating on/ Time's ruins" (*CPP* 41).[40]

Yet knowing Pater's works intimately and accrediting them are two very different phenomena.[41] From 1915 to 1919, as Eliot tried to establish himself as a critical presence in English (especially) and American intellectual circles, his occasional reviews cited Pater—disparagingly, most often, but also to substantiate his own cultural conversance.[42] Considering the possibilities of generic hybridity in "The Borderline of Prose," Eliot informs readers that the prose-poem is doomed to failure. Pater's essay on "Style" is not quoted directly, but Eliot's argument constantly rebuts Pater's key suggestion that "those who have dwelt most emphatically on the distinction between prose and verse, prose and poetry, may sometimes have been tempted to limit the proper functions of prose too narrowly" (*Ap* 1). To emphasize his disagreement, Eliot uses Pater's own words for his rebuke: "'All the arts *approach* the condition of music.' Yes! but not by being less themselves" (1917:159). Specific mention of Pater is withheld until the final paragraphs: "I have purposely avoided Pater's 'Mona Lisa'," Eliot intones, "—because I am not sure that it is good prose" (1917: 159). Doubt is cast again in a review of Bertrand Russell's *Mysticism and Logic:* "It is quite as good prose as Pater's, but it is not Mr. Russell's best prose"; "[Mr. Balfour's] hardness is of the surface, and conceals an affinity to Walter Pater. But Mr. Russell's hardness is from within" (1918b:768, 769). A survey of "Recent British Periodical Literature in Ethics" will not list Pater among the "eminent" or "distinguished critics" of Socrates and Plato, but Eliot praises P. S. Burrell's work because "among [the] noteworthy theories [he] oppose[s]" is that offered in *Plato and Platonism:* "Justice does not as Pater thought 'supervene' upon the other virtues; it is what makes them possible" (1918a:270–271). As if to prove uncategorically that "whatever Mr. Yeats's influence may have been" it is now passé, that his is a mind "foreign" to contemporary English letters, Eliot's 1919 review of *The Cutting of an Agate* pauses to expose a passage that borrows liberally from the "Conclusion" to *The Renaissance:* "It is a style of Pater," Eliot concludes, "with a trick of the eye and a changing of the nether lip that come from across the Irish Channel. . . . Mr Yeats sometimes appears, as a philosopher of aesthetics, incoherent. But all of his observations are quite consistent with his personality, with his remoteness"

(1919a:553). Although the circulation numbers of some periodicals to which he contributed were comparatively small, the tentacles of Eliot's persuasive opinions reached extensively. As he boasted in 1919 to his mother, who was always anxious for his success, he was "known to be disinterested" as a critic, and was in a good position to "influence London opinion and English literature. . . . I really think that I have far more *influence* on English letters than any other American has ever had, unless it be Henry James. I know a great many people, but there are many more who would like to know me" (*LE* 280).

Pater's first published essay was a study of "Coleridge's Writings"; "The Perfect Critic," the essay that begins Eliot's first volume of criticism, *The Sacred Wood* (1920), commences by acknowledging Coleridge as "perhaps the greatest of English critics" (*SW* 1) and then proceeds to imply that Pater is surely among the lesser.[43] One named mention of Pater is buried among comments establishing Arthur Symons's critical genealogy: in the history of "'aesthetic criticism' or 'impressionistic criticism,'" Symons is the "successor of Pater, and partly of Swinburne" (*SW* 2–3). Thereafter, Eliot is free to engage with Pater's ideas at a safe remove—as attributed to Symons.[44] Otherwise he can take potshots at "the type" of critic who "reacts in excess of the stimulus, making something new out of the impressions, but suffer[s] from a defect of vitality or an obscure obstruction which prevents nature from taking its course" (*SW* 6). (The delicate hints of something unnatural about Pater, an "obscure" problem, seem almost Jamesian.) The second essay, "Imperfect Critics," also names Pater mockingly (this time in negative contrast to Swinburne), yet Eliot's assessment of George Wyndham's romanticism is framed in decidedly Paterian terms: "What is permanent and good in Romanticism is curiosity . . . a curiosity which recognizes that any life, if accurately and profoundly penetrated, is interesting and always strange. Romanticism is a short cut to the strangeness without the reality, and it leads its disciples back upon themselves" (*SW* 31).[45] One of the two most famous essays in the collection, "Hamlet and His Problems" (the other being "Tradition and the Individual Talent"), concludes its first paragraph with an almost Wildean riposte at Pater's expense: having castigated Goethe and Coleridge for substituting "their own Hamlet for Shakespeare's," Eliot then adds, "We should be thankful that Walter Pater did not fix his attention to this play" (*SW* 95).[46] The witticism had its desired effect; many critics have subsequently quoted it to slight Pater. Few, however, have also noted Eliot's constant, even nagging need to pronounce and render Pater's writings obsolete.[47]

Walter de la Mare provided the occasion for further, extensive interment: to his 1930 collection of studies, *The Eighteen-Eighties,* Eliot contributed "Arnold and Pater," the essay that revisits the interstices of aesthetic, religious, cultural, and ethical discourses in order to demonstrate that Pater's best work (on "art for art's sake") is derivative, an "offspring of Arnold's Culture" (*SE* 439); that *Marius the Epicurean* is moral yet "incoherent; . . . its content . . . a hodge-podge of the learning of the classical don . . . and a prolonged flirtation with the liturgy" (*SE* 440–441);[48] and that Pater's "influence," overall, was and is confined to "one moment in the history of thought and sensibility in the nineteenth century" (*SE* 442).[49] There is a fine temporal-spatial precision to Eliot's placement of Pater and his writings: he is of another century; *Marius* only "marks indeed one of the phases" of religious culture in England (*SE* 438); the "right practice of 'art for art's sake' was the devotion of Flaubert and Henry James; Pater is not with these men," these proto-modernists, "but rather with Carlyle and Ruskin and Arnold, if some distance below them" (*SE* 443). Whereas Arnold's writings are "skilfull," Pater's are merely "competent" (*SE* 437). The only "gift" that Eliot is willing to discern is Pater's "taste for painting and the plastic arts"—and it is *a taste* at that, not a talent or forte or ability, in a subject "to which Ruskin had introduced the nation" (*SE* 437).[50] The "famous dictum" from *The Renaissance* is quoted—"'for art comes to you professing frankly to give nothing but the highest quality to your moments as they pass, and simply for those moments' sake'" (*SE* 439)—but its chief term is turned against Pater to insist that his "moment" in the critical spotlight has passed. The essay seems to be yet another Eliotic exercise in critical insight and civility, but insinuated into the discussion are terms—*subversive, degradation, virulent, peculiar, suspect, perverse, morbid, malady, perversion, absurd, incoherent*—which speak to another, moralistic agenda. The reader is told that the "view of art expressed in" *The Renaissance* actually "propagated some confusion between life and art which is not wholly irresponsible for some untidy lives" (*SE* 442), a circumlocution all the more damning for the effort required to understand its meaning. Although completely unnecessary, there is a reference to Oscar Wilde in the essay ("If we wish to understand painting, we do not go to Oscar Wilde for help. We have specialists, such as Mr. Berenson, or Mr. Roger Fry" [*SE* 438]) that goes a long way toward contextualizing the intimations of *subversive, suspect,* and *perversion.*

Public notice of Pater's writings, therefore, is inevitably a matter of denunciation for Eliot, a series of disclaimers and negative judgments—in Carol Christ's terms, a strategic "smokescreen" to "produc[e] a climate of appreciation for his own work and obscure the genuine continuities between him and his immediate predecessors" (157). As the speaker of "Portrait of a Lady" likes to imagine, "I keep my countenance, / I remain self-possessed" (*CPP* 20). Nonetheless, as the remainder of this chapter demonstrates, there is a sustained and sometimes intense discursive engagement with key Paterian concepts and resonant, almost haunting phrases. As Conlon and Blisset concur, "some of the tastes they display, the images they use, the preoccupations they evince, have appeared and reappeared in Eliot's work" (Blisset 267; Conlon 1982a).

Once enumerated, the extent of Paterian "under-currents" flowing in Eliot's canon is quite astonishing. From the nature of experience to the relationship between thought and feeling in creative and critical endeavors, from correlatives to confounding metamorphoses, a Pater text has introduced a term, connected epistemological and aesthetic issues, or provided "hints and guesses" that Eliot pursues in positive or negative fashion. I am not referring to those passages in which Eliot uses his considerable gifts for parody to lampoon Pater and perhaps a secondary object of critical attention—when he remarks that "the poet aspires to the condition of the music-hall comedian" (*UPUC* 32) or, in a much more complex intertextual gesture, compares Spinoza and Copernicus by suggesting that "the presence that, a little later than Bruno, rose so strangely beside the waters of the Zuyder Zee, is symbolical of all that in the ways of the sixteenth century the humanist was not" (1919a:1015).[51] The most significant intertextual gestures in Eliot's prose and poetry are sometimes only "footfalls" that "echo in the memory," shadows "hidden in the shrubbery" (*CPP* 171, 172). To express the "fundamental belief" that "man requires" a "*formula* to be imposed upon him from above," Eliot invokes *askesis* (1916: 284), for Pater the defining characteristic of Marius's life and a more general "self-restraint, a skilful economy of means" (*Ap* 14) such as one finds in the prose of Flaubert or the "austere" and "earliest phases" of the Renaissance (*TR* xxiii). Several years before coming to terms with the antiempiricist approach to "Experience and the Objects of Knowledge in the Philosophy of F. H. Bradley"[52] Eliot was taken with another Oxonian formulation, one that emphatically argues, "The service of philosophy, of speculative culture, towards the human spirit, is to rouse, to startle it to a life of constant and eager observation. . . . Not the fruit of experience, but experience itself, is the end. A counted number of pulses only is given to us of a variegated, dramatic life. . . . To burn always with this hard, gem-like flame, to maintain this ecstasy, is success in life" (*TR* 188–189). The latter sentence will be parodied in the poems to mock self-assertive smugness ("My self-possession flares up for a second," the speaker of "Portrait of a Lady" declares; "My self-possession gutters; we are really in the dark" [*CPP* 20–21]), but there is always a felt pressure, seldom honored, to experience fully, to know "the awful daring of a moment's surrender" (*CPP* 74). The contemplative speaker of "East Coker" can intone, "There is, it seems to us, / At best, only a limited value / In the knowledge derived from experience" (*CPP* 179), but another voice in *Four Quartets* wryly admits, "We had the experience but missed the meaning" (*CPP* 186).

Pater defines the Renaissance as "that movement in which, in various ways, the human mind wins for itself a new kingdom of feeling and sensation and thought" (*TR* 5). Throughout his writings, *sensation* is the foundation of aesthetic experience; *thought* and *feeling* must be inextricably connected. Eliot would not have it otherwise. The best Renaissance writers, in his opinion, "had a quality of sensuous thought, or of thinking through the senses, or of the senses thinking, of which the exact formula remains to be defined" (*SW* 23).[53] As Christ comments, "Eliot, like Pater, achieves a universality for private experience by depending upon sensation as the experience art offers. Objects implicitly contain the power of evoking particular sensations" (82–83). Reviewing *Tarr*, Eliot observes: "Intelligence, however, is only a part of Mr. Lewis's quality; it is united with a vigorous physical organism which interests itself directly in sensation for its own sake. The direct contact with the senses, perception of the world of immediate experience with its own scale of values, is like Dostoevsky" (1918e:105). In "The Perfect Critic" Eliot reiterates the fact that, "Not only all knowledge, but all feeling, is in perception" (*SW* 10). Readers of *Chapbook* are reminded that "it does not follow that these are two distinct faculties, one of imagination and one of reason, . . . or that 'feeling,' in a work of art, is any less an intellectual product than is 'thought'" (Eliot 1921a:9). The highest accolade Pater can grant Prosper Mérimée is that he "felt intelligently" (*MS* 19); Eliot concurs that "the material of the artist is not his beliefs as *held*, but his beliefs as *felt*" (*UPUC* 136). Marius's quest for spiritual enlightenment is also a life- long attempt to unify thought and feeling, to connect the sensations of life with the lessons of philosophical and religious discourse. Metaphysical poets and Jacobean dramatists, according to Eliot,

> were notably men who incorporated their erudition into their sensibility: their mode of feeling was directly and freshly altered by their reading and thought. In Chapman especially there is a direct sensuous apprehension of thought, or a recreation of thought into feeling, which is exactly what we find in Donne. . . . Tennyson and Browning are poets, and they think; but they do not feel their thought as immediately as the odour of a rose. A thought to Donne was an experience; it modified his sensibility. (*SE* 286–287)[54]

Crashaw's poetry, on the other hand, is flawed because feeling and thought are unbalanced; "Crashaw is one of those who are on the side of feeling rather than thought" (*VMP* 163).

Eliot might just as easily have said that a Crashaw text offers "a short cut to the strangeness without the reality" of religious experience (*SW* 31). Condemning a closet romanticist in Paterian terms would provide a particular pleasure; after all, it is Pater's seemingly excessive claim that, "A certain strangeness, something of the blossoming of the aloe, is indeed an element in all true works of art . . . and this strangeness must be sweet also—a lovely strangeness" (*TR* 57). Yet, for both Pater and Eliot, an acute response to that which is "rich and strange" underscores the artist's creative abilities and the transformative possibilities of literary and aesthetic discourse. Not only are both men familiar with Ariel's song from *The Tempest*—"Those are pearls that were his eyes: / Nothing of him that doth fade,/ Both doth suffer a sea-change / Into something rich and strange" (1.2.399–402)—time and again they cite its promise of transmutation and transformation. But this is more than a shared, unconnected metaphorical enthusiasm. The intertextual link is found in the Benson biography of Pater praised by Eliot. "Those who cannot see with Pater's eyes," Benson observes,

> may look in vain, in the writings or the pictures of which he speaks, for the mysterious suggestiveness of line and colour which he discerns in them. They have suffered in passing through the medium of his perception, like the bones of the drowned king, "a sea-change into something rich and strange." . . . [I]n the hands of Pater these pictures out of the past have been transmuted by a secret and deep current of emotion into something behind and beyond the outer form. They are charged with dreams. (36)

Eliot informs readers of *Dial* that "what is needed of art is a simplification of current life into something rich and strange," an ideal that few writers attain (1921b:214). Years later he tried to explain that the poet attempts "to fabricate something permanent and holy out of his own personal animal feelings . . . to transmute his personal and private agonies into something rich and strange, something universal and impersonal" (*SE* 137). One cannot help but note that "feelings" were much more suspect in 1927, a year of personal and religious upheaval for Eliot; the critic astringently avows the "universal" and "impersonal" dimension of texts as an escape from animalistic impulses or all-too-human suffering.

Transmutation can be imagined in several different discursive modes. I have already quoted Eliot's suggestion that "the exact formula" for sensuous thinking "remains to be defined" (*SW* 23). Pater anticipated Eliot's attempts to make aesthetic experience seem more concrete and necessary by resorting to scientific discourse and its aura of objective truthfulness. "The function of the aesthetic critic," Pater observes,

> is to distinguish, to analyse, and separate from its adjuncts, the virtue by which a picture, a landscape, a fair personality in life or in a book, produces this special impression of beauty or pleasure. . . . His end is reached when he has disengaged that virtue, and noted it, as a chemist notes some natural element, for himself and others. . . . Few artists, not Goethe or Byron even, work quite cleanly, casting off all *débris,* and leaving us only what the heat of their imagination has wholly fused and transformed. Take, for instance, the writings of Wordsworth. The heat of his genius, entering into the substance of his

work, has crystallised a part, but only a part, of it; and in that great mass of verse there is much which might well be forgotten. (*TR* xx-xxii)

Transformation is thereby grounded in natural fact. Eliot extends "the suggestive analogy" in "Tradition and the Individual Talent" when, in unwittingly Paterian terms, he remarks with much greater scientific specificity,

> There remains to define this process of depersonalization and its relation to the sense of tradition. It is in this depersonalization that art may be said *to approach the condition of science.* I therefore invite you to consider, as a suggestive analogy, the action which takes place when a bit of finely filiated platinum is introduced into a chamber containing oxygen and sulphur dioxide. . . . The analogy [is] that of the catalyst. When the two gases . . . are mixed in the presence of a filament of platinum, they form sulphurous acid. This combination takes place only if the platinum is present; nevertheless the newly formed acid contains no trace of platinum, and the platinum itself is . . . unaffected. . . . The mind of the poet is that shred of platinum. It may partly or exclusively operate upon the experience of the man himself; but, the more perfect the artist, the more completely separate in him will be the man who suffers and the mind which creates[.] (*SE* 17–18; my emphasis)

Whereas Pater addresses "disengagement" in terms of the critical enterprise, Eliot (as always) focuses on the possibilities of separating the work of art from the artist or performer—"a being," Eliot once explained in relation to dancers, "a personality, a vital flame which appears from nowhere, disappears into nothing and is complete and sufficient in its appearance" (*SE* 113). On all occasions, he positions himself against an emphasis on "personality" ("in the romantic sense of the word" [*SE* 352]) long and commonly associated with *The Renaissance* and other writings (hence the "flame" motif). What the reader may not realize, however, is that Eliot's arguments in favor of "depersonalization" repeatedly feature terms first put into circulation in English letters by Pater himself.

In the first two decades of his philosophical and cultural studies, Pater adumbrates the historically-specific "conditions" that produce texts and artifacts, but also focuses on the extent to which an individual's personality—"the secret places of his nature" and "strange veil of sight" (*TR* 81, 87)—is "stricken into colour and imagery," and becomes part of the alchemical process at the "moment of invention" (*TR* 89). As Child and Conlon have noted, Pater's exploration of French literature in the late 1880s, notably the works and correspondence of Gustave Flaubert and Prosper Mérimée, introduced him to the doctrine and potential of impersonality (Child 32–33; Conlon 1982b:142–144). "If the style be the man," Pater declares in *Appreciations,* "in all the colour and intensity of a veritable apprehension, it will be in a real sense 'impersonal'" (*Ap* 35). Yet the assertion is equivocal, as is his assessment of Mérimée's "central aim" in his "literary art," his "*impersonality*":

> Personality *versus* impersonality in art:—how much or how little of one's self one may put into one's work: whether anything at all of it: whether one *can* put there anything else:—is clearly a far-reaching and complex question. Serviceable as the basis of a precautionary maxim towards the conduct of our work, self-effacement, or impersonality, in literary or artistic creation, is, perhaps, after all, as little possible as a strict realism. . . . [But] to his method of conception, Mérimée's much-praised literary style, his method of expression, is strictly conformable—impersonal in its beauty, the perfection of nobody's style—thus vindicating anew by its very impersonality that much worn, but not untrue saying, that the style is the man:—a man, impassible, unfamiliar, impeccable, veiling a deep sense of what is forcible, nay, terrible, in things, under the sort of personal pride that makes a man a nice observer of all that is most conventional. (*MS* 35–36)

Eliot's essays and reviews brook no such "after all" or indecisiveness. Critical journalism from 1918 to the early 1930s, especially "Tradition and the Individual Talent," promulgates the notion that the "progress of an artist is a continual self-sacrifice, a continual extinction of personality," an "escape from personality"—and Pater's reputation and discursive influences (*SE* 17, 21). Subsequently, in *The Use of Poetry and the Use of Criticism* (1933) and "The Frontiers of Criticism" (1958), Eliot abandons this strictly objectivist stance (Shusterman 40). Yet, as he candidly remarked to E. M. Forster in 1929, "As for the 'impersonality' doctrine, it has its personal motives of course, and is neither more true nor more false that [*sic*] the opposite doctrine; but I believe that it may have been of some value in its time."[55]

Perhaps no essay seems so decisively, completely Eliotic as "Tradition and the Individual Talent," yet I have identified several specific ways in which the critic adapts Pater's own terms and precepts to construct a tradition, and imagine a critical enterprise, from which the Oxford don is wholly excluded. Fundamentally, the essay's imperatives—to think historically when assessing individual works and eras, to place the artist in a cultural context, including "many of those who worked before him, and in many others down to our own time" (*TR* 102)—are catalyzed by and transmuted from *The Renaissance* and other Paterian texts that speak to the ongoing presence of the past.[56] "The study of many an earlier adventurous theorist satisfied his curiosity," the narrator of "Sebastian Van Storck" observes; "It was a tradition—a constant tradition—that daring thought of his; an echo, or haunting recurrent voice of the human soul itself, and as such sealed with natural truth, which certain minds would not fail to heed" (*IP* 107). Heeding and hailing are two very different things in Eliot's writings, however; Pater's special role as interlocutor is silenced, any possibility of his writings taking a place in the "simultaneous order" of the acknowledged "tradition" eliminated (*SE* 14).

Other intertextual elements could be teased out in detail, including a fascination with the tortuous psychic and physical states of would-be saints—what Richter terms the "aesthetics of pain"—or the way in which Eliot situates his early reviews and critical essays against the "appreciation" mode popularized by Pater. Time and again Eliot insists to readers that "what is needed is not sympathy or encouragement or appreciation" (1920c:635; see also 1927:259), or pronounces someone "an appreciator and not a critic" (1919b:909). In 1932 he accommodates the concept by suggesting that "appreciation" is merely the second of three stages in "our understanding of poetry" (following "enjoyment" but surpassed by "reorganization" [UPUC 19]). For Pater, considering the intersections of music, language, and art are not confined to one pithy phrase, "*All art constantly aspires towards the condition of music*" (*TR* 106). He praises du Bellay, for example, because he "recognised of what force the music and dignity of languages are, how they enter into the inmost part of things" (*TR* 129–130). Eliot continued to argue against the "School of Giorgione" paradigm for decades; in the 1951 essay "Poetry and Drama," regarding those feelings "beyond the nameable, classifiable emotions and motives of our conscious life," he states that this "peculiar range of sensibility can be expressed by dramatic poetry, at its moments of greatest intensity. At such moments, we touch the border of those feelings which only music can express. We can never emulate music, because to arrive at the condition of music would be the annihilation of poetry, and especially of dramatic poetry" (*OPP* 87). ("The Music of Poetry," 1942, also continues to answer Pater.) Eliot's famous suggestion that poetry can communicate before it is understood because the "auditory imagination" responds to the "musical qualities of verse" (*UPUC* 118–119) is an adaptation of Pater—as Eliot acknowledged to a Johns Hopkins University audience in 1933. It is "often a useful exercise," he observed, "to take a figure of speech to pieces: if it can be put together again it is all right. Walter Pater observes that 'the meaning' (of poetry)—I should say rather of some kinds of poetry—'reaches us through ways not distinctly traceable by the understanding'" (*VMP* 269–270).

A comparison of their essays on Pascal indicates just how divergently they would approach a subject—Pater focuses on the controversial years of Pascal's life, the *Letters to a Provincial by one of his Friends*, rather than "Pascal in his final sanctity, his detachment of soul from all but the greatest matters" (*MS* 63), the phase and writings most admired by Eliot—yet the shared interest in one who had "the knowledge of worldliness and the passion of asceticism" (*SE* 411) is most revealing, as is the discursive strategy of interweaving aesthetic, religious, and scientific discourse.[57] Also apparent is Eliot's recurring need to rebut Pater (and those writers he deemed culturally crucial), for reasons effectively summarized in his complaining assessment of Montaigne:

> One cannot destroy Pascal, certainly; but of all authors Montaigne is one of the least destructible. You could as well dissipate a fog by flinging hand-grenades into it. For Montaigne is a fog, a gas, a fluid, insidious element. He does not reason, he insinuates, charms, and influences; or if he reasons, you must be prepared for his having some other design upon you than to convince you by his argument. It is hardly too much to say that Montaigne is the most essential author to know, if we would understand the course of French thought during the last three hundred years. (SE 409–410)

Eliot would hardly say the same about the "essential" Pater, yet his continual recourse to Pater's writings would suggest otherwise. In the essay on "Style," Pater summarizes and reformulates Flaubert's theory that a parallel exists between "a relative, somewhere in the world of thought, and its correlative, somewhere in the world of language—both alike . . . somewhere in the mind of the artist, desiderative, expectant, inventive" (Ap 27), a concept he then applies to Greek culture, so that a "correlative" of the "Platonic quality" of thought may be found in "Greek clay, in Greek marble, as you walk through the British Museum" (PP 283). Pater did not "fix his attention" on Hamlet, but Eliot's essay on the play depends greatly on the theory of an "objective correlative" (SE 145), the very definition of which is redolent with Paterian possibilities.[58] Ironically, in this and so many other situations Eliot was at his critical best when trying to best Pater.

Eliot's unrealized, three-volume "criticism of the English Renaissance" (VMP 41) may have been one such project, a "trilogy" forecast as The School of Donne, Elizabethan Drama, and The Sons of Ben, which only survives in occasional essays and the Clark and Turnball Lectures (1926, 1933). Clearly Pater's book had convinced Eliot of the epoch's cultural diversity, and the discursive opportunities of Renaissance studies. One could also say that Pater's Renaissance persuaded Eliot that an entirely different account of its intellectual, artistic, and religious productions was needed, one that not only stressed the English contributions to "the most interesting period in the history of the mind" (TR 48) but countermanded Pater's version of religious history, in which a "crabbed Protestantism" and the "Protestant principle in art" ultimately "cuts" nations off "from the supreme tradition of beauty" and the "pagan grandeur in the Roman Catholic religion" (TR 149). The Clark Lectures especially chide the emotional religiosity of sixteenth and seventeenth-century English Catholic writers, their incipient romanticism (learned, in part, from the teachings of Ignatius Loyola and the Jesuits [*VMP* 76]), and begins to construct an alternative canon of astringent, metaphysical,[59] or differently mystical poets and authors (a canon that will include Dante and selected poets of the *Trecento,* Donne and his fellow metaphysical poets, Dryden, and such latter-day "manifestations" as Baudelaire, Laforgue, and Rimbaud [*VMP* 59]). Yet even this gesture is Paterian: *The Renaissance* extends the temporal and national boundaries of the period to include other expressions of "a many-sided but yet united movement, in which the love of the things of the intellect and the imagination" (*TR* 1), from Dante's Italy and medieval France to the German studies of Winckelmann and Goethe in the eighteenth century. The insight that Dante's work expresses "a Renaissance in the end of the twelfth and the beginning of the thirteenth century, a Renaissance within the limits of the middle age itself" (*TR* 1) was particularly important to Eliot (see *VMP* 98–99, pages in which Pater is cited for negative purposes).

I have identified the intertextual tangle of Eliot's critical response to Pater fully aware of Eliot's admonishing comment that the "important debt does not occur in relation to the number of places in one's writings to which a critic can point a finger, and say, here and there he wrote something which he could not have written unless he had [X] in mind" (*TCC* 132). Yet the volume of references, allusions, caustic remarks, and serious intellectual engagements demonstrates that Pater's writings are anything but dead in Eliot's capacious mind or writings. However much Eliot tries to distance himself and his works from all that was "suspect or perverse" (*SE* 439), time and again a Paterian trope or idea resurfaces textually as "the symbol of the modern idea" (*TR* 99). Yet discursive revisitations are not confined to the prose writings. In each of three major phases of Eliot's lyric poetry—the aestheticized "observations" of personalities and environments epitomized by "The Love Song of J. Alfred Prufrock"; mapping the "hollow" realms of "Gerontion," *The Waste Land,* and "The Hollow Men"; the poetic recovery of the religious "lost word" in *Ash-Wednesday* and *Four Quartets*—"strange affinities" (*TR* 98) with Paterian texts are discernible and significant. For the most part, critics' awareness of these Paterian traces has been intermittent, or suspicious—sightings of aliens near Roswell, New Mexico rather than "the sudden look of some dead master" (*CPP* 193). Ricks, for example, possibly finds an allusion to *The Renaissance* in "Suite Clownesque" (*IMH* 35, 172); Fleissner and Monsman individually note that Prufrock's pathetic denial, "No! I am not Prince Hamlet" (*CPP* 16) echoes, in rhythm and substance, the observation, "No, Shakespeare's kings are not, nor are meant to be, great men" (*Ap* 207); Janowitz links Marius's medical simile—"For a moment the whole world seemed to present itself as a hospital of sick persons; many of them sick in mind" (*ME* 2:174)—with the speaker's suggestion that "the whole earth is our hospital" in "East Coker," Part IV. It is more productive, I would suggest, to consider the Paterian "under-currents" of Eliot's poetic discourse when any one of six problematics or motifs is approached: subjectivity, crises of masculinity and imagined femininity, vigils and peregrinations, the "intense moment," the terrors of spring, the "presence of the past" (*GDL* 22), and the "perpetual *agonia*" of doubt. Although sometimes contradictory in their effects, the "intimate impress" (*TR* 49) of the intertextual gestures are always felt.

The "Conclusion" to *The Renaissance* is evocative when theorizing a contingent and mobile subjectivity as "that continual vanishing away, that strange, perpetual, weaving and unweaving of ourselves" (*TR* 188), yet Pater's canon as a whole privileges three other interconnected metaphors, two architectural and one geometrical, to render "the narrow world of thought and feeling" (*TR* 187) in terms of isolation and imprisonment. When the "narrow chamber of the individual mind" is probed, one learns that, "Experience, already reduced to a group of impressions, is ringed round for each one of us by that thick wall of personality through which no real voice has ever pierced on its way to us, or from us to that which we can only conjecture to be without. Every one of those impressions is the impression of the individual in his isolation, each mind keeping as a solitary prisoner its own dream of a world" (*TR* 187–188).[60] Marius's "philosophical reading" confirms this view: "we are never to get beyond the walls of the closely shut cell of one's own personality" (*ME* 1: 146); Sebastian van Storck, "perhaps" because of "some inherited satiety or fatigue in his nature," cannot intellectually or emotionally penetrate "the circumference of . . . one infinite creative thinker," and lives according to the "truth, the beatific calm, of the absolute selfishness, which could not, if it would, pass beyond the circumference of itself" (*IP* 107–109). Shifting from aesthetic and narrative discourse to the philosophical, one finds that *Plato and Platonism* also explores "those dark chambers of his individuality, of himself, into which none but he can ever get" (*PP* 190). So governed and confined by circularity is the society sketched in "The Love Song of J. Alfred Prufrock" that even the miasmic yellow fog "Curl[s] once about the house" (*CPP* 13); the speaker may have "lingered in the chambers of" the mind too long for his erotic pleasures, but the quotidian round of "evenings, mornings, afternoons" devoted to "tea and cakes and ices" is even more dangerously stultifying, or infernal, to the paradoxical point that "human voices wake us, and we drown" (*CPP* 17). ("Prufrock" was completed in 1911, several years before Eliot began his Bradley studies.) Pater's "solitary prisoner" is reduced to fragmented artifacts in Eliot's subsequent poetry: the "key" of memory that threatens in "Rhapsody on a Windy Night" resurfaces in the "memories" haunting the penultimate movement of *The Waste Land*:

> *Dayadhvam:* I have heard the key
> Turn in the door once and turn once only
> We think of the key, each in his prison
> Thinking of the key, each confirms a prison[.]
>
> (*CPP* 74)[61]

If the "sympathy" extolled by the Thunder refers to "a kind of receptivity to intimations and signs" (L. Gordon 114), the final lines of the poem do not indicate that "thinking of the key" has produced enlightenment or empowerment, let alone freedom. The apocalyptic style and ambience of *The Waste Land* is very different from the claustrophobic, *fin-de-siècle* salon world of "Prufrock," but the Paterian spectre of someone "imprisoned now in the narrow cell of [his] own subjective experience" (*MS* 12) remains constant. Furthermore, Eliot must have been struck by the way in which Pater imagines an external world parallel to this inner state: it is variously the "hollow ring of fundamental nothingness under the apparent surface of things" (*MS* 14) detected by Mérimée or "the vast unseen hollow places of nature, of humanity, just beneath one's feet or at one's side" apprehended by Pascal (*MS* 82). "Between the conception / And the creation" of "The Hollow Men" (*CPP* 85) falls the shadow of Pater's prose; "*Here we go round the prickly pear*" (*CPP* 85) differs in discursive register, not ontological insight, from "Experience . . . is ringed round for each one of us by that thick wall of personality through which no real voice has ever pierced on its way to us" (*TR* 187).[62]

Gendered identity crises punctuate the first and second phases of Eliot's poetry, masculinity and its burdens only a little less terrifying than the spectacles of femininity represented. Some commentators who have shied away from the Paterian elements of "Prufrock" or "Portrait of a Lady" seem to have done so for fear of conflating the dandy and the "nancy-boy." As Moers and Sinfield have demonstrated, however, the dandy was originally "a heterosexual philanderer" (Sinfield 37), an identity marked by misogyny rather than homophobia when Eliot appropriated it. After all, it was Baudelaire who celebrated the dandy and his "cult of the self" in "The Painter of Modern Life," section IX (1995:27). Sinfield points out that the dandy was "good at entertaining and being entertained by women; he enjoyed activities that were coded 'feminine'—trivia, chit-chat, flirting, gossip, scandal" (42). "Far more than sexuality," the dandy signals

class. . . . The [late-Victorian] dominant middle class justified itself by claiming manly purity, purpose, and responsibility, and identified the leisure class, correspondingly, with effeminate idleness and immorality. In the face of this manoeuvre, there were two alternatives for the wealthy and those who sought to seem wealthy. One was to attempt to appear useful and good; the other was

to repudiate middle-class authority by displaying conspicuous idleness, immorality, and effeminacy; in other words, by being a dandy. (Sinfield 38)

Felski also suggests that the dandy was identified with women because he
too could be "perceived in aestheticist doctrine as quite useless; exalting appearance over essence, decoration over function, he voices a protest against
prevailing bourgeois values that associate masculinity with rationality, industry, utility, and thrift" (1096). By "the energies of genius," Feldman observes, the dandy managed to "escape" the "prison of dichtomous gender"
and thus exist "on the divide" of societal norms (17). Specific dandies of the
1880s and 1890s might have enjoyed contesting or fracturing the "fault-
lines" of class, gender, and aesthetics, creating "a disturbance of categories
that reache[d] beyond the oppressive terms" then in circulation (Sinfield
46), but discomfiture rather than pleasure marks the textual existence of
male speakers who endure "among velleities and carefully caught regrets"
(*CPP* 18) in "Prufrock" and "Portrait of a Lady." And it is critics, unwittingly perpetuating the homosexual panic of the Men of 1914, who reduc-
tively dismiss the "slightly 1890-ish, lily-pale atmosphere that hangs over"
the pre-*Waste Land* poems (Stead 66) rather than identify the extent to
which the Eliot dandy is paralyzed by the demands of heterosexual masculinity or forestalled by female figures who reiterate the stereotypes that
Eliot, like Pater before him, inscribes in his texts.

However strange it may sound, there is an energy and discursive bite to
the antifeminist poems missing from *Ash-Wednesday* and *Four Quartets*—
their Ladies, "veiled in white and blue" (*CPP* 94), desexualized, alternatively
silenced or enshrined, inspire the religiously searching male speaker without
threatening (or awakening) his masculinity. But Part III of *Ash-Wednesday*
lyrically recalls a moment of poignant desire aroused by a woman's long hair:
"Blown hair is sweet, brown hair over the mouth blown, / Lilac and brown
hair" (*CPP* 93). The sensual representation of such a "distraction" owes
everything to Prufrock's voyeurism—"I have seen them riding seaward on
the waves/ Combing the white hair of the waves blown back/ When the
wind blows the water white and black" (*CPP* 17). Yet in these images Eliot
also replicates the same conventions of the femme fatale[63] that Pater discerns
in Leonardo da Vinci's paintings: the "delicate brown flesh and woman's hair
no one would go out into the wilderness to seek" (*TR* 124). As well, a conjunction of hair, rocks, and femme fatality helps to explicate the allusively
complex yet stereotypically unsubtle figure of "The Lady of the Rocks,/ The
lady of situations" found within Madame Sosostris's "wicked pack of cards"
in *The Waste Land* (*CPP* 62).[64]

Normative regimes of gender binaries "ente[r] into the very fastnesses
of character" (*PP* 272) as it is imagined in Pater's texts: "men are linked to

intellect, imagination, and breadth, women to emotion, fancy, and close observation" (Shires 25); "the creative behaviour and potential of boys and men signal energy, assertiveness, ability, and persistence, while girls and women are clearly associated with subservience, ignorance, and domesticity" (Casteras 1992:125). And so it is with *La Gioconda*. "Present from the first incorporeally in Leonardo's brain," Pater suggests, "she is found present at last in *Il Giocondo's* house" (*TR* 98). Thus "she" becomes "a sort of impersonation of [masculine subjectivity] itself, its projected reflex or ideal" (*TR* 148) or Other, a painterly (and textual) "presence" predicated on the absence of female subjectivity. Replete with references to Greek goddesses, Leda, Saint Anne, the Borgias, and "the modern idea," Pater's peroration reproduces and extends what Alice Jardine terms "inherited genealogies of the feminine" (261). "The presence that rose thus so strangely beside the waters," the famous passage intones,

> is expressive of what in the ways of a thousand years men had come to desire. Hers is the head upon which all "the ends of the world are come," and the eyelids are a little weary. . . . She is older than the rocks among which she sits; like the vampire, she has been dead many times. . . . [A]s Leda, [she] was the mother of Helen of Troy, and, as Saint Anne, the mother of Mary[.] (*TR* 98–99)

Pater's description actually reconciles, or conflates, several works by da Vinci: *La Gioconda*, the *Virgin and Child with St Anne*, and the two versions of the *Virgin of the Rocks* (one now housed in the Louvre, the other in London's National Gallery). Boundaries between the secular and the sacred become blurred, but the typology of "woman," as a unified and historically constant figure, remains unchanged. Pater may "invoke the universal or generic when he wishes to imagine subjectivity," as Katz admits, "but he is really only dealing with male subjectivity much of the time" (171).[65] So it is that Pater's representation of a primordial "she" is reformulated for a modernist audience by Eliot, who introduces the "Lady of the Rocks" in Part I of *The Waste Land* as augur of the alternatively nightmarish, devouring, pathetic, or surreal femininity displayed in the subsequent four sections of the poem.

Eliot had planned one satirical reference to Pater in *The Waste Land*, but the lines, and the entire section of the manuscript, never made it past Ezra Pound's lacerating editorial gaze.[66] Yet the "Fresca" episode—which originally began "The Fire Sermon," the physical center of the poem and thematic core of the neo-Augustan urban satire—is extremely pertinent to an understanding of Eliot's sexist typologies, and revealing as to the way in which misogyny and homophobia can be mutually supportive (in part as a response to a double-sided threat to the speaker's masculinity: he is trying to distance himself from the oppressive operations of female-male desires and the "demotic" possibilities of male-male desire, such as Symonds and Pater enjoyed, and Mr Eugenides suggests in the published Part III). Like Joyce's Molly Bloom, Fresca[67] is confined to the domestic (and sexually available) sphere of the bedchamber, and the degrading chamberpot. But this would-be siren, who "blinks, and yawns, and gapes, / Aroused from dreams of love and pleasant rapes" (*Facs* 39), does not wholly conform to the heterosexual script. Eliot's latter-day Belinda moves through Pope-esque couplets to her "steaming bath":

> Fresca! in other time or place had been
> A meek and lowly weeping Magdalene;
> More sinned against than sinning, bruised and marred,
> The lazy, laughing Jenny of the bard.
> (The same eternal and consuming itch
> Can make a martyr, or plain simple bitch);. . . .
> [A] strolling slattern in a tawdry gown,
> A doorstep dunged by every dog in town.
> For varying forms, one definition's right:
> Unreal emotions, and real appetite.
> Women grown intellectual grow dull,
> And lose the mother wit of natural trull.
> Fresca was baptised in a soapy sea
> Of Symonds—Walter Pater—Vernon Lee.
>
> (*Facs* 41)

At the heart of the labyrinthine, "Unreal city" one finds its most sinister monster (by "fate misbred"): a woman of "unreal emotions" whose "appetite," all too real, ranges from the "natural" (as written, say, by St Paul or Rossetti) to the unnatural desires of Symonds, Pater, and Lee, Fresca's tripartite "Uranian muse" (Koestenbaum 126). Small wonder, then, that her verse is "gloomy" but entirely of a piece with its "sort of can-can salonniere" creator (*Facs* 41).

The presence that bathes thus so strangely within the soapy waters of the manuscript also occasions its most blatantly repulsive lines: "Odours, confected by the cunning French, / Disguise the good old hearty female stench" (*Facs* 39).[68] Although very different in tone and lexicon from the description that begins "A Game of Chess"—

> In vials of ivory and coloured glass
> Unstoppered, lurked her strange synthetic perfumes.
> Unguent, powered, or liquid—troubled, confused
> And drowned the sense in odours
>
> (*CPP* 64)

—the substance of the antifeminist observations remains constant.[69] Ostensibly, the phrasing of the passage is ambiguous: the seated woman could be "troubled, confused," or the man who watches her. I would argue, however, that he is undoubtedly the drowning man, helpless before a figure whose "hair [is] / Spread out in fiery points" (*CPP* 65), as was Prufrock before him when "perfume from a dress / . . . makes [him] so digress," and the speaker of "Portrait of a Lady" when the scent from "a bowl of lilacs" or "the smell of hyacinths across the garden" (*CPP* 15, 19, 20) reduces him to the gutterish "dark" of gendered inadequacies. All of this Eliot remembers and returns to the cauldron of discursive possibilities, so that four years after *The Waste Land* is published he can inform a Cambridge audience that, in the "History of Sensibility," St. Theresa is responsible for a particularly strong line of "sentiment[al]" and romantic writing, to the extent that,

> In much English prose, even the finest, of the nineteenth century, I find more than a trace of intellectual psychologism, and just the faintest, undefinable perfume of femininity. I find it in Newman and Francis Bradley as well as in Ruskin and Pater. Or it is as if such prose had been written in a low fever; there is a slight temperature to it. (*VMP* 92)

Presumably the "low fever" of femininity is entirely different from the "forms of illness [that] are extremely favourable, not only to religious illumination, but to artistic and literary composition" (*SE* 405) such as Pascal experienced. If one reads the Clark Lecture in the context of the pre-1927 poetry, the "perfume" is neither faint in its textual effects nor undefinable. Pater is available to Eliot's scorn whether he is feminized or accused of unnatural and unmanly "perversions."

As Lyndall Gordon first discerned, "The Love Song of J. Alfred Prufrock" was at one stage in its development a "vigil" poem, one of several composed in 1910 and 1911. In the central section of the manuscript, "Prufrock's Pervigilium" (*IMH* 43–44), a personified midnight "turned and writhed in fever," the dawn "realized itself / And turned with a sense of nausea," and the speaker remains isolated from the world, experiencing it from "the window" rather than confronting directly "lonely men in shirtsleeves," women "spilling out of corsets," and "evil houses leaning all together / Point[ing] a ribald finger at me" (*IMH* 43).

Thoughts of Pater would seem far removed from this urban, heterosexualized scene that ironically gestures to the *Pervigilium Veneris*, a Latin poem from the third or fourth century A.D. in which public celebrations to honor spring and Venus are juxtaposed with the speaker's private, amorous longings and artistic doubts (quoted by Eliot in the final concatenation of lines for *The Waste Land*).[70] But, as Williamson and Ricks acknowledge, "the crucial evocation of the *Pervigilium Veneris* for [Eliot's] generation was that" found in *Marius the Epicurean* (*IMH* 177; Williamson 148–149). In Pater's fictional account, the poem was composed by Flavian as he "lay at the open window of his lodging, with a fiery pang in the brain. . . . It was but the fatal course of the strange new sickness," the plague that travelled home with Aurelius and his soldiers "from the East" (*ME* 1:112, 111). The composition is described as "a nuptial hymn" that celebrates "the preliminary pairing and mating together of all fresh things, in the hot and genial spring-time" (*ME* 1:113), suggesting a relevance to *The Waste Land* (the "sudden spasm of spring" is marked by rebirth and death, and thereafter constitutes a powerful "memory" for Marius) as well as "Prufrock."[71] But unremarked in the intertextual transformation are the encodings of male-male desire in Pater's representation of the "pure and disinterested friendship" between Marius and Flavian (*ME* 1:49), who lays "amid the rich-scented flowers—rare Paestum roses, and the like—procured by Marius for his solace" (*ME* 1:112–113). Marius keeps watch throughout "the patient"'s last night; the "thunder which had sounded all day among the hills, with a heat not unwelcome to Flavian, had given way nightfall to steady rain" (*ME* 118).[72] It is a "strange vigil" one would expect to find echoing in Whitman's poetry, not Eliot's.[73]

The narrative of *Marius the Epicurean* juxtaposes static scenes such as vigils and moments of heightened awareness with symbolic peregrinations that further the pagan pilgrim's steps along the path to death, or, at "the midway of life" (*ME* 2: 208), effect a return to his boyhood home, a circling back to his beginnings which instigates "something of a *meditatio mortis,* ever facing towards the act of final detachment" at a time of trouble, natural and social, of "wild fracture . . . [and] sudden upheaval and depression" (*ME* 2: 209, 201).[74] Connections with the mood and movements of *Ash-Wednesday* and *Four Quartets* are obvious. Marius also internalizes the journey motif, sensing "some other companion, an unfailing companion, ever at his side throughout. . . . It was as if there were not one only, but two wayfarers, side by side, visible there across the plain. . . . [a] fantasy of a self not himself, beside him in his coming and going" (*ME* 2: 67–68), an "apprehension" he later rewrites in his journal[75] in this manner: "'If a particular tutelary or *genius* . . . according to old belief, walks through life beside each one of us, mine is very certainly a capricious creature" (*ME* 2: 172). In Part V of *The Waste Land*, Marius's benign companionship merges with figures from Luke (24: 15–16), Prufrock's imaginary ("Let us go then, you and I"), and Shackleton's frigid hallucinations; for Eliot's apprehensive speaker, the would-be affiliate is menacing, marked by sexual and racial indeterminacy:

> Who is the third who walks always beside you?
> When I count, there are only you and I together

> But when I look ahead up the white road
> There is always another one walking beside you
> Gliding wrapt in a brown mantle, hooded
> I do not know whether a man or a woman
> —But who is that on the other side of you?

(*CPP* 73)

The intimate community of "you and I together" is disrupted by a "hooded figure" who could be the advance party for the "hooded hordes swarming / Over endless plains" (*CPP* 73); mirroring the abject persons who populate it, the "cracked earth" is so "[r]inged by the flat horizon" (*CPP* 73) that renewal or resurrection is impossible.

The *flânerie* of *The Waste Land* is not simply a reiteration of Baudelaire; da Vinci, according to *The Renaissance*, "as if catching glimpses" of the "extremes of beauty and terror" in "the strange eyes or hair of chance people, . . . would follow such about the streets of Florence till the sun went down" (*TR* 82). Sebastian van Storck's peregrinations are also solitary, but he "escape[s] to the sea" for rejuvenation, in order to "make 'equation' between himself and what was not himself, and set things in order" (*IP* 113–114). One could simply argue that the intertextual resource, for Pater as well as Eliot, was Isaiah (38:1); I have demonstrated, however, that the "interfusion" of Pater's writings in the final 30 lines of *The Waste Land* is dense and palimpsestic. To cite Pater, "we have a constant sense in reading him, that his thoughts, however little their positive value may be, are connected with springs beneath them of deep and passionate emotion," imagery, and phrasing that spring up in Eliot's poetic discourse time and time again.

The Waste Land is animated by vignettes and fragments in which "the awful daring of a moment's surrender" (*CPP* 74) is never realized. *Four Quartets* theorizes "the moment" differently from the "Conclusion" to *The Renaissance* in order to rescue it from a Paterian relativism and restore its transcendent possibilities at the interstices of aesthetic and religious discourse (Janowitz 590, McGrath 115). But the speaker of "East Coker" cannot imagine otherwise without invoking the very words being refuted:

> As we grow older
> The world becomes stranger, the pattern more complicated
> Of dead and living. Not the intense moment
> Isolated, with no before and after,
> But a lifetime burning in every moment
> And not the lifetime of one man only
> But of old stones that cannot be deciphered.

(*CPP* 182)

The speaker has answered Pater's claim that "[t]his at least of flame-like our life has, that it is but the concurrence, renewed from moment to moment, of forces parting sooner or later on their ways" (*TR* 187), but he can only do so in images and assertions hopelessly "complicated" by their intertextuality. In "The School of Giorgione," Pater praises dramatic poetry because "it presents us with a kind of profoundly significant and animated instance . . . some brief and wholly concrete moment . . . which seem[s] to absorb past and future in an intense consciousness of the present" (*TR* 118). Translated into the philosophical discourse with which Marius is most familiar, we have the Cyrenaic theory of "the μονόχρονος ἡδονή, as it was called—the pleasure of the 'Ideal Now'—if certain moments of their lives were high-pitched, passionately coloured, intent with sensation, and a kind of knowledge" (*ME* 2:21–22). In Eliot's religio-aesthetic discourse, the intersection of "Time present and time past / . . . both perhaps present in time future" is "renewed, transfigured, in another pattern": "Quick now, here, now, always—/ A condition of complete simplicity / (Costing not less than everything)" (*CPP* 171, 195, 198), a glimpse of redemption that is nonetheless indebted to Pater's imaginative articulations.

The "ideal now" of religious certainty and the blessings of "pentecostal fire" are not easily represented in concrete, memorable terms, but Eliot does not shy away from the challenge. Self-reflexively answering the dire, cruel, and stillborn springtime of *The Waste Land*, "Little Gidding" begins with the compelling yet paradoxical images of a "midwinter spring":

> Midwinter spring is its own season
> Sempiternal though sodden towards sundown,
> Suspended in time, between pole and tropic.
> When the short day is brightest, with frost and fire,
> The brief sun flames the ice, on pond and ditches,
> In windless cold that is the heart's heat,
> Reflecting in a watery mirror[76]
> A glare that is blindness in the early afternoon. . . .
>   This is the spring time
> But not in time's covenant. Now the hedgerow
> Is blanched for an hour with transitory blossom
> Of snow, a bloom more sudden
> Than that of summer, neither budding nor fading,
> Not in the scheme of generation.
> Where is the summer, the unimaginable
> Zero summer?
>
>   (*CPP* 191)

Despite the interrogative gesture that ends the passage, the lines are assured and reassuring; they impress because of their taut binaries, the acute attention to natural detail, and the cumulative rhythmic power of the phrasing (produced through a deft combination of enjambments and medial caesurae). Decades before composing the passage, Eliot read that in "Michelangelo's poems, frost and fire are almost the only images—the refining fire of the goldsmith; once or twice the phoenix; ice melting at the fire; fire struck from the rock which it afterwards consumes" (*TR* 68). In *Plato and Platonism*, Pater identifies "a quest (vain quest it may prove to be) after a kind of knowledge perhaps not properly attainable. Hereafter, in every age, some will be found to start afresh quixotically, through what wastes of words! in search of that true Substance, the One, the Absolute, which to the majority of acute people is after all but zero" (*PP* 40). *Four Quartets* is less a defense of the absolute truth of Christianity than an "exploration" of poetic resources to name the Love "[b]ehind the hands that wove / The intolerable shirt of flame / Which human power cannot remove" (*CPP* 196) and human discourse can only approximate. There is a profound irony to the fact that, at every turn in Eliot's quest to communicate, Pater's voice is "heard, half-heard, in the stillness / Between two waves" of new verse; not a welcome guest, certainly, "accepted and accepting," but one cannot "resolv[e] the enigma" of *Four Quartets* or *The Waste Land* or "Prufrock" without admitting Pater to the dance of words.

A particular kind of Eliot purist does not enjoy finding Pater's voice among "the tongues" of *Four Quartets,* but the evidence is overwhelming— as the narrator of *Gaston de Latour* almost predicts, referring to the "very presence of the past" in books "which had already found tongues to speak of a still living humanity—somewhere, in the world!—waiting for him in the distance" (*GDL* 22). Pater makes a similar comment, in a religious context, in the introduction to C. L. Shadwell's translation of the *Purgatorio,* citing "the belief in a constant, helpful, beneficent interaction between the souls of the living and the dead, in the immense grace still obtainable for the departed by prayer here" (Pater 1892:xxi). Eliot concludes the first part of "Little Gidding" by defining the grace that is prayer and faith:

> And what the dead had no speech for, when living,
> They can tell you, being dead: the communication
> Of the dead is tongued with fire beyond the language of the living.
> Here, the intersection of the timeless moment
> Is England and nowhere. Never and always.
>
>   (*CPP* 192)

The compelling presence of Pater in Eliot's writings could not be better summarized: never and always.

Posterity in "Surroundings of Antagonism"

In retrospect, there is another, unrecorded reason why the Men of 1914 were willing to accept Whistler rather than Pater as iconoclastic precursor and bravura champion of aesthetic independence and cultural hybridity. Long before 1895, Whistler had a famous falling-out, a "notable enmity" (Seitz ed. 66)[77] with Oscar Wilde. Although not a self-proclaimed enemy of Wilde because of his sexual preferences and practices, Whistler's relations with him did become extremely adversarial and acrimonious. Afterward, in the decades following Whistler's death, such a public denunciation of Wilde made it easier for the cult of ugliness to find room for Whistler in its pantheon of privileged predecessors.

How did the Butterfly attempt to trample the Green Carnation? Friends in the 1870s and early 1880s, Whistler and Wilde were so widely recognized as conjointly important figures in the new aestheticism that Gilbert and Sullivan parodied both in *Patience* (1881)[78] and George du Maurier caricatured both in the pages of *Punch* (Wilde "as the poet Maudle and Whistler as the painter Jellaby Postlethwaite" [Anderson and Koval 247]). To publicize their shared wit in 1883 they allowed the *World* to publish telegrams they had exchanged. But each man, confirmed in his own artistic self-importance, chafed under the press's persistent badinage, and resented being reduced to the position of aestheticism's Tweedledum or Tweedledee. Predictably, pugnaciously, Whistler decided to prove who was the serious cultural icon, and best lecturer, by making Wilde the initial, thinly-veiled object of contempt in the *Ten O'Clock Lecture* of February 1885.[79] Instead of being praised for popularizing aestheticism, Wilde is denounced as one of the "false prophets" of Art, who "have brought the very name of the beautiful into disrepute, and derision upon themselves" (*GA* 136). Rather than silencing Wilde, however, Whistler only prompted further bravura and witticisms. In his review of the lecture for the *Pall Mall Gazette,* Wilde criticized the "miniature Mephistopheles, mocking the majority" (*CWW* 10:64), but acknowledged his text as a "masterpiece." Both comments were excised from the excerpt of the review as Whistler published it in *The Gentle Art of Making Enemies.* Interestingly, he did include Wilde's observation, "That an artist will find beauty in ugliness, *le beau dans l'horrible,* is now a commonplace of the schools" (*CWW* 10:66; *GA* 161), yet eliminated the lines which follow:

> but I strongly deny that charming people should be condemned to live with magenta ottomans and Albert-blue curtains in their rooms in order that some painter may observe the side-lights on the one and the values of the other. Nor do I accept the dictum that only a painter is a judge of painting. I say that only an artist is a judge of art; there is a wide difference. (*CWW* 10:66)

For Whistler, differentiation was the only means of protecting his aesthetic authority. Subsequently, his negative judgments of Wilde helped to ensure that modernist writers could comfortably discount Wilde and at the same time number Whistler among the "great men" (*GA* 137) of art since the 1870s.

Such selective ranking has also obscured the many interesting parallels between Whistler and Pater as champions of beauty in the late nineteenth century. Pater first published *The Renaissance* in 1873; the following year, Whistler held the first exhibition of his works in London.[80] Both forays into the public arena were greeted with intensely mixed critical responses. Yet Pater deemed Whistler's "style" to be "at once highly picturesque, finished, and temperate" (*LWP* 31).[81] In 1877, Pater published the second edition of his study, but this time without the controversial "Conclusion."[82] Several months later Whistler paintings featured in the opening of the Grosvenor Gallery attracted the vociferous attention of John Ruskin, whose various lectures as Oxford's Slade Professor of Art between 1870 and 1885 implicitly and explicitly challenged Pater's writings.[83] In 1885, the same year that Pater's *Marius the Epicurean* appeared, Whistler delivered his *Ten O'Clock Lecture*.[84] In 1889, Pater may have attended a celebratory dinner for Whistler in London, at the conclusion of which the artist, secure in "the warm glow of . . . friendship," referred to "the surroundings of antagonism" in which he had conducted his career.[85] Pater would have appreciated the survivalist theme. References to Whistler are scarce in Pater's writings, but always laudatory.[86]

Arthur Symons was almost alone in his appreciation of their parallel achievements, which he articulated in the 1906 work *Studies in Seven Arts*. After assessing the careers of Ruskin and William Morris, Symons juxtaposes the critical acumen of Pater and Whistler:

> Had Walter Pater devoted himself exclusively to art criticism . . . he would have been a great art critic. There are essays scattered throughout his work, the essay on "The School of Giorgione," for instance, in which the essential principles of the art of painting are divined and interpreted with extraordinary subtlety. . . . But with him art criticism was but one function of a close, delicate, unceasing criticism of life. . . . As it was, he corrected many of the generous and hasty errors of Ruskin, and helped to bring back criticism to a wiser and more tolerant attitude towards the arts.
>
> Everything that Mr. Whistler has written about painting deserves to be taken seriously, and read with understanding. Written in French, and signed by Baudelaire, his truths, and paradoxes reflecting truths, would have been realised for what they are. Written in English, and obscurely supposed to conceal some dangerous form of humour, they are left for the most part unconsidered by the "serious" public[.] (1906:36–37)

To borrow Symons's term, the discursive practices of Pater and Whistler were both deemed "dangerous" by various audiences, yet only Pater's writings and articulations of desire were deemed to be deviant by the Men of 1914. In October 1910, Laurence Binyon informed readers of the *Saturday Review* that, "Current criticism of art . . . derives from Pater's essay on the school of Giorgione, helped out by memory of some of Whistler's witty sayings" (413). Six months later, Paul Elmer More would begin the campaign not only to alter the currents of criticism but to drown out any praise for Pater.

Ironically, the careers and posthumous reputations of both Pater and Whistler were enormously altered by, refracted through the lens of, celebrated trials. But of the two, only Whistler instigated the legal action that would shape his public stature.[87] Pater had been dead for less than a year when Wilde's trials began; in the immediate aftermath, his public and critical standings were dealt a near-mortal blow. Lionel Johnson insisted upon Pater's cultural importance in various reviews and essays, but his own premature death in 1902 ended the supportive gestures. Friends and intellectual admirers such as Gosse and Benson tried to defend Pater's writings by sanitizing his life, reconstructing him as a retiring, asexual don, "whose adult life was spent in the seclusion of his study in Oxford or Kensington" (Rawlinson vii).[88] Symons too did his best, yet insisted on identifying Pater's "genius and his at times perverse and exotic imagination" (1932:5). Publication of the 1910 Library Edition of Pater's works by Macmillan prompted commendations from Binyon and Buchan (Seiler ed. 402–406), and thoughtful consideration in the pages of the *Times Literary Supplement* (Seiler ed. 406–412), but a final, ambiguous reference in the *TLS* to Pater's preference for Sparta could also curtail a reader's approving nod.[89] Saintsbury praised Pater's prose "exuberant[ly]," but the Regius Professor of English at Edinburgh University "may have clouded and damaged Pater's reputation more than he helped it by identifying Pater's aestheticism with his own extreme interpretation of 'art for art's sake'" (Court 43). By 1929, J. C. Squire tried to protest that, "In the casual allusions of current criticism Pater is often the victim of injustice. . . . The common conception of him is that of an a-moral scholar" (vii), but Squire's own moment in the critical spotlight had ended. Yeats launched the *Oxford Book of Modern Verse* (1936) with a relineated, vers libre version of the "Mona Lisa" passage, insisting in his Introduction that Pater's writings continue to impress and instruct because of their "revolutionary importance," but the critics were not impressed.[90] With rare exception, there would be no time for Pater in modernist scholarship for half a century and more.[91]

Chapter 3 ∽

Diagnosis, Hate, and Masculine Difference: Delineating the "Cult of Ugliness"

Look the negative in the face and live with it.

—G. W. F. Hegel (92–93)

Now that realism, for the time at least, is exhausted, abstraction of some sort has become a necessity. Abstraction implies omission, and, if it is to be novel, the omission of something which has never been omitted before. Such art will therefore at first seem incomplete to the public eye, and, if it be vigorous too, its vigour will appear odd, awkward, or even ugly. This is not so preposterous as it sounds. Oddity, incompleteness, ugliness, and even stronger terms, have been freely used by contemporary critics.

—C. J. Holmes (206)

Marionettes play a special role in modern poetry thanks to Jules Laforgue and his aptest pupil, T. S. Eliot. If I were prefacing this chapter with theatricals, however, I would ignore the marionettes and dust off a Punch-and-Judy show. But instead of one Punch, we would see four perform—Eliot, Wyndham Lewis, Ezra Pound, and T. E. Hulme. (Judy would have to go, alas: gender has its privileges in modernist culture, and this is a spectacle in and of masculinist sensibilities.) First, our Punches would read outsized books with titles such as *Les Fleurs du Mal* and *Saison dans l'Enfer*. Inspired, they would grab their cudgels and smash the statues of Plato, Milton, Wordsworth, and Tennyson ringing the stage. Overwhelmed with success, they would turn upon the audience and begin to assault eyes, ears, and minds. Suddenly, stage right, a glorious model of Botticelli's Venus would rise up from a papier maché shell. Initially, the Punches would lavish her with praise—then abruptly begin to pummel her with their clubs. Beauty defeated, they would next turn on each other, battering away until the curtain, reluctantly, fell.

Is this too fanciful an introduction for so important a discussion? I take my cue from Wyndham Lewis, who in 1919 lampooned his harshest critics in this way:

> But what you want to know—you who insist on regarding "modern art" as a melodrama, in which Beauty is foully done to death by a villainous figure disguised as a Cube—you principally want to know when the pistol is next going off. What new technical surprises will you be expected to submit to? This really rests with the Italians. You always got your bloodiest bits from them, and always will. No one made such a ranting, gory job of the doing-in of Beauty as Marinetti. (*CH*:47)[1]

A thorough account of the "doing-in of Beauty" perpetrated by the self-styled Men of 1914—that sometimes closely, sometimes loosely-associated group of Anglo-Americans who, between 1908 and the early 1920s, mostly lived in London and tried to effect radical changes in aesthetic theory and practices—begins with an analysis of their "cult" mentality. The chapter then proceeds to canvas the ways in which antipathy to modernity shaped aesthetic policies and practices; their diverse intertextual resources; the contest for "ugliness" among avant-garde groups; satire's generic edge in cult writing; and the consequences of a commitment to rhetorical "violence." The discussion concludes with an analysis of the cult of ugliness in the marketplace of modernisms.

Was It Really a Cult and Could Anyone Join?

In his 1913 essay "The Serious Artist," Pound defends the "delineation of ugliness" with great resourcefulness:

> As there are in medicine the art of diagnosis and the art of cure, so in the arts, so in the particular arts of poetry and of literature, there is the art of diagnosis and there is the art of cure. They call one the cult of ugliness and the other the cult of beauty.
>   The cult of beauty is the hygiene,[2] it is sun, air and the sea and the rain and the lake bathing. The cult of ugliness, Villon, Baudelaire, Corbière, Beardsley are diagnosis. Flaubert is diagnosis. Satire, if we are to ride this metaphor to staggers, satire is surgery, insertions and amputations.

Beauty in art reminds one what is worth while. I am not now speaking of shams. I mean beauty, not slither, not sentimentalizing about beauty, not telling people that beauty is the proper and respectable thing. I mean beauty. You don't argue about an April wind, you feel bucked up when you meet it. You feel bucked up when you come on a swift moving thought in Plato or a fine line in a statue.

Even this pother about gods reminds one that something is worth while. Satire reminds one that certain things are not worth while. It draws one to consider time wasted.

The cult of beauty and the delineation of ugliness are not in mutual opposition. (*LEEP* 45)

The initial invocation of medical discourse and its aura of facticity, objectivity, and necessity provides Pound with a substantial context for his theorizing. By inventing and then subsequently borrowing from unnamed authorities ("they call one the cult of ugliness"), he elevates his own idiosyncratic appraisal to the status of an understood truth. If ugliness is part of our world, the passage suggests, one must cultivate it, steep oneself in it, in order to move beyond it. Invoking Baudelaire's name is strategic, because Pound is identifying a new group of writers and artists who will assume the manly role of "hero" in modern life.[3]

"Cult of ugliness" effectively overstates the intense personal and intertextual ties that generated what one now thinks of as the first wave of modernism in Anglo-American culture just prior to and after World War I.[4] Certainly the "set politics of London" (*LWL* 104) had everything to do with the emergence of this particular group's densely-encoded aesthetic as *the* dominant mode of artistic discourse and production.[5] Yet their elevation to absolute cult or hegemonic status (as, in Jameson's words, "an exclusive and overisolated pantheon" [1979:87]) was not secure until successive generations of critics and historians, unable or reluctant to pursue more than one narrative of modernism, learned to refer to Pound, Hulme, Lewis, Eliot (and Joyce) as a "constellation" (Svarny 13) or a "literary republic of interdependent 'originals'" (*BLAST* 3:15). Not surprisingly, the notion of a cult was never invoked to define or explicate the literary politics of the Men of 1914, nor were the competitive power relations of Edwardian and Georgian art groups working to accumulate "symbolic capital" (Bourdieu 1986:132) discussed in those terms. Recently, a more reflective Levenson has acknowledged "the ambition of [modernist] writers and artists to set the terms by which they would be understood, where this often meant setting the terms by which others would not qualify for understanding. The circle of initiates was closed not only against the unwashed public, but also against rival artists who were excluded from the emerging narrative of Modernism triumphant" (1999:2).[6] He stops short of recognizing, however, that many of the "circles" cherished by the academy featured creative "men bonding with men to do without women" (McDonald 87).[7]

Two interrelated questions should be considered: what constituted this cult mentality, and why did they cherish it, nurture it, so assiduously? Fundamentally, these writers were the products and purveyors of what Mannheim has defined as the "generational" ideology that creates distinction for members of an age group through repudiation of their elders. In Pound's taxonomic terms, it was a matter of "parties"—"the dead, the accepted[,] the young" (*P/L* 192). "Our alliance," he informed readers of *The Egoist* in March 1914, "must be with our own generation" (Zinnes ed. 185). "We were of course," boasted Lewis, "a youth racket—oh yes! among other things. This may have contributed to that impression of 'haughtiness,' experienced at contact with us by the middle-aged observer" (*BB* 254).[8] The latter, after all, was undoubtedly entrenched in his or her own "phalansteries, sets, cells, or cliques" (*DPDS* vii). In the case of Lewis, Pound, and peers, they shared, to borrow Evelyn Waugh's portmanteau word, a post-Victorian "Youngergenerationconsciousness," a determination that the "new attitude of mind . . . should be the twentieth-century mind, if the twentieth century is to have a mind of its own" (Eliot 1924a:231).[9] Bourdieu has suggested that the "primacy" given to youth in "the field of cultural production" is a ruse, a means of claiming "indifference to power or money and the 'intellectual' refusal of the 'spirit of seriousness'" (1986:158). Nonetheless, "to bring a new producer, a new product and a new system of tastes onto the market at a given moment," recourse to a "system of symbolic distinctions between groups" to help discredit and displace established producers within the cultural field is crucial (1986:160–161). As Jensen observes in the context of the visual arts, "These 'isms' are not just the great creative flow of a generation, but a mentality, haunted by the need for originality, by the need to supercede one's competitors, by the desire to get a piece of the market share, to be discussed" (15). The "youth racket" of Eliot, Pound, and Lewis was as shrewd in its operations as it was noisy.

Within this historically-specific "alliance," claiming membership in a cult, however playfully, was actually a further strategy of self-representation, a defense against personal, socioeconomic, and artistic marginalization. To be an "outlaw," "enemy," or "exile"[10] is to occupy a subject position determined by exclusion; it is, to some degree, a position of subjugation and otherization. To create a cult, on the other hand, is to construct a community that provides meaning and significance, both of which are magnified by the requisite inclusivity and elitism. Members of the cult experience an enhanced degree of agency and self-determination. There could also be residual pleasures from being involved in something clandestine, mysterious, almost dangerous. From their readings of mythologists, anthropologists, and historians of religion such as James Frazer, Jane Harrison,[11] and Evelyn Underhill—and in Pound's case, his exposure to Yeats's personal involvement with Rosicrucianism and the occult[12]—the cult leaders also found adaptable notions of a secret, special knowledge shared only by initiates, of texts accessible only to privileged readers of extraordinary perception.[13] As Pound later explained in the *Guide to Kulchur,* some mysteries must be protected from "the fools": "Fools can only profane them. The dull can neither penetrate the secretum nor divulge it to others" (*GK* 145). Similarly, Lewis insisted,

> in every generation [nature endows] a handful of people with invaluable and mysterious gifts, in the special fields of science, and of art, or . . . general ability, making them fertile and inventive where other people are for the most part receptive only. . . . And when the herd-animus that it has been necessary to arouse, aimed originally at social privilege and wealth alone, is turned against this other type of man, privileged by nature according to some law that, until its secret is revealed, must be accepted by all of us . . . then you can see how the very rationale of true Revolution or salutary change is exploded. (*DPDS* 128)

Lewis's own animus against the "herd"-like masses confirms Huyssen's remarks about the modernists' acute "anxiety of contamination" from the marketplace (vii). The quotation also reminds one that cult membership was restricted to a special "type of man"; women were presumed not to qualify for this band of "exceptional creatures" (*DPDS* 130). Instead, the women could content themselves with what Pound termed "damd female tea parties who . . . committeeize themselves" (*P/Q* 27).[14] Woolf certainly understood these unwritten arrangements. In a 1917 review, she criticized the undemocratic inclinations of essayist Henry Sedgwick by summarizing his argument thus: "The men of genius and learning are to constitute a priesthood, held in special reverence; and the intellectual traditions of generations of educated men should be taught by them as a special cult" (Woolf 1990:81). Her response? "[W]as there ever a plan better calculated to freeze literature at the root than this one?" (Woolf 1990:81).[15]

Antipodal to a Whitmanesque, "lyrical cult of a universal brotherhood" (*Hit* 106), this "gang"[16] of like-minded, rebellious writers and artists valued individualism but responded to the allure of exclusivity and understood the advantages of assistance from peers whom they respected. A "crisis of differentiation" (Lyon 1992:104) pervaded avant-garde groups at that time; thinking through the cult mentality enabled Pound or Lewis to develop other "brands" of self-identification and assert a special "authenticity."[17] As Pound told the readers of *New Age* in 1919, "Nothing is more certain than that men of letters suffer from not meeting . . . men who really know whole systems of things which they themselves do not know" (1919:424). On the one hand they were setting themselves apart from a general public they disparagingly referred to as "the mob," the "masses" that were "persistently described [in "magazines and newspapers"] in terms of a feminine threat" (Huyssen 52).[18] As Lewis insists in *The Art of Being Ruled,* "Like the woman, whose psychic state is determined less by the grounds of abstract reason than by an indefinable emotional longing for a force which will complement her nature . . . likewise the masses love a commander more than a petitioner" (*Art* 42). On the other hand, they refused to be assimilated into existing "sets."[19] Instead, they participated in a self-fashioned "movement of individuals, for individuals, for the protection of individuality" (Zinnes ed. 191). When Eliot derided *The London Mercury* in 1920, it was because "it is run by a small clique of bad writers. J.C. Squire, the editor, knows nothing about poetry; but he is the cleverest journalist in London. If he succeeds, it will be impossible to get anything good published" (*LE* 358). Success, on their own terms, became paramount; ugliness would be their masculinized sign of difference.[20]

Songs of exclusivity echo throughout Pound's canon. In the early lyric "Au Salon," the speaker asks for "Some circle of not more than three / that we prefer to play up to, / Some few whom we'd rather please / than hear the whole aegrum vulgus / Splitting its beery jowl / a-meaowling our praises" (*Per* 52; *P/EP* 173-174). "In Durance" is more plaintive in tone, medieval in its cast:

> For I am homesick after mine own kind
> And ordinary people touch me not.
> 　　　Yea, I am homesick
> After mine own kind that know, and feel
> And have some breath for beauty and the arts.
> Aye, I am wistful for my kin of the spirit
> And have none about me save in the shadows.
>
> 　　　　　　　　　　　　　　　　　　(*P/EP* 86)

Kin and kind are elsewhere defined as the "flesh-shrouded bearing the secret" of the new; like Lewis, Pound insists that this is a communion with "my fellows" only (*P/EP* 86). "Causa," a work that first appeared in *Lustra* (1916) and was then republished in the *Selected Poems* of 1928 edited by Eliot, articulates both a specific and a general strategy of address,

> I join these words for four people,
> Some others may overhear them,
> O world, I am sorry for you,
> You do not know these four people.
>
> 　　　　　　　　　　　　　　　　　(*P/SPo* 70)

Section X of "Und Drang" pays homage to "an exquisite friendship," promising that "where these have been . . . the ground is holy" (*P/EP* 173). And where Pound's poetry has been once, it revisits with a vengeance in the *Pisan Cantos*. Among the mournfully defiant memories of *Canto* LXXX one finds old Colonel Jackson saying "to Yeats at a vorticist picture show: / 'You also of the brotherhood?'" (*Can* 504). With a nod to the Pre-Raphaelites' energetic efforts to work among "fellow" writers and artists and to promote each other's work, *Canto* LXXX includes among its "brotherhood" Henri Gaudier-Brzeska, Arnold Dolmetsch, Edmond Dulac, Stéphane Mallarmé, Edoard Manet, James McNeill Whistler, and Wyndham Lewis.[21]

Fundamentally, the purpose of cult activities was to compose avant-garde works and to provide fitting sites of dissemination—at a time when "the woild-uv-letturs" (*P/L* 35) was indifferent to or unaware of the cultists' efforts. As Pound explained to Dorothy Shakespear in March 1914, "Lewis is starting a quarterly 'BLAST.' He has gone off with eleven nice blasty poems of mine. At last there's to be a magazine one can appear in without a feeling of degradation—without feeling that one is slumming among mentalities of a loathsomely lower order" (O. Pound ed. 316). Always hierarchically atuned and ready to discriminate, Pound imagined a Dantesque "paradiso" for his chosen elite. "We want," he informed readers of "On Criticism in General," a few "barbs under the gate somewhere if our literary paddock is not to be filled with the bores and time-wasters. We do want some sort of paradiso, some sort of place where we can meet, preferably, superiors, or, in any case, mental equals" (1923:145–146). Such a meeting place could, metaphorically, be a "cenacle," the kind of supping room or upper chamber mentioned in accounts of Christ's Last Supper (Pound could never be accused of humility): "All civilisation has proceeded from cities and cenacles. If there are three hundred people worth writing to, they would do better to organise in some stricter fashion. One would like a list of the resolute, of the half-thousand exiles and proscripts who are ready to risk the coup" (1923:143). According to Pound's agenda, the cult would gradually expand its base of operations and then use its augmented strength to effect changes in the production, circulation, and reception of modernist culture.

Characteristically, Lewis offers contradictory statements about the "youth racket" and its cult activities in *Blasting and Bombardiering*.[22] Reminiscing about the "Great London Vortex" in the early sections of the book, he refers to it as an "organized disturbance," "Art behaving as if it were Politics" (*BB* 35). Subsequently he mocks "the solemn groupification" practiced by artists and critics alike:

> We are all familiar [Lewis explains] with the solemn groupification that occurs every year or so of, usually, a half-dozen "poets" or artists, introduced to the

world by their impresario as the team chosen (by him if not by destiny) to represent the absolute newest generation. Today these terms age and disintegrate
with alarming rapidity. But new ones take their place. And always the rationale of their assemblage is that their members were all born of women about
the same time. (*BB* 289)[23]

(Again one notes that such groups are "born of women" rather than constituted by men and women.) On the very same page, however, Lewis celebrates his former clique as "the literary band, or group, comprised within the
fold of Ezra Pound—the young, the 'New,' group of writers assembled in
Miss Weaver's *Egoist* just before and during the war" (*BB* 289).[24]

In the *Blasting and Bombardiering* passage, Lewis seems to be struggling
for an adequate or apposite name for his cohorts. Surveying the texts produced by the "youth racket," however, one finds an indisputable moniker of
preference: Modern. There is remarkable consistency in the textual construction of individual and group identities. Unwilling to be classified by
others (perhaps inaccurately or disparagingly), these tireless propagandists
christened themselves "moderns," thereby endorsing a model of human subjectivity, and an aesthetics, inextricably defined by time. "We are a number
of modern people," Hulme observed in his "Lecture on Modern Poetry"
(1955:680).[25] Sculptor Henri Gaudier-Brzeska lauded "WE the moderns"
(158); Pound preferred the folksier "us moderns" (*LEEP* 10). Burdened by
their existence within what Lewis called a "conscious and clamorous modernity" (*CH* 29), they dedicated themselves to "modes of extreme modernism"
(*CH* 248). The latter phrase is taken from Lewis's 1934 retrospective essay,
"Plain Home-Builder: Where is Your Vorticist?" T. E. Hulme used the same
locution in his "Lecture on Modern Poetry," which was "first delivered in
1908 or 1909" (1955:viii).[26] As Pound's poem "Hugh Selwyn Mauberley"
laments, "The age demanded an image / Of its accelerated grimace, / Something for the modern stage, / Not, at any rate, an Attic grace" (*P/SPo* 61–62).
And what the age demanded, the Men of 1914 provided.

Conjointly and independently, Hulme, Pound, Eliot, and Lewis rebelled
against artistic practices and theories that they felt to be outmoded and ineffective. With enviable "political"[27] savvy, they identified and repudiated
carefully-chosen "enemies," promoted work (theirs and their friends') which
embodied "a new attitude of mind" (Eliot 1924a:231), and developed a
multi-purpose, multi-voiced polemic that was deliberately quarrelsome, lavish in its praise and condemnation, as reactionary as it was revolutionary.[28]
Trailblazers for art, they knew, in Lewis's phrase, that "the road to understanding . . . the 'inhumanity,' the 'abstractness,' the 'ugliness' of extreme
contemporary art, is not . . . an easy one" (*CH* 247). A willingness to travel
such a path only magnified their self-constructed and self-proclaimed notion

of being among the elect. *Men Without Art* memorializes this secret society of artist-critics:

> We so called "satirists" [Lewis observes], or today just "artists," or whatever we are, must be great experts in this in the objective and material world in order to do our work properly: and so we must, paradoxically perhaps, relish our task. We must possess *an appetite* for what you regard as "the horrors" that we "perpetrate." But when I said "what you regard"—it was there that the essentials of this statement are to be looked for. What you regard as hideous has the same claims on us even as your ravishing self. We are the reverse of squeamish. Nay, there is no doubt about it, from the standpoint of the sentimental lady-reviewer, we are "coarse." Picasso's hands are caked with paint and clay—my own are never free of paint or ink. This *matière* which composes itself into what you regard I daresay as "abortions," is delightful to us, *for itself.* However regrettable that may be, it is the price of success in art. Materialist to that extent the artist *must be.* No artist has yet experienced any personal repulsion for a grotesque that sprang up beneath his hand. On the contrary. He is on the side of the "ugly" as much as "the beautiful," as far as subject-matter is concerned. . . . Beauty-doctors we are not, and have no intention of being: but we have a notion of beauty which is all our own—it is our secret, and it is strictly no one's business but ours. From *your* standpoint, no doubt—and from that of the average mystic, the ascetic of any order or degree—our work is a horrible one. . . . But all the time we are as happy as sandboys: we do not feel that way about it in the least. (*MWA* 229)

Dismissing competing aesthetic interests or values as "illusion[s]" is typical of Lewis's strategic combativeness. Membership in the "we"[29] is apparently as secret as the new "notion of beauty." What it means to "relish" the "horrible" will be anatomized in the following section; the misogynistic tactics (the need to construct, for the purposes of mockery and counter-definition, a "sentimental lady-reviewer") will be discussed subsequently.

Delineating and Exploiting "Ugliness"

Privileging the new, in sometimes clamorous tones, was paramount for these writers and artists. "The motive power behind any art," Hulme observed, "is a certain freshness of experience which breeds dissatisfaction with the conventional ways of expression because they leave out the individual quality of this freshness. You are *driven to new means* of expression because you persist in an endeavour to get it out exactly as you felt" (1936:162; emphasis added). Ironically, however, what was freshest and most compelling about their personal, cultural, and artistic experiences was the apprehension of an all-pervasive ugliness. At the simplest level, ugliness was used as a *cri de coeur,* a way of condemning an acutely industrialized, urbanized, over-crowded world. (What they abhorred, the Futurists embraced). In that sense, paradoxically, it typified the antimodernity position of these very modern subjects. Lewis is his most Ruskinian when he observes that the function of the artist is "to show you the world, only a realler one than you would see, unaided" (*Art* 32). According to McLuhan, "he set out to educate the eye by means of deft organization of gestures. . . . The artist's personality at hostile grips with the environment is dramatically offered not for its pathos . . . but as a means of clairvoyance" (1980:67). As testimony to the "importunate" burden of diagnosing the conditions of modernity—what Matthew Arnold had already taught them to think of as "this strange disease of modern life" (261)—the reader is offered numerous examples.

Pound's condemnation of urban blight is Ruskinian in a 1920 contribution to *The Apple (of Beauty and Discord)*. London, his readers are informed, is "a hideous city to look at. . . . [T]here is not enough public taste to ensure one building that is not an eyesore; there has not been a decent doorway constructed for eighty years. *And Paris is worse than London.* Since the assassination of architecture by the Beaux Arts, Paris has been under the curse" (Pound 1920a:22). The eyesore is decried, yet it nonetheless furnishes an opportunity for editorializing. "The Exploitation of Vulgarity," Lewis's 1914 *BLAST* essay, advances a complementary argument in typically acidic tones:

> When an ugly or uncomely person appeared on the horizon of their daily promenade, Ingres' careful wife would raise her shawl protectingly, and he would be spared the sight that would have offended him.
>
> Today the Artist's attention would be drawn, on the contrary, to anything particularly hideous or banal, as a thing not to be missed.
>
> Stupidity has always been exquisite and ugliness fine. . . .
>
> But the condition of our enjoyment of vulgarity, discord, cheapness or noise is an unimpaired and keen disgust with it.
>
> It depends, that is, on sufficient health, not to relinquish the consciousness of what is desirable and beneficial.
>
> Rare and cheap, fine and poor, these contrasts are the male and female, the principle of creation to-day.
>
> This pessimism is the triumphant note in modern art.
>
> A man could make just as fine an art in discords, and with nothing but "ugly" trivial and terrible materials, as any classic artist did with only "beautiful" and pleasant means. (*BLAST* 1:145)

The conflation of "manliness" and aesthetic stamina is bolstered by the highly conventional otherization trope: male is to rare and fine as female is to cheap and poor. For Lewis, the modern artist struggles with a range and degree of *concordia discors* that would have quelled a Virgil or even a Pope.

Subsequently, the discord of war only heightened Lewis's apprehensions; the discursive strategies were already in place. Thus he writes from France, in October 1917, "I could no doubt (the changes of war permitting) remain here another 6 months, and another after that. But there is one thing to be remembered. Nature and my training have made me curiously sensitive to ugly and stupid influences. The whole point of *Me* is that. . . ." (*P/L* 110). A month earlier, he had also shared with Pound the terrible, anguished irony of waging war in the French and Belgian countryside: "The beauty of these farms, by Christ! = But I shall forget the ugliness as soon as I turn my back on it, and it helps me to forget it communicating it to you" (*P/L* 103). While the politicians and diplomats were busy constructing the Treaty of Versailles, Lewis was explaining to readers of the parabolical *Caliph's Design* that the artist is "*nourished*" by stupid utterances and "every beastly, ill-made, or tasteless object that abound in life to-day" (*WLA* 221). At one and the same time, he grants that "there *could* be such a thing as too much ugliness, or foolishness" (*WLA* 221) yet adumbrates "this ugliness, this commonness and squalor. . . . It is what meets the eye in any London street, in any railway, bus, teashop, restaurant or hotel in our capitol city, or in the official art which is to be found annually displayed in Burlington House [home of the Royal Academy]" (*WLA* 224). Somewhat disingenuously, he admits that he enjoys the appetizing spectacle yet questions its efficacy:

> With men trying their hardest to eliminate ugliness, injustice, or imbecility from the world, has there ever been any absence of these commodities for the delectation of the artist? Is there ever likely to be? It is true that the artist can gorge himself to-day as never before. But is that the best thing for his talent? (*WLA* 222)

Lewis's detractors would answer the last question with a resounding No. Those sympathetic to his work, such as Normand, Quéma, and Edwards, would argue that his talent was only realized because of the stimulii provided.

Concurrent with Lewis and Eliot's surveys of an "unreal city" turned wasteland, and Stevens's pronouncements from a dump, long before Yeats celebrated the "foul rag-and-bone shop of the heart," Hulme was summarizing his views in a fragmented text entitled "Cinders: A Sketch of a New Weltanschauung." "The truth remains that the world is not any unity, but a house in the cinders," he muses; all one can discern is a "landscape, with occasional oases. So now and then we are moved—at the theatre, action, a love. But mainly deserts of dirt, ash-pits of the cosmos, grass on ash-pits" (Hulme 1936:223, 225). Yet from the ash-pits, Hulme had begun to fashion his modernist aesthetic, a "new classical spirit" that would, in its "dry hardness," repudiate and repair romanticism's excesses (1936:113, 133). The notion that ugliness is both a scourge and an opportunity is echoed in Eliot's 1920 appreciation of "Dante"[30]: "The contemplation of the horrid or sordid or disgusting, by an artist, is the necessary and negative aspect of the impulse toward the pursuit of beauty. But not all succeed . . . in expressing the complete scale from negative to positive. The negative is the more importunate" (*SW* 169). So compelling did Eliot find his argument that he repeated it more than a decade later. "We mean all sorts of things, I know, by Beauty," Eliot advised readers of "Matthew Arnold," but "the essential advantage for a poet is not, to have a beautiful world with which to deal: it is to be able to see beneath both beauty and ugliness; to see the boredom, and the horror, and glory" (*UPUC* 106). And what the poet sees, his readers experience anew. For all four writers, ugliness as subject matter was legitimized by ensconcing it within a dynamic binary with beauty. Thus dichotomized, it enabled the artist (and only the artist) to play Jekyll against carefully-selected Hyde-bound predecessors. And such manoeuvres promised, in previously unimaginable terms, to lead to glory.

Acknowledging the ugliness that constitutes modern life, working with ugly words and images (plastic and verbal), was, I would reiterate, a coveted mark of distinction for the Men of 1914; it confirmed their places and privileges within a self-selected coterie. Eliot's favorite terms for this secret new aesthetic were *horror, sordid,* and *terror,* a lexicon adapted from Baudelaire, Laforgue, and Conrad. When, for example, derogatory statements about Joyce and Lewis were published in the *New Age,* Eliot replied,

> The *New Age* is "mystified, bewildered, repelled." That is quite intelligible. *Ulysses* is volatile and heady, *Tarr* thick and suety, clogging the weak intestine. Both are terrifying. That is the test of a new work of art. . . . But this attractive terror repels the majority of men; they seek the sense of ease which the sensitive man avoids, and only when they find it do they call anything "beautiful." (1918d:84)

Perhaps one should rechristen the Men of 1914 the "Attractive Terrorists."

Who Taught Them to Think This Way?

The passage from "The Serious Artist" quoted above identifies a tradition or genealogy of cult leaders. Every sect has its spiritual masters, its special hoard of privileged texts, and these male modernists were no exception. Whether schooled in comparative literature at university, as were Eliot and Pound, or self-taught admirers, like Hulme and Lewis, they found—and then appropriated—stimulating textual models and precedents. Nineteenth-century French writers such as Baudelaire, Laforgue, Verlaine, and Rimbaud were canonized for their avant-garde textual practices and their thematic insistence that "le Beau, le Bien, le Vrai" must be subjected to the experiences of contemporary metropolitan life. Baudelaire's ironic and barbed insistence on *l'héroisme de la vie moderne*,[31] even or especially with its attendant sordidness and squalor, was particularly affective, and perhaps partially responsible for the posturing of these twentieth-century artistic-martyrs-in-the-face-of-life's-ugliness. As Pound observed in 1915, "Baudelaire and Verlaine generally ring true, and their horrors and squalors and miseries and audacities have the value and virtue of touching the reader to something of compassion or meditation" (*LEEP* 365).

In many cases, the Anglo-Americans' first exposure to these continental writers was Symons's 1898 study, *The Symbolist Movement in Literature*.[32] (His original choice of paradigm and title was the *Decadent* movement in literature; Yeats persuaded him to make the changes.) Revealingly, Symons praised five crucial elements of the French texts: a generic preference for satire; symbolic urban landscapes; the evocation of "modern emotion[s] and sensation[s]," especially "horror" (46, 52); formal experimentation, especially with vers libre; and, a "revolt against" yet attraction to "the ugliness" of contemporary life (77). Throughout, there is a commitment to truth-telling as the artist's paramount responsibility; as Symons later said of Rodin, "art has no meaning apart from truth" (1906:3). Baudelaire is cited in *The Symbolist Movement* as the developer of a new discursive formation: he "invented," Symons claims, "a new vocabulary for the expression of subtle, often perverse, essentially modern emotion and sensation" (1898:46). (To share these difficult lessons in turn, Pound organized the February 1918 issue of *The Little Review* around an anthology of late-nineteenth, early-twentieth-century French poetry. Works by Laforgue, Corbière, and Rimbaud were featured.)

Of the numerous paeans to the French writers penned by Anglo-American modernists, Eliot's is the most informative:

> I think that from Baudelaire I learned first, a precedent for the poetical possibilities, never developed by any poet in my own language, of the more sordid aspects of the modern metropolis, of the possibility of fusion between the sordidly realistic and the phantasmagoria, the possibility of the juxtaposition of the matter-of-fact and the fantastic. From him, as from Laforgue, I learned that the . . . source of the new poetry might be found in what had been regarded hitherto as the impossible, the sterile, the intractably unpoetic. That, in fact, the business of the poet was to make poetry out of the unexplored resources of the unpoetical[.] (*TCC* 126)

Eliot's response to Baudelaire's texts is scripted to repeat the master's discoveries while reading Edgar Allan Poe: they shared, Baudelaire observed in

"Avis du traducteur," a common sensibility and common pursuit of a new aesthetic, "un genre de beauté nouveau" (1918 1:348). In addition to his exotic status as the poet who became a *succès de scandale,* Baudelaire established ties between the visual arts, literature, and critical journalism that the modernists fervently pursued. Furthermore, Baudelaire and his peers fixed their gaze on two almost interchangeable sites of modern ugliness: the "fourmillante cité" (see Chapter 4) and a woman's body, "comme un astre inutile, / La froide majeste de la femme sterile" (1918 1:233, 56).

Competing for Ugliness: Marinetti

The first modernist text quoted in this chapter features Lewis's comments about "the Italians": "You always got your bloodiest bits from them," he informed his readers. "No one made such a ranting, gory job of the doing-in of Beauty as Marinetti" (*CH* 47). Are these words meant as a "blast" against a perceived enemy, or a "blessing" for a like-minded aesthetic movement? With consistently paradoxical intensity, the answer is: both. As the work of Lyon and Hansen has shown, points of intersection between the Men of 1914 and the Futurists are significant, especially concerning the development of publicity strategies for their enterprises, including manifestos and "sensational headline-grabbing" (Lyon 1992:105). When Marinetti delivered his "Futurist Speech to the English" at London's Lyceum Club in 1910, Lewis, Hulme, and Pound took anxious note. "The unexpected ease with which Futurism was articulated to popular culture," Lyon summarizes, "precipitated a crisis of differentiation within the English avant-garde" (1992:104). Marinetti's return in March 1912, to speak at "Bechstein (now Wigmore) Hall produced headlines in all the major newspapers" (Rainey 1999:38). Competition was a keen catalyst; it enabled the Men of 1914 to concentrate their aesthetic theories and practices, so that "the Italian intruder," as Lewis put it, could be "worsted" (*BB* 33; Hansen 362). The first issue of *BLAST* in 1914 was part Whistler, part Marinetti, and entirely a Lewis-Pound fusion of competing interests: showcasing the work of "new" talent, insisting upon an ongoing dialogue between the literary and visual arts, praising the cultural contributions of a select few, and exposing the "Melodrama of Modernity." The latter, exemplified by the Futurists, heroizes the future, vilifies the past, and "romances" science and its current manifestations: automobiles, airplanes, speed (*BLAST* 1:143). (That the hero "gets" the girl will be discussed below.) "Time equals speed was the fulcrum of Marinetti's revolutionary theory"; the Futurists disapproved of any cultural work that did not express its fascination with an immediate, "dynamic, accelerating world" (Guiati 125), or share a "destructive, antitraditionalist principle" (Marinetti 80). For Lewis and those who cherished "mythic methods," who succeeded in "making the historical and cultural past into an ever-accessible present, ready and waiting to serve modern cultural needs" (Rado 285), the Futurists' inability to respect the past or "tradition" (mere *Passéism,* according to Marinetti) was a principle failing; declarations such as the following were anathema: "we hate our glorious intellectual fathers, after having greatly loved them: the grand Symbolist geniuses, Edgar Poe, Baudelaire, Mallarmé, and Verlaine. We despise them now for having swum the river of time with their heads always turned back toward the blue far spring of the past" (Marinetti 66). The dismissal of Baudelaire is particularly disingenuous: Marinetti savors the notion of "heroism" in modern life and is willing to explore the possibilities to an absurdist extreme.[33]

And yet: although one is grateful that Lewis and Pound were not swayed by the "excited, pugnacious, dreamlike, improvising, utopian" vision and exploits of this rival culture worker, shared "proto-Fascist and Fascist mentalities" were certainly operational (R. W. Flint 5). Without question, they absorbed what Marinetti termed "the characteristic gift of the Latin races"— the ability *"to hate"* (89).[34] Comparisons between modernists and Futurists are also instructive because one can discern how and why the Men of 1914 were more selective in their repudiations, less ideologically extreme, and more focused on literary projects. They would change the culture at large by changing literature; the Futurists wanted to change everything, and everyone, immediately. For cubists, space was the new frontier of experimentation; for Futurists, time. Modernists attempted to reconfigure the spatial/temporal relations of creativity and aesthetic engagement.

And yet: regarding three key topics—sentimentality, beauty, and ugliness—keen intertextualities are evident, and each is inextricably connected with a masculinity currently under siege by "distracting" femininity. "We Abjure Our Symbolist Masters" repudiates "the poetry of nostalgic memory" (Marinetti 67) and praises the new "man whose roots are cut, of the multiplied man who mixes himself with iron, who is fed by electricity and no longer understands anything except the lust for danger and daily heroism" (Marinetti 67). Lewis was right, one could hastily assume: this sounds like the overblown rhetoric of melodrama, and the protagonist's moustache is askew. Yet Marinetti goes on to identity the four major "intellectual poisons that we want to abolish forever," among them "romantic sentimentality drenched with moonshine that looks up adoringly to the ideal of Woman-Beauty" (68). Subsequently, "Against *Amore*" insists that "sentimentality and lechery" are the "least natural thing[s] in the world. There is nothing natural and important except coitus" (Marinetti 72), notions reiterated in *War, the World's Only Hygiene,* which looks forward to the time when the "young modern male" will surpass "the double alcohol of lust and sentiment" (Marinetti 92).

The Futurists' attack on sentimentality is rather narrowly focused, but typical of the antifeminism animating their socio-aesthetic texts. Whether attacking the dangerously "supplicating arms" of women in "Let's Murder the Moonshine" (1909) or "domesticated" sexual activities in "Down with the Tango and Parsifal" (1914), "scorn for women" is never far from Marinetti's thoughts and words. The phrase, in fact, was made dictum in "The Founding and Manifesto of Futurism," featured on the front page of *Le Figaro* on February 20, 1909. The ninth of 11 commandments "sings" the glories of war ("militarism, patriotism, the destructive gesture of free-dom-bringers") and intones "scorn for woman" in a gesture that reduces all women to one negative type (Marinetti 41). Number ten pledges to "destroy the museums, libraries, academies" and to "fight moralism, feminism" (Marinetti 42). Two years later, Marinetti updates the femme fatale script in order to blame "the woman-poison,[35] woman the tragic trinket, the fragile woman, obsessing and fatal, whose voice, heavy with destiny, and whose dreaming tresses reach out and mingle with the foliage of forests drenched in moonshine" (Marinetti 72). Except for the coarse alliteration in "tragic trinket," one could imagine that Yeats and Pound, ensconced in Stone Cot-tage, had composed this particular mantra of misogyny for a lark.

Items four and seven in the Futurists' manifesto suggest the kind of "new beauty" they applauded: "the beauty of speed" ("a roaring car that seems to ride on grapeshot . . . is more beautiful than the *Victory of Samothrace*") and the beauty of "struggle" and aggression (Marinetti 41). In other words, by aestheticizing their call for cultural and social upheaval, they hoped to make it acceptable. The Men of 1914 would not "sing," like inverted, latter-day Whitmans, the "vibrant nightly fervor of arsenals and shipyards blazing with violent electric moons; greedy railway stations . . . factories hung on clouds by the crooked lines of their smoke; . . . the sleek flight of planes" (Marinetti 42) and declare these things, with "aggressive optimism," examples of a "new beauty" to be called "Geometric and Mechanical Splendor" (Marinetti 97). *War, the World's Only Hygiene* clarifies Marinetti's efforts to separate, once and for all, the "two ideas Woman and Beauty." His rationale ardently clar-ifies the basis of all masculinist discomfiture with "the beautiful" as a cate-gory of value:

> [One needs to] understand one of our principal Futurist efforts, namely the abolition in literature of the seemingly unchallengeable fusion of the two ideas Woman and Beauty, which has reduced all of romanticism to a kind of heroic assault leveled by a bellicose and lyric male against a tower that bristles with enemies who cluster around the divine Beauty-Woman. . . . It is a matter of a dominant leitmotiv, tiresome and outworn, of which we want to disembarrass literature and art in general. (Marinetti 90)

The Men of 1914 refused to "exalt love for the machine" as compensation for this radical severance, but "Beauty-Woman" (or, beauty = woman) was not featured in the new compensatory truths they would proffer. They certainly learned that capturing attention in the crowded field of cultural production depended upon "hastening the grotesque funeral of passéist Beauty (romantic, symbolist, decadent)" (Marinetti 97). Hence a cult of ugliness that distinguished their works from the Futurists' but promulgated the same kind of arresting rhetoric guaranteed to raise eyebrows and sell books and journals. One must remember, however, that Marinetti often referred to "cults" ("the aggressive optimism that results from the cult of muscles and sport" [97]), saluted the "so-called ugliness of locomotives, trams, automobiles" (56), and, in the May 1912 "Technical Manifesto of Futurist Literature," declared,

> They shout at us, "Your literature won't be beautiful! Where is your verbal symphony, your harmonious swaying back and forth, your tranquilizing cadences?" Their loss we take for granted! And how lucky! We make use, instead, of every ugly sound, every expressive cry from the violent life that surrounds us. We bravely create the "ugly" in literature, and everywhere we murder solemnity. Come! Don't put on these grand priestly airs when you listen to me! Each day we must spit on the *Altar of Art*. (89)

Eliot would never spit, and Pound relished his airs. Undoubtedly, however, they could separate the insights from the bombast in Marinetti's writings.

The Truths of Satire

Marinetti had little use for satirical effects in his writings; the latter involve irony and subtlety, and thus slow the pace of the writing and reading experiences. The modernists were more deliberative. In his "Vers pour le portrait de M. Honoré Daumier," Baudelaire observes,

> C'est un satirique, un moqueur;
> Mais l'energie avec laquelle
> Il peint le Mal et sa sequelle,
> Prouve la beauté de son coeur.
>
> (1918 1:23)

"Satirist" was an honorific title among Eliot and his peers; satire shaped their essays, short lyrics, and experimental epics-gone-awry. As Symons had argued, "Satire . . . is the revenge of beauty upon ugliness, the persecution of the ugly; it is not merely social satire, it is a satire on the material universe by one who believes in a spiritual universe" (1898:27). In "Irony, Laforgue, and Satire," Pound's praise for Laforgue as "a purge and a critic" (*LEEP* 282) reminds us of how readily they borrowed from the French the discursive strategy of "diagnosing" the sick world in which they found themselves. A March 1914 newspaper interview provided Pound with an opportunity to share these insights with common readers:

> "Poetry," continued Mr. Pound, "is the one art in which mediocrity is unpardonable. Literature is the poor man's bridge to the beautiful. A shepherd, a ploughman or a miner may never be able to see the best art or the best sculpture, but he need never be shut out from the best poetry. To my mind, the object of poetry is to focus the light on something, and I do not care what the reader sees in a poem so long as he sees beauty. There are two ways of presenting beauty—by satire, which clears away the rubbish and allows the central loveliness to reveal itself; and by the direct presentation of beauty itself." (O. Pound and Litz eds. 324–325)

If readers of the *Daily News and Leader* ever found themselves in the company of "Hugh Selwyn Mauberley" or "Les Millwins," they would undoubtedly realize that the "direct presentation of beauty itself" was never Pound's first instinct. Given the daily, debasing spectacles of "τὸ καλόν [the beautiful] / Decreed in the market place" (*P/SPo* 150), satire's cleansing powers were most frequently invoked.

"I believe with a Calvinistic uncompromisingness that one cannot be too hard on the stupidities of one's neighbours," Lewis privately advised Augustus John in 1910 (*LWL* 45). Publically, Lewis adumbrated the "goodness" of satire in terms of its coldness, externality, and fortitude:

> Satire is *cold* [*Men Without Art* advocates], and that is good! It is easier to achieve those polished and resistant surfaces of a great *externalist* art in Satire. At least they are achieved more naturally than can be done beneath the troubled impulse of the lyrical afflatus. All the nineteenth century poetry of France, for instance, from the *Fleurs du Mal* onwards, was stiffened with Satire, too. There is a stiffening of Satire in everything good, of "the grotesque," which is the same thing—the non-human outlook must be there (beneath the fluff and pulp which is all that is seen by the majority) to correct our soft conceit. . . . Satire is *good!* (*MWA* 121; Lewis's italics)

One can only presume that the stiffening described by Lewis is a metaphor for phallic (and phallogocentric) tumescence, not a sign of rigor mortis. So intent was Lewis on discrediting any writing or work of art that did not fulfill his expectations that he took the brilliantly extreme stance of declaring "that all art is in fact satire today" (*CH* 12).

Lewis devotes *Men Without Art* (1934) to the twofold project of defending satire as the privileged weapon in the cultist's discursive arsenal and identifying its most appropriate targets. Introducing himself to readers as "a notorious satirist" (*MWA* 14), he emphasizes that the Satirist is not "a moralist: and about that I make no bones either" (*MWA* 87). Eschewing the subject position of moralist or ethical guardian, Lewis instead happily occupies the chair of Platonic shadow-catcher and scientific truth-teller: "Satire in reality often is nothing else but *the truth*—the truth, in fact, of Natural Science. The objective, non-emotional truth of the scientific intelligence sometimes takes on the exuberant sensuous quality of creative art: then it is very apt to be called 'Satire,' for it has been bent not so much upon pleasing as upon being true" (*MWA* 99).[36] Like Ruskin before him, Lewis asserts a "new series" of literary truths by taking refuge in scientific discourse, naturalizing his "ugly" words in the process. General science skillfully segues into medical discourse (Pound's preferred strategy) in order to proclaim that satire is "called upon to deal" with "man, and not with manners. . . . It is a *chronic* ailment (manifesting itself, it is true, in a variety of ways) not an *epidemic state,* depending upon 'period,' or upon the 'wicked ways' of the particular smart-set of the time" (*MWA* 102).[37] Satirist against "man," cult members against the "smart-set": the Men of 1914 learned quickly, if idiosyncratically, and disseminated that knowledge in as many media as possible.

Aesthetic Values, Not Sentiments

In his 1914 lecture "Modern Art and Its Philosophy," Hulme observed that,

> The thought or vocabulary of one's period is an extraordinarily difficult thing to break away from. While an artist may have emancipated himself from his own period as far as his art is concerned, while a spectator may have emancipated himself by looking at the art of other periods in museums, yet the mental, or more accurately speaking, the linguistic emancipations of the two may not have gone forward parallel with the artistic one. . . . Most of us cannot state our position, and we use adjectives which in themselves do not explain what we mean, but which, *for a group for a certain time,* by a kind of tacit convention become the "porters" or "bearers" of the complex new attitude which we all recognize that we have. . . . At the present time you get this change shown in the value given to certain adjectives. Instead of epithets like graceful, beautiful, etc., you get epithets like austere, mechanical, clear cut, and bare, used to express admiration. (1936:76, 95, 96; emphasis added)[38]

"Ugliness," therefore, could be used as both a documentary epithet and a new articulation of abiding aesthetic values. This claim for a radical complementarity between "ugliness" and "beauty" was discussed at length in

Hulme's animadversions on "Cinders." Beauty, we are told, is merely a "counter" or token of value that has become exhausted, emptied of its previous significance:

> For the purposes of communication they [a group of persons who want to communicate] invent a symbolic language. Afterwards this language, used to excess, becomes a disease, and we get the curious phenomena of men explaining themselves by means of the gossamer web that connects them. Language becomes a disease in the hands of the counter-word mongers. It must constantly be remembered that it is an invention for the convenience of men; and in the midst of Hegelians who triumphantly explain the world as a mixture of "good" and "beauty" and "truth," this should be remembered. . . . Symbols are picked out and believed to be realities. People imagine that all the complicated structure of the world can be woven out of "good" and "beauty." These words are merely counters representing vague groups of things, to be moved about on a board for the convenience of the players. (Hulme 1936:217–218)

Ugliness is the new "counter" necessitated by the burden of modernity; the Platonic triad could only be preserved by reformulating it in terms of the Ugly, the Good, and the True. As Ezra Pound admonished, "The cult of beauty and the delineation of ugliness are not in mutual opposition" (*LEEP* 45).[39]

One crucial dimension of their project to reanimate aesthetic ideals through wholesale redefinition was the need to reinterpret the nature and function of emotion in aesthetic production and reception. Repeatedly, any "school of sentimental aesthetics" (Pound 1916a:26) or "sentimentalizing about beauty" (*LEEP* 45), any "sentimental" attachments to "the production of what [was once] called beauty" (Hulme, 1936:104), was declared outmoded.[40] As Clark has persuasively argued, "this reversal against the sentimental helped to establish beleaguered avant-garde intellectuals as a discourse community, defined by its adversarial relationship to domestic culture" (1). Hence Lewis's special barb against "sentimental lady-reviewers." Discrediting women, women writers, and the "literary past" (Clark 1) was carried out as variously as possible. As Williams stridently insists in *Paterson*, "There's nothing sentimental about the technique of writing" (*Pat* 269).

Sentimentalism was perceived as a multifaceted and ever-present danger, an abherrant or unexamined emotional enthusiasm that could flourish in the most unexpected places. Marinetti said as much in his critique of "Marriage and the Family" (*Futurist Democracy*, 1919), which flamboyantly insists, "We proclaim that Sentiment is the typical virtue of vegetables, for digging down and growing roots. It becomes a vice in animals, a crime among men, because it fatally restrains their dynamism and swift evolution" (77). Yet the attacks on Futurism launched by Lewis in *BLAST* focus on the

Futurists' "sentimental" attachment to speed and mechanization. This is his opening salvo, another exercise in "we"-ness:

> AUTOMOBILISM (Marinetteism) bores us. We don't want to go about making a hullo-bulloo about motor cars, anymore than about knives and forks, elephants or gas-pipes.
>
> Elephants are VERY BIG. Motor cars go quickly.
>
> Wilde gushed twenty years ago about the beauty of machinery. Gissing, in his romantic delight with modern lodging houses, was futurist in this sense.
>
> The futurist is a sensational and sentimental mixture of the aesthete of 1890 and the realist of 1870. (*BLAST* 1:8)

Nonacceptance is therefore a crucial part of Lewis's aesthetic ideology—represent the ugliness in the world, he admonishes, but do not romanticize or fall in love with it. Reference to "the aesthete of 1890" demonstrates that Lewis is prepared to indict the opposition in any way possible: Marinetti is either too much like a woman, or too much like a "womanly" man. The general denunciation of nineteenth-century culture is expanded upon by Lewis in *The Caliph's Design*. "The Victorian age," he insists, "produced a morass of sugary comfort and amiableness, indulged men so much that they became guys of sentiment—or sentimental guys. Against this 'sentimentality' people of course reacted. So the brutal tap was turned on. For fifty years it will be the thing to be brutal, 'unemotional'" (*WLA* 268). Evidently, the construction of masculinity is no less important to Lewis than the cultivation of the arts: real men must cleanse themselves in the waters of brutality to wash off the stains of historically-determined gender contamination.

Sentimentalism, then, was to be routed from aesthetic productions and criticism, part of a wholesale purge of emotional objectives and effects. The "new art," Hulme promised, was "aiming at the satisfaction of a different mental need altogether" (1936:104–105). Claims for this nonspecified but crucial difference were also articulated in Hulme's study of "Bergson's Theory of Art":

> In the state of mind produced in you by any work of art there must necessarily be a rather complicated mixture of the emotions. Among these is one which can properly be called an essentially aesthetic emotion. It could not occur alone, isolated . . . but it is, as far as any investigation in the nature of aesthetics is concerned, the important thing. (1936:145)

Had a character in *Alice in Wonderland* offered such a tautology, one would think it an amusing example of Carrolline satire. Coming from Hulme, it was embraced by Pound and others for its oracular insights.[41] Eliot, for example, devoted several essays, including "Hamlet and his Problems," to enumerating the distinctions between the feelings experienced by the writer and the emotions generated by the text.

Just as attacks on sentimentality were gender-encoded, so too were the concerted efforts to distinguish hierarchically between beauty and that which is merely "pretty." In "Bergson's Theory of Art," for example, Hulme tried to explain "what happens in the decay of any art. Original sincerity, which is often almost grotesque in its individuality, slackens off in the rounded curves of 'prettiness'" (1936:161). When Lewis severed ties with Roger Fry and the Omega Workshop, he informed the public that,

> [Their] Idol is still Prettiness, with its mid-Victorian languish of the neck, and its skin is "greenery-yallery,"[42] despite the Post-What-Not fashionableness of its draperies. This family of Strayed and Dissenting Aesthetes, however, were compelled to call in as much modern talent as they could find, to do the rough and masculine work without which they knew their efforts would not rise above the level of a pleasant tea-party, or command more attention. (*LWL* 49)

Characters changed in Lewis's ongoing allegorical narrative of then-contemporary cultural movements, but the hyperbolic combination of misogyny and homophobia never faltered. Perhaps he was familiar with Andrew Lang's approach to disparaging Pater's writings: in a dispeptic review of *Greek Studies*, Lang accuses Pater of "prettifying" and thereby falsifying the ancient Greeks and their culture; "The book is full of pretty and even poetic ideas which the relics of Greece suggested," he observes, but "I really do not think that the Greeks (or any other people) were like Mr. Pater's Greeks" (Lang 332).

Accusations of "prettiness," a categorization intended to feminize and humiliate the opposition, proved to be useful for the cultists on many occasions. Pound once dismissed almost all sculptors *other* than Jacob Epstein and Henri Gaudier-Brzeska because they were still creating "pretty-pretties" (1916a:109); he tried to persuade John Quinn that the coloration of Lewis's canvasses was wholly "distinct from the pretty brightness of Picabia or 1910 Paris" (*P/Q* 41). "Matisse is best," Lewis begins an assessment designed to blame, not praise the painter, "at a very circumscribed, thin, gay, and pretty cleverly arranged effect; and many small canvasses of his for what they set out to be, are good enough" (1924b:110). Five years earlier, in *The Caliph's Design*, he pronounced that in London "and in Paris Cézannism is being side-tracked into a pretty studio-game" (*WLA* 315). "The artist's function," he insisted, "is to create—to make something; not to make something pretty, as dowagers, dreamers, and art-dealers here suppose" (*WLA* 258).[43] Excluded from the ranks of art producers, disparaged as cultural contaminants and threats to masculinity, women were also belittled in their roles as consumers and patrons.[44]

Interestingly, Baudelaire employed analogous terms to distinguish between the conventional paintings of his day and the genius of Delacroix, who did not stoop to painting merely "pretty women" (1965:65–66). And in "Peintures et Aqua-Fortistes," he lamented that, "le sens du beau, du fort et même du pittoresque a toujours été diminuant et se degradant. [Ainsi] . . . Il y a . . . sans contestation la peinture proprette, le joli, le niais, l'entortille" (Baudelaire 1918 2:111). The passage not only laments the diminishment of "le sens du beau," it alludes to a concomitant degradation. With alacrity, Hulme, Pound, Eliot, and Lewis carried forward a self-defined crusade against the alleged corruption of the visual and literary arts. At all times, their work was motivated by a profound "distrust" of "the Feminine in literature" or everyday life (*LE* 1:204). The phrase is Eliot's: he is lamenting to Pound his ordeals as a staff member for the *Egoist:* "I struggle to keep the writing as much as possible in Male hands, as I distrust the Feminine in literature, and also, once a woman has had anything printed in your paper, it is very difficult to make her see why you should not print everything she sends you" (*LE* 1:204). A myth of female insatiability is easily transferred from the sexual to the literary realm. As Nelson suggests, gender "is at once its own subject and a stand in for other anxieties about cultural life" (325). Eliot's correspondent would have nodded along in agreement as he read. In his article on "Suffragettes" for the *Egoist* (1914) Pound asserts that Christabel Pankhurst has "about as much intellect as a guinea-pig," then concludes that, "The *Male* mind does not want to be bothered with Asquith or Wright or their kind. Politics is unfit for men; it may be good enough for women, we doubt it. The male mind does not want a state run by women" (1914a:254, 256).[45] What the male mind needs, according to Canto 29, is to assert a gender essentialism that disenfranchises women as creatively as possible:

> the female
> Is an element, the female
> Is a chaos
> An octopus
> A biological process . . .
> "Nel ventre tuo, o nella mente mia"[.]
>   [in your belly, or in my mind]
>
> (*Can* 144)

Lewis, as always, was just as forthright and just as committed to debasing women through pseudobiological signifiers. According to *The Code of a Herdsman* (1917), "As to women: wherever you can, substitute the society of men . . . treat them kindly, for they suffer from the herd, although of it, and have many of the same contempts as yourself. . . . But women, and the processes for which they exist, are the arch conjuring trick" (1917:48). Anyone puzzled by the reference to women's "processes" would have to wait a year for clarification. "A woman was a lower form of life," the narrator of *Tarr* observes; "[e]verything was female to begin with. . . . Above a certain level of life sex disappeared, just as in highly organized sensualism sex vanishes. And, on the other hand, everything below that line was female" (*Tarr* 334).[46] There is nothing pretty about the "combination of misogyny and triumphal masculinism" that defines "modernist work by men" (DeKoven 1999:175).

"No Beauty Without Disgust"

Approaching aesthetics in terms of a reception theory enabled Hulme, on several occasions, to work toward a new definition of beauty. According to his unexecuted "PLAN FOR A BOOK on Modern Theories of Art," Chapter 3 would have addressed,

> Complicated mixture of different questions involved in question "What is Art"?. . . . Taking modern arts as known, ask this question—Is there any specific emotion which characterises them all and is found in no other activity?— a specifically aesthetic emotion, the experiencing of which constitutes beauty. (Hulme 1936:262)

Noticeably, the one emotion or emotional experience that is never considered, theoretically or practically, is "pleasure."

How can "beauty" be derived from ugliness? For Hulme and Pound especially it is a matter, in very Ruskinian terms, of "accuracy" of representation. "You could define art, then, as a passionate desire for accuracy," *Speculations* reports, "and the essentially aesthetic emotion as the excitement which is generated by direct communication" (Hulme 1936:162–163). Once again Pound deftly appropriates the discourse of science to elevate the truth claims of his aesthetic (and morally encoded) projects. "The serious artist," he proclaims, "is scientific in that he presents the image of his desire, of his hate, of his indifference as precisely that. . . . The more precise his record the more lasting and unassailable his work of art" (*LEEP* 46). Furthermore, the "arts, literature, poesy, are a science," Pound insists, "just as chemistry is a science. Their subject is man, mankind and the individual. . . . This brings us to the immorality of bad art. Bad art is inaccurate art. It is art that makes false reports" (*LEEP* 43). Lewis makes a similar point when discussing *Tarr:* "The language is not travaille: any beauty it may possess depend[s] on the justness of the psychology,—as is the case in the Russian novels, I suppose" (*LWL* 65).

The paradoxical dimensions of this emergent aesthetic are formidable. The notion of an ugliness that pervades and blights the physical world and the human spirit is predicated on a nostalgic belief in a quality of beauty that once existed. "Disgust with the sordid," Pound observes in a review which champions Joyce's writing, "is but another expression of a sensitiveness to the finer thing. There is no perception of beauty without a corresponding disgust" (*LEEP* 415). An unrelenting delineation of the ugliness of contemporary life does not prevent Hulme, Pound, Lewis, or Eliot from claiming beauty as an indisputable category for describing the intentions of the artist/writer or the response of the viewer/critic to the successful or accomplished aesthetic artifact. "Art creates beauty," Hulme declares in the crucial "Beauty, Imitation, and Ecstasy" section of his "Notes on Language and Style"; art does not copy "the beauty in nature: beauty does not exist by itself in nature, waiting to be copied" (1936:97). Consider beauty as a mark of approbation in the following remarks by Pound: "Vorticism means that one is interested in the creative faculty as opposed to the mimetic. . . . It is only by applying a particular and suitable force that you can bring order and vitality and thence beauty into a plate of iron filings, which are otherwise as 'ugly' as anything under heaven" (1915b: 277–278). After all, as Pound had declared in 1913, "tradition is a beauty which we preserve and not a set of fetters to bind us" (*LEEP* 91). Beauty had become a quintessential measure of technical mastery, not a description of subject matter or an "archaic" fidelity to representational realism (Hulme 1936:84). Hence Pound's praise for Rodin's *La Vielle Heaulmière:* "the 'beauty' of the work depends in no appreciable degree on the subject, which is 'hideous.' The 'beauty' is from Rodin. It is in the composition, as I remember it; in silhouettes" (1916:98). (Intertextual gestures to Symons's *Studies in Seven Arts* are noteworthy.) The site of beauty has been displaced from the object to the mind of the artist and the informed viewer—as Lewis boasted in *BLAST* 1, "Intrinsic beauty is in the Interpreter and Seer, not in the object or content" (7). Or, as Pater observed first in the "Preface" to *The Renaissance,* "What is this song or . . . book, to *me?* What effect does it really produce on me?" (*TR* xix-xx).

Hulme once drolly observed that the "lexicon of the beautiful is elastic" (1955:98). In male modernist culture, beauty was privileged as a "category of appreciation," to borrow Eliot's phrase (*UPUC* 109), invoked to link the accomplishments of contemporary art—and its burdensome but imperative presentation of ugliness—with previous aesthetic achievements. Talk of beauty connected them with the past; a commitment to ugliness made them distinct, avant-garde, perfectly poised for the serious work of *épater le bourgeois.* (That it also purchased significant "symbolic capital" is discussed below.) Objectivist aesthetic theories, and productions of selective predecessors, had been decried and dismantled, but the moderns were quick to construct new criteria, to restabilize the significance of aesthetic judgment itself. As a consequence, their writings seem unimpeachably to demonstrate Terry Eagleton's contention that,

> The aesthetic is thus the wan hope, in an increasingly rationalized, secularized, demythologized environment, that ultimate purpose and meaning may not be entirely lost. It is the mode of religious transcendence of a rationalistic age—the place where the apparently arbitrary, subjectivist responses which fall outside the scope of such rationalism may now be moved to the centre and granted all the dignity of an eidetic form. That which is purely residual to bourgeois rationality, the *je ne sais quoi* of taste, now comes to figure as nothing less than a parodic image of such thought, a caricature of rational law. (1990a:88)

Breaking Up Is Hard to Do

Pound's accolades for Whistler in 1912 include the fact that he "tried and pried/ And stretched and tampered with the media" (*Per* 243). When Eliot praises Yeats in his 1940 tribute lecture, he cites "the violent and terrible epistle dedicatory of *Responsibilities*" (*OPP* 256). The first issue of *BLAST* promises to be "an avenue for all those vivid and violent ideas that could reach the Public in no other way" (*BLAST* 1:1). There is a great deal of exuberance in modernist discourse—an unmistakable energy and combative enthusiasm, a willingness to be and to cause "a disturbance" (Pound 1920b:168).[47] Pound and Lewis playfully acknowledge this in their correspondence: Pound would write to "WynDAM" and the latter, to "Ez-*roar*" or "Ezroar" (*P/L* 126, 171, 201). But there is also a disturbing refrain of "brutality": not just predictably in postwar texts, but repeatedly in the texts of 1908 to 1914. In 1912, Ezra Pound also said that his goal was "saving the public's soul by punching its face" (*LEP* 58), perhaps echoing the third tenet of the Futurists' manifesto: "We intend to exalt aggressive action . . . the punch and the slap" (Marinetti 41).[48] "Let it be an authentic earthquake!!!" Lewis advises Augustus John in 1914, jesting that he should have been born on a "volcanic island . . . the sort of place where aesthetic structures have a slight shake-up every day and are periodically swallowed up altogether" (*LWL* 64). The "more expansive" male, Pound informs Marianne Moore, should not be "discredit[ed] for 'taking up cudgels'"—just the opposite (Scott ed. 362). Eliot preferred biblical weapons, however metaphorically: he instructs Schofield Thayer (editor of the *Dial*) to "be to the inhabitants of Greenwich Village a flail, and to the Intellect of Indianapolis a Scourge" (*LE* 1:236). The first issue of *BLAST* boasts that it "sets out to be an avenue for all those vivid and violent ideas that could reach the Public no other way"

("Long Live the Vortex!" 7). (Vorticism, Lewis subsequently summarized, is "a violent central activity attracting everything to itself, absorbing all that is around it into a violent whirling—a violent central engulfing" [*CH* 378].) Lewis later praises Pound for having been "a tireless agitator. A most healthy destructive force" (*BB* 285).[49] Eliot disparages the Georgian poets because they "caress everything they touch" (Julian Symons 19); the modernists preferred to slap and explode. Just as the pointillist Georges Seurat refers to his canvases as "'toiles de lutte'" or canvases of combat, and speaks of "'toiles de recherches et si possible de conquête [research canvases, conquests if possible]'" (R. Herbert 5), so the Men of 1914 produced combative poems, essays, fictions, and manifestos determined to contest and remake aesthetic values and at the same time discipline readers to behave and appreciate differently. Violence begets violence, as Lewis imagines the contemporary cultural scene: "all true *revolution*," all "radical change must depend, for its birth and fulfillment, upon the existence of leadership" of singular men who have "invaluable and mysterious gifts," but "these 'individuals' we are taught to mistrust and hate, to hobble, clip, hunt, and wipe out" (*DPDS* 130).

As Levenson acutely observes, "So much of the story that these figures told themselves was a tale of tyranny and resistance. The name of the tyrant changed—the Editor, the Lady, the Public, the Democrat—but whatever the scenario, the narrowness of the oppressor was seen amply to justify the violence of the art" (1999:2). One needs to consider Moon's suggestion, however, that not all forms of violence are "expressive of a general masculine consciousness"—certain "forms of masculinity are constructed 'with a door open' toward violence" (195, 197). By approaching the problem structurally, he observes, one finds that "the notion of patriarchal power, patriarchal violence, is potentially more useful than the notion of 'masculine' violence. The former designates a structure in which gender and power are systematically linked, and which gives rise to forms of consciousness, and to ideologies; whereas the latter implies power's obedience to consciousness" (Moon 201). For the Men of 1914, the ability to imagine, hope for, and instigate violence, rhetorical or otherwise, was certainly a "prerogative" of the patriarchal power they enjoyed and enjoined.

"One of the main achievements of the nineteenth century was the elaboration and universal application of the principle of continuity," Hulme observes; "[t]he destruction of this conception is, on the contrary, an urgent necessity of the present" (1936:3). Pound approvingly defines the Wagnerian "aesthetic ideal" in these terms: "'you confuse the spectator by smacking as many of his senses as possible at every possible moment'" (1924:321). Later in the same essay he praises new, difficult modes of art as "a scaling of eyeballs, a castigating or purging of aural cortices; a sharpening of verbal apperceptions. It is by no means an emollient" (Pound 1924:322). Lewis fears that the advances of emetic cultural productions will be reversed by the "swarming 'intellectualist' and artistic tribe of sub-supermen": "So often what Art has produced in order *to purge*," he laments, "has come into the hands finally of people who wish not to 'purge,' but to poison and murder" (*DPDS* 94).[50] I concur with Mao that Lewis writes "with all the fury of apostasy" (97); the texts "of the late twenties and the thirties regarded as a whole . . . [place] the accent more firmly on crushing than on the resistance" (95). In 1931, the former artillery specialist refers to his typewriter as a "*Corona* rattling away like a machine-gun" (*DPDS* viii); his comrade-in-letters Pound entreats in "Redondillas, or Something of that sort" (a poem withdrawn from *Canzoni*), "We speak to a surfeited age, / Grant us keen weapons for speaking" (*P/EP* 217). As Pound later recounts in one of his last letters to Lewis (February 1957), "Still think you'd have saved time if yu had plugged for a milder philosophy, BUT it might hv/ taken bump out of style where bump was needed, and HOW" (*P/L* 302). As McDonald observes, "disdain" may have been Eliot's "characteristic tone," but "rage" was Pound's (110). "'You let *me* throw the bricks through the front window,'" Pound allegedly advised his friend, "'You go in the back door and take the swag'" (qtd H. Carpenter 264).

Common to the texts of Lewis, Hulme, Pound, and Eliot is the desire to "break"[51]—to "break-up" the "Renaissance humanistic attitude" (Hulme 1936:78, 79), to "break away" from conventional attitudes and artistic techniques (1936:93). As Lewis advises in *Code of a Herdsman:* "In order to live, you must remain broken up" (1917:7). It is entirely "necessary to break moulds and make new ones," Hulme insists in "Bergson's Theory of Art": "[in each era we find that] a certain individual artist was able to break through through the conventional ways of looking at things which veil reality from us at a certain point" (1936:150). The "heap of broken images" littering *The Waste Land* is the tangible result of a violent aesthetic famously summarized in "The Metaphysical Poets": the "poet must become more and more comprehensive," Eliot argues, "more allusive, more indirect, in order *to force, to dislocate* if necessary, language into his meaning" (*SE* 249; emphasis added). The passage uncannily echoes Hulme's assessment of the artist's efforts "when he tries to express the individual thing which he has seen. He finds then that not only has his mind habits, but that language, or whatever medium of expression he employs, also has its fixed ways. It is only by a certain tension of mind that he is able to force the mechanism of expression out of the way in which it tends to go and into the way he wants" (1936:160). Hulme's art criticism articulates a complementary process: in the new "angular" and "geometrical" art, he advises, "the human body . . . is often entirely non-vital, and distorted to fit into stiff and cubical shapes" (1936:82); Cézanne is especially skilled in producing compositions in which "all the lines are ranged in a pyramidal shape, and the women are distorted to fit this shape" (1936:101).

"Forms have to be broken and remade," Eliot later summarizes in "The Music of Poetry" (*OPP* 37). For these modernist poets and essayists, the necessary breakage of forms includes an all-out assault on normative poetic discourse, especially the hegemony of iambic pentameter.[52] As Pound likes to recall in Canto 81, "(To break the pentameter, that was the first heave)" (*Can LXXXI/* 518). Within the modernists' "ugliness projects," vers libre is axiomatic. Poised between Books I and II of Williams's *Paterson* is a poetic credo disguised as a quote from John Addington Symond's *Studies of the Greek Poets,* which explains how Hipponax, "to bring the meter still more within the sphere of prose and common speech," was able to do "the utmost violence to the rhythmical structure" of his texts by ending his iambic lines with "a spondee or a trochee. . . . These deformed and mutilated verses . . . communicated a curious crustiness to the style," a metrical pattern well-suited to the "snarling spirit of the satirist" (*Pat* 53). What worked for Hipponax certainly inspired the man who insists the "free verse" is "the ONE verse form that embodies the quality of thought which can be designated as modern. And it is only the modern which is worth expressing" (W. C. Williams 1919:30). Literally, figuratively, and typographically, vers libre makes possible a poetry of radical de-composition and dislocation. When one compares the free verse of Rimbaud and Laforgue (especially in *Derniers Vers*) with that of *The Waste Land* and the *Cantos,* the English-language texts seem technically hyperbolic. Like the sylvan Philomel resurrected in *The Waste Land,* verse has been mutilated, "rudely forc'd" (*CPP* 64). Theory and praxis are consubstantial. By disfiguring and destabilizing poetic discourse, modernist free verse becomes truly performative.[53] It also reaches the limits of articulation. As Randall Jarrell observes in 1942, "How can poems be written that are more violent, more disorganized more obscure, more—supply your own adjective—than those that have already been written?" (81).

The literary modernists' insistence on fragmented, multilated forms complements the methods and critical arguments advanced by European visual artists a generation before. As Nochlin explicates, the "theme of the body in pieces or the fragment as a metaphor of modernity" (1994a:37) dominated aesthetic theories and practices. In the late eighteenth century, French visual artists introduced "a distinctly *modern* view of antiquity-as-loss, a view, a 'crop,' that will constitute the essence of representational modernism" (Nochlin 1994a:8). Subsequently, "[f]ragmentation, mutilation, and destruction might be said to be the founding tropes of the visual rhetoric" of Manet, Monet, Cézanne, and Pissarro (Nochlin 1994a:9). In their cityscapes she discerns a shared "sense of things falling apart, fragmented by revealed brushwork"; linking the paintings with other discourses, she identifies the "social, psychological, even metaphysical fragmentation that so seems to mark modern experience—a loss of wholeness, a shattering of connection, a destruction or disintegration of permanent value" (Nochlin 1994a:26, 24). Importantly, however, she also perceives an antithetical response that has its counterpart in literary modernism. It is "by no means possible to assert that modernity may *only* be associated with, or suggested by, a metaphoric or actual fragmentation," Nochlin asserts;

> On the contrary, paradoxically, or dialectically, modern artists have moved toward its opposite, with a will to totalization embodied in the notion of the *Gesamatkunstwerk,* the struggle to overcome the disintegrative effects—social, psychic, political—inscribed in modern, particularly modern urban, experience, by hypostatizing them within a higher unity. One might, from this point of view, maintain that modernity is indeed marked by the will toward totalization as much as it is metaphorized by the fragment. (1994a:53)

Ugliness, I would argue, is one such totalizing, compensatory schema; it partakes of the Absolute so desperately sought, in disparate ways, by Hulme, Pound, Lewis, and Eliot.

Although violence against female figures is also a staple of modernist texts, the rape fetish of male modernists has received little critical attention. In Lewis's *Tarr* (1918), the rape of Bertha by Kreisler is presented as the just desserts of "an erotic object who can only distract and degrade the artist" (V. Parker 215). After all, the novel claims, a woman is "a lower form of life" (*Tarr* 334); hence the "violence" of the assault is dismissed as a "loathsome, senseless event, of no meaning" to Bertha, much less Kreisler (*Tarr* 195). To quote Scott, "Lewis adjusts the point of view so that we experience the whirlpool off-center, in a violent, chaotic juxtaposition of images that denies connections in time, personal identity, or male responsibility" (1:106).[54] *The Waste Land* is obsessed with "the change of Philomel" (*CPP* 64), but the speaker protects himself from the reality of the event by aestheticizing it through indirect phrases and metaphors; rather than specifying that the mythical Philomel was sexually violated by her brother-in-law and then mutilated, the reader is merely told she was "so rudely forced" by "the barbarous king" (*CPP* 64). As weaver of the telling tapestry and then as nightingale of "inviolable voice," Philomel transforms her suffering into art, but the reader should resist any facile consolations.

Ironically enough, by "absorbing" violence into sexuality (Carroll 148) in "Leda and the Swan," giving "canonical authority to a particular kind of experience of subjectivity and social power" (Pollock 1999:103), Yeats most emphatically stakes his claim for belonging in the annals of male modernism. "Leda and the Swan" has prompted diverse critical interpretations, from the most misogynistic (Levine's suggestion that the poem reveals Leda to be the aggressor, not the victim [114–119]) to the feminist determination that the poem is pornographic (Cullingford 152). Cullingford partially defends the poem in terms of its textual history, reading it as a political protest: reacting in "horror" to the new puritanism of the Irish Free State that gave "Catholic moral standards the backing of the State," Yeats revised and published the poem "to arouse controversy and flout censorship" (142). Yeats himself informs readers that the more he worked on the poem, "bird and lady took such possession of the scene that all politics went out of it" (1966:828). One would like to explain to Yeats that the "political" actually extends to the utter objectification, disempowerment, and violation of female figures. Said, who persuasively presents Yeats as a "poet of decolonization" (84), states that the violence of "Leda and the Swan" is in some sense "necessary" (90–91); regrettably, gender norms and presumptions, and their culturally damaging implications, are not considered. I would argue against the convention of using rape as the best possible trope to represent the relationship between oppressor and oppressed, or to express abject liminality— each reinscription of a rape scene unwittingly serves to perpetuate its normativity. To paraphrase Carroll's study of Rubens's *Rape of the Daughters of Leucippus,* in "claiming something like a truth value" for the poem's "celebratory depiction" of rape, both truth and "what is natural in human sexuality" are mystified (140).

It could be argued that in William Carlos Williams's *Paterson,* episodic violence against women is staged to consolidate the "verisimilitude" (*Pat* 74) of the long poem: documenting the "legs, scarred (as a child)/ by the whip," the "busted nose" that "all / desired women have had each / in the end," the farm wife whose husband "broke" her "cancerous jaw because she was too weak, too sick, that is, to / work in the fields for him" (*Pat* 152, 153, 168) allows the central speaker to diagnose the diseased state of male-female relations. But the juxtaposition of "senseless rapes—caught on hands and knees / scrubbing a greasy corridor; the blood / boiling as though in a vat" with the "forthright beauty" of "Plaster saints, glass jewels," their "tranquility and loveliness," in Book I of *Paterson* (*Pat* 51), belittles the victims as it protects the perpetrators. Williams privileges the quotidian or antidream world, Yeats, the mythic and "high dream" realm, but both are "caught" up in fantasies of domination that are degrading to women *and* men.

A Liberatory Aesthetic?

This chapter has demonstrated the extent to which a "thwarted desire for beauty" (*LEEP* 415) motivated and informed modernist aesthetic ideology and discourse. The beautiful was still functional as a superlative expression of value, but always employed in radical juxtaposition to the ugliness believed to be inherent in the material conditions of the world, the artist, or the artifact (whether plastic or verbal). Exposing the "realler" truths of modernity, however, was only part of their self-constructed mandate. More profoundly, the cult of ugliness was a daring critique of judgment itself: it signified a complexly-coded matrix of ideologically-determined aesthetic and personal values, ones which assailed foundational notions of art as social knowledge, cultural criticism, and as a vehicle for transcendent emotional and spiritual experiences.

By referring to the pre- and post–World War I writings of Hulme, Pound, Lewis, and Eliot, I have underscored the fact that theirs was very much a pre-war ideological formation; the slaughter and destruction of World War I intensified their commitment to a cult of ugliness, but did not, in the first instance, inspire or shape its discourse. Lewis stresses this point in an April 1919 essay, "What Art Now?": "The war has not changed our industrial society," he observes, "or the appearance of our world; nor has it made men desire different things, only possibly the same things harder still. . . . The innovations in painting, pressed everywhere before the war, have by their violence and completeness exhausted the scope of progress on that point" (*CH* 46). Pound is equally adamant that the war had only and thoroughly proved that the new truths of "ugliness" had to be told: "if Armageddon has taught us anything," he writes in May 1918, "it should have taught us to abominate the half-truth, and the tellers of the half-truth in literature" (*LEEP* 415).

"Regarding this pother about the Greeks," Pound advises in 1914, "Some few of us are at last liberated from the idea that 'THE BEAUTIFUL' is the caressable, the physically attractive. Art is not particularly concerned with the caressable" (Zinnes ed. 185). But what kind of liberation had they constructed, this selective "few"? Certainly they were free to diagnose the horrors of the world as they found them, to salute the most productive artistic diagnosticians, in the most "uncompromising" terms (*BLAST* 1:148). After all, Baudelaire had taught them to boast: "As you see, we are now in the hospital of painting. We are probing its sores and its sicknesses; and this is by no means among the least strange or contagious of them" (1965:96). In the process of cultivating their "diagnostic" skills, however, they constructed and disseminated an aesthetic of impoverished essentials. "It is essential to prove that beauty may be in small, dry things," Hulme insists (1936:131); his review of the London Group showing of 1914 can only praise "the beauty of banal forms" (1955:131). Taken together, the cultists champion a poetry of "discouragingly 'unpoetic' modern surroundings" (*LE* 1:101); produce prose works that are "not merely a depiction of the sordid . . . [but the] swift alternation of subjective beauty and external shabbiness, squalor, and sordidness" (*LEEP* 412); exhibit and praise paintings and sculptures that give expression to "the hard, the cold, the mechanical, the static" (Lewis 1935: 17). New standards of aesthetic legitimation and appreciation are created, but the rules and the rulemakers justify, vociferously, "the 'inhumanity,' the 'abstractness,' the 'ugliness' of extreme contemporary art" (*CH* 247). As Foucault observes in *The Order of Things,* during and since the nineteenth century

> literature becomes progressively more differentiated from the discourse of ideas, and encloses itself within a radical intransitivity; it becomes detached from all the values that were able to keep it in general circulation during the Classical age (taste, pleasure, naturalness, truth), and creates within its own space everything that will ensure a ludic denial of them (the scandalous, the ugly, the impossible). (1973:300)

Denying or radically redefining beauty's once-traditional place in the Platonic triad was the most productive means of combatting (if not eliminating) a "bad metaphysical aesthetic" (Hulme 1936:131).[55] But it served other purposes, other gender-defined cultural imperatives, as well. As citations throughout the chapter have indicated, the poems, essays, and tracts produced by the self-constructed "brethren" of the new reinscribed traditional misogynistic prejudices and articulated fresh anxieties concerning the roles women could or might want to play in the production and social reception of art. That is why Lewis, replying to Pound in 1916, defended his practices of coloration by blasting "the stupidity" of English taste "most crudely displayed in red pillar boxes, soldier's vermillion coats, and the cold bright dashes of colour females choose" (*P/L* 47). Lewis also worried in print whether "the word 'modern'" would be fatally traduced by association with "such clichés as 'Miss Modern' or 'a modern girl'" (*WLA* 20); Hulme ranked "emancipated women" among the "spectacled anaemics" responsible for the "cinders" of contemporary life (1936:242). Pound applauded the virile mode of writing that was only possible "whenever poetry emerges from the lavender sachet and bric-à-brac category" (1960:237). Perhaps only Lewis would state publically, categorically that

> To-day it is the dregs of the female nature, all that is stupidest in the mere *being a woman,* that is stimulated, and allowed to triumph (to force our society into a rapider disintegration): it is the dregs in everything whatever that is encouraged (male or other) as our democracies become more and more enfeebled: and, with the female, emotion is nearer the surface—that is all that is meant by "feminine" (*DY* 245)

—but Eliot's "Hysteria" and *The Waste Land,* Pound's "Portrait d'une Femme" and "Hugh Selwyn Mauberley," Hulme's "Cinders" and "Romanticism and Classicism," share a similar subtext. Hence the need not only to decry "prettiness" but to promote an aesthetic that eludes the trap of the physically beautiful woman as object of desire and embodiment of perfection. Constituted initially as a response to a "conscious and clamorous modernity" (*CH* 29), a cult of ugliness also afforded the means to liberate aesthetic discourse from all things even remotely female, feminine, and womanly. This shift from premodern to modernist sensibilities is dramatized in Ezra Pound's often overlooked poem, "The Study in Aesthetics":

> The very small children in patched clothing,
> Being smitten with an unusual wisdom,
> Stopped in their play as she passed them
> And cried up from their cobbles:
> > *Guarda! Ahi, guarda! ch'è be'a* [*bella*]!
>
> But three years after this
> I heard the young Dante, whose last name I do not know—
> For there are, in Sirmione, twenty-eight young
> Dantes and thirty-four Catulli;
> And there had been a great catch of sardines,
> And his elders
> Were packing them in the great wooden boxes
> For the market in Brescia, and he
> Leapt about, snatching at the bright fish
> And getting in both of their ways;
> And in vain they commanded him to *sta fermo!*
> And when they would not let him arrange
> The fish in boxes
> He stroked those which were already arranged,
> Murmuring for his own satisfaction
> This identical phrase:
> > *Ch'è be'a.*
>
> And at this I was mildly abashed.

(Per 96–97)

Why is Pound's speaker confounded by the boy's utterance? Because previously, the contemplation of what is "bella" could only be imagined and articulated in terms of a woman's physical appearance; aesthetic discourse was little more than beauty-watching and reporting, hopelessly contingent upon female figurations. But "the young Dante" is animated by a different order of aesthetic pleasures: arranging shapes and colors, composing the scene, and appreciating the extraordinary sights to be found within quotidian reality. Who would prefer fish to "she"? Only those who believed that "the business of the poet was to make poetry out of the unexplored resources of the unpoetical; that the poet, in fact, was committed by his profession to turn the unpoetical into poetry" (*TCC* 126). Only the immature and unschooled, the "very small," stop short for mere feminine beauty; the rare Dantes find "greatness" among the mundane, discerning what is truly "bright." And all of this for one's own "satisfaction"—a state of gratification desired by Pound and Hulme—a different "desire and mental need" (Hulme 1936:84). The piscine allusion to Christ and his disciples might seem a little strained, but what a fitting intertextual gesture for an exercise in cultist didacticism. As Pollock observes, "The canon is held in place by the power of the stories it tells about artists. These mythologies are not all the same. Some call upon images of personal suffering that have an almost religious aura; others stress a secular, overtly sexual character. Both the sacrificial and the virile are elements of a construction of modernist masculinity" (1999:39).

Nothing Short of "Consecration"

The lessons to be learned by considering the social production of art were first sketched in the Introduction. At this point, working more specifically, I would like to recast the discussion of the cult of ugliness in terms of market consciousness, dominant power relations, and the opposition between "consecrated art and avant-garde art, or between orthodoxy and heresy" (Bourdieu 1986:139). One of Bourdieu's most influential contributions to the study of twentieth-century culture has been his analysis of art's "symbolic capital" and the "system of symbolic distinctions between groups" (1986:160–161); he challenges one to reconsider "what 'makes reputations'" in the cultural field, and the relations of power among established artists, newcomers, critics, publishers, and anyone else who participates in the production, sale, and reception of art. Competition and success within the cultural marketplace becomes a less romanticized but more coherently understood phenomenon if one considers the dialogue and tensions among the established figures who dominate "the field of production and the market through the economic and symbolic capital they have been able to accumulate"—and therefore have the power to confer status upon or "consecrate" new works and artists—and the "newcomers," heretical or avant-garde figures who compete with both the establishment and with "other newcomers with whom they vie in novelty" (Bourdieu 1986:139).

As interpreted and furthered by Jensen in the visual arts and by Lyon and Dettmar and Watt, for example, in literary studies, Bourdieu's insights have led to an ongoing reconfiguration of the institutions and individuals who promoted, resisted, and furthered modernism in the cultural marketplace.[56] In this context, one realizes that the work of Lewis, Pound, Eliot, and Hulme to champion "ugliness" and claim allegiance to a privileged cult or coterie was all part of the struggle to create "a new position" in the literary field, to "introduce *distinctive marks*" in a world

> in which the only way to *be* is to be *different*, to "make one's name," either personally or as a group. The names of schools or groups which have proliferated . . . are pseudo-concepts, *practical* classifying tools which create resemblances and differences by naming them; they are produced in the *struggle for recognition* by the artists themselves or their accredited critics and function as *emblems* which distinguish galleries, groups and artists and therefore the products they make or sell. (Bourdieu 1986:159)

Pound and Lewis were especially savvy in terms of calculated, emboldened public gestures, naming or "branding" their work, and judiciously including a select few in their struggle for recognition. Marinetti's theatrical, headline-grabbing appearances in London were particular spurs, ones that sharpened their rhetoric and taught them the value of fashioning manifestos that would "polarize rather than negotiate" readership (Lyon 1991:102). Pound made his start in London dressing like Whistler; quickly he learned to capitalize on the Combative Expatriate's subject position. Lewis was comfortably at odds as the Enemy. Hulme was an important instigator, decrying romanticism, adapting Bergson, all in an attempt to name and be part of a new aesthetic domain. Eliot, always canny, was as connected as he had to be. Diepeveen suggests that Eliot was "socially and aesthetically aloof," and did not "belong to a single set of writers" (39). He was not antagonistic in the same obvious ways as Lewis and Pound, but, as the many citations of this chapter have demonstrated, the articulation and dissemination of cultist principles would not have been the same without him. As McDonald observes, "Eliot was the more skilful at managing his image; Pound sometimes seemed wilfully to mismanage his" (63).

Two related elements of Bourdieu's argument, the "capital of consecration" and the "'charisma' ideology," are especially apposite in relation to the major figures cited in this study. Ruskin led the way, I would argue, in positioning the aesthetic and literary critic as he who "consecrates," someone who, having made "a name for [himself], a known, recognized name," enjoys and expends "a capital of consecration implying a power to consecrate objects . . . or persons" (Bourdieu 1986:132). Ruskin would not have recognized himself as someone who "*consecrates* a product which he has 'discovered'" and "exploits the labour of the 'creator'" (Bourdieu 1986:133), but his work on behalf of Turner and the Pre-Raphaelites, and *against* Whistler, was just that. "Above all," Bourdieu remarks, this person "'invests his prestige' in the author's [or artist's] cause, acting as a 'symbolic banker' who offers as security all of the symbolic capital he has accumulated" (1986:133). Ruskin, in fact, began accumulating capital as he shaped his defense of Turner in *Modern Painters*. His subsequent investment in the Pre-Raphaelites assured them a more judicious evaluation (and better sales) in the Victorian art arena. Whistler, on the other hand, was a painter in whom Ruskin refused to invest. To continue the metaphor, his "pot of paint" accusation declared Whistler and his canvases to be aesthetically and morally bankrupt. Whistler, for his part, believed in nothing so much as the "'charisma' ideology" or "ideology of the creation, which makes the [artist or] author the first and last source of the value of his work" (Bourdieu 1986:133). Consequently he was tireless in his efforts to condemn any person or institution that dared to pass an independent judgment. Retrospectively, one realizes that Whistler was a skilled operative in the field of cultural commodities, someone who, to borrow Gendron's phrase, "significantly expanded the scope of aesthetic production beyond the primary work" (6–7) to include exquisitely planned exhibitions, newspaper commentaries, *very* public rows (with patrons, peers, editors), and activities within an established art organization (the Society of British Artists) guaranteed to bring additional attention to his own aesthetic enterprises.[57] Fiercely believing in his talent, Whistler wanted fame, financial success, and proof that his works were highly valued as cultural commodities by having them purchased by and hung in the most important galleries and museums. The litigious debate over the "worth" of his paintings highlights the impossible bind to which he and Ruskin were committed: only those works of art deemed the most "sacred" command the highest prices, yet the monetary considerations despoil the illusions of a sacrosanct icon or artifact.[58]

Lewis and Eliot especially refused to "consecrate" Pater's writings because of their antipathy to his "trademark" decadence and their abhorrence of his homosexual reputation. The mission of their disparaging remarks and negative assessments was to withdraw Pater's works from circulation, to render him null and void as a cultural figure. In effect, they resorted to the same moralistic critical practices of Ruskin or Matthew Arnold before them: they assumed that the work must be unworthy if the individual who created it is suspect, and presumed to decide who and what is morally sanctionable. By the 1920s, Lewis was a more marginal figure in the modernist cultural marketplace. Eliot, on the other hand, was moving from strength to strength. The acclaimed (or at least, notorious) poet of *The Waste Land* also profited greatly from his growing reputation as a critic; editorial direction of the *Criterion* from 1922 to 1939, his work at Faber from the mid-1920s until the 1960s, and his second creative career as a playwright furthered his powerful, multifaceted position within the field of Anglo-American letters and encouraged untold readers, critics, audiences, and cultural producers to invest in his authority. Only when one returns to his writings from 1910 to the

1930s and places them alongside those of Hulme, Lewis, and Pound does one realize the Eliot was as much a cultist as they were, just as committed to the development of artistic charisma and devoted to consecrating as *the* modernist experience the "contemplation of the horrid or sordid or disgusting" (*SW* 169).

Common to all of these aesthetic practices and productions was an unswerving belief in the special individual's ability to know and articulate the truth—about art, about life, about the inadequacy of conventional beauty in a modernized world. Almost all women were excluded from this elite, self-determined group, which peppered its aesthetic, cultural, and social commentaries, its "consecrated" writings, with antifeminist truisms. Yet the gender politics of their utterances and activities were as unexamined as they were adamant—and remained so until the 1980s.

Chapter 4 ∿

"O City City":
Gendered Topographies
in Modern American Poetry

The city is, properly speaking, more poetic even than a countryside, for while nature is a chaos of unconscious forces, a city is a chaos of conscious ones. . . . [T]here is no stone in the street and no brick in the wall that is not actually a deliberate symbol—a message from some man, as much as if it were a telegram or a post card. The narrowest street possesses, in every crook and twist of its intention, the soul of the man who built it, perhaps long in his grave. Every brick has as human a hieroglyph as if it were a graven brick of Babylon[.]

—G. K. Chesterton, "A Defence of Detective Stories"

We cannot comprehend political and economic history at all unless we realize the city, with its gradual detachment from and final bankrupting of the country, is the determinative form to which the course and sense of higher history generally conforms. *World history is city history.*

—Oswald Spengler, *The Decline of the West*

The city has its cunning wiles, no less than the infinitely smaller and more human tempter. There are large forces which allure with all the soulfulness of expression possible in the most cultured human. The gleam of a thousand lights is often as effective as the persuasive light in a wooing and fascinating eye.

—Theodore Dreiser, *Sister Carrie*

A "complex and interactive network" of relations, the city links together "a number of disparate social activities, processes, and relations, with a number of imaginary and real, projected or actual architectural, geographic, civic, and public relations. The city brings together economic and informational flows, power networks, forms of displacement, management, and political organization, interpersonal, familial, and extra-familial social relations, and an aesthetic/economic organization of space and place to create a semipermanent but ever-changing built environment or milieu" (Grosz 244). It is almost axiomatic that a study of "modern" literature, whether American, British, Anglo-American, or international, will pause to consider "the city as the privileged locus or image for modernism" (Blanchard 24).[1] As Heller observes, "by the nineteenth century, the city had firmly become the central mental environment of Western if not of nearly all culture, . . . in literature and poetry, even of the most pastoral or nature-inspired, the city is a presence, a foil, an entity to resist" (87). Similarly and more searchingly, Pollock has argued that modernity, "a product of the city," is

a response in a mythic or ideological form to the new complexities of a social existence passed amongst strangers in an atmosphere of intensified nervous and psychic stimulation, in a world ruled by money and commodity exchange, stressed by competition and formative of an intensified individuality, publicly defended by a blasé mask of indifference but intensely "expressed" in a private, familial context. Modernity stands for a myriad of responses to the vast increase in population leading to the literature of the crowds and masses, a speeding up of the pace of life. . . . [C]entres of cities such as Paris and London become key sites of consumption and display producing what Sennett has labelled the spectacular city. (1988:66)

Within each city text, however, one must consider whether or not the "unacknowledged but presumed" spectator is masculine (Pollock 1988:75), and the extent to which female figures function as the ultimate urban spectacle. The following discussion will assess such strategies of representation—what Linda Nochlin terms the "construction of the perceivable" (1994a:75)—in the works of Eliot, Pound, William Carlos Williams, Carl Sandburg, and several other poets. But agreeing that "space is, after all, a form of representation" (Colomina vii), and insisting that one must consider "the problems of historicizing particular spatial practices" (M. Morris 3), this chapter goes two crucial steps further by factoring both gender and race into the argument. The city texts of Langston Hughes will be presented to suggest that African American male speakers can find a nurturing community and confirm human dignity in urban environments—under specific conditions. The ways in which poets such as H. D., Edna St. Vincent Millay, and Elinor Wylie *resisted* the city as predominant topos for their texts will be examined, and their works correlated with those of Helene Johnson and Angelina Weld Grimké. With major critical consequences, modern women's poetry typically focused on the exploration of "wild" and affirmative natural spaces.

Comparing the overwhelming presence of urban tropes in texts by male writers and the relative absence of metropolitan sites in texts by female writers will not only reorganize one's understanding of early-twentieth-century poetic discourse, but call attention to the presumptions and prejudices of various canon-makers. A poet's refusal to engage with cityscapes, most commonly construed as a *lack* of engagement, made it even easier for critics to marginalize or completely overlook her work.

Typically, white male poets flourish in oppositional environments. They write of the city, but against the urban locus; the latter is the site of alienation, angst, aggression, and ennui. City texts, under these conditions, revel in the negative: they are poetic devotions to and for the cult of ugliness.[2] For African Americans, however, who associate fields with slave labor and the scent of southern pine trees with sexual exploitation, the city provides differently. Female poets, on the other hand, black and white, favor complementary environments. They write themselves into nonurban locii, natural landscapes that allow for a range of responses. Nature texts, for the women, become strategies of resistance: they resist the city because they refuse to be engaged with a locus that is inherently life- and self-denying. It falls to readers, however, to determine whether these natural landscapes unwittingly furthered the tradition of representing women as being "apart from men, controlled by nature rather than in control of it" (Duncan 94). As anthropologist Sherry Ortner and many others have demonstrated, patriarchy has thrived by identifying women with nature, and men, oppositionally, with culture—a hierarchical binary that underscores myriad oppressive structures and institutions.

Stone Deserts and Semantic Fields

To ruminate about city texts and textual cities is to confront some of Western culture's most basic assumptions, accomplishments, and catastrophes. For instead of coming to terms with one "normative city meta-narrative," one learns about the city as both "the physical embodiment of the Utopian community" (Preston and Simpson-Housley 8, 2) and "the tradition, all but co-extensive with culture itself, which looks upon the city as inherently suspect" (Howe 40). "Utopia," "Vanity Fair," "Babylon Revisited," "Apocalypse Now"; market, theatrical spectacle, labyrinth, prison: the city as lived experience and cultural emblem is undoubtedly a polyvalent signifier.[3] Raymond Williams has taught us to rethink the Town and Country dichotomy as a fiction that "promote[s] superficial comparisons" and "prevent[s] real ones," namely those of economic and power relations (1973:54). Writers from Virgil to Virginia Woolf have asked us to consider whether the necessity of building and living within cities is a human imperative or a gendered burden. Some have imagined a "Just City" on earth; many others have imputed to an actual place the mythic dimensions of the "Trivial Unhappy Unjust City" (Auden, *The Enchaféd Flood)* or what Rilke's "Tenth Duino Elegy" terms "Pain City."[4]

In the nineteenth century, European urban centers like Vienna and Paris were being vigorously (and for many, traumatically) redeveloped;[5] the population of London grew from 1,335,000 in 1825 to 6,480,000 in 1900 (Sutcliffe 7), and the city was overwhelmed by "the raw facts of poverty, poor housing, and social malaise in the congested metropolis of the first industrial revolution" (P. Hall 19).[6] American cities such as New York, Philadelphia, and Chicago were experiencing unprecedented population growth due to European and Russian immigration and the northern exodus of African Americans. The population of New York, for example, was reported at 1,700,000 in 1825; one hundred years later, 7,774,000 people had a New York address. At that time, it was the most populated city in the world (Paris had approximately 4,800,000 people in 1925; Berlin, 4,013,000) (Sutcliffe 7). Concomitant crises in housing, employment, mass transit, and ethnic relations ensued. The town became a city and then a metropolis; national capitols became World Cities. As historian Arthur Schlesinger summarized in 1933, people were participating in "'the momentous shift of the center of national equilibrium from the countryside to the city'" (qtd Davidson 103).

From the early nineteenth century well into the twentieth, not only did the city increasingly preoccupy creative writers as diverse as Blake, Wordsworth, Dickens, Poe, Gaskell, Gissing, and Dreiser, it emerged as *the* object of scrutiny and debate among social commentators, civic planners, and politicians (particularly in the wake of Engel's *The Condition of the Working Class in England*). Then-emerging disciplines in the social sciences were especially keen to claim the city as their primary topos, to debate, probe, praise, and lament its cultural, moral, and political dimensions. By looking briefly at the ways in which sociologist Georg Simmel and historian Oswald Spengler assessed the social and psychic "costs" of urban life in the early twentieth century, one can become familiar with the discursive terrain that poets repeatedly traversed.

Simmel knew that cities had comparatively high death rates and low birth rates; he believed that instead of providing cohesive social experiences, the city produced lives marked by isolation and gradual enervation. Secure in the wisdom of his gendered and also post-Darwinian perspective, Simmel expounded about the "metropolitan man" who had developed a "different" and more intense "consciousness" than that of his rural counterpart (48). Thus, "the metropolitan type of man—which, of course, exists in a thousand individual variants—develops an organ protecting him against the threatening currents and discrepancies of his external environment which would uproot him. He reacts with his head instead of his heart. In this an increased awareness assumes the psychic prerogative" (Simmel 48). The consequences of this new intense "intellectuality" (49) are multifold, Simmel conjectured. On the one hand, "metropolitan man" acquires an "unmerciful matter-of-factness" in his daily encounters with others; on the other hand, this "reserve" functions "in turn as the form or cloak of a more general mental phenomenon of the metropolis: it grants to the individual a kind and an amount of personal freedom which has no analogy whatsoever under other conditions" (Simmel 53). Eventually, however, because of "the *intensification of nervous stimulation*" within the city, a requisite "matter-of-factness" leads to a debilitating and chronic "blasé attitude":

> The blasé attitude [Simmel insists] results first from the rapidly changing and closely compressed contrasting stimulations of the nerves. . . . [T]hrough the rapidity and contradictoriness of their changes, more harmless impressions force such violent responses, tearing the nerves so brutally hither and thither that their last reserves of strength are spent: and if one remains in the same milieu they have no time to gather new strength. An incapacity thus emerges to react to new sensations with the appropriate energy. (Simmel 49, 51)

In the sections that follow I shall compare the ways in which some poetic texts privilege the representation of neuraesthenic figures while others find a new "strength" by identifying positively with "appropriate" but decidedly nonurban milieus.

Simmel concentrated on the new species of "man," presumed to be white, created by the metropolitan environment; Spengler made the city itself chief emblem of the historical deterioration and degeneration of the naturally agrarian Nordic "race." Volume one of *The Decline of the West* announced this theme in 1918; volume two, published in 1922, features an arresting and catastrophically-minded chapter entitled "The Soul of the City." Whereas a town "confirms" the country, in Spengler's view, the "Late City," the "gigantic megalopolis, the *city-as-world,*" actively "denies" and tries to annihilate the country (70). Spengler shares with Simmel the notion that the intellect becomes overly developed in urban dwellers: "There, separated from the power of the land—cut off from it. . . . Being comes more and more languid, sensation and reason more and more powerful. Man becomes intellect, 'free' like the nomads, whom he comes to resemble, but narrower and colder than they" (67). Yet Spengler's anthropomorphized city-soul, vividly and alternatively figured as demon, insatiable giant that "sucks the country dry"(79), and self-destructive tyrant, is also a figure of apocalyptic doom. "This, then, is the conclusion of the city's history," he predicts:

> growing from primitive barter-center to Culture-city and at last to world-city, it sacrifices first the blood and soul of its creators to the needs of its majestic

evolution, and then the last flower of that growth to the spirit of Civilization—and so, doomed, moves on to final self-destruction. . . . Finally, there
arises the monstrous symbol and vessel of the completely emancipated intellect, the world-city[.] (Spengler 85, 75)

Using imagery that suggests Ruskin's Gothic "greatness" interleaved with
Eliot's dreaded wasteland, Spengler argues that we are all both creatures and
victims of the "Final City":

> The stone Colossus "Cosmopolis" stands at the end of the life's course of every
> great Culture. The Culture-man whom the land has spiritually formed is seized
> and possessed by his own creation, the City, and is made into its creature, its
> executive organ, and finally its victim. This stony mass is the *absolute* city. . . .
> The spirit-pervaded stone of Gothic buildings, after a millennium of style-
> evolution, has become the soulless material of this demonic stone desert. (76)

More so than any speaker in Eliot's poem, Spengler shows his reader "fear in
a handful of dust" and insists that the historical process he is delineating is
fatefully inevitable. To some extent, he is also suggesting that it is deserved.
Spengler's insistence on defining the city as a moral landscape is only typical,
however. So too is his implicit suggestion that the Absolute City is, at times,
a female entity: "once the full sinful beauty of this last marvel of all history
has captured a victim," he observes, "it never lets him go" (Spengler 79).

American Ambivalence

Simmel, Spengler, and after them, Lewis Mumford, represent a European
tradition of assessment and writing that was only gradually persuaded of the
city's perniciousness.[7] For Mumford, the city is a container that is always
"bursting," exceeding itself (1938:451). In the following sections, the cities
of excess in modernist male poetry will be examined: spaces of excessive
pleasures, poverty, and danger; most especially, spaces in which excessive
femininity flourishes. As several scholars of American culture have demonstrated, the urban phenomenon has always been suspect to its writers: Jefferson's representation of the city as being "'pestilential to the morals, the
health and liberties of men'" was just the beginning of a hostile discursive
tradition (White and White 17). To cite the influential conclusions of Lucia
and Morton White,

> [America's] most celebrated thinkers have expressed different degrees of am-
> bivalence and animosity toward the city. . . . We have no persistent or perva-
> sive tradition of romantic attachment to the city in our literature or in our
> philosophy, nothing like the Greek attachment to the *polis* or the French

writer's affection for Paris. And this confirms the frequently advanced thesis that the American intellectual has been alienated from the society in which he has lived, that he has been typically in revolt against it. For while our society became more and more urban throughout the nineteenth century, the literary tendency to denigrate the city hardly declined; if anything, its intensity increased. (13–14)

More recently, Leo Marx has considered what he calls "The Puzzle of Anti-Urbanism in Classic American Literature," and concludes that "the attitude the Whites and others have mistaken for anti-urbanism is better understood as an expression of something else: a far more inclusive, if indirect and often equivocal, attitude toward the transformation of society and of culture of which the emerging industrial city is but one manifestation" (64). Although he agrees that "important" writers such as Howells, Wharton, Norris, Crane, Dreiser, Dos Passos, Wright, Baldwin, and Bellow have devoted their texts to "the actualities of urban experience in America" (66, 63), Marx—who is clearly engaged in a canon-making exercise—contends that the "classic" American writers such as "the works of the poets in the main line that leads from Emerson to Whitman, Frost, and Stevens, or in the central tradition in prose that includes Cooper, Emerson, Hawthorne, Melville, James, Twain, Fitzgerald, Hemingway, and Faulkner" all "neglected" cityscapes and urban realities in the interests of a "pastoral impulse" that is "seldom rewarded with success" (75). Marx's analysis is only convincing if one overlooks crucial dimensions of, for example, *The American Scene* and *The Ambassadors,* "Crossing Brooklyn Bridge," *The Great Gatsby* and *The Beautiful and the Damned,* and neglects completely the work of female and African American writers. Surveying the work of Mencken and then James will clarify my point.

In the 1920s, satirist and social critic H. L. Mencken expressed his urban "prejudices" in two distinctly different ways. "Metropolis" is his paean to New York and its excesses, his argument that "serious artists" (rather than mere "performers") should seize the opportunity to document its diverse energies, even its "organized badness" (Mencken 210). "New York is not all bricks and steel," Mencken insists; there are "hearts there, too, and if they do not break, then they at least know how to leap. It is the place where all the aspirations of the Western World meet to form one vast master aspiration, as powerful as the suction of a steam dredge" (Mencken 211–212). "I hymn the town without loving it," he maintains, but nonetheless adumbrates its "immense" possibilities and literary potential: "What I contend is that this spectacle, lush and barbaric in its every detail, offers the material for a great imaginative literature. There is not only gaudiness in it; there is also a hint of strangeness; it has overtones of the fabulous and even of the diabolical. . . . [It] certainly holds out every sort of stimulation that the gifted literatus may plausibly demand" (Mencken 214). Every word of reproach or condemnation withheld from New York is lavished on the cities and towns of southern Pennsylvania. *Prejudices: Sixth Series* also includes "Five Little Excursions," the fifth of which describes a train ride from Pittsburgh "through the coal and steel towns of Westmoreland county" (Mencken 187). "I am not speaking of mere filth," Mencken protests:

> One expects steel towns to be dirty. What I allude to is the unbroken and agonizing ugliness, the sheer revolting monstrousness, of every house in sight. . . . It is as if some titanic and aberrant genius, uncompromisingly inimical to man, had devoted all the ingenuity of Hell to making [the villages]. They show grotesqueries of ugliness that, in retrospect, become almost diabolical. One cannot imagine mere human beings concocting such dreadful things, and one can scarcely imagine human beings bearing life in them. (187–188, 190–191)

Initially, Mencken can only define his objects of censure by interweaving strands of religious and aesthetic discourse. Such traditional strategies, however, are inadequate to his task. The twentieth-century man can only characterize the area's "appalling desolation" adequately, and castigate those responsible for the "dreadfully hideous" center of "industrial America," by imagining a new psychosis: "The Libido For the Ugly." "Here is something," Mencken states,

> that the psychologists have so far neglected: the love of ugliness for its own sake, the lust that makes the world intolerable. Its habitat is the United States. Out of the melting pot emerges a race which hates beauty as it hates truth. The etiology of this madness deserves a great deal more study than it has got. There must be causes behind it; it arises and flourishes in obedience to biological laws, and not as a mere act of God. What, precisely, are the terms of those laws? And why do they run stronger in America than elsewhere? Let some honest [citizen] apply himself to the problem. (193)

As Mencken was undoubtedly aware, a number of writers were busy doing just that.[8] Many were predisposed to find "uglinesses" in American cities because Henry James had already cited them (*TAS* 472).

James's importance to Edwardian and modern literature is indisputable; his innovations in narrative focalization, impressionistic techniques, the foregrounding of moral complexities, and devotion to nuance and exquisite sensibilities were as significant to Eliot and Pound as they were to countless novelists.[9] One particular text, I would suggest—an exercise in life-rewriting only recently "recovered" by literary critics—is indispensable to a discussion of literary urban analysis: *The American Scene,* a narrative of his travels from New England to Florida in the early 1900s.

James regards New York, Boston, and Chicago with an aesthetic eye much like Whistler's: he is always prepared to register or generate impressions of beauty, the "particular felicity" of a scene or object of desire (*TAS* 472).[10] All too quickly, however, James concludes that America's northeastern cities have been overrun by "mere masses of brute ugliness," or skyscrapers, that "overtower" every architectural site of "quality" (*TAS* 546). Whatever the "combination of uglinesses" he documents, James promises his readers that "we may bind up the aesthetic wound . . . quite as promptly as we feel it open" (*TAS* 472). Yet the particular "intensity" of New York injures more grievously than James would like to admit.[11] Compounding the "mysteries of the City Hall" one encounters politicians, civil servants, and other "types, running mainly to ugliness and all bristling with the taste of their day" (*TAS* 1907:437). The city is alternatively a "monstrous organism" (*TAS* 418), a once-lovely "charmer" now "so violently overpainted" (*TAS* 447, 359), or a wasteland. Imagine Eliot avidly reading James's admission:

> Were I not so afraid of appearing to strike to excess the so-called pessimistic note, I should really make much of the interesting, appealing, touching vision of waste—I know not how else to name it—that flung its odd melancholy mantle even over one's walks through the parts of the town supposedly noblest and fairest. . . . The whole costly uptown demonstration was a record . . . of individual loneliness; whence came, precisely, its insistent testimony to waste—waste of the still wider sort than the mere game of rebuilding. (*TAS* 486–487)

Undoubtedly James has laid foundations for the canon of Eliotic poetry: the "insistent testimony" of urban "waste" will feature "caged" speakers with their "smothered visibility," the "throbbing" of buildings and denizens alike, "raw fog" and assaultive winds, "rat-holes" and "league-long bridges" (*TAS* 420–421, 424, 446, 422). And as antidote, the texts will also pause to mark rare old churches that survive to offer "this charm, this serenity of *escape and survival* [that] works as a blind on the side of the question of their architectural importance" (*TAS* 432–433; emphasis added). In other words, the most "real" and "unreal" features of the poetic cities are textual, or virtual, as much as they are vivid representations of actual urban environments; the discursive die was cast by James, among others, long before the March Hare began to compose his own "inventions."

Survival emerges as one of the major preoccupations of *The American Scene:* individual and national endurance or extinction, as well as architectural, social, cultural, and especially ethnic hardiness are examined. Extensive travel since the 1870s had supposedly accustomed James to the "hazard[s] of *flânerie*" (*TAS* 511); a return to America, after an absence of more than 20 years, was planned as an opportunity to write a book[12] in which memories and new observations would fruitfully intermingle. "I was to return," the preface states, "with much of the freshness of eye, outward and inward, which, with the further contribution of a state of desire, is commonly held a precious agent of perception" (*TAS* 353). Rather than being "fresh," however, James's perceptions were already preconditioned by the ideological and discursive practices that inform *English Hours* (1905), a text in which "the real London-lover" rehearses impressions of a "dreadful, delightful city" (James 1905:18) and its hinterland formed in 1880s.[13] Gustatory imagery is crucial; London's "savour" (1905:19) is usually as delicious as its sights. Furthermore, because London is "a collection of many wholes," the discerning *flâneur* can avoid altogether or selectively the city's "queer corners, the dark secrets" (1905:43); thus the "uglinesses, the 'rookeries,' the brutalities, the night-aspect of many of the streets, the ginshops" can be acknowledged but effectively overlooked in his "genial summary" (1905:35). Although it lacks the deliberate architectural symmetry and style of Paris, "the splendid city" (James 1905:22), London features pleasingly "accidental" street-vistas and a "congregation of parks" that "constitute an ornament not elsewhere to be matched and give the place a superiority that none of its uglinesses overcome" (James 1905:24). Parks are identified geographically, but class is the underlying criterion for making distinctions. In phrases that anticipate Pound's "Kensington Gardens" and "Les Millwins," James notes that the "character" of Green Park "comes from its nearness to the Westminster slums. . . . There are few hours of the day when a thousand smutty children are not sprawling over it, and the unemployed lie thick on the grass and cover the benches with a brotherhood of greasy corduroys" (James 1905:29). Distressingly untidy they may be, but at least they are *English*. Impressionism and racism combine in James's urban analyses: London is a great city because, in the 1880s at least, "aliens" are greatly absent. To say that London is a city held fast by "the bond of our glorious tongue" is only a well-mannered way of praising the fact that "the capital of our race" is culturally and ethnically homogeneous (1905:38). James can understand and respond to "the deep, perpetual voice of the place" (1905:20) because it speaks to him in English alone. Certainly there are dialects to be heard everywhere—Cockney and Anglo-Irish voices, especially—but "aliens" such as these easily "submi[t] to Londonisation" because they are, after all, part of "our being" (James 1905:21, 39). Long before James surveys the American scene, then, the "literary scene" of *English Hours* becomes a "crucially important site of racial formation, in and through which distinctly American, Anglo-American, and 'Anglo-Saxon' racial feelings, entangled with the pursuit of taste and the cultural good, evolve" (Blair 1996:3).[14]

Therefore, James may disembark in New York or Richmond and declare himself a "restless analyst," a "palpitating pilgrim," and a "pilgrim from afar" (*TAS* 655, 662), but his tales will never be far from the discursive marks previously established. Consider his fundamental dilemma, the crisis that conditions the entire text: after 20 years of being the American in Europe, he returns "home" only to find that Europe is already there. *The American Scene* is destabilized at every turn by the new relations of heterogeneity being forged, and their implications for the "American" identity. Gone is the "fond tradition of homogeneity" he liked to imagine as the defining characteristic of America; the melting pot has overflowed and "the aliens," in all of their "monstrous, presumptuous" might, have become entrenched (*TAS* 427). New York assails him with difference: "the swarming ambiguity and fugacity of race and tongue" are not only "luridly strong" but almost overwhelming (*TAS* 520). Boston, no longer "'my' small homogenous Boston of the more interesting time," features "gross aliens to a man" now in "serene and triumphant possession" of the city, "labouring wage-earners" speaking "a rude form of Italian" (*TAS* 545).[15] New England, like much of the rest of the eastern seaboard, is now "a huge applied sponge, a sponge saturated with the foreign mixture" that passes "over almost everything I remembered and might still have recovered" (*TAS* 545–546). Instead of cleansing, this ethnic and racial sponge dirties all that it touches, besmirching the "supreme relation" with "one's country" that James had taken for granted (*TAS* 427). (Power relations are always at the fore in James's stories of survival and escape.) He had not counted on confronting otherness in order to define himself anew. Only in Philadelphia can he contemplate the "soothing truth" of a city "solely and singly itself"; the "hordes" may be "gathered" in "some vast quarter unknown" to James, but he will not speculate further, nor will he even steal a "glimpse" (*TAS* 586). The "social equilibrium" of Philadelphia is praised, but James's real interest in the city "as a human group" focuses on its *consanguinity,* an exquisitely polite euphemism for its racial purity. Philadelphia is not a "place" so much as a "state of consanguinity," the reader is assured, "which is an absolute final condition. . . . Consanguinity provides the marks and features, the type and tone and ease, the common knowledge and the common consciousness" necessary for the narrator's "equilibrium" as much as the general population's (*TAS* 582–584). Stated more bluntly, Philadelphia is a city to love because of "this elimination of the foreign element" (*TAS* 586).[16]

Even in the midst of Cambridge's Harvard Yard, while admiring the young and WASPish undergraduates, the very "types of youth" and their "*milieu,*" reminders of the "foreign element" intervene. The narrator interrupts the visual pleasures of Cambridge to recall and foreshadow the constant "plenishing of our huge national *pot au feu,*" the "introduction of fresh . . . foreign matter into our heterogeneous system" daily occurring on Ellis Island in "the bay of New York" (*TAS* 408). The specter of Ellis Island is so powerful that he cannot suppress it; it is the trauma that disturbs everything and anything he encounters. James begins and ends the first part of "New York Revisited" with "spring" impressions of the Bay area; finally, after pointed references to Zola and "his energy of evocation" (*TAS* 424), the "dense raw fog" of the scene disperses to reveal "the facts of the terrible little Ellis Island, the first harbor of refuge and stage of patience for the million or so of immigrants annually knocking at our official door" (*TAS* 425).[17] The text is not unsympathetic to the "hundred forms and ceremonies" to which they are subjected, to the ways in which they are "marshalled, herded, divided, subdivided, sorted, sifted, searched, fumigated, for longer or shorter periods" (*TAS* 426). Yet "the effect of [this] prodigious process, an intendedly 'scientific' feeding of the mill" is never understood in terms of the immigrants themselves, but rather limited to the consternation of the American observer: "[it gives] the earnest observer a thousand more things to think of than he can pretend to retail" (*TAS* 426). Difficulties extend beyond the problem of classification, however: the place of observation is threatened, and the observer's identity transformed by radically altered power-knowledge relations. "Indeed," James admits,

> the simplest account of the action of Ellis Island on the spirit of any sensitive citizen who may have happened to "look in" is that he comes back from his visit not at all the same person that he went. He has eaten of the tree of knowledge, and the taste will be forever in his mouth. He had thought he knew before, thought he had the sense of the degree in which it is his American fate to share the sanctity of his American consciousness, the intimacy of his American patriotism, with the inconceivable alien; but the truth had never come home to him with any such force. In the lurid light projected upon it by those courts of dismay it shakes him—or I like at least to imagine it shakes him—to the depths of his being; I like to think of him, I positively *have* to think of him, as going about ever afterwards with a new look, for those who can see it, in his face, the outward sign of the new chill in his heart. So is stamped, for detection, the questionably privileged person who has had an apparition, seen a ghost in his supposedly safe old house.[18] Let not the unwary, therefore, visit Ellis Island. (*TAS* 427)

Unlike a figure in one of his ghost stories, James cannot awake from the nightmare that immigration has produced. Small wonder that James eventually exclaims of the "alien," "Is not the universal sauce essentially *his* sauce, and do we not feel ourselves feeding, half the time, from the ladle, as greasy as he chooses to leave it for us, that he holds out[?]" (*TAS* 453). The recurring figure of "appetency" (Blair 1996:173) makes the intrusive presence of immigrants in urban America seem that much more intimate and permanent.

Faced with a "houseful of foreigners, physiognomically branded as such" (*TAS* 561), the narrator fears that no form of collective let alone national identity will survive; the city—and by extension, the country—is overrun by strangers, marked by the disparate juxtapositions of "queer" differences. The integrity of national and individual identities can only be traced nostalgically: "There was no escape from the ubiquitous alien into the future, or even into the present; there was an escape but into the past" (*TAS* 428). *The American Scene* is actually a phantom; the "scenery" may not have changed much in rural New England or swampy Florida, but everything else has. Scientific discourse offers little protection: whether the narrator enumerates the strangers, acknowledges "migrations" as necessary "measures" to populate the country, reduces an immigrant to a "dog who sniffs round the freshly-acquired bone,"[19] or creates "categories of foreigners" (such as Italians, Negroes, Chinamen, Jews), he cannot escape from the new reality of "the sordid and the squalid" spectacle (*TAS* 468), nor shrug off the post-Darwinian fear that survival of the fittest, in American terms, means survival of those most likely to adapt: the "aliens."

"Consideration of an African type" has been delayed in this analysis because James postpones it, deliberately, until Chapter XII of *The American Scene,* when the reader arrives in Richmond, "the tragic ghost-haunted city," the "centre of the vast blood-drenched circle" (*TAS* 658). For all of its early obsession with "the 'ethnic' outlook" of the larger northern cities (*TAS* 463), this is a journey to the heart of "a vividly tragic" and race-stained past from which the Confederate states cannot or will not escape. Geography alone is not responsible for a narrative that begins in New England and ends in Florida; a North vs. South "plot" animates James's carefully organized travels. Consequently the hierarchy of aliens culminates, or reaches its nadir, with "members of the negro race" (*TAS* 697), a strategy that effectively de-Americanizes the African Americans.[20] Just as Conrad's Marlow will grope for words to define Africans who "were not inhuman" (37), James is "discomposed" yet compelled to recall his first impression, back in America, of "the intimate presence of the negro":

> [In Washington] I was waiting, in a cab, at the railway-station, for the delivery of my luggage . . . while a group of tatterdemalion darkies lounged and sunned themselves within range. To take in with any attention two or three of the figures had surely been to feel one's self introduced at a bound to the formidable question, which rose suddenly like some beast that had sprung from the jungle. There were its far outposts; they represented the Southern black as we knew him not, and had not within the memory of man known him, in the North; and to see him there, ragged and rudimentary, yet all portentous and "in possession of his rights as a man," was to be not a little discomposed, was to be in fact very much admonished. (*TAS* 662)

In this and other passages, primitivist discourse enables James to separate blacks from the ranks of genuine or white Americans "of the right complexion" (*TAS* 681); he also avails himself of sexualizing remarks ("the negroes, though superficially and doubtless not at all intendingly sinister, were the lustier race" [*TAS* 681]) to encode the subtleties of his racist apprehensions. The same narrator who, chapters earlier, rejects the "greasy" ladle of the immigrant finds himself in Richmond and Charleston "tasting of the very bitterness of the immense, grotesque, defeated project—the project, extravagant, fantastic, and today pathetic in its folly, of a vast Slave State (as the old term ran) artfully, savingly isolated in the world that was to contain it and trade with it" (*TAS* 659). In his dramatic retelling of the Tale of Dixie, a feminized and now neuraesthenic South is "condemned to a state of temper, of exasperation and depression," burdened by "a horrid heritage she had never consciously invited" and facing a future in which "the negro . . . could absolutely not fail to be, intensely 'on the nerves'" (*TAS* 663). Having been brutalized by the armies of the North, she is imprisoned in the shabby, "vacant cage" of post-bellum realities, populated everywhere by "black teamsters who now emphasized . . . with every degree of violence that already-apprehended note of the negro really at home" (*TAS* 697, 664).[21] James can no longer feel "at home" in the cities of the North or the South because America no longer enjoys nor allows for a "*whole* national consciousness as that of the Switzer and the Scot" (*TAS* 428)—its racialized parts are too overwhelming. Hence the "sense of dispossession" that informs the text like a "reviving ache" (*TAS* 427, 734)—and prompts, in 1915, James's decision to become a "naturalized" British subject. Affronted by the "dire backwardness of the Northern spring" and the "want of forwardness of the Southern" the narrator of *The American Scene* finally "settle[s], at the eternal car window, to the mere sightless contemplation, the forlorn view, of an ugly—ah, such an ugly, wintering, waiting world" (*TAS* 732).

Sexualized Spaces and Female Signifiers

Only in Part V of his London essay does James focus on the city's negative features; for that work, the city must be feminized. "London is so clumsy and brutal," he admits, "and has gathered together so many of the darkest sides of life, that it is almost ridiculous to talk of her as a lover talks of his mistress, and almost frivolous to appear to ignore her disfigurements and cruelties. She is like a mighty ogress who devours human flesh. . . . It is not in wantonness that she fills her maw, but to keep herself alive and do her tremendous work. She has no time for fine discriminations" (James 1905:30).[22] James's narrative self, however, has all the time in the world; the finer the discriminations, the more obvious the confluence of misogyny, racism, and class prejudice through which he filters his precious impressions.

Quite clearly, "city" names both locus and discursive field. In "Semiology and the Urban," Barthes argues that "the city is a discourse and this discourse is truly a language: the city speaks to its inhabitants, we speak our city, the city where we are, simply by living in it, by wandering through it, by looking at it" (92). What Barthes does not acknowledge, however, is that the city has been a traditionally masculinist discourse, that the "we" to which he refers is a privileged cultural and political utterance masquerading as a universal truth. Furthermore, the suggestion that "we" speak on behalf of the expressive yet voiceless city wholeheartedly reifies the Western tradition of gendering the city female. The essentializing impetus of Barthes's approach is even more apparent when he discusses its "eroticism and sociality" (96). "The eroticism of the city is the lesson we can draw from the infinitely metaphorical nature of urban discourse," he contends; "essentially and semantically," the city is "the place of our meeting with the *other*" (96). In similar vein, de Certeau insists that the "city," "founded by utopian and urbanistic discourse," is in itself "a *universal* and anonymous *subject*," without once considering that universality is also a discursive fantasy.

I would agree with de Certeau that "'[t]he city,' like a proper name, thus provides a way of conceiving and constructing space on the basis of a finite number of stable, isolatable, and interconnected properties" (94)—but he has not considered gender, race, or class as the foundational elements of the "properties" involved.[23] Fortunately, Mulvey, Sedgwick, and Pollock have persuasively explained how the representation of *all* space is "overdetermined by the connotations implicit in the masculine/feminine binary opposition" (Mulvey 55); traditions of naturalizing and spatializing gender in Western culture are all-pervasive. Colomina usefully summarizes their work by suggesting that the "politics of space are always sexual, even if space is central to the mechanics of the erasure of sexuality" (vii). This is not to claim, however, that space is "yet another symptom of sexuality, repressed or otherwise. It is not a question of looking at how sexuality acts itself out in space, but rather to ask: How is the question of space already inscribed in the question of sexuality?" (Colomina viii).

The ancient Greeks developed the term *metropolis, mater + polis,* to identify "a mother city from which smaller cities [colonies] have been settled" (Sutcliffe 3). "The city is almost always a female," as Jane Marcus comments:

> The male writer perceives the city as subject or object, as mother or whore, through the subjectivity of his sex. The city is to be conquered, raped and subjugated, or idealized in a quest, captured in a war, wooed like a lover, spurned like a wife. He bedecks it with jewels to reflect his own glory; he masks his own aggression by claiming that his battles for cities were fought for women instead of power. (140)[24]

Ascribing a feminine identity to the city facilitates a masculinist desire to control a complex and often forbidding environment. And if control is lost, if the city proves inviting yet dangerous, untrustworthy and ultimately deadly—all the more reason to invent a female adversary. One thinks almost immediately, for example, of Ruskin's preoccupation with Venice as the alluring, once-beautiful Gothic lady now aging, gracelessly, as the Roman Catholic whore of the Adriatic. Following suit, James represents Venice, throughout *Italian Hours,* as the beguiling woman of social and sexual intrigue. Pound is more graphic but not really more reductive when he defines creativity as "driving any new idea into the great passive vulva of London" (1958: 207). Jung effectively summarizes masculinist mythmaking for the twentieth century when he reinscribes as universal archetypes, or the "numinous, structural elements of the psyche" (232), patriarchy's preferred and prejudicial tropes: when all is well-balanced, the city is "maternal," a "woman who harbours the inhabitants in herself like children"; but in addition to the "earthly city-mother" there can be both the "Higher City" and the mother as "underworld, the City of the Damned" in and for which the "mother of every hellish horror" is herself ultimately responsible—after all, we have Babylon as the "the symbol of the Terrible Mother, who leads the peoples into whoredom with her devilish temptations and makes them drunk with her wine" (Jung 213–232).

The extent to which an eroticized male gaze obsessively genders place in order to exercise some measure of discursive and psychic domination is especially evident in works by modern American male poets. One must remember, further, that for many poets, "only women possessed gender in any way that was distinctive and problematic enough to warrant conscious reflection. However imperiled it might have seemed, male gender was often . . . taken as a normative condition from which deviation was the only difference possible" (Nelson 324). Rather than peruse too-familiar texts, however, I would like to present several typical but now largely forgotten examples. Pound's early poem "N.Y." alternates voices to express a fractured, antithetical perspective:

> My City, my beloved, my white! Ah, slender
> Listen! Listen to me, and I will breathe into thee a soul.
> Delicately upon the reed, attend me!
>
> *Now do I know that I am mad,*
> *For here are a million people surly with traffic;*
> *This is no maid.*
> *Neither could I play upon any reed if I had one.*
>
> My City, my beloved,

Thou art a maid with no breasts,
Thou art slender as a silver reed.
Listen to me, attend me!
And I will breathe into thee a soul,
And thou shalt live for ever.

(*Per* 62)

It is as if a Whitmanesque urban paean were interrupted, rudely, by a brash, plain-speaking, very modern "E.P." However love-laden, the speaker's command, "Listen to me, attend me!" emphatically announces that he wields the power in their relationship. (A kinder reading would suggest that the city is young simply because it is American, and therefore a mere child compared with European metropoloi.) Twice the reader is told that the female city is soulless until animated by the poet's words.[25]

A somewhat more subtly gendered but also conventional poem is John Hall Wheelock's "In the Dark City," which begins:

There is a harper plays
Through the long watches of the lonely night
When, like a cemetery,
Sleeps the dark city, with her millions, laid each in his tomb.

(*SofC* 206)[26]

Similar sentiments lurk beneath the typographical innovations of e. e. cummings's "writhe and" (1923):

peacefully,
lifted
into the awful beauty
        of sunset

            the young city
putting off dimension with a blush
enters
the becoming garden of her agony[.]

(cummings 61)

Williams prefers a bluntly dichotomized symbolic landscape:

        T
    Ro   sq   e
G   E   U

.   The city has tits in rows.
The country is in the main—male,

> It butts me with blunt stub-horns,
> Forces me to oppose it
> Or be trampled.
>
> The city is full of milk
> And lies still for the most part.
> These crack skulls
> And spill brains
> Against her stomach.
>
> (1991 1:49–50)

The crude pun of the first line debases both its bird imagery and the feminized city, a gesture that also controls the second stanza. Caesura and dash in the second line underscore the forcefulness of the male or "country" principle that the text claims as its worthy opponent. Equally crude in its lascivious representation of the city is Don Marquis's "New York," which pronounces:

> She is hot to the sea that crouches beside,
> Human and hot to the cool stars peering down,
> My passionate city, my quivering town,
> And her dark blood, tide upon purple tide,
> With throbs as of thunder beats,
> With leaping rhythms and vast, is swirled
> Through the shaken lengths of her veined streets—
> She pulses, the heart of the world. . . .
> I have thrilled with her ecstasy, agony, woe—
> Hath she a mood that I do not know?
> The winds of her music tumultuous have seized me and swayed me,
> Have lifted, have swung me around
> In their whirls as of cyclonic sound; . . .
> O wholly human and baffled and passionate town!
> The throes of thy burgeoning, stress of thy fight,
> Thy bitter, blind struggle to gain for thy body a soul,
> I have known, I have felt[.]
>
> (*SofC* 335–336)[27]

Soulless in and of itself, the city—implicitly "known" to the speaker both intellectually and carnally—is "wholly human" and wholly feminized. Through a remarkable sleight of hand, in this and countless other poems, a fascination with female signifiers produces texts that reiterate the "masculine signified" (Felman 28). To gender the city female is to objectify and commodify it—and thereby gain some distance from it.[28]

Two notable exceptions to this general rule should be mentioned: Chicago, as it is figured in Sandburg's earliest texts, and Williams's Paterson, New Jersey. Sandburg repeatedly, energetically celebrates the brawn and diversity of his "City of the Big Shoulders"; even its brutality elicits positive poetic swaggering:

> And they tell me you are brutal and my reply is: On the faces of
> > women
> > and children I have seen the marks of wanton hunger.
> And having answered so I turn once more to those who sneer at this my
> > city, and I give them back the sneer and say to them:
> Come and show me another city with lifted head singing so proud to be
> > alive and coarse and strong and cunning.
> Flinging magnetic curses amid the toil of piling job on job, here is a tall
> > bold slugger set vivid against the little soft cities;
> Fierce as a dog with tongue lapping for action, cunning as a savage
> > pitted
> > against the wilderness. . . .
> Under the smoke, dust all over his mouth, laughing with white teeth,
> Under the terrible burden of destiny laughing as a young man laughs,
> Laughing even as an ignorant fighter laughs who has never lost a
> > battle[.]
> > > (Sandburg 3)

The "soft little cities" are presumably those lacking in ferocity or the energy of the "young man." Sandburg's combative and manly Mid-western city is "pitted against the wilderness," its very existence a victory against hostile nature. Williams, on the other hand, repeatedly imagines "a man like a city" and a city, like a man, that reconciles the natural and the urban as much as possible.

As Halter and Kuspit point out, Williams initially learned from the photographers and painters he admired, particularly John Sloan and Alfred Stieglitz, to juxtapose "urban and technological dimension[s]" with "elements of nature" (Halter 87), to create a feeling of being "at home with" modern buildings and urban development by treating them as "natural organisms, or as organic parts of nature" (Kuspit 68; see also Corn).[29] Whereas the Men of 1914 and their "camp" specialized in an urban poetics of rejection,[30] Williams produced the poetry of compromise and acceptance, in which human, natural, and environmental "antagonistic forces" (Halter 93) are integrated. Most importantly, Paterson, New Jersey is a community[31] and a "town" rather than an alienating city, one that fully combines the built world and nature: "Paterson lies in the valley under the Passaic Falls/ its spent waters forming the outline of his back" (*Pat* 14). It is not too fanciful to suggest that Williams's Paterson thrives because it is not a *metropolis,* neither woman-identified nor outsized.

What Sandburg's speaker hollers, Williams's speaker reiterates in measured tones. Not until the male-focused agenda of *Paterson* has been established in the 66 lines of the preface and the first 32 lines of verse, when the reader fully appreciates "a nine months' wonder, the city / the man, an identity" (*Pat* 12), is a female counterpart mentioned—and then, to establish the sexualized dichotomies that control *Paterson:*

> A man like a city and a woman like a flower
> —who are in love. Two women. Three women.
> Innumerable women, each like a flower.
>
> > But
> only one man—like a city.
>
> > > > > (*Pat* 15)

It is difficult to find a plainer declaration of masculinist singularity; "I, Paterson, the King-self" has spoken (*Pat* 272).[32] Ultimately, every person, every "thing" in *Paterson* is defined, understood, and experienced according to "the female of it facing the male" (*Pat* 74).

Book I of *Paterson* was published in 1946; the fifth and final book, in 1958. On many levels it is the last city-focused modernist long poem; it tries to answer Eliot and anyone else who made a name for himself canvassing the "unreal," life-denying cities of modernity. In Book III (1949), an angry interlocutor demands, "Do / you still believe—in this/ swill-hole of corrupt cities?/ Do you, Doctor? Now?" (*Pat* 132). Williams's continued commitment to the *Paterson* project provides its own answer: he will no more give up on his "town" than he will "Give up / the poem. Give up the shilly-/shally of art" (*Pat* 132). Art and urban life constitute "the universal" as Williams understands them, both of which can be grasped when the poet learns "to write particularly" and the reader, to read attentively (*Pat* 6). As the first sentence of the Author's Note declares, "a man in himself is a city, beginning, seeking, achieving, and concluding his life in ways which the various aspects of a city may embody" (*Pat* 3).

Man and city eventually "become estranged from woman and nature" in Williams's text (Sharpe 134); to effect a rapprochement, the poem concludes by reversing its gender patterning and evoking a feminized, sexualized city-as-woman who "embodies both whore and virgin" (Sharpe 135).[33] The fragmentary representation of Paris in Book IV signals this symbolic switch: "Paris. / the soft coal smell, as she / leaned upon the window before de-/ parting, for work. /—a furnace, a cavity aching / . . . a hollow, / a woman waiting to be filled" (*Pat* 206). If one does not share Nelson's view that Williams's "perspective on women is rich and varied and generally affirmative," one can at least agree that "charges of sexism" are appropriate (349).

The "Ebony Muse"[34] and the "City of Refuge"

Henry James was appalled by an American "scene" that featured too many "tongues," too many nonwhite or non-Northern European faces, too many people whose class and/or race disqualified them from refinement and sameness.[35] His text is crucial testimony to the "reiminaging [of] the city as a psychosocial space of racial contact, definition, and exchange" (Blair 1996:164) from the 1890s onward. Yet James, at least, enjoyed "sanctified" childhood memories of a unified, stable, WASP American identity. T. S. Eliot did not. Even as a member of a privileged white family, he felt displaced and alienated. As he later informed Herbert Read, "'Someday I want to write an essay about the point of view of an American who wasn't an American, because he was born in the south and went to school in New England as a small boy with a nigger drawl, but who wasn't a southerner in the South because his people were northerners in a border state and looked down on all southerners and Virginians, and so was never anything anywhere'" (qtd Sigg 110).[36] Personal feelings of displacement became social critique: in *After Strange Gods,* Eliot observed that, "The population should be homogenous; where two or more cultures exist in the same place they are like either to be fiercely self-conscious or both to become adulterate" (1933b:20). Miscegenation is not a theme of "Gerontion" or *The Waste Land,* but the destabilization of city life, exacerbated by the enforced movement of peoples during and after World War I, is anxiously noted. The speaker of "Gerontion," who identifies himself as "an old man in a dry month" shedding tears "shaken from the wrath-bearing tree" (*CPP* 37, 38), inveighs against deracination and other "supple confusions" of the epoch. "My house is a decayed house," he laments allegorically,

> the Jew squats on the window sill, the owner,
> Spawned in some estaminet of Antwerp,
> Blistered in Brussels, patched and peeled in London. . . .
>   . . . Mr Silvero
> With caressing hands, at Limoges
> Who walked all night in the next room;
>   . . . Hakagawa, bowing among the Titians;
>   . . . Madame de Tornquist, in the dark room
> Shifting the candles; Fräulein von Kulp
> Who turned in the hall, one hand on the door.

(*CPP* 37–39)

The coherence of home has been supplanted by the squalor of a "rented house," the tenement of the overcrowded, urbanized, industrialized city. In *The Waste Land,* disorders of class, race, gender relations, and ethnicity are all threatening. In the would-be apocalypse of Part V, an unknown, spectral "hooded" figure materializes and is immediately displaced by

> . . . those hooded hordes swarming
> Over endless plains, stumbling in cracked earth
> Ringed by the flat horizon only
> What is the city over the mountains
> Cracks and reforms and bursts in the violet air
> Falling towers
> Jerusalem Athens Alexandria
> Vienna London
> Unreal[.]
>
> (*CPP* 73)

Demographic chaos carries out the work that a world war left unfinished.[37]

As doctor and poet, Williams attempts to treat "colored" figures respectfully. Some of the early lyrics note the abject poverty that conditions their illnesses (1:59, 70). The textual gaze, however, often intensifies its representation of the racialized other in predictable ways. "[C]ome with me," the reader is summoned in "Sub Terra," "poking into negro houses / with their gloom and smell! / in among children / leaping around a dead dog!" (Williams 1991 1:64). A male speaker and an "old black-man" bond long enough to appreciate a memory of "six women, dancing / a set-dance, stark naked below / the skirts raised round / their breasts" (Williams 1991 1:78). However much the speaker appreciates the "old emotion," the eroticization is further evidence of the "multiple jeopardy" of discrimination that black women experience, the "interactive oppression" of gender, race, and class that "circumscribes" their lives (King 220). When "3 colored girls . . . stroll by" the speaker, he is quick to note that they are "of age" or legally available for sex; they are exotic, "dissociated" in his mind "from the fixed scene," "their color flagrant, / their voices vagrant / their laughter wild" (*Pat* 66). Although I argue below that female poets insist upon different kinds of "wildness" to assert independent spirits, the word has other connotations in Williams's poetic discourse. *Paterson* acknowledges blacks in the general populace, but denies them status as *American* citizens. After an historical account of the introduction of "mulattoes" to colonial New Jersey (*Pat* 21–22), which unobtrusively yet decidedly establishes their non-"native" lineage, the first concentrated appearance of black women is staged. They are not featured, however, as emblems of everyday Ameri-

cana; instead they are barbaric, sexualized, and paganized, curiosities lifted
from the pages of *National Geographic:*

> I remember
> a *Geographic* picture, the 9 women
> of some African chief semi-naked
> astraddle on a log, an official log to
> be presumed, heads left:

> Foremost
> froze the young and latest,
> erect, a proud queen, conscious of her power,
> mud-caked, her monumental hair
> slanted above the brows—violently frowning.
>
> > *(Pat* 22)

The source of the photograph supposedly endorses its scientific/anthropo-
logical veracity, "confirming a stereotype of blackness . . . in which the
Negro is rendered synonymous with sex and instinct, lacking the more
highly developed capacities of reason" (Boone 223). All of the female figures
in *Paterson,* I would argue, black and white, are inevitably related to and
measured against this primitivist tableau. Even as the text diminishes the
possibilities of basic humanity for females, it worries about their "power"
and propensity for violence. Immediately after this passage, the profound
"mystery of a man" is juxtaposed with all things "womanlike" and "menacing—yet abashed" (*Pat* 23). In Williams's texts, the systemic construction of
demeaning differences is always vigilant, industrious.

In racist discourse, skin color is presumed to mark both external and internal inferiority; as Pollock suggests, it is the "bodily sign of an internal otherness that becomes a self-alienation" (1999:256). To counter that lived
tradition, African American poets developed two distinct and highly gendered responses: Langston Hughes, Claude McKay, and their male peers asserted the worth and vitality of individuals in urban settings; Angelina Weld
Grimké, Georgia Douglas Johnson, and many other women resisted oppression by writing themselves into enabling natural topographies. In other
words, the gender-specific discursive paradigms I am identifying in the poetry of white Americans holds true for black Americans as well.

"The census of 1920," Douglas reports, "declared America for the first
time in its history an urban nation, and New York was the largest city in that
urban nation" (4).[38] The population of New York "doubled between 1910
and 1930" (Douglas 15), in part because of the final phase of the massive
"out-migration" of African Americans from the south to the industrialized
cities of the north. Some 170,000 "made the exodus out of the South during

the first decade of the twentieth century, while 450,000 followed suit in the 1910s, peaking in a flood tide of 750,000 black émigrés during the 1920s" (Kalaidjian 309). Between 1920 and 1930, "118,792 whites left Harlem" (Douglas 311–312).

Bremer persuasively reminds one that the "alienating images" of the "Euro-American vision of the living-dead megalopolis" are almost wholly absent from the work of African American writers of this period: "[d]uring those same megalopolitan 1920s, some of New York's most powerful ethnic minority writers bravely claimed the city—at least, their neighborhood microcosm of the city—as a home for the transient outcasts of American society. . . . Collectively, they developed a vision of an urban home that was at once an organic place, a birthright community, and a cultural aspiration" (1990:48). As the special March 1925 issue of *Survey Graphic* proclaimed, Harlem was "The Mecca of the New Negro": not a "fringe," as Boone explains, "not a slum, nor . . . a 'quarter' consisting of dilapidated tenements" but a "city within a city" (James Weldon Johnson's phrase) that was "on one level, 'central' to the whole city" even if it was "symbolically invisible" in relation to "mainstream white New York" (213–214). Just as importantly, the *textual* existence of Harlem and its cultural "renaissance" was both evocative and inspirational. "From the very beginning of Harlem's ascendance as an urban and a cultural phenomenon," Boone states,

> a series of evocative spatial metaphors—refuge, mecca, paradise, home—were deployed to describe its promise and appeal. . . . One such designation, "the city of refuge," taken from the title of story by Rudolph Fisher, was quickly adopted . . . to evoke the safety experienced within the boundaries of this geographically and symbolically complete world. (221)[39]

Prose works such as Claude McKay's *Home to Harlem* (1928), James Weldon Johnson's *Black Manhattan* (1930), and Nella Larsen's *Passing* (1929)[40] vividly conveyed the complexites of Harlem, but the poetry was and is equally important as historical record, cultural statement, and aesthetic challenge. Langston Hughes's poetry brings inner city life to the page with incomparable verve. Unconventionally, he often focused sympathetically on the everyday lives of women, but did not need to feminize the city either to grapple with or overcome all that it offers or denies.[41] Just as importantly, Hughes developed a poetic discourse featuring the vernacular idioms of working-class and underclass African Americans without condescension, and normalized them within a middle register of formal utterance that neither black nor white readers could ignore. At the time, Hughes was faulted by white and black critics alike for his "low rent" focus, for failing to ascribe to a "racial uplift" program in an obvious way;[42] in the last two decades, the politics of his aesthetic choices have been roundly applauded.

In the 1920s, audiences newly conditioned by Eliot, H. D., and Williams to accept vers libre found in Hughes's superficially unassuming works an easily accessible collage of blues and jazz cadences, the spoken word, and expressive lyricism. Although somewhat detached like Baudelaire's *flâneur*, Hughes's poetic self is not indifferent to the lives he documents in "the great Negro city in the World" and other major urban centers.[43] Eliot has always been the modern poet praised for the panoply of fragmented "voices" featured in *The Waste Land*. A comparison with Hughes's method is very revealing. To generate a sense of heterogeneous chaos in the "unreal cities," Eliot juxtaposes silent, ennui-ridden crowds and telling snippets of overheard conversations and confessions, in several "dead" and current Indo-European languages. Women's voices are emphasized to convey spiritual, emotional, and sexual bankruptcy; in the most highly-charged emotional moments (with the "hyacinth girl" in Part I, the woman whose "'nerves are bad to-night'" in Part II), females speak and men think (only the reader is privy to their thoughts). Eliot is a miniaturist, and a caricaturist: personalities are intimated, exaggerated with a few deft strokes or images; class, gender, and ethnicity are carefully encapsulated elements of the satirical representation. Hughes, on the other hand, is a dramatist in verse: a community is given voice in his works, each painful or pleasure-seeking life generously allowed a moment in the footlights. It is very instructive to distinguish among the folk ballads, the blues poems (highly structured, repetitive, focusing on suffering *and* endurance), and the jazz poems (stylized to seem improvisational, multivoiced) in Hughes's canon. From another perspective, the sophistication of Hughes's discourse is best appreciated by considering the various registers constructed: poems of sonorous reflection featuring a familiar yet educated, poetically learned voice, American but not idiomatic[44] ("Aunt Sue's Stories," "Song for Billie Holiday," "Uncle Tom"); poems featuring the near-seamless fusion of registers and voices ("Ballad of the Fortune Teller," "Little Old Letter"); exercises in verbal mimesis that dramatize, without patronizing, the diversity of peoples' lives ("Early Evening Quarrel," "Sylvester's Dying Bed," "Crossing"); and poems in which the disruptive juxpositioning of formal utterance and song or speech heightens the reader's awareness of the poem's politicized narrative ("The Weary Blues," "Mulatto," and *Montage of a Dream Deferred*). As he states in the introduction to his play *Tambourines to Glory*, the "complexity of simplicity" is the governing principle of all his writings.

The Waste Land is noisy: everything from the wind to a "throbbing" motor makes itself heard, to the point of symbolic cacophony. The text gestures toward cultural inclusivity by citing "that Shakespeherian Rag" as well as Wagner's *Parsifal*, music hall ditties and operatic arias; the lyricism so often squelched in the poem is heightened by the musical motifs that literally and figuratively underscore the text. Nonetheless, the reader of *The Waste Land* cannot help but fear for the ultimate degradation of high culture; it cannot withstand the onslaught of ugliness much longer.[45] Hughes's poetry, on the other hand, not only enshrines blues and jazz lyrics and rhythms to garner respect and cultural acceptance for them, he elevates ordinary lives to "the condition of music," in Pater's phrase, in order to promote his great argument that "Beautiful, also, are the souls of my people" (1994:36).[46] Appreciating the important cultural work that "beauty" can still perform, Hughes repeatedly aestheticizes his political message in order to encourage black readers and educate white readers. Long before it became a volatile slogan of 1960s radicalism, "Black is Beautiful" was Hughes's message of the streets.[47] Some African American writers and cultural leaders like James Weldon Johnson argued that "Negro Authors" should confound and overturn racist stereotypes by rising "above race," "reach[ing] out to the universal in truth and beauty" (481). Hughes was too much of a realist to depend on a myth of transcendence. As he counterargued in "The Negro Artist and the Racial Mountain" (1926) and everything he penned,

> Let the blare of Negro jazz bands and the bellowing voice of Bessie Smith singing Blues penetrate the closed ears of the colored near-intellectuals until they listen and perhaps understand. Let Paul Robeson singing 'Water Boy,' and Rudolph Fisher writing about the streets of Harlem . . . cause the smug Negro middle class to turn from their white, respectable, ordinary books and papers and catch a glimmer of their own beauty. . . . But this is the mountain standing in the way of any true Negro art in American—this urge within the race toward whiteness, the desire to pour racial individuality into the mold of American standardization, and to be as little Negro and as much American as possible. (Hughes 309, 304)

Hughes's urban poetry is aurally complex and visually limited. If asked to describe Hughes's cities, the reader would give vivid accounts of the people—Susanna Jones, Big Boy, Aunt Sue, Sylvester, the Preacher, Widow Woman, Alberta K. Johnson—but only sketchy details about crowded streets or "weary" avenues, pawn shops, gospel halls, front stoops where people congregate, blues clubs where pianos "moan with melody" (1994:50). Overall, one notes the homogeneity of the community he represents; the rare white figures are interlopers, figures of exploitation. The absence of interest in built environments reminds one of the invisible but palpable "lines" separating black and white neighborhoods and workplaces even in cities where Jim Crow laws were not on the books.[48] The poems of the 1920s and 1930s focus on community life, creating a sense of coherence, even safety, within specific areas. Yet Hughes later disparages implicit or explicit urban segregation, and condemns those who are interested in black neighborhoods only as cultural /tourist attractions. "Visitors to the Black Belt" offers a challenging lesson in racist human geography:

> You can talk about
> *Across* the railroad tracks—
> To me it's *here*
> On this side of the tracks.
>
> You can talk about
> *Up* in Harlem—
> To me it's *here*
> In Harlem.
>
> You can say
> Jazz on the South Side—
> To me it's hell
> On the South Side:
> Kitchenettes
> With no heat
> And garbage
> In the halls.
>
> Who're you, outsider?
>
> Ask me who am I.
>
> (Hughes 1994:215)

Montage of a Dream Deferred (1951) further documents the physical parameters of oppression in cities like Chicago[49] and New York. "Passing," addressed to African Americans, accuses "the ones who've crossed the line / to live downtown" of abandoning "Harlem of the bitter dream" and thus contributing to its socioeconomic and cultural decline ("grandma cannot get her gospel hymns" on the radio "on account of the Dodgers" broadcast) (Hughes 1994:417).

For Claude McKay, Jamaica was the realm of natural beauty and "high days" of happiness; he was a man in the British West Indies, not a black man. Consequently, a speaker tries to recall "The Tropics in New York," a poem that juxtaposes the "benediction" of the Caribbean countryside (McKay 1953:31) with the reality of urban blight much like Yeats's "Lake Isle of Innisfree" contrasts rural Ireland and London. A similar textual strategy informs the very accomplished "When Dawn Comes to the City,"[50] and "Subway Wind," in which the "perfume" of "the Trades" is invoked to heighten the reader's response to the "sick and heavy air" circulating in the subway tunnels, "the city's great gaunt gut" (McKay 1953:75). "Dawn in New York," a sonnet, and "On Broadway," a lyric, recycle the conventions of the "mighty city" and its cheerless skyline, "pushing" crowds, and ghostly or pleasure-seeking denizens (McKay 1953:65, 67). Three other poems, "The City's Love" and the starkly named sonnets "The White City" and "The White House," can only intensify their speakers' emotional reaction to being "an alien guest" (McKay 1953:66) through female stereotypes. In "The City's Love," the "great, proud city, seized with a strange love," embraces the grateful man; in "The White City," a "life-long hate" is best expressed if the city's features "Are sweet like wanton loves because I hate" (1973:125).[51] McKay's most arresting urban poem, I would argue, is the one in which Williams's notion of "a man like a city" is explored for its negative capabilities. "My spirit is a pestilential city," the speaker begins; the subsequent spectacle of "sewers, bursting," "contagious" air, interior and exterior "decay" expresses an abject sense of self at the same time as it catalogues urban blight (McKay 1953:52). This is not, however, an American city; only an arrestingly exotic site, reminiscent of that explored in "A Farewell to Morocco," will suffice for a poem in which male subjectivity is paramount.

As Douglas notes, "NewYork was one of the few big cities in the nation that did not experience mass convulsions of racial violence between 1916 and 1930" (315). The violence was especially terrible in Atlanta,[52] Chicago, and St. Louis; New York was the site of "the famous silent protest parade of July 28, 1917 in which nearly ten thousand women and children dressed in white and men in dark clothing marched silently down Fifth Avenue to the beat of muffled drums to protest the bloody East St. Louis riot in which hundreds of blacks were killed" (Early 14). Small wonder, then, that several black male poets focused on the "bitter dream" of urban life in their poetry of the 1920s. McKay's "Rest in Peace" summarizes the "the city's thorny ways, / The ugly corners of the Negro belt" and the "nights of unabating bitterness" experienced because of the "city's hate, the city's prejudice" (1953:77). Lewis Alexander's approach to urban "Streets" is effectively imagistic: "'Avenues of dreams / Boulevards of pain / Moving black streams / Shimmering like rain'" (qtd Boone 220). Waring Cuney salutes the "True Love" of a woman who "loves in a tenement / Where the only music / She hears / Is the cry of street car brakes / And the toot of automobile horns / And the drip of a kitchen spigot / All day" (Cullen ed. 213). For Sterling Brown, Harlem's pleasures are ruinous: Maumee Ruth lays dead in her coffin but her children are unaware because the son is "Hiding in city holes / Sniffing the 'snow,'" and the daughter is "Sodden with gin" amid "Harlem's din" (Cullen ed. 134). Even Countee Cullen, who never wavered from his Yeatsian "high dream" of what poetry should be, rehearses the scars of racism first experienced in the city: the speaker of "Incident" recalls "riding in old

Baltimore," eight years old and "very small" when he encounters a white boy "no whit bigger, / And so I smiled, but he poked out / His tongue and called me, 'Nigger'" (Cullen ed. 187). No one had taught the white child that Baltimore could be somebody else's Mecca.

Intertextual Cities

In the early twentieth century, San Francisco was a horrific reminder of the true fragility of the city: the April 1906 earthquake and subsequent fires destroyed much of the downtown area. Chicago, on the other hand, was acknowledged as the fastest growing city in the world; its phenomenal buildings by Louis Sullivan, Frank Lloyd Wright, and Mies van der Rohe, and then the "skyscrapers" of New York, provided a startlingly new architectural definition for the modern metropolis, an urban aesthetics that "took form," in Carl Sandburg's words, by "Wrecking, / Planning, / Building, breaking, rebuilding" the city centers (3).

Some texts by male poets localize their references to represent a "real" city in all of its chaotic complexity. Sandburg's "Chicago" is an excellent example:

> Hog Butcher for the World,
> Tool Maker, Stacker of Wheat,
> Player with Railroads and the Nation's Freight Handler;
> Stormy, husky, brawling,
> City of the Big Shoulders[.]
>
> (Sandburg 3)

More often, however, a generalized urban locus is created, both "real" and "unreal." In poems such as "Perpetuum Mobile: The City," Williams struggles to connect the city as erotic "dream / a little false / toward which / now we stand / and stare transfixed" (1991 1:430) with quotidian figures such as truck drivers-cum-thieves. A perpetual array of possibilities both for "pleasure" and "waste," the "impossible" city constantly evades the speaker's gaze:

> There!

> There!

> There!

> —a dream

> of lights
>   hiding
> the iron reason
>   and stone
> a settled
>   cloud—
> City[.]

(Williams 1991 1:434–435)

According to Heller, the "disjunctive deployment of images" in the text "present us with the ganglia of emotions the modern city might induce" (93). As Molesworth suggests, Williams "makes us aware of the city as a place where no coherent perspective is possible" (18).

Nonetheless, Williams's ubiquitous, any-city poems of the 1920s and 1930s never descend into a figurative abyss of incoherence or chaos; the speakers are accepting rather than condemnatory, always prepared to be "astonished"[53] rather than revolted. In the texts of many contemporaries, however, the common thematics are city blight and city nightmare. This is Robert Swasey, circa 1916, writing of "The City in Summer":

> A dusty vista
> Down which a cat
> Darkly moves.
> Bleak doors
> And bleaker windows;
> A withered vine
> Patters against the wall.
> A newspaper
> Shambling in the gutter;
> A ragged child
> Stands at the corner
> Beside a hungry dog
> Looking in a dust can.
> A murky
> Silence over all:
> The city dead.

(SofC 134)

In countless city texts produced by white male poets during this period the imagery, attitudes, and death-in-life experiences are remarkably similar. Just as Collier has found in the late-nineteenth-century city poetry of Paris, this "urban imagery is generated as much from linguistic processes as from referential observation" (39). Because of this, one needs to think in terms of "intertextual cities," linguistic sites that owe as much to the satiric traditions of

Juvenal, Dryden, and Johnson, and the textual tropes of Wordsworth, Dickens, Poe, and Dreiser, as they do to the actual topographies of New York, Chicago, or London. Modernist poets were extremely attentive to the work of their peers; as a result, the collective self-referentiality of their texts is as striking as it is pervasive.[54]

Sandburg and Eliot share a fog—brown, yellow, catlike, and menacing—with each other, Oscar Wilde,[55] and Max Bodenheim; citizens swarm before the gaze of Eliot, Pound, and W.M. Letts;[56] ragged people gather and their "lost footsteps" echo on "motionless pavements" for William Rose Bénet, John Gould Fletcher, and Williams. Each new intertextual gesture adds figurative force to the signifier. A selection of titles by Maxwell Bodenheim effectively summarizes the most familiar tropes of the textual city: "The Rear-Porches of an Apartment Building," "The Cafeteria," "In the Park" (which features the most marginalized, economically disadvantaged people: African Americans and old women), "Streets," "Sunday in a certain city suburb," and "Summer evening: New York Subway-Station." One text, "Fifth Avenue," is distinctive because it blends urban spaces and western American topography:

> Seasons bring nothing to this gulch
> Save a harshly intimate anecdote
> Scrawled, here and there, on paint and stone.
> The houses shoulder each other
> In a forced and passionless communion[.]

> *(SofC* 104)

Eliot identifies the "arid plain" of modernity with Old Testament deserts; Bodenheim's figural ground is similar yet homelier.

Two prominent nineteenth-century intertextual cities are reinscribed in these modernist works: Paris as represented by Charles Baudelaire and the New York of Walt Whitman.[57] Mention should also be made of the short story that had a profound impact on Baudelaire and thus, directly or indirectly, on the Americans: Edgar Allan Poe's "The Man of the Crowd" (1845). An unnamed narrator, still recovering from an illness, sits at the window of a London coffeehouse, pleased to be "in one of those happy moods which are so precisely the converse of *ennui*" (Poe 3: 134). Late in the day, the narrator becomes "absorbed in contemplation" of the crowds milling by, a "tumultuous sea of human heads" (Poe 3: 135). The catalogue of human types that ensues is particularly revealing in terms of class, ethnicity, and gender relations: in "descending" order, one is told about "the decent" ("noblemen, merchants, attorneys, tradesmen, . . . men of leisure and men actively engaged in affairs of their own"), "the tribe of clerks," the "gamblers," and then "Jew pedlars," "professional street beggars," and "feeble and ghastly invalids." Only then are women observed: "modest young girls returning from long and late labor," the "women of the town of all kinds and of all ages," ranging from "the unequivocal beauty" to the prostitutes and "drunkards innumerable and indescribable." Coming after them are the "pie-men, porters, coal-heavers, sweeps; organ-grinders, monkey-exhibitors and ballad mongers . . . ragged artizans and exhausted laborers" (Poe 3: 138–139). Initially, the narrator is content to "read" these faces of "the mob" at a distance. But when "a decrepit old man" suddenly comes into view, the narrator is so "singularly aroused, startled, fascinated" by his countenance—which speaks "of triumph, of merriment, of excessive terror, of intense—of extreme despair"—that he has "to know more of him" (Poe 3:140). Bizarrely but unquestioningly, for the next 24 hours the narrator follows the man throughout the city, a clandestine journey that takes him from scenes of crowded communality to squalor and solitude. The old man enters shops, but purchases nothing; he brushes by people, but does not interact with them. In the "most noisome quarter of London," where "horrible filth festered in the dammed-up gutters," and the "whole atmosphere teemed with desolation," they reach a Gin "palace" (Poe 3: 144). Sunrise finds them back at the street where the narrator first caught sight of the man; for another 12 hours, the stranger walks "to and fro" but accomplishes nothing. Finally, with a second night approaching, the narrator, now "wearied unto death," stops and looks the stranger "steadfastly in the face": "He noticed me not. . . . 'This old man,' I said at length, 'is the type and the genius of deep crime. He refuses to be alone. *He is the man of the crowd*'" (Poe 3: 145).

Poe's innovative exercise in textual *flânerie* begins and ends with an apprehension of "horror," a keen sense of crimes that remain "undivulged" and "secrets which do not permit themselves to be told" (3:134). Illness seems to have evacuated the narrator's life; vicariously but also parasitically, he lives through the strangers whom he contemplates and also commodifies. In terms of textual strategies, the narrator's "absorbed" gaze determines the content and plot of the story. The city is rendered in terms of faces, glances, and "aching sensations" of sights and sounds; in addition to the fog, the park, and labyrinthine streets, there are "wild effects of the light" from natural and gas-lamp sources. But the more that we know about the city and the external appearance of its inhabitants the less we can discern about the quintessential "stranger"—except that one should fear him.

"The Man of the Crowd" vividly established "fundamental ways of appropriating urban experience" (Molesworth 15). An inspired Baudelaire seized upon Paris as hospital, brothel, hellish underworld, and penal colony.[58] Crucially, he positioned Paris as an environment in which a "consciousness of modernity" (Foucault 1984:39) would flourish, albeit burdened with melancholia. As Foucault suggests, "modernity for Baudelaire is not simply a form of relationship to the present; it is also a model relationship that has to be established with oneself. The deliberate attitude of modernity is tied to an *indispensible aestheticism*. . . . This ironic heroization of the present, this transfiguring play of freedom with reality . . . Baudelaire does not imagine that these have any place in society itself, or in the body politic. They can only be produced in another, a different place, which Baudelaire calls art" (1984:41, 42). At the outset of "The Painter of Modern Life," Baudelaire suggests that beauty is two-dimensional: it is "made up of an eternal, invariable element, whose quantity is expressively difficult to determine, and of a relative, circumstantial element, which will be . . . the age, its fashions, its morals, its emotions" (1995:3). The ugliness of Parisian life, "the shocking, raw immediacy of his sense impressions of the new urban reality" (Buck-Morss 1986:122), constitute the particular circumstances of his poetry. Death taints and tinges everything; to quote Blanchard, "it seems that the precondition for the shock of the new is [a] negative consciousness" (83).

As Walter Benjamin first observed, Baudelaire's metropolitan locus also begat a *species,* the poet/speaker as *flâneur,* an ambiguous figure "sometimes verging on that of the mere stroller, at other times elevated to that of the detective, to the decipherer of urban and visual texts" (Frisby 82).[59] Part voyeur and part gossip, the *flâneur* is entirely an emotional parasite who "reads the city as he would read a text—from a distance" and is "entertained, not distressed, by the ever changing urban spectacle" available for his "dream of domination" (Ferguson 1994:31). A "prince enjoying his incognito" (Baudelaire 1995:400), he is the "sovereign of the chance meetings of the city stage which has no spaces forbidden to him" (Tester 5). Self-empowered to render the city and its inhabitants exceptional or banal, to use a discrete technology of "otherization" that imaginatively appropriates lives in order to compensate for his own status as modernity's "hollow man," the poet/*flâneur* diverts himself and his readers from the "tedium" of life (Buck-Morss 1986:112). Shields aptly summarizes the operative relations of power: "As a consumer of sights and goods, the *flâneur* is a vicarious conqueror, self-confirmed in his mastery of the empire of the gaze while losing his own self in the commodified network of popular imperialism. . . . The *flâneur* closes the gap in the cultural formation of empire between the citizen and the state, brings the two together in the social imaginary in a collusive project of possession" (78, 75). Although debilitated by ennui, the *flâneur's* exceptional sensibility distinguishes him from the unindividuated masses. The multitude, in fact, teaches him to cherish his solitude. He may be enervated by the conditions of modernity in post–Haussmannian Paris, but he is liberated by his city-inspired fantasies.[60] Nonetheless, his privileges are ironically enjoyed. As Benjamin often noted, Baudelaire's writings stress the *flâneur's* sense of estrangement; "although he was born there: 'No one felt less at home in Paris than Baudelaire.' . . . The world in which Baudelaire had become 'a native' did 'not thereby grow any more friendly'" (Buck-Morss 1991:186).

As Tester insists, "Baudelaire's poet is the man *of* the crowd as opposed to the man *in* the crowd. The poet is the center of an order of things of his own making even though, to others, he appears to be just one constituent part of the metropolitan flux" (3). Without question, however, the *flâneur* is a *man*. According to Baudelaire and subsequent purveyors of *flânerie,* no woman "can disconnect herself from the city and its enchantments. No woman is able to attain the aesthetic distance so crucial for the *flâneur's* superiority" (Ferguson 1994:27).[61] Ferguson, Wolff, Nord, and Urch have effectively demonstrated that "the notion of the *flâneuse* or 'female dandy' is impossible" because a "female cannot transcend the marked body to engage in the kind of modern observation of crowds practiced by the *flâneur*" (Urch 23). Simply put, a woman walking the streets in the nineteenth century was not presumed to be a lady of leisure consuming the view—it was assumed she was working the streets, literally, a sexual commodity waiting for the next available customer. As Pugh summarizes Baudelaire's favorite metaphors, any loitering woman is presumably "'la grande horizontale,' the 'landscape,' signifier of the 'virgin forest' of the city" (1990b:155).

As revised and reissued in 1857, *Les Fleurs du Mal* consists of five sections: "Spleen et idéal," "Tableaux parisiens," "Le Vin," "Fleurs du Mal," and "La Mort." The Parisian scenes of the second section focus upon the strange and the estranged; for the speaker, everything is graphically real and at the same time "allegorical." Through the speaker's tireless gaze, one encounters red-haired beggars, a dying swan "bathing his wings in dust" (Baudelaire 1993:175), old men, old women with their "appalling charms" (1993:181), "old whores" (1993:195), and "la brune echanteresse" (1993:128).[62] Some are physically maimed, others are blind; all are emotionally and psychically damaged. Somewhat surprisingly, the built environment is rarely mentioned beyond references to the streets, arcades, and the "charnel house" (1993:191); it is as if the redevelopers of the Second Empire had forgotten to replace all the homes, buildings, and monuments they had razed.

Reading *Les Fleurs du Mal* through Walter Benjamin, critics today tend to confine their comments to Baudelaire's project of rendering "the modern" texture of life in "enormous cities." But the gender dynamics of the collection also deserve comment. The prefatory poem, "Au Lecteur," establishes that this is to be a homosocial textual relationship: its final line, which Eliot admired so much that he borrowed it to conclude the first section of *The Waste Land,* is an apostrophe and challenge to "—Hypocrite lecteur,—mon semblable,—mon frère!" ("—Hypocrite reader,—fellow man,—my twin!" [Baudelaire 1993:6, 7]). "Spleen et idéal" returns time and again to the "femme impure" (Baudelaire 1993: 52) to whom the speaker has assigned the role of embodying "Ô fangeuse grandeur! sublime ignominie!" ("O filthy grandeur! o sublime disgrace!" [Baudelaire 1993:54, 55]). In some poems, female figures are merely dishonored or debased. In a text entitled "Une charogne" ("A Carcass"), defilement is horrific because the speaker insists upon correlating his lover's body and "the object" they encounter on the path, a dead woman's body now serving as carrion for a host of predators. Yet the speaker's willful desecration is more shocking:

> Her legs were spread out like a lecherous whore,
> Sweating out poisonous fumes,
> Who opened in slick invitational style
> Her stinking and festering womb.
>
> (Baudelaire 1993:59)

As Pollock has generally observed, the "gaze of the *flâneur* articulates and produces a masculine sexuality which in the modern sexual economy enjoys the freedom to look, appraise and possess" (1988:79). Eliot's praise for Baudelaire's urban poetry eloquently articulates a dream of phallic empowerment and transcendence:

> It is not merely in the use of imagery of the sordid life of a great metropolis, but in the elevation of such imagery to the first intensity—presenting it as it is, and yet making it represent something much more than itself—that Baudelaire has created a mode of release and expression for other men. (*SE* 377)

Apparently, writing and reading textual cities can be truly seminal experiences.

Baudelaire's self-appointed role of *le poet maudit,* the writer whose shock tactics inform theme and imagery alike, should be remembered as well as his textual reconstructions of Paris and Parisians. Also innovative—and of great interest to twentieth-century writers, women and men alike—was the *poème-en-prose* genre, a "hybrid literary form" (Soucy 70), which he helped to introduce. As the introduction to *Le Spleen de Paris* explains, "it is especially from the frequenting of enormous cities, from the intersecting of their innumerable connections, that this ideal [of a prose-poem] arises" (Baudelaire 1918 1:276). One should consider carefully the argument's causality: modernity, and its chief space, the city, are the *cause* of and impetus for avant-garde modes of writing. Fifty years after Baudelaire, Williams presents an almost identical rationale to his readers: "To hell with singing the States and the plains and the Sierra Nevadas for their horses' vigour," Williams exclaims in an editorial.[63] It is time to write the "new"—urban life—in the

"ONLY form [free verse] that CAN CARRY THE NEW MEANING that is imperatively required today. . . . And it is only the modern which is worth expressing" (Williams 1919:31).[64]

Although the ennui pervading Baudelaire's Paris could not be further removed from the unbridled energy of Walt Whitman's New York, the poetry of both men insists that there is something fundamentally "heroic" about modern life. Baudelaire not only entitled one section of the *Salon de 1846,* "De l'héroisme de la vie moderne," he continually returned to this theme in his poems. Whitman's texts repeatedly identify, with great exuberance, the "heroic deeds" that characterize life on the open road and within the city, "glories strung like beads on my smallest sights and hearings, on the walk in the street and the passage over the river" (1:167). For those modern American poets who preferred heroic gestures with a nationalistic flare, the legacy of Whitman's organic and orgiastic city was crucial.

Characteristically, a Whitman text offers a catalogue of urban sights and sounds, a palimpsest of past and present impressions:

> You flagg'd walks of the cities! you strong curbs at the edges!
> You ferries! you planks and posts of wharves! you timber-lined
>   sides! you distant ships!
> You rows of houses! you window-pierc'd façades! you roofs!
> You porches and entrances! you copings and iron guards!
> You windows whose transparent shells might expose so much! . . .
> You gray stones of interminable pavements! you trodden crossings!
> From all that has touch'd you I believe you have imparted to yourselves,
>   and now would impart the same secretly to me,
> From the living and dead you have peopled your impassive
> surfaces, and the spirits thereof would be evident and amicable with me.
>   (Whitman 1:158)

The poet needs the city as muse and topos, but the city, one is told, needs the poet to speak on its behalf. The teeming life of "Broadway," for example, all but begs for his interpretive utterance:

> What hurrying human tides, or day or night!
> What passions, winnings, losses, ardors, swim thy waters!
> What whirls of evil, bliss and sorrow, stem thee!
> What curious questioning glances—glints of love!
> Leer, envy, scorn, contempt, hope, aspiration!
> Thou portal—thou arena—thou of the myriad long-drawn
>   lines and groups!
> (Could but thy flagstones, curbs, façades, tell their
>   inimitable tales;

Thy windows rich, and huge hotels—thy side-walks wide;)
Thou of the endless sliding, mincing, shuffling feet! . . .
Thou visor'd, vast, unspeakable show and lesson!

(Whitman 1:442)[65]

As much an emotional space as it is a built environment, this textual city
bespeaks a multitude of events, impressions, and personalities that the
poet reads as a mirror for his multidimensional self. Whether the text is
"Crossing Brooklyn Ferry," "A Broadway Pageant," or the prose-poem-
cum-sermon *Democratic Vistas* (which is *not* unreservedly positive in its
assessment of urban life), Whitman is not simply observing other bodies
and structures: he is representing himself in the act of discovering his own
body. "I too walk'd the streets of Manhattan island," he declares in
"Crossing Brooklyn Ferry," "I too felt the curious abrupt questionings stir
within me, / In the day among crowds of people . . . / In my walks home
late at night or as I lay in my bed . . . / I too had been struck from the
float forever held in solution, / I too had receiv'd identity by my body"
(Whitman 1:169).

Baudelaire's Paris has been robbed of its past; the future can only be projected as a tomb. Whitman's "Mannahatta" draws its strength from an im-
brication of history and myth, and remarkable confidence in "high growths"
to come:

I was asking for something specific and perfect for my city,
Whereupon lo! upsprang the aboriginal name.
Now I see what there is in a name, a word, liquid, sane, unruly,
    musical, self-sufficient,
I see that the word of my city is that word from of old,
Because I see that word nested in nests of water-bays, superb,
Rich, hemm'd thick all around with sailships and steamships, an
    island sixteen miles long, solid-founded,
Numberless crowded streets, high growths of iron, slender,
    strong, light, splendidly uprising toward clear skies, . . .
Immigrants arriving, fifteen or twenty thousand in a week,
The cars hauling goods, the manly race of drivers of horses, the
    brown-faced sailors. . . .
The mechanics of the city, the masters, well-form'd, beautiful-
    faced, looking you straight in the eyes . . .
A million people—manners free and superb—open voices—
    hospitality—the most courageous and friendly young men,
City of hurried and sparkling waters! city of spires and masts!
City nested in bays! my city!

(Whitman 1:409–410)

Not only is "Mannahatta" a place for all seasons, it is a city that has not been alienated from the country. In Richard Chase's words, it is "a paradoxically urban-pastoral world of primeval novelty" (95). It is also a space in which a homoerotic gaze freely appreciates that which is "manly," "well-form'd" and beautifully masculine. In contrast, Baudelaire offers his readers several textual encounters with lesbians, but they are little more than further examples of urban malnormality.

City Women

As different as they are in ambience and human possibilities, Baudelaire's Paris and Whitman's New York share one common, abject figure: the prostitute.[66] The men who populate the city are dissimilar and varied; the women are pathetically typecast (mother-city degraded to inner-city whore), "always objectified, always 'other' and always instrumental in making the social or existential statement he is after" (Nord 1991:353). "The Painter of Modern Life" devotes an entire chapter to "Women and Prostitutes"; courtesans invade the streets of Baudelaire's city as much as they overrun his speaker's dreams. When the evening, "amiable soir," arrives,

> Against the glimmerings teased by the breeze
> Old Prostitution blazes in the streets;
> She opens out her nest-of-ants retreat;
> Everywhere she clears the secret routes,
> A stealthy force preparing for a coup;
> She moves within this city made of mud,
> A worm who steals from man his daily food.
>
> (Baudelaire 1993:193)

In Baudelaire's allegory of modern life, "an 'erotology of the condemned,'" only Prostitution defiantly maintains and exudes the forcefulness that Ennui has drained from everyone and everything else in the city; "the debasement of erotic life is presented in all its facets, and in Satanic lividness" (Buck-Morss 1986:122).

A Whitmanesque prostitute can be victimizer or victim. In "Song of Myself" Section 15 ("The Memorial History of the City of New York"), the note struck is one of pathos:

> The prostitute draggles her shawl, her bonnet bobs on
>   her tipsy and pimpled neck,
> The crowd laugh at her blackguard oaths, the men jeer
>   and wink to each other,
> (Miserable! I do not laugh at your oaths nor jeer you[.])
>
> (Whitman 1:74)

Although the speaker's tone may suggest acute sensitivity, the text is nevertheless exploitive, condemning the woman to a male economy of desire in
which she is expendable and easily exchanged—the ultimate commodity
fetish. With considerable metaphorical thrift, Whitman's "The City Dead-
House" fuses morgue, brothel, and female genitalia to expose the city's dead-
liest, most corrupting reality:

> Dead house of love—house of madness and sin, crumbled, crush'd,
> House of life, erewhile talking and laughing—but ah, poor house,
>   dead even then,
> Months, years, an echoing, garnish'd house—but dead, dead, dead.
>   (1:329)

At the monstrous heart of the most insidious streets in the modern textual city, the prostitute's dangerously appetitive (and often diseased) body is
the ultimate site of horror, degradation, and emasculation.[67] Nonetheless, it
is her secret carnal knowledge that the text wants to penetrate, time and
again. The brothel figures as "the privileged other space of the city in its masculine urban geography, the house that is not a home, in Linda Nochlin's
phrase" (Pollock 1999:222). Picasso knew as much when he identified the
women in his ground-breaking cubist spectacle as *Demoiselles d'Avignon,* the
"Avignon being not the Provençal home of the anti-Popes, but the Nighttown of Barcelona" (Scholes 2:9). Joyce stages "Circe," the cathartic and
punningly nonclimactic episode of *Ulysses,* in Dublins's Nighttown, which
valorizes "the phallic arena" of the text as it "foster[s] and satisf[ies] male fantasies" (Boone 157).[68]

In Bodenheim's "South State Street, Chicago," the "spectral night" juxtaposes one "woman/ Sleekly, sulkily complacent, / Like a tigress nibbling bits
of sugar" and "a snowy girl/ Whose body blooms with cool withdrawal"
(*SofC* 208). In Edgar Lee Masters's Chicago-inspired narrative poem, "The
Loop," almost the only females who populate the text are fallen women:
"obese women" who cater to "skeleton men," and "a fair girl who is a late re-
cruit/ To those poor women slain each year by lust" (*SofC* 123). In a man's
city, the woman is always identified in terms of prostitution: is she, is she
not, could she be, would she be. A public woman is presumed to be "fallen
woman," as Nord explains: "she may function as a projection of the male
stroller's alienation or as an emblem of social contamination that must be
purged" (1991:374). Sandburg's textual gaze identifies female "traffickers" in
flesh (61) wherever it goes—from Chicago to New York, "chippies" and
"floozies" (164) are to be found either "on the knee" of some man, or underneath him (191). "They tell me you are wicked and I believe them," the
speaker of Sandburg's "Chicago" declares: "for I have seen your painted

women under the gas lamps luring the farm boys" (3). The possessive pronoun carefully absolves the speaker of any responsibility for these women, who must be disowned to facilitate guiltless sexual possession.

With the exception of the "young slatterns, bathed in filth" in Williams's 1923 text "To Elsie" (1991 1:217) and the "marvelous old queen" who haunts "The Wanderer" (1991 1:29), prostitutes are scarce in his early imagistic lyrics. Their figuration is crucial to *Paterson*, however. In Book III, Henri Toulouse-Lautrec[69] is invoked as *the* emblematic artist (Book V is dedicated to him), someone who "made brothels [his] home" and whose canvases, like his mind, became "the locus / where two women meet" and are "recorded" (*Pat* 134–135). Homage to Joyce[70] is featured in Part Five, in the letter from "G. S." that regales "Doc Paterson" with tales of foreign sexual adventures, both promised and achieved. Initially, G. S. was exposed to the "'whores grasping for your genitals, faces almost pleading ... "two dolla, two dolla" till you almost go in with the sheer brute desire straining at your loins, the whisky and the fizzes and the cognac in you till a friend grabs you ... "No ... to a real house, this is shit." ... *Casa real? Casa de putas?* and then the walk through the dark streets, joy of living, in being drunk and walking with other drunks, ... and there are women ready to love for some paper in your pocket'" (*Pat* 249). Subsequently, thinking of "'Baudelaire and Rimbaud and a soul with a book in it,'" the correspondent pays to have sex with a young girl, noting "'the clean hair of her and the beauty of her body in the orchid stench, in the vulgar assailing stench the fragility. ... [T]here is nothing to smile at but smile absurdly ... heat and passion bright and white ... [brighter] than the gin fizz white and deep as birth, deeper than death'" (*Pat* 250). "Doc" is a latter-day Ulysses at this moment: he hears the siren's song, but is distanced from actual sexual contact. Williams's discursive strategy is noteworthy: the text enjoys the vicarious sexual experience but the letter, and its prose medium, prevent any degradation to the poetry.

As Sharpe and Rodgers have thoroughly discussed, *Paterson* is obsessed with "the whored virgin" as "sacrificial victim" of the modern city" (Rodgers 107). If one returns to the retrospective Book V, however, one finds that platitudinous comments do not disguise the power dynamic relished by the speaker. "[E]very married man carries in his head," the speaker admits, "the beloved and a sacred image / of a virgin / whom he has whored" (*Pat* 272). A phallic imagination is being "consecrated," not a woman. The speaker protects his image of his wife by conferring whoredom upon another female, at one and the same time proving that he is the active member, so to speak, while the unnamed woman is the recipient of his definitive heterosexuality. As I discussed in Chapter 3, poets such as Williams readily represent fleshly female bodies that can be violated and overpowered: they are occasions for domination in partial compensation for the powerlessness that characterizes everyday life. Yet, as Nord suggests, the prostitute's "meaning" is "by no means monolithic. The sexually tainted woman can stand variously as an emblem of social suffering or debasement, as a projection of or an analogue to the . . . alienated self, as an instrument of pleasure and partner in urban sprees, as a rhetorical and symbolic means of isolating and quarantining urban ills in the midst of an otherwise buoyant metropolis, or as an agent of connection and contamination" (1991:353–354).

Among those figures featured in the "lunar synthesis" of Eliot's "Rhapsody on a Windy Night" is

> " . . . that woman
> Who hesitates towards you in the light of the door
> Which opens on her like a grin.
> You see the border of her dress
> Is torn and stained with sand,
> And you see the corner of her eye
> Twists like a crooked pin."
>
> (*CPP* 24)

Sand stains connect her with the "sawdust restaurants" and the mermaid-haunted shores of "The Love Song of J. Alfred Prufrock." Whores and their madams are easily located in the Sweeney poems and *The Waste Land,* but "refinement"[71] prevents middle- and upper-class male figures from taking advantage. Eliot, like Ezra Pound, is more interested in prostitution as a metaphor for all female activity. Throughout their canons, middle- and upper-class "ladies" and wives sell themselves into safe marriages and relationships: consider Eliot's "Portrait of a Lady" and the neuraesthenic woman of "A Game of Chess" in *The Waste Land,* and Pound's "Portrait d'une Femme" and "In a Garden."[72] Madame Sosostris prostitutes the male art of prophecy in *The Waste Land;* the latter rightly belongs to Ezekiel, Isaiah, Tiresias, Buddha—and the doom-speaking "I" of the text.[73]

Prostitutes also ply their trade in the poems of Claude McKay and Langston Hughes, but to different effect. For both, the females' "sexual barter" is a response to "poverty"; the "weary, weary feet" of the women are "thinly clad" as they trudge along city streets looking for trade (McKay 1953:60). Yet McKay's speaker in "The Harlem Dancer" cannot wholly separate himself from the "eager, passionate gaze" of those who "devou[r]" the dancer's "shape"; the natural imagery he uses ("To me she seemed a proudly-swaying palm") may seem to dignify her, but also makes her exotic, less of a person. And this despite the earnest sensitivity of the final line, "I knew her self was not in that strange place" (McKay 1953:61). Typically, the McKay poems serve to reinforce the speaker's social awareness, not the prostitutes' individuality. Hughes, on the other hand, not only refuses condemnation, but insists that the women have just as much voice in the community as anyone else. (This same approach is taken in his fiction and drama [Nelson 339].) Thus some texts are presented from the prostitutes' subject position. How *does* the reader feel to be reduced to banal come-ons for sailors in "Port Town" and "Natcha"? As Hughes's life and art become more radicalized, the analysis of prostitution and its metaphorical potential become more pointed, and race-related. "Ruby Brown" tells the complex story of beautiful, "gold" young "colored" woman whose life offers no outlet for "the clean flame of joy / That tried to burn within her soul" (Hughes 1994:73). Consequently, while "polishing the silver" one day for her white employer,

> She asked herself two questions
> And they ran something like this:
> What can a colored girl do
> On the money from a white woman's kitchen?
> And ain't there any joy in this town?
>
> Now the streets down by the river
> Know more about this pretty Ruby Brown
> And the sinister shuttered houses off the bottoms
> Hold a yellow girl
> Seeking an answer to her questions. . . .
> But the white men,
> Habitués of the high shuttered houses,
> Pay more money to her now
> Than ever they did before,
> When she worked in their kitchens.
>
> (Hughes 1994:73)

The economics of exploitation could not be clearer. "Habitués" would seem to protect the anonymous white men, cloaking them in a French word that disguises their identities as sexual predators—but the unexpected term, and the heavy alliteration of the line, only draw attention to their demeaning, dishonorable behavior. As Leslie Sanders observes, "In the economy of the ghetto, few women have access to wealth: the sex trade . . . always represented opportunity of a kind" (201). In the American domain, Hughes exposes white supremacy in the "magnolia-scented South" as a "dark-eyed whore, / Passionate, cruel, / Honey-lipped, syphilitic" (1994:27). His examination of racism abroad, however, is more complicated. "Negroes from Senegal" visiting the capitol of their colonial oppressors (who "amuse themselves" with their visitors) are allowed to consort with "the three old prostitutes of France—/ Liberty, Equality, Fraternity—And all three of 'em sick," but the "disease" that they carry home with them ("From the boss to the bossed / disease") could potentially infect the Africans with live-saving political ideals (Hughes 1999:91–92).

Two final points about the prostitution and brothel fetish should be mentioned: the masculine privilege it enshrines, and its alternative symbolic potential. As Scholes admits, "modernism was never a level playing field but was a gendered movement, driven by the anxieties and ambivalences of male artists and writers . . . [a] masculinist activity that positioned women voyeuristically and turned would-be agents into patients to an astonishing extent" (1:2, 1). If one is repeatedly exposed to the objectification and degradation of textual women, how readily could one imagine—or respect, or publish the works of—a different kind of woman? Strangely enough, the brothel-bound female of male modernist poetry is inversely analogous to the *Japoniste* figures in Whistler's canvases. Whistler dehumanizes through beauty; the Men of 1914, through ugliness. The prostitute, a projection of the male mind, embodies what he fears most about the world (it is dangerous, devouring, yet seductive) and what he dreads to accept about himself. As the first issue of *BLAST* declares, "The past and the future are the prostitutes Nature has provided. Art is periodic escape from this Brothel" (1:148). The Lewis/Pound observation echoes Baudelaire but does not pursue his insight that the prostitute exemplifies the artist's situation in "modern, capitalistic Europe" (Scholes 1:6). Yet Baudelaire fully acknowledges "this divine prostitution of the soul giving itself entire, all its poetry and all its charity, to the unexpected as it comes along, to the stranger as he passes" (1995:20). Similarly, "The Venal Muse" in *Spleen and Ideal* reiterates the damaging truth that publication is tantamount to prostitution. As the prostitute sells her body, so the poet sells his ideas and words.[74]

Policing the Phallic City

Male texts frequently catch the scent of a woman before they catch sight.[75] Olfactory imagery, I would argue, intensifies the presentation of woman as animalistic Other. Sandburg sniffs out women in "Whiffs of the Ohio River at Cincinnati" as much as Eliot does in "Rhapsody on a Windy Night" ("all the old nocturnal smells /. . . . female smells in shuttered rooms" [*CPP* 25]) and "Prufrock" ("Is it perfume from a dress/ That makes me so digress?" [*CPP* 15]). Pound eliminated from the typescript of *The Waste Land* the vignette that is obsessed with "Odours, confected by the cunning French, / [To] Disguise the good old hearty female stench" (*Facs* 39). In the "Broadway" segment of "The Wanderer" (1914), Williams's speaker, an Alastor- by-way-of-Whitman figure, is "struck" by his female daemon in this way: "for the first time, / I really scented the sweat of her presence / And turning saw

her and—fell back sickened! / Ominous, old, painted" (1991 1:29). Paterson repeatedly scolds a woman, "You smell as though you need / a bath. Take
off your clothes and purify / yourself" (*Pat* 128). Confirmation of his own
point of view, however, is really what the man-city-poet seeks:

> (Then, my anger rising) TAKE OFF YOUR
> CLOTHES! I didn't ask you
> to take off your skin. I said your
> clothes, your clothes. You smell
> like a whore. I ask you to bathe in my
> opinions, the astonishing virtue of your
> lost body (I said)[.]

(*Pat* 128–129)

All women, therefore, are multiply victimized: by modern city life—its excessive violence, economic deprivations, and spiritual malaise—and by modern male poets, who feed, textually speaking, on female debasement, and
habitually reinscribe these victims as unnatural or demonic victimizers.

The text's ultimate revenge, in many instances, is to dismember the female body, to carve up the corrupting site. It has been argued by many that
disembodiment—fragmented body imagery—pervades modern city poetry,
a technique that vividly symbolizes the extent to which urban environments
maim their inhabitants physically as well as emotionally.[76] Nochlin's excellent 1994 study outlines the extent to which impressionist and post-impressionist paintings foreground "the theme of the body in pieces or the
fragment as a metaphor of modernity" (1994a:37). "Fragmentation, mutilation, and destruction," she observes, "might be said to be the founding
tropes of the visual rhetoric" of modern art (Nochlin 1994a:9).[77] It is within
this context that one should reconsider the modern male poet's preoccupation with female vivisection. The eponymous "Old Men" of Williams's 1916
poem "have studied / every [female] leg show / in the city" (1991 1:96). The
female accident victim of "The Last Turn" (first published 1941; reworked
and reissued in 1944) is brutally dismembered by a car crash[78]—and the
gaze of the male speaker, who does not flinch from sharing every "distress-
ing detail" of "a half purple half naked woman's / body whose bejeweled guts
/ the cars drag up and down" (Williams 1991 2:27). The anonymous
woman, reduced to "pigment upon flesh," is "nothing recognizable," but her
mutilation is an occasion for masculine creativity (1991 2:83).

Eliot's J. Alfred Prufrock is particularly adept at itemizing those features
of the female anatomy that tantalize and torment him most: "the faces that
you meet," a head "settling [on] a pillow," "Arms that are braceleted and
white and bare," "Arms that lie along a table, or wrap about a shawl" (*CPP*

14–16). Stevens has not been mentioned thus far because he is exceptional among his male peers for his non-urban gaze. Nonetheless, of the "Six Significant Landscapes" that he explores in 1916, the second is as follows:

> The night is of the color
> Of a woman's arm:
> Night, the female,
> Obscure,
> Fragrant and supple,
> Conceals herself,
> A pool shines,
> Like a bracelet
> Shaken in a dance.
>
> (Stevens 16)

This speaker and Prufrock should have compared dance cards. As Rubin advises, "we never encounter the body unmediated by the meanings that cultures give to it" (276–277).

However brutal or criminal the dismemberment of metropolitan females may seem to us, the typical white male modernist text not only allows it, but sanctions it. This is one of the ways in which the text controls both its boundaries and its central problems. Eliot's original, Dickensian title for *The Waste Land,* "He Do the Police in Different Voices," is usually cited as a gesture toward the ventriloquism of the text. Just as significant, I would suggest, is the notion of the text as a system for imposing order on the most unstable, chaotic, and threatening elements of modern urban life. In the poetic systems of Eliot and his male contemporaries, bag ladies are allowed to roam the parks and gutters, and prostitutes are not kept from the streets—after all, a girl has to make a living—but most women and ladies are marshalled into domestic, interior textual spaces. Linguistic force, in this sense, combats the turmoil of the city. In the ancient Greek city-state, the original *polis,* women, like slaves, were not included in the ranks of *polites,* or citizens. In modern male textual cities, women are similarly disenfranchised.

This privileged homosociality—for male citizen and writer alike—is especially apparent in the works of Sandburg and Eliot, two poets rarely spoken of in the same critical breath because Sandburg's Whitmanesque urban paeans seem thematically and stylistically anachronistic when compared with Eliot's modernist delineations of urban nightmares. Nevertheless, both poets share a dream of the re-gendered phallic city. For Sandburg, the *muscular* phallic city exists *now:* it can be experienced in Chicago, Buffalo, New York, Cincinnati—any urban space where "men grappling [with] plans" and men working with their hands and machinery build the most imposing phallic monument possible, the skyscraper. "Strong men put up a city," declares Sandburg's "Four Preludes on Playthings of the Wind" (183), a textual city that is then inhabited by manly figures of toil and tenacity.[79] For Eliot, the *spiritual* phallic city is visited only in glimpses:

> O City city, I can sometimes hear
> Beside a public bar in Lower Thames Street,
> The pleasant whining of a mandolin
> And a clatter and a chatter from within
> Where fishmen lounge at noon: where the walls
> Of Magnus Martyr hold
> Inexplicable splendour of Ionian white and gold.

> *(CPP 69)*

These lines occupy the thematic as well as the physical center of *The Waste Land;* only this promise of exclusive male-male bonding prompts the text to gaze at the splendid rather than the sordid.[80] Significantly, this is the sole reference to a "city" in the poem that is not qualified by the word "unreal." Granted, the speaker overhears rather than experiences the providential homosocial exchange, but sensory contact with the "fishmen" also links the modernist *flâneur* with Christ and his disciples, the Grail legend, and other ostensible origins of patriarchal Western civilization ("Ionian white and gold").

Writing Oneself Out of the City

Given all that the modern male textual city is, and is not, small wonder then that many female contemporaries of Eliot, Sandburg, Williams, and McKay elected to write themselves out of the urban locus, away from the bastion of male prerogatives where women were "exiled by sexuality, relegated to marginality, silenced, objectified, expunged" (Squier 102). (The same is not true about women novelists from this period, but that, as they say, is another story.[81]) Some would argue that in doing so, in turning their gaze away from the city, poets such as H. D., Marianne Moore, Angelina Weld Grimké, and Helene Johnson were simply capitulating to stereotype, adhering to the tradition of gendered spaces that banished women from public centers of culture and relegated them instead to the merely natural or domestic. I would suggest that they elected to occupy an alternative dialogical position, in that way both ensuring and politicizing personal and vocational survival. These poets sought an imaginative locus in which they could achieve independence and mobility, where their perceptions of themselves and the world were clarified and confirmed, not denigrated and denied.[82] They returned to "nature" to denaturalize gender conventions that pronounce women passive and weak yet fertile when necessary—to overcome the prejudices so aptly summarized by James, that nature is "that quite other happy and charming thing, *feminine* . . . feminine from head to foot, in expression, tone, and touch, mistress throughout of the feminine attitude and effect. . . . It seemed to plead, the pathetic presence, to be liked, to be loved, to be stayed with, lived with, handled with some kindness, shown even some courtesy of admiration" (*TAS* 372–373). As women and as Americans, they were "doubly drawn to the natural world, expressing through that affinity their resentment and fear of a perceived patriarchal civilization, symbolized so well by the city, that conquers the landscape 'by imposing an alien and abstract pattern upon it'" (Grace 195). Rather than thinking of these feminist-naturalist poems as acquiescent exercises in an outmoded discursive tradition, or "conventional and sentimental, out of step with the militant, rebellious race consciousness of the period" (N. McKay 1–2), one could just as easily consider them as potent refusals to reduplicate city text clichés—refusals in the modern tradition of the impressionists' Salon des Refusés.

Although gender politics are not part of his brief, Pugh aptly summarizes the position that "landscape imagery" is also "contested political terrain"; how "landscape is 'read' illustrates the primary role that discourses of landscape play in the field of cultural contestation" (1990a:2). However naturalistic the effects of a poem, it never presents a "transparent transcription of nature" (Bermingham 97); as the works by modern women poets amply demonstrate, landscape is not "an object to be seen" but a "process by which social and subjective identities are formed" (Mitchell 1994a:1). Fabricant was one of the first to explain specifically how "feminized landscape[s]" in works by men encode cultural meanings and values; her ground-breaking study of Augustan prose and poetry demonstrates that when men write about gardens and nature, they are simultaneously uttering "statements about how power was conceived and wielded during this period" (113). When modern women write themselves into natural environments, they are not only using the natural elements for "self-understanding and self-representation" (Mitchell 1994b:22), but repossessing the discursive means of mediating erotic, social, and aesthetic experiences. Where once a Pope or Addison, Wordsworth or Whitman exercised their "fantasies of power," control, and conquest (Fabricant 123), modern women began asserting and legitimating new realities. To borrow Bourdieau's terms, the poets work through natural tropes to consecrate the discursive events and their creative rights.

Sometimes a text will begin with a speaker who "is sick of the city, wanting the sea" (Millay 105), and move quickly from a restrictive urban locus to an enriching natural one. (Prufrock, of course, tried to do the same, but was too emotionally paralyzed to enjoy his freedom.) As Bessie Mayle observes, "Skylines / Are marking me in today" (Honey ed. 207). "These burning streets shall know / My songs no more," Marjorie Marshall's speaker promises herself, "And I shall guard my ears / Against the rigid cry / Of steel on stone" (Honey ed. 190). Anita Scott Coleman is most explicit: the "jammed" and "drab street" is a "white man's street" (Honey ed. 109). "Wild Peaches" by Elinor Wylie not only rejects the cityscape of Baltimore, but denies the appeal of a quintessential male fantasy, a "homespun" Thoreau-esque retreat into a "milk and honey" rural scene. Instead, the final lines of the text effect another kind of solitary possession:

> I love the look, austere, immaculate,
> Of landscapes drawn in pearly monotones.
> There's something in my very blood that owns
> Bare hills, cold silver on a sky of slate,
> A thread of water, churned to milky spate
> Streaming through slanted pastures fenced with stones.
>
> (Wylie 12)

Ownership, austere fecundity: the textual gaze constructs and then benefits from its landscape of difference.

To remain city-focused would have narrowed the intellectual and emotional registers of the texts. As H. D. summarizes in her 1919 *Notes on Thought and Vision,*

> Our minds, all of our minds, are like dull little houses, built more or less alike—a dull little city with rows of little detached villas, and here and there a more pretentious house, set apart from the rest, but in essentials, seen from a distance, one with the rest, all drab, all grey.
>   Each comfortable little home shelters a comfortable little soul—and a wall at the back shuts out completely any communication with the world beyond. (Scott ed. 103)

Psychological and emotional discomfort prompt the speaker of Wylie's "Where, O Where" to find a means of escaping both a repressive "little home" and any thoughts of suicide:

> I need not die to go
> So far you cannot know
> My escape, my retreat,
> And the prints of my feet
> Written in blood or dew;
> They shall be hid from you,
> In fern-seed lost
> Or the soft flakes of frost. . . .

You shall see me no more
Though each night I hide
In your bed, at your side.

(Wylie 153)

On the one hand, the speaker imaginatively exercises the wandering "feet" so feared or disparaged by writers such as Yeats. On the other hand, the relief is temporary at best, textual rather than actual. Similarly, Georgia Douglas Johnson imagines that "The Heart of a Woman" begins each day as "a lone bird," "restlessly" exploring the world, but each night returns home and "enters some alien cage in its plight . . . / While it breaks, breaks, breaks on the sheltering bars" (Stetson ed. 58).[83] This scenario of defeat, however, is countered by the speaker of Johnson's "Your World," who admits that "I used to abide / In the narrowest nest in a corner, / My wings pressing close to my side," but now soars with "rapture, with power, with ease!" (Honey ed. 63).

In *Achievement in American Poetry*, Louise Bogan praises twentieth-century women poets for continuing, "unbroken," the "line of feeling" in American poetry, that "poetic intensity which wavers and fades and often completely fails in poetry written by men" (1951:19). As I discussed in Chapter 3, "feeling" was presumed, by male authors and critics alike, to be synonymous with "sentimentality," and therefore to be avoided. Yet the poetry of H. D., Millay, and their peers represents a deliberate break from the genteel, asexual, unquestioningly inspirational verse of their nineteenth-century female predecessors, texts that celebrated the quiet joys of domesticity or the spiritual benefits of God's creation. (I am referring to the kind of poetry written by Emma Embury, not Emily Dickinson.) Those women, to quote a Bogan poem,

Women have no wilderness in them,
They are provident instead,
Content in the tight hot cell of their hearts
To eat dusty bread. . . .
They wait, when they should turn to journeys,
They stiffen, when they should bend.
They use against themselves that benevolence
To which no man is friend.

(Bogan 1954: 25)

As the text insists, women have no "wilderness in them" because their culture teaches them otherwise. Masculinist discourse is not only promulgated by men; for centuries, women have been complicit in their own oppression, working "against themselves" in the name of gender stability and "benevolence." Bogan, Millay, Moore, and H. D. were the "new" women whose natural locii were "wild" zones that made possible original discursive and cultural practices. Searching for a new clarity of vision, they abandoned phallic, urban *hinder*-lands in favor of textual hinterlands of their own making. Within the latter, as Millay writes, "The mind is free / One moment, to compute, refute, amass, / Catalogue, question, contemplate, and see" (721). Figuratively speaking, by leaving behind the city these poets refused physical, cultural, and creative incarceration.

H. D., Moore, and Bogan laid claim to nonurban locii like prospectors seizing upon a new vein of gold. Similar to Georgia Douglas Johnson and Effie Lee Newsome, Wylie and Millay typically used conventional poetic discourse to articulate nontraditional ideas about female aspirations and sensations. Yet as Nelson argues, "to ask what gendered legacy modern poetry has bequeathed," one must "set aside the long-honored division between experimental and traditional forms in modern poetry. It is reasonable to claim . . . that our fixation on the story of experimentalist triumph—the hallmark of modernism as it has been marketed by academics for fifty years—has blinded us to other ways of configuring modern poetry" (323). One does not find critics faulting "modern" Baudelaire for writing sonnets; just as the "fixedness" of genre is "a mirage" in his canon (C. Scott 270),[84] so too Millay's sonnets such as "What lips my lips have kissed" (602), "I shall forget you presently, my dear" (571), and "I too beneath your moon, almighty Sex" (688) gingerly invigorate the discourse with vernacular tones and wisdom, and subvert generic expectations. Nothing is sacred in these texts, and everything is open to negotiation: desire, sexual satisfaction, the construction of femininity and masculinity, the potential of the form. "Sonnets from an Ungrafted Tree" is a stunning 17-text sequence that follows a wife's death-watch for her husband. Elliott and Wallace's insights regarding Natalie Barney's poetry are especially apposite for poets such as Millay or Helene Johnson; Barney's strategy was "not simply *adopting* but consciously *adapting* archaic forms" (46):

> [T]he need to summon authority by placing one's work in a recognized cultural tradition is a particularly pressing problem for women who have more often than not been exiled from prevailing literary and artistic canons. Frequently a conflict arises between wanting to be taken seriously and legitimized as a writer or artist (which usually means working in either conventional or *recognizably* avant-garde forms) and a need to explore alternative forms and issues that relate to one's position as a woman. (47)

Once poetic paradigms and cultural patterns are both reconfigured, not only will the work of Barney, Millay, and Grimké cease to be devalued, but so too the poetry of other twentieth-century authors such as Frost, Hardy, Lawrence, and Yeats.

Especially interesting is the subtle way in which Millay and many of her peers interrogated the traditional (masculinist) "charms" of the *locus amoenus:* the gardens, springs, meadows, flowers, soft breezes, and birdsong. They resisted reinscribing themselves within the conventions of *descriptio locii,* I would suggest, because of inherent cultural assumptions about that which is "soft," fertile, passive (and feminine) and that which is "hard," generative, active (and masculine).[85] Millay's speakers are not content to be "flowers" or harmless fauna; they express themselves as "hungry" hearts, trees, and "clean cliff[s]" of "ragged islands." Despite the pangs of separation, they require movement, not stasis: "the long white road; / A gateless garden, and an open path" (Millay 67). Many of Millay's texts are apostrophes to, or dialogues with, Life, Death, and Desire; she never confuses love with sexual need, nor fails to assess the costs of "being born a woman and distressed / By all the needs and notions of my kind" (601). Not content with being counted among "the lilies of the field," her speakers enjoy the hard labor of creativity. "Still will I harvest beauty where it grows," one sonnet declares: "in ditch and bog / Filmed brilliant with irregular rainbows / Of rust and oil" (Millay 603). Louise Bogan also resisted both urban sites and the "charms" of patriarchal nature poetry. "The Crows" is typical in its tropes:

> The woman who has grown old
> And knows desire must die,
> Yet turns to love again,
> Hears the crows' cry.
> She is a stream long hardened,
> A weed that no scythe mows.
> The heart's laughter will be to her
> The crying of the crows,
>
> Who slide in the air with the same voice
> Over what yields not, and what yields,
> Alike in spring, and when there is only bitter
> Winter-burning in the fields.
>
> (Bogan 23)

Usually, a Bogan text situates speaker and reader alike in an unsettled natural "zone" where the "wind breaks over us, / And against high sharp angles almost splits into words" (115).

Similarly and consistently, H. D. challenged the established symbolic order through such extended metaphors as the "Sheltered Garden." Eschewing masculinist conventions that relegate woman-as-wax-lily to the confines of the *hortus conclusus*—a legacy of "beauty without strength" as enshrined in texts

such as Ruskin's "Of Queens' Gardens"—H. D.'s speaker articulates astringent
subjective and aesthetic imperatives:

> I have had enough—
> border-pinks, clove-pinks, wax-lilies,
> herbs, sweet-cress.
>
> O for some sharp swish of a branch—
> there is no scent of resin
> in this place,
> no taste of bark, of coarse weeds,
> aromatic, astringent—
> only border on border of scented pinks. . . .
> For this beauty,
> beauty without strength,
> chokes out life. . . .
> O to blot out this garden
> to forget, to find a new beauty
> in some terrible
> wind-tortured place.
>
> (H. D. 1983:19–21)

One of many texts forging an impersonal lyric discourse that deeply encodes
gender issues but does not address them directly, "Sheltered Garden" insists
that the ground of subjectivity should be *difference*. To remain in the garden
of patriarchal imperatives is to have one's "life" choked out. The "astringent"
rewards of agency are figured in terms of a fruit-full existence:

> Have you seen fruit under cover
> that wanted light—
> pears wadded in cloth,
> protected from the frost,
> melons, almost ripe,
> smothered in straw?
>
> Why not let the pears cling
> to the empty branch?
> All your coaxing will only make
> a bitter fruit—
> let them cling, ripen of themselves,
> test their own worth,
> nipped, shrivelled by the frost,
> to fall at last but fair
> with a russet coat.
>
> (H. D. 1983:20)

Experience will inevitably bring a "taste of frost," but the latter is surely "exquisite" when compared with the "smothering" effects of patriarchal culture. "Sheltered Garden" reminds us that irony can have many subtle inflections in modern poetry. As with Hughes's texts, surface simplicity should not be mistaken for a simplistic utterance; H. D.'s accessible diction, metrics, and imagery restore "virtue" to poetic discourse.[86]

As Marianne Moore observed in 1923, "nature in its acute aspects" is to H. D. "a symbol of freedom" (1986:80). Beginning with her celebrated first volume, *Sea Garden* (1916), the discerning reader[87] is aware that "standard poetic representation[s]" are challenged at every turn; "the vast power of the sea" (DeKoven 1999:189) is evoked to erode or wash away notions of women as, in Moore's splendid phrase, "the eternally sleeping beauty, effortless yet effective in the indestructible limestone keep of domesticity" (1986:82). Hence the "Sea Rose," although a "marred" and "meagre flower, thin, / sparse of leaf" is adamantly "more precious / than a wet rose / single on a stem" (H. D. 1983:5). Similarly, the "Sea Lily" is wrested from Marian or Pre-Raphaelite conventions of timidity and virginity, presented not only "slashed and torn," "shattered/ in the wind" but defiantly and "doubly rich" for the experience (H. D. 1983:14). In the new gender order imagined by the speaker, defiant female figures are no longer "drift[ing] upon temple-steps," worshipped for a beauty that actually victimizes them; "though the whole wind / slash at your bark, / you are lifted up" to new subjective and cultural possibilities.

Moore's praise for H. D.'s "wiry diction, accurate observation" and the ability to represent life "denuded of subterfuge" with "the clean violence of truth" (1986:80) was occasioned by *Hymen,* the 1921 volume that continues the work of redefining female subjectivity by reconfiguring beauty in a "cold splendour of song" (1983:127). The volume is remarkable for its generic and emotional range: the ritualized verse drama "Hymen"; dramatic monologues such as "Demeter," "Circe," and "Hippolytus Temporizes"; and lyrics such as "Leda," "The Islands," and "Egypt." "Hymen" is a poetry/prose hybrid that anticipates the discursive method of *Helen in Egypt,* the theme of which—a new vision of Helen's story unlike anything rehearsed by Homer—is forecast in "Eygpt," which dares to enunciate "forbidden knowledge, / wisdom's glance" in terms of the following vision:

> in the mid-most desert—
>
> great shaft of rose,
> fire spred across our path,
> upon the face grown grey, a light,
> Hellas re-born from death.

> (H. D. 1983:141)

H. D. was a careful reader of Yeats's poetry;[88] it is not too fanciful to suggest that her multifaceted "great" rose not only answers and reworks, in a general way, the female signifiers of Yeats's early verse, but replies, visionary to visionary, to the "pitiless" and "vast image out of *Spiritus Mundi*" presented in "The Second Coming," in which the "sands of the desert" reveal a "shape with lion body and head of a man," a "rough beast" whose hour has "come round at last" (1966:402).[89] The rebirth imagined in her text is life-affirming, not a "nightmare" of cyclical inevitability. One wonders too if Yeats's interest in the Leda and the Swan story was spiked by H. D.'s "Leda," which first appeared in *The Monthly Chapbook* in 1919. Those only familiar with Yeats's violent version of the fateful union are unprepared for the erotic fantasy of H. D.'s lyric, a reverie text ("no more regret / nor old deep memories / to mar the bliss") in which the opportunity for human and godly congress is profoundly naturalized. Yeats's speaker is fascinated by the perversion of the sexual act; in H. D.'s refashioning, the event is wholly displaced from the river nymph's body and sanctioned in terms of the inevitable meeting of the "slow river" and "the tide." On this occasion, the lily is "caressed" into a deeper color by the "level ray" of the phallic sun, and then welcomes sexual satisfaction:

> where the low sedge is thick,
> the gold day-lily
> outspreads and rests
> beneath soft fluttering
> of red swan wings
> and the warm quivering
> of the red swan's breast.

(H. D. 1983:121)

Some readers would prefer a more outrageous retelling of the myth; H. D.'s poem stresses shared erotic pleasure.

"Circe" and "Hippolytus Temporizes" explore the consequences of denying satisfaction from different gendered subject positions. The heterosexual plot pursued in the monologues, "Hymen," and many other texts is offset by the Sapphic "heat, more passionate / of bone and the white shell" of "Fragment 113," which employs "the plunder of the bee," the "sweet / stain" of honey, and the "tall stalk / of red twin-lilies" to naturalize lesbian desire.[90] In other words, H. D.'s texts are always writing the body, but using natural tropes to translate the body and mind into new narratives of possibility. Demeter's maternal body is juxtaposed with her deity not only to remind readers of alternative, matriarchal religious and mythic heritages, but to reclaim "strength" as a characteristic of and for women. "My fingers," the goddess exclaims,

Now they are wrought of iron
to wrest from earth
secrets; strong to protect,
strong to keep back the winter
when winter tracks too soon . . .
strong to break dead things,
the young tree, drained of sap,
the old tree, ready to drop,
to lift from the rotten bed
of leaves, the old
crumbling pine tree stock[.]

(H. D. 1983:114)

H. D.'s texts do not imagine, or promise, a woman's strength at the expense of a man's. As *Trilogy* and *Helen in Egypt* demonstrate at length, gender equilibrium is the ultimate desideratum, but the difficult work of achieving balance is always at the forefront.

Many of H. D.'s texts are dramatic monologues whose mythic speakers (Eurydice, Circe, Demeter, Helen, Iphigenia) interrogate the misogynistic assumptions of Western culture, and challenge the ideological work that classical myths have carried out. Like James, Pound, and Eliot, H. D. felt it necessary to relocate in Europe in order to find a suitable environment in which to live and work. But this ex-patriate was also determinedly ex-patriarchal and ex-urban in her writing, a politicized aesthetics best articulated in "All Mountains." To quote just a portion of this splendid text:

Give me all mountains:
city,
town,
the precinct
of temple,
the crowded town-gate,
I have no love for . . .
give me the stream's cold path,
the grove of pine,
for garden terrace
the unclaimed,
bleak
wild stretches
of the mountain side. . . .

Give him white marble,
him the luminous white
of sheltering porch,

> carved pillar,
> portico;
> give him the wharf,
> the quay,
> the street,
> the market,
> street corner
> and the corner of the street; . . .
>
> ah Zeus,
> ennoble,
> shelter these
> thy children,
> but give me the islands of the upper air,
> all mountains
> and the towering mountain trees.

> (H. D. 1983:288–290)

With remarkable and refreshing directness, feminist nature answers, and re-pudiates, the phallic city.

Two of Lowell's most accomplished narrative poems, "Patterns" and "A Roxbury Garden," also use the "sheltered garden" motif to decry the stulti-fying confinement and sameness of women's lives. At the same time, her witty exercise in recovering a women's literary tradition, "The Sisters," high-lights the contrast between Sappho and Elizabeth Barrett Browning by sketching their respective environments. Thriving in the "crisp sea sun-shine," the ancient Greek poet was, especially when "loving,"

> like a burning birch-tree
> All tall and glittering fire, and . . . she wrote
> Like the same fire caught up to Heaven and held there,
> A frozen blaze before it broke and fell.

> (Lowell 459)

But if Sappho's example is akin to the "tossing off of garments," Barrett Browning reminds us of a life "squeezed in stiff conventions" (Lowell 459). Whether her address was Wimpole Street or Casa Guidi, Barrett Brown-ing remains for Lowell an example of the woman who spent her life "tied down to the sofa" (460), her work and her existence tethered by the no-tion that her husband was the superior artist, the "genius" whose needs must come first.

Sappho's "frozen blaze" is seen again in one of Lowell's best imagistic texts, "Opal":

You are ice and fire,
The touch of you burns my hands like snow.
You are cold and flame.
You are the crimson of amaryllis,
The silver of moon-touched magnolias.
When I am with you,
My heart is a frozen pond
Gleaming with agitated torches.

(214)

Strategically available for hetero- or homoerotic narratives, the poem imagines an "unimaginable / Zero" moment quite unlike Eliot's day of "frost and
fire" in "Little Gidding" (*CPP* 191). Like H. D.'s texts, Lowell's poetry transgresses in its very insistence that all desire is "natural" if honestly and intensely experienced. One can readily find in her canon the construction of
natural landscapes for the purposes of self-fashioning, expressing desire, or
seeking a congenial stateside environment. In a very Whitmanesque way,
"Lilacs" pays tribute to "this my New England" (Lowell 446) and the act of
poetic repossession:

Lilacs,
False blue,
White,
Purple,
Colour of lilac.
Heart-leaves of lilac all over New England,
Roots of lilac under all the soil of New England,
Lilac in me because I am New England,
Because my roots are in it,
Because my leaves are of it,
Because my flowers are for it,
Because it is my country
And I speak to it of itself
And sing of it with my own voice
Since certainly it is mine.

(Lowell 447)

Conventional or not, the "heart-leaves" are an effective naturalistic means of
claiming an independent, creative "voice."

African American women poets of the era also favored natural settings for
their works—for the same affirmative reasons cited above, and sometimes
because of a complicated desire to reaffirm the cultural and historical importance, the racial "pride," of Africa. Their texts eagerly participated in the
radical shift of metaphorical paradigms with which the fragile flowers of

masculinist discourse transformed themselves into the "new beauty" of (pro)feminist strength and diversity. Nonetheless, the black poets tested the resources of natural tropes knowing that the fields and moonlit nights of the South were not just vivid, polyvalent symbols but the actual means of assault, rape, and murder;[91] the trees particularly were instruments of death, the sign of absolute powerlessness when a lynch mob turned a human being into the "strange fruit" of racist terrorism.[92]

Gwendolyn Bennett's speaker associates herself with "the lonely splendor / Of the pine tree" (Stetson ed. 73), but also insists upon an ennobling African "Heritage." "We claim no part with racial dearth," Bennett insists in "To Usward"— "We want to sing the songs of birth!" (Stetson ed. 77). Effie Lee Newsome's aesthetic is proudly politicized: it is a "noble gift to be brown," she proclaims,

> Like the strongest things that make up this earth,
> Like the mountains grave and grand,
> Even like the trunks of trees—
> Even oaks, to be like those!
> God builds His strength in bronze. . . .
> I thank God, then, I am brown.
> Brown has mighty things to do.
>
> (Honey ed. 117)

The second stanza cites "brown" birds such as thrush, lark, and wren; one might appreciate the association with song, but protest that Newsome is uneasy with "mighty" self-referential images. The final natural example, however, "Eagles are of this same hue," indicates that Newsome's speaker is no longer confined to reaffirming a symbolic status quo. The speakers of Grimké and Georgia Douglas Johnson often place themselves at "the horizon's edge" (Honey ed. 73), preparing themselves and their readers for new possibilities, "launching" the dreams that are prerequisites for personal and racial accomplishment.

"My soul is like a tree," Mae Cowdery exclaims, "Lifting its face to the sun" (Honey ed. 194).[93] "A Winter Twilight" by Grimké concentrates on the "group of trees, lean, naked, and cold / Inking their crests 'gainst a sky green-gold," but the solitary "fir" tree, "lonely, apart, unyielding" (Honey ed. 181) is a suggestive emblem of subjectivity. Anita Scott Coleman defines "Negro laughter" as "a stem of joyousness, a hardy tendril / Thrusting through the moraines / of long distress"—in sharp contrast to those who "force their distrait mirth / through thin pale lips" (Honey ed. 111). The construction of whiteness in African American poetry is often a matter of deliberately denying "those others" fully human or natural status (Honey ed. 111). In Anne Spencer's dense short lyric "Lady, Lady," the long-term effects of a black woman's arduous physical labors are inscribed in body and soul, symbolized by her "hands, / Twisted, awry, like crumpled roots, / Bleached poor white in a sudsy tub, / Wrinkled and drawn" (Honey ed. 56). Trees cannot flourish in a racist culture that punishes difference down to its "roots."

Like many African American poets, both Angelina Weld Grimké and Helene Johnson combine images of moonlight and silhouettes to construct new possibilities of "black" beauty. In Grimké's texts, however, moonlight is also best for acknowledging desire and sexual difference. "The Want of You" is evocative whether the desired other is female or male:

> A hint of gold where the moon will be;
> Through the flocking clouds just a star or two;
> Leaf sounds, soft and wet and hushed;
> And oh! the crying want of you.
>
> (Honey ed. 150)

Helene Johnson prefers to feature Sappho in a heterosexual narrative: "Summer Matures" is a dramatic monologue in which the ancient poet enjoins her lover Phaon, a boatman of Lesbos, to "sleep like the stars at dawn with her" (Stetson ed. 82). (According to legend, Phaon's ultimate rejection was the catalyst for Sappho's suicide.) Johnson's very accomplished "Trees at Night" focuses on a local rather than a mythic landscape:

> Slim sentinels
> Stretching lacy arms
> About a slumbrous moon;
> Black quivering
> Silhouettes,
> Tremulous,
> Stencilled on the petal
> Of a bluebell. . . .
> The jagged rent
> Of mountains
> Reflected in a
> Still sleeping lake;
>   . . . And
> Printed 'gainst the sky—
> The trembling beauty
> Of an urgent pine.
>
> (Stetson ed. 81)[94]

Power and urgency, however, signify very differently in Grimké's "Tenebris," a fascinating text:

> There is a tree, by day,
> That, at night,
> Has a shadow,
> A hand huge and black,
> With fingers long and black.
> All through the dark,
> Against the white man's house,
> In the little wind,
> The black hand plucks and plucks
> At the bricks.
> The bricks are the color of blood and very small.
> Is it a black hand,
> Or is it a shadow?
>
> (Cullen ed. 40–41; Honey ed. 185)

Those inside the "white man's house" are currently safe, but the deliberately menacing scenario produced by the speaker suggests that a day will come when they will pay for the "blood" of blacks that they have exploited or shed. The reader is made aware of this future possibility, but the inhabitants of the house cannot "see" the tense anthropomorphic and metonymic signs. Ending with a question adds to the unsettling quality of the poem. I would disagree, therefore, with Nellie McKay's suggestion that Grimké composed "non-racial" and "Imagistic nature poems" and saved the exploration of sexual oppression and racism for her plays and short stories (4).

It Is Not All (Urban) Waste

Despite the sheer number of poems that Lowell produced in her comparatively short career (her first volume was published in 1912; she died in 1925), her ability to find her "own voice" was inconstant. "Circus Tents by Lake Michigan" playfully acknowledges the positive dimensions of creative indebtedness:

> I looked from my window at the great lake,
> And Shakespeare, and Keats, and Whitman stood beside my chair
> And pointed out to me things I might not have seen.
>
> (Lowell 570)

All too often, however, Lowell's poetry seems preoccupied with repeating the discursive manoeuvres of others, including H. D., Moore, and Pound. Of the experiments in "translating" Chinese texts into English that appeared in *Fir-Flower Tablets,* those concentrating on condensed natural images are the most successful. Her collected and uncollected verse also includes a number of poems that focus on urban sites. They have titles such as "New York at Night," "A London Thoroughfare. 2 A.M.," "Wakefulness," and "The Sixteenth Floor," and rarely do more than repeat already-established tropes. But one text, "May Evening in Central Park," clearly identifies a crucial reason why Lowell falters in such a male-identified mode:

> Lines of lamp-light
> Splinter the black water,
> And all through
> The dim part
> Are lamps
> Hanging among the trees. . . .
> I am a swimmer
> In the damp night,
> Or a bird
> Floating over the sucking grasses,
> I am a young man,
> In Central Park,
> With Spring
> Bursting over me[.]
>
> (Lowell 591–592)

Gendered social positioning and poetic practice have collided. To station herself within the city, as an active participant in the work and leisure of urban life, Lowell can only imagine herself as "a young man." "May Evening in Central Park" vividly demonstrates the dilemma facing most women poets in the early twentieth century: participate in a poetic discourse that erases your gendered identity, concentrate on metropolitan topoi in which you are marginalized at best, or privilege naturalistic symbolic landscapes that may seem—to readers, critics, and yourself—removed from contemporary life.

Helene Johnson, on the other hand, writes several accomplished city poems to assert the "splendid" aspects of African American men. Both "Sonnet to a Negro in Harlem" and "Poem" ("Little brown boy, / Slim, dark . . .") assume the power of the gaze to anatomize the "perfect body" and "supercilious" bearing of the "jazz prince" (Cullen ed. 217–218). Rather than commodifying the figures, however, the speakers work diligently to counter demeaning stereotypes of the so-called "lower orders." The speaker of "Bottled," a more complex narrative poem, reclaims "the derogatory epithets of racists" (N. McKay 27) as she learns to see a young man "dressed fit to kill / In yellow gloves and swallowtail coat / And swirling a cane" not as a cartoonish and preening "darky" but as a black man whose self-worth has been bottled up, like the sand "taken from the Sahara desert" now on display in the "135th Street library / in Harlem" (Cullen ed. 221). As Rado observes,

"African-American women struggled to negotiate between their loyalties to their race and to their sex" (297). In these three texts, the identification of people who are "dignified and *proud!*" (Cullen ed. 222), and the effort to claim city streets for blacks, is mutually beneficial.

Not including *Trilogy* and *Helen in Egypt* (feminist revisions of the epic), H. D.'s canon offers more than six hundred pages of spare but lyrically energized, imagistic poetry. Yet one has to look very hard to find the handful of urban motifs she uses. One text, the starkly-named "Cities," confronts the tropes of her male peers, but does so in generalized terms. "Can we believe," the poem begins,

> —by an effort
> comfort our hearts:
> it is not waste all this,
> not placed here in disgust,
> street after street,
> each patterned alike,
> no grace to lighten
> a single house of the hundred
> crowded into one garden-space.
>
> (H. D. 1983:39–40)

Outlining the cycles of growth, decay, and destruction which all cities—male creations—undergo, the poem summons the reader to do more than simply "await the new beauty of cities" (H. D. 1983:41). It is a poetic call to action, a plea for urban renewal that begins with the citizens' imaginations. In her review of *Responsibilities,* H. D. challenges Yeats and "we few, the remnant who still persist in the worship of beauty other than the grace of the steel girder" to counter the "black magic of triangles and broken arcs," of those who praise guns and love "the beauty of machines" (1914:129). "Can we not spiritually join our forces," she asks, "and chastened with old calamities, redefine and reconstruct boundaries and barriers, and reinvoke some golden city, sterner than the dream-cities, and wrought more firm to endure than those riveted of steel and bleak with iron girders" (1914:129)?

From the technically experimental and thematically probing texts of H. D. and Moore we learn that poetry can be erudite and urbane without being urban. "It is human nature," suggests a Moore text entitled "A Grave," for "human nature to stand in the middle of a thing" and thus claim it, experience it, and explain it (1981:49). But Moore's speakers never stand in the middle of a city. Rarely do they engage with humans at all, preferring instead the nongendered realm of a "proliferating bestiary of creatures in protective armour and camouflage" (Ostriker 52). Most importantly, her speakers seek out diversity and admire strength in the natural world: the "defiant edifice" of an underwater cliff; the proud bearing and voice of "A Prize Bird" whose "brazen claws are staunch against defeat"; the incomparable "Indian buffalo"; the "hell-diver" frigate pelican with "wings uniting levity with strength"; "a not long / sparrow-song" that is "tuned reticence with rigor/ from strength at the source" (1981:32, 31, 28, 25, 149).

A "precisionist," to borrow a term from her poem "Bowls," Moore continually demonstrates her belief that the mind "is an enchanting thing" (1981:134). It is "a power of / strong enchantment. It / is like the dove- / neck animated by / sun" (1981:134), not a wound, a prison, or a keyless door (images prevalent, for example, in Eliot's canon). Of the 45 texts in Moore's 1935 *Selected Poems,* only one, "New York," addresses the city. The latter, however, contrasts "the plunder" of contemporary metropolitan life with "the savage's romance" of the past, when people lived with, rather than exploited, nature and each other. The first text in her carefully-selected volume, entitled "The Steeple Jack," explores "a town like this" rather than a depersonalizing city. Characteristically, the town is chosen for its proximity to the sea (the leitmotif of preference in Moore's oeuvre), and is principally described, not in terms of who lives there, but what grows there. In her own reticent way, Moore attempts to transform "opposed urban/ rural codes into a new system of dynamic interrelatedness" (Grace 206).

Generic Possibilities

Cities preoccupy male modernists. For African Americans, the city is always a "border line" between opportunity, community, and abjection (Hughes 1994:325). Texts by the poetic Men of 1914 and those who emulated them could best be described as ironic urban elegies: they mourn the loss of a life-affirming environment and at the same time lament the death of personal and cultural coherence. But what is one to call the nature-focused poems of so many modern female poets?

"Pastoral" comes readily to mind. Marx has identified profound pastoral strains in American literature; Marcus uses the term to define a certain kind of women's novel from this period; Friedman has discussed H. D.'s early poetry in terms of the "the modern pastoral." "Feminist pastoral" is an appealing coinage, at first glance. After all, the works of Sappho, ancient precedent for women's uncompromisingly shrewd yet lyrical and passionate nature-focused texts, were being unearthed from neglected antiquities in the very decades in question. But to speak of women's pastoral poetry, feminist or otherwise, is to ensconce these modern poems and their makers in a literary history that has ignored or silenced them, sometimes both simultaneously, and to reaffirm a tradition of reading "nature" within a matrix of power relations in which all things typed "feminine" are presumed to be unequal and destined to be subjugated. Since Theocritus sang of Sicily's charms, the pastoral has consigned female figures to Delia-hood (the Delia, Celia, Camilla, or Cynthia who is the object of the shepherd's desire, never the working poet). Additionally, given the "pastoral" poetry of the 1910s and 1920s that was produced by such Georgian masters of emotional treacle as John Drinkwater, Lascelles Abercrombie, and Walter de la Mare,[95] one would hesitate to employ such a generic label in relation to the astringent works of Millay, Moore, Bogan, or H. D. The latter were not indulging in the countryside conventions of Crabbe or Goldsmith, producing poems that were, in Raymond Williams's phrase, "a dissolving of the lives and works of others into an image of the past" (1973: 77). Nor were the women simply reviving the seventeenth- and eighteenth-century topographical poem (Denham's "Coopers Hill," Pope's "Windsor-Forest," Thomson's *The Seasons*) and ignoring the gendered cultural norms disseminated by such texts.

Traditionally, the pastoral is a luxurious, escapist genre: city dwellers who have the education and the means to write creatively imagine themselves into another time and a wholly different environment. Even Theocritus was writing anachronistically. Students of African American poetry should be familiar with the searing antipastoralism of Elma Ehrlich Levinger and Abel Meeropol. Levinger's "Carry Me Back to Old Virginny" ironically juxtaposes lyrics from the folksong with the harsh thoughts of a speaker who not only refuses but angrily refutes the comfortable sentimentalism of "white folks":

> *"There's where the birds warble sweet in the springtime."*
> That's when it used to stink most down in nigger town;
> We slept six in a room and the drains never worked right;
> Lots of scarlet fever on account of them drains,
> But folks got to expect it;
> My little sister, she died of it in the springtime.
>
> (Honey ed. 71)

The second stanza of Meeropol's "Strange Fruit" is equally frank and unflinchingly graphic: "Pastoral scene of the gallant South, / The bulging eyes and the twisted mouth, / Scent of magnolia sweet and fresh, / And the sudden smell of burning flesh!" (qtd Margolick 312). Billie Holiday's *explication du texte* is chilling. As Margolick summarizes, "In *The Heart of a Woman*, Maya Angelou recounts how, during a visit to Los Angeles in 1958, in a hoarse and raspy voice, Holiday sang 'Strange Fruit' as a bedtime song for her son, Guy. 'What's a pastoral scene, Miss Holiday?' the young boy interjected. 'Billie looked up slowly and studied Guy for a second,' Angelou writes. 'Her face became cruel, and when she spoke her voice was scornful.

"It means when the crackers are killing the niggers. It means when they take a little nigger like you and snatch off his nuts and shove them down his goddam throat. That's what it means. . . . That's what they do. That's a goddamn pastoral scene"'" (320).

Another reason should also be mentioned. Among modern poets, the person who accomplishes the most as an "urban pastoralist" is Williams. I take my cue from Pugh, who explicates Benjamin's notion that the *flâneur* "'goes botanising on the asphalt'" in these terms: he is "part of the surging crowd, yet apart from it as an observer, . . . part of and apart from nature. . . . In important respects, the *flâneur* grew out of the pastoralist. Both attempted to privatise social space by arguing that passive and aloof observation was adequate for a knowledge of social reality" (1990b:156–157). Communities still exist in Williams's world; rather than posing as a downtown Jeremiah, he continues to imagine the city as an "Emersonian village" that is not "alien to individuality" (Kuspit 69). The series of "Pastorals" Williams published in 1914 and revised for 1917 establish his willingness to be "astonished" by sparrows *and* gutters (1991 1:42–43, 70–71); another speaker is "stirred" by the "beauty of / the terrible faces / of our nonentities" (1991 1:70). Gasoline "smells mingle with leaf smells" in his texts (1991 1:81), but the speaker never suggests that he and his "townspeople" should pull up stakes. Williams's America features the alluring, ubiquitous "city," but enjoys everyday life in towns "where the streets end / in the sun / and the marsh edge" (1991 1:170). *Spring And All,* the 1923 volume designed to answer and rebuke the antipastoralism of Eliot's *The Waste Land* ("April is the cruelest month . . ."), asserts that the world is only partially symbolized by a "contagious hospital," only "lifeless in appearance"—"the profound change" and promise of renewal "begin to awaken" natural and human realms alike (1991 1:183). As Schmidt and Halter both suggest, in the "majority of his poems about the city . . . we have exactly this juxtaposition of man, nature, and the city in which the natural functions as an ameliorative or alleviating element" (Halter 99). What neither critic considers, however, is that the "gendered projects in Williams's work . . . [features] elements of patriarchal totalization, elements . . . that remain disabling" (Nelson 356). Paterson, New Jersey depends topographically and spiritually upon "the Park / upon the rock, female to the city /—upon whose body Paterson instructs his thoughts / (concretely)" (*Pat* 57). Rather than resort to the extremism of a cult of ugliness, William's urban pastoralist compromise finds "the most marvelous" in "the classic attempt / at beauty / at the swamp's center: the / dead-end highway" or in a run-down building's entryway where "two potted geraniums" flourish regardless (1991 2:191–192).

Currently, a number of critics are exploring the "ontology of the sublime" in order to define the function of natural elements and the structure of subject/object relations in women's poetry (Alfrey 48), especially the texts of Emily Dickinson.[96] Although the textual insights produced by this work are considerable, I hesitate to adopt this approach for modern women's poetry for three reasons. To begin with, it is impossible to separate the theoretical category from the antifeminist inclinations underscoring it. Like Ruskin's grotesque, theories of the sublime from Longinus and Burke to Wordsworth and Victor Hugo are based upon gendered power relations. Beauty, according to those who prefer sublimity, is fundamentally inadequate; it generates feelings of "vibrant stillness, of animated rest" (Kurrik 49), but nothing more exceptional. Not surprisingly, therefore, beauty is assigned a "female" identity in these theoretical circles; it is associated with that which is smooth and regular, fundamentally passive, and unrelated to powerful emotions or scenes of mighty force. "The beautiful offers a fusion of subject and object," Yaeger explains, "a world of pleasure, while the sublime offers more complex feelings—a movement of action and reaction, a negative pleasure in the checking of vital powers" (208). Alfrey's definition of the sublime is redolent with masculine-identified, militaristic characteristics: "while the sublime's transmission of power and knowledge . . . requires the subject's encounter with the world outside the self, this encounter is usually recognized as agonistic. The difficulty surmounted in the experience of the sublime can be understood as a sort of ontological struggle, a battle between the self and other in which only one side can emerge victorious" (48). Surely it is possible to "invent, for women, a vocabulary of ecstasy and empowerment, a new way of reading feminine experience" (Yaeger 191) without reinscribing the shop-worn and also culturally damaging clichés of patriarchical aesthetics. The second reason hearkens back to an argument broached in the Introduction to this study: a reluctance to assume that admission to a previously male canon, or generic/ typological grouping, is advantageous or enlightening. Yaeger's perceptive work offers "a new architectonics of empowerment" by suggesting that women writers eschew the "vertical sublime which insists on aggrandizing the masculine self over others" and privilege instead a "horizontal sublime that moves toward sovereignity or expenditure," and can include "the sociable" (191, 195). Yet would one want the final word on H. D. or Wylie, Millay or Grimké, to be that she "domesticat[ed] the Romantic sublime as a literary mode" (Yaeger 209)? Finally, all theorists of the sublime, whatever their politics, endorse what Thomas Weiskel terms the "structure of transcendence," a belief that the speaker of the text (and vicariously, the reader) achieves a kind of "transport" or exaltation (Yaeger 192, 199). *Transcendence* is the goal of the Men of 1914: their adversarial texts alternatively revel or grovel in ugliness in order to prove that the speaker can overcome it, whether physically, emotionally, or psychologically ("I sat upon the shore / Fishing, with the arid plain behind me" [*CPP* 74]). Ultimately, like Baudelaire's *flâneur,* they are both "aloof" and untouched

by the environments, natural and human, in which they are forced to **dwell.**
The white male modernists' ability to transcend, even imaginatively, not
only involves rising above that which is terrible, disgusting, or antihuman,
but the cultural power to identify, objectify, and denigrate that which has
to be overcome—whether a woman's body, an African American's out-
stretched hand, an impoverished cityscape, or mass culture. Transcendence
is such an exquisite goal, or dream, because the reality from which it offers
relief is so dire: death.[97]

Transformation, on the other hand, is the empowering narrative offered
by many modern female poets. Subjectivity is the territory most often explored; long denied in canons of patriarchal culture, it is the energizing focus
of innumerable poems. This confederate commitment to life, however, is
neither disingenuously nor naïvely optimistic; the poets are only too aware
of what it means "being born a woman and distressed / By all the needs and
notions of my kind" (Millay 601). Yet they chose not to be aloof; theirs is
the poetry of commitment, recognition, and redefinition.

If one must have a label, consideration should be given to *modern
women's geo-graphies,* a phrase that emphasizes that these writers turned
away from debilitating urban environments and instead seized the opportunity to write and reimagine the earth—natural and also "wilder" spaces—
in order to explore multiple subject positions and artistic possibilities.
Firmly rooted in the now, a present they accept with all of its limitations,
these *geo-graphers* elected to engage with tropes that affirm, however strin-
gently. As Moore contends, poetry is, despite "all its fiddle," "a place for the
genuine"; it offers exasperating, vital, and illuminating glimpses of "'imaginary gardens with real toads in them'" (Ellmann and O'Clair eds. 457).[98]
Bogan's "M., Singing," reaches "within the deep / Night of all things" to
find a "fresh voice"; the words, albeit "melancholy," provide a "long harvest
which they reap / In the sunk land of dust and flame" (Ellmann and O'-
Clair eds. 596).

But Is It Modernist?

The extent to which the urban "crisis" poem became formulaic in the first
three decades of the twentieth century is clearly demonstrated by cummings's short lyric "e":

    e
    cco the uglies
    t

    s
    ub
    sub

urba
n skyline on earth between whose d
owdy

hou
se
s

l
ooms an eggyellow smear of wintry sunse
t[.]

(788)

Although typographically avant-garde—the form of the poem playfully mimics the impoverished glimpses of sunset to be had between the "dowdy houses" that constitute suburbia—the work is structured in terms of firmly established tropes that stress the curse of modern ugliness. Urban landscapes are decidedly problematic in the texts of cummings, Eliot, Pound, Williams, even Sandburg—they are sites of decay and deprivation, symbol and summary of the sterility characterizing life in an alienating, industrialized world. Hughes and McKay are more resigned to urban environments, sometimes even optimistic, but the "smear" of racism taints all experience. Vilified or not, the city is fully exploited; negative textual topographies are central to the processes of signification. In contrast, the absence of the city in many women's texts is wholesale and deliberate. Whether one is talking about well-known writers like Moore and H. D., or lesser known but imaginatively vital women like Bogan, Wylie, or Georgia Douglas Johnson, their texts are engaged with nonurban, enabling "geo-graphies," what Anna Hempstead Branch has termed those "wilder zones."

Modern male poets were framing textual impressions of alienation, of physical and metaphysical discomfort. For those projects, negative city images proved to be the most effective. Modern female poets, on the other hand, were working towards self-definition, and could only do so by inscribing themselves within natural, life-affirming landscapes. Writing to confirm a self, they deliberately looked outside the city—outside the public realm—for reifying metaphorical ground. There were modern female poets who wrote about the city (Lowell and Helene Johnson, as I have discussed, and Sara Teasdale), just as there were male poets (Stevens and Frost) who privileged natural metaphorical spaces. For the most part, however, white male poets—who had been secure in their cultural inheritance for centuries—went into the modern city to enact scenes of willful disinheritance.[99] Female poets, on the contrary, left the cities—real, unreal, textually traditional—to claim a new inheritance for themselves in *contrata*. Some of the female poets were just as technically experimental, just as defiantly conflictive and oppositional in their art, as one has long been taught that modernists should be. Why, then, were (and are) their texts excluded from, or slighted within, the received canons of modernist poetry? Because they fail the once-infallible locus test—the one that dictates that the city is requisite scene and subject? Partly. And partially because, until the past two decades, almost all of the definitions and canon-making decisions were unquestioningly made according to priorities inherited from the Men of 1914. As a symbol of the chaotic, disturbing complexity of twentieth-century life, the city is unsurpassed: if it had not existed, those advancing a cult of ugliness would have invented it. Yet an international interest in metropolitan culture should not be mistaken for a universal aesthetic or cultural necessity—nor should a "modernist" aesthetic, in all of its specificity and success, be misappropriated to define other works, other discursive modes, flourishing from the 1900s to the 1940s.

Afterword

"We are the first men of a Future that has not materialized. We belong to a 'great age' that has not 'come off.' We moved too quickly for the world. We set too sharp a pace" (*BB* 258). With these melancholy words, Wyndham Lewis explains to readers of *Blasting and Bombardiering* (1937) why, "whatever happens to the world during the next century or so, there will be no society present upon the globe to think, live, and speculate in a manner conducive to the production of such works as *Bouvard and Pecuchet* [Flaubert], *Ulysses* [Joyce], *The Hollow Men* [Eliot], *The Ambassadors* [James], *The Portrait of Carlyle* [Whistler], to name a few" (*BB* 257–258). Ironically but not surprisingly, one must agree *and* disagree with Lewis. The Men of 1914 were right to feel threatened: a future marked by social homogeneity, gender essentialism, and the continuing, tenacious domination of their particular aesthetic ideology did not materialize. Other aesthetic principles and cultural values outpaced their own; writers who were or would have been anathema to them emerged and their accomplishments were eventually recognized; the dangerous political implications of radical conservatism were exposed, by the 1940s, to the entire world. Culture work did not remain the preserve of gifted men. Although a substantial number followed where the cultists had led, many others explored the burdens and possibilities of modern art and life in different "manners." Yet *The Waste Land* is still a remarkable work; Lewis's artistry in all media commands one's attention; Pound's *Imagisme* changed the way in which poetry is written and received and the *Cantos* challenged Eliot, Crane, Williams, H. D., and many more to rethink the possibilities of the sequential long poem.

The Cult of Ugliness provides new ways of acknowledging the aesthetic innovations and cultural critiques produced by these modernists, but also cautions, as Kant reminded us, that every revolution has its destructive elements and consequences. Literally, of course, there was never any "cult": no secret meetings and membership lists, ritualized worship, nor devotion to a leader at all costs. But the concerted efforts by a small, interconnected group of men, however "disparate and unassimilable" (*BB* 254), to install themselves as a self-proclaimed, adversarial "youth racket" are unmistakable. So too is the radical shift in aesthetic priorities that they endorsed and disseminated, the insistence on representing "the horrid or sordid or disgusting" conditions of modernity (*SW* 169). The story of modern literature that I have outlined is one of competing truth claims, strategies of legitimation, and individual and collective efforts to impose new definitions of artistic and social reality (Bourdieu 1986:155). Furthermore, I have expanded the temporal and spatial horizons of "modern" inquiries in order to promote unfamiliar juxtapositions—Ruskin and Hulme, Whistler and Pound, Pater and Lewis and Hughes, H. D. and Grimké, *The Waste Land* and *The Weary Blues*—that unsettle canonical categories and enable one to rethink the pursuit of beauty and ugliness in literary culture. Focusing on different combinations of texts and authors, and following the cult of ugliness as it was propagated, I have not only highlighted a dimension of modernist culture that others have overlooked, but have suggested the implications of ignoring the political productivity of ugliness.

In denominating "cults of beauty" and "ugliness," Pound was anticipating the classificatory tendencies of the LitCrit profession. At the time, being able to identify the "new" works and authors worth reading, and "booming" their efforts, had positive effects: attention was paid in the cultural marketplace, and readers, patrons, and publishers were alerted. Today, the persistence of categories in institutional criticism not only encourages single-minded approaches and limits readers to limiting canons, it consolidates reading practices that are often insensitive to and intolerant of the inscriptions of gender, race, and sexual difference.

Learning from the work of many accomplished people, and answering to the astonishing range of the texts being considered, I have presented a series of readings and a politics of reading. Focusing on one exclusive binary opposition, I have suggested strategies for effecting inclusive change. Agitating for a new set of categories, devising new terms, has not been my goal: it would be foolhardy, for one thing, and more importantly, too exclusionary despite my best intentions. Instead, by offering new terms of address, one story among many that promotes dialogic textual encounters, I have demonstrated that transformative reading practices are what the heterogeneous "conditions" of modern literature demand.

Notes

Introduction

1. In March 1913, John Yeats also warned his son, "A strenuous modern . . . will go into a garden and find nothing so agreeable as the pungent smells of a dung-heap" (J. B. Yeats 157). The letter arrived when William Butler Yeats was developing his *Responsibilities* volume (1914). Had the poet already succumbed, textually speaking, to the "dung-heap" due to the persistent editorial pressures of his part-time secretary, Ezra Pound? From the early 1900s onward Yeats consistently, independently labored to divest his poetry of an attachment to female beauty and any hints of sentimentality. To have "wrought" and celebrated "beautiful lofty things" was always secondary in Yeats's poetic discourse; even before a "vision of beauty" was superseded by a "vision of terror" (1966:619), the reaffirmation of the poet's creative power was paramount. The poet may have served beauty, in his fashion, but beauty always served the writer's purposes. Yeats, who defended Ruskin against his father's harsh criticism on several occasions (see 1972:19), was most Ruskinian when asserting the primacy of truth-telling through art (whether those truths are aesthetic, spiritual, political, and/or cultural).

   Yeats's refusal to experiment in vers libre resulted in texts that initially seem quite different from the cultists' works. Further inspection, however, reveals that the "artifice" of poetic tradition only masks entrenched commonalities. With or without Pound's suggestive interference, Yeats was dedicated to promulgating an aesthetic program that was elitist, antidemocratic, and intensely gender-inflected. Rather than "break the pentameter," he proceeded to assault female-identified motives for creativity. In the final lyric of *Responsibilities,* a vulnerable speaker decries that "*all my priceless things / Are but a post the passing dogs defile*" (1966: 321). Yeats's modernism is achieved by mastering the techniques of poetic defilement; he too developed an aesthetic of repudiation. Few twentieth-century artists were more "cult"-minded than Yeats, more committed to "secret" knowledges, aesthetic and otherwise. As a cultural archive, his canon provides an exemplary opportunity to reexamine the way in which a male writer functions within the imaginative parameters of patriarchal culture and myth, how "woman" as a discursive category is historically reconstructed, rather than contested, and the extent to which the narratives of "sexual interaction" (Mann 25) available to the poems were both prescribed and severely limited. Yet, the "fearful misogynistic response to the New Woman" that Yeats shared with Pound, Eliot, and Lawrence was not complicated by "self loathing and sexual abjection" (DeKoven 1999:17); his poems can require or relish the presence of female figures without respecting them (DeKoven offers the opposing view, 1999:17–18).

Unlike Cullingford or Keane, I would not try to prove that Yeats's writings are not sexist. Texts such as "The Seven Sages" (*VP* 486–487) and *A Vision* reaffirm exclusively male paths of cultural entitlement; throughout the poetic canon, female figures are alternatively acclaimed for their femme fatality, condemned for operating within public spheres, or infantilized into roles of "the girl" or "the child." In the final chapter, I adumbrate the ways in which EP, TSE, and Williams use tropes of the female body to represent the travails of contemporary urban life: its pleasures, temptations, and desecrations. Yeats's poetry, on the other hand, concentrates on female figures to articulate the consequences of political action, a cyclical theory of history, the necessary rigidity of class demarcations, and the struggle to remain a privileged enunciator of aesthetic discourse in the post–World War I era. Writing at a time when competing interpretations of "being a woman" were available, Yeats—like Whistler, whose paintings he praised on numerous occasions—tried to preserve and extend the traditions of the ahistorical, symbolic Woman. Eventually, when the representation of such a figure became impossible, his negative poetic responses were both graphic and dismaying ("Leda and the Swan" and the Crazy Jane poems are but the most familiar examples). Increasingly, poems with specifically male speakers come to attack or disfigure female physical beauty, comparing the latter to "unshapely things," things "uncomely and broken" (1966:143, 142). These texts should be read as a protest against suddenly "uncontrollable" changes in the cultural definition and activities of women, who acquired "opinions" and insisted upon assuming public roles. More and more the Yeats canon chastises and rebukes the female figures it has created; repeatedly, almost ritualistically, the poems try to discipline a transgressive woman (because she is too forthright, or ambitious, or "wandering"). Attitudes toward the conditions of possibility for achieving beauty in the world are inextricably linked to increasingly de-idealizing representations of female figures. Gradually but intensely, the texts shift from marking norms of gender differentiation to articulating a particularly satiric antifeminism. One might have assumed that the patron Celtic deity for Yeats's canon would be Aengus, "the god of youth, beauty, and poetry" (1966: 794). But only "poetry" actually emerges as a "supreme" value to be endorsed—poetry, and truth-telling.

For an excellent analysis of the Yeats-EP personal and working relationships, see Longenbach 1988. More recently, he has argued: "It has often been said that . . . Ezra Pound 'modernized' Yeats's style, toughening his attitude and roughening his diction. . . . But it now seems clear that Yeats was far more influential in determining the direction of Pound's career" (Longenbach

1999:106). See also Elizabeth Cullingford, *Gender and History in Yeats's Love Poetry* (Cambridge: Cambridge University Press, 1993); Patrick Keane, *Terrible Beauty: Yeats, Joyce, Ireland, and the Myth of the Devouring Female* (Columbia: University of Missouri Press, 1988); Gloria Kline, *The Last Courtly Lover: Yeats and the Idea of Woman* (Ann Arbor: UMI Research Press, 1983). An invaluable resource is Jahan Ramazani, *Yeats and the Poetry of Death: Elegy, Self-Elegy, and the Sublime* (New Haven: Yale University Press, 1990).

2. Examples of this work include Benstock's *Women of the Left Bank,* Scott's *Refiguring Modernism: The Women of 1928* (2 vols.), Elliott and Wallace's *Women Artists and Writers: Modernist (im)positionings,* and *The Gender of Modernism,* ed. Scott.

3. Scholes concludes that "modernism, especially around its Parisian center of activity, was indeed a masculinist activity that positioned women voyeuristically and turned would-be agents into patients" (1:1). Dettmar and Watt "recognize a plurality of modernisms, whether or not they are canonized or sanctioned by the academy" (6), yet the essays in *Marketing Modernisms* demonstrate that considerations of gender and race remain the exception in modernist studies.

4. "Foucault's analyses of historical writing, of discursive formations and their practical institutionalization, provided a necessary instrument for feminist probing of the archive, . . . of the selective resources of historical research which secure masculine hegemony in the recirculation by one generation of a previous generation's ideological structurings of knowledge" (Pollock 1988:92).

5. WL coined this phrase retrospectively, in *Blasting and Bombardiering* (1937); it will be used hereafter without quotation marks. As Svarny suggests, the "obvious" reference "to those who fought in the First World War" was deliberate; the "military metaphor captures the antagonistic, often rebarbative, cultural posture of these writers" (2). Issues of gender are absent from Svarny's considerations.

6. Both JR and WHP studied at Oxford. TSE received his B.A. and M.A. from Harvard; he completed his doctoral dissertation on the philosophy of F. H. Bradley but did not take the degree. EP received his B.A. and M.A. from the University of Pennsylvania. TEH did not complete his undergraduate studies at Cambridge. WL attended Rugby, among other schools, before enrolling at the Slade School of Art. TEH and TSE attended Henri Bergson's lectures at the Sorbonne.

7. "Outlaw" and "enemy" were WL's favorite personae; each cultist created his own revolutionary mask(s).

8. Eagleton argues that the "moment of modernity" is "characterized by the dissociation and specialization of these three crucial spheres of activity [the aesthetic, ethical, and cognitive]. Art is now autonomous" (368).

9. I have chosen the Jowett translations, despite their flaws, because they were the most well-known at the time. Citations will include the name of the dialogue and the Jowett edition page reference. Regarding the politics of translating Plato in the late nineteenth century, see Higgins 1993.

10. One should "promote the recognition of more orders of 'meaning' than one," WL observes, "there are several and they should exist side by side upon equal terms" (*CH* 196).

11. Despite the call for "rendering a fuller account" of modernism in Levenson's perceptive "Introduction," the essays in the *Cambridge Companion* do little to counter the long standing "narrative of Modernism triumphant" (1999:2). Except in two essays written by women and Longenbach's survey of modern poetry, the impact of 20 years of work by feminist, postcolonial, and African American scholars is negligible.

12. "Misogyny" signals "a more constitutive and thorough-going antagonism toward women than that suggested by *sexism*" (Nelson 358).

Chapter 1

1. Foucault challenges "the pursuit of the origin": rather than locating a (predetermined) "timeless and essential . . . truth of things," the genealogist works historically to "cultivate the details and accidents that accompany every beginning" and in the process reconsiders "the events of history, its jolts, its surprises, its unsteady victories and unpalatable defeats" (1984:78, 80).

2. *Fors Clavigera: Letters to the Workmen and Labourers of Great Britain* was published monthly from January 1871 to December 1884 (except when Ruskin was too ill to write). More than 600,000 words were written in 96 pamphlets. See Birch, "Introduction," *Fors Clavigera,* ed. Birch (Edinburgh: Edinburgh University Press, 2000). Hilton agrees that *Fors* is "Ruskin's masterpiece" (xi; see Birch 1999b:175). *Fors Clavigera* "has a large circulation among artists and art patrons," JW's lawyer observed in his opening statement; "the fact of its large circulation is of importance" (qtd Merrill 1992:139).

3. JR had seen JW's works in the 1871–72 or 1872–73 Dudley Gallery exhibitions (Shrimpton 137). JR's public denunciation of JW began in October 1873: first, to auditors of his Oxford lectures, and then to readers of *Val d'Arno.* "I never saw anything so impudent," JR exclaimed; "it was a daub professing to be a 'harmony in pink and white' (or some such nonsense); absolute rubbish, and which had taken about a quarter of an hour to scrawl or daub—it had no pretence to be called painting. The price asked for it was two hundred and fifty guineas" (*WJR* 23:49). JR wanted the index for *Fors* to include "'Whistler, Mr, impudence of'" (Hilton 480; see *WJR* 29:609-676). When JW sold *The Falling Rocket* to Samuel Untermeyer of New York for 800 guineas he "exulted that this was in Ruskinian terms the equivalent of 'four pots of paint'" (McMullen 246).

4. "Whistler's own defence was more memorable," Hilton states, "since he seemed to regard the court as a theatre in which he was the principal actor" (398). Henry James informed readers of *The Nation* that the trial was "'a singular and most regrettable exhibition. If it had taken place in some Western American town, it would have been called provincial and barbarous'" (qtd Prideaux 129).

5. Sir Coutts Lindsay's Grosvenor Gallery opened in London's fashionable Mayfair district on May 1, 1877; it closed in 1890. Initially the Gallery played a pivotal role in showcasing new art and defying the Royal Academy's authority. The inaugural exhibition (209 paintings and sculptures) featured works by G. F. Watts, Albert Moore, James Tissot, Edward Burne-Jones, and JW, who contributed four *Nocturnes* and the portrait of Thomas Carlyle. In 1884, JW had a falling out with Lindsay (Koval 92). See Susan Casteras and Colleen Denney, eds., *The Grosvenor Gallery: A Palace of Art in Victorian England* (New Haven: Yale Center for British Art, 1996); Christopher Newall, *The Grosvenor Gallery Exhibitions: Change and Continuity in the Victorian Art World* (Cambridge: Cambridge University Press, 1995).

6. This text constitutes the second part of JW's exaggerated, self-serving account of the trial in *The Gentle Art of Making Enemies, as pleasantly exemplified in many instances, wherein the serious ones of this earth, carefully exasperated, have been prettily spurred on to unseemliness and indiscretion, while overcome by an undue sense of right.* All quotations are from the enlarged, second edition of 1892.

7. Both men completed self-portraits in 1873; both feature the unflinching, hard-staring face of a determined man. JW, *Arrangement in Grey, Self-Portrait* (1871–1873, oil on canvas); JR, *Self-Portrait with a Blue Neckcloth* (1873, watercolor).

8. Counsel for the plaintiff consisted of John Humphreys Parry, Serjeant-at-law, and William Petheram; for the defendant, Sir John Holker, attorney-general, and Charles Bowen.

9. Cox defined JW's method as the art of "eliminations" (1904:637).

10. The doubly inappropriate "Cockney" remark was addressed by Parry in his summation: "It was said that Mr. Ruskin had a right to call the plaintiff a cockney; though Mr. Whistler was not born within the sound of Bow Bells; but 'cockney' means something dirty and disagreeable. I hope the jury will tell Mr. Ruskin he cannot use such language with impunity." In his jury instructions, Baron Huddleston insisted upon a geographically-specific definition of "cockney" (quoted from Samuel Johnson's 1755 *Dictionary*), because "there are plenty of cockneys who would not condescend to do an ungenerous or ungentlemanly act." But he too admitted a class-inflected frame of reference when he advised the jury, "'Cockney,' therefore, appears to mean a man who does not know much beyond his own sphere" (qtd Merrill 1992:186, 193).

11. JW "slowly succeeded in educating the more sensitive that . . . a person looking at a picture should be moved to exclaim, 'How beautiful!' rather than 'How true!'" (Werner xii).

12. "That element of binding and blending in Ruskin can hardly be emphasized enough," Fellows states; "[c]ategories, like his 'overflowing' books, are containers that do not categorize" (1981:xvi).

13. Millet considers the text "senile eroticism addressing itself to beautiful ignorance" (90).

14. Bloom praises the visionary, heroic dimensions of JR's aesthetic writings; feminist critics, for more than two decades, have exposed the degree to which sociological texts such as *Letters and Advice to Young Girls and Young Ladies* (1870, a compilation of passages from "Of Queen's Gardens," the second preface to *Sesame and Lilies,* and selections from *Fors Clavigera*) promote the subjugation of women. Millet's polemical denunciation of JR in *Sexual Politics* (1970) brought widespread attention to texts that, in recent years, had interested only specialists. Millet terms Ruskin's definition of women and their domestic/social role a dangerous "concoction" of "nostalgic mirage, regressive, infantile, or narcissistic sexuality, religious ambition, and simplistic social panacea" (107). Millet focuses solely on *Sesame and Lilies,* stressing its importance as one of the "central documents of sexual politics in the Victorian period" (89). Yet by isolating "Of Queen's Gardens," she (and many others) unwittingly detach it from the canon and the contexts that produced it. One of the first people to argue against *Sexual Politics* was Sonstroem. As Sawyer points out, however, Sonstroem's 1977 essay "looks convincing until one returns to the text and finds the phrases" he omits (Sawyer 1990:289). More recently, both Birch and Bauer have made it their mission to "reclaim" JR's writings from "powerful" feminists (Birch 1988:308; see Bauer 79). Sawyer's cogent work is also typical of the schism in Ruskin studies. A 1985 appraisal of JR's "poetic argument" does not address the effects of a gendered aesthetic discourse; a 1990 article offers a judgmental view of Ruskin's social criticism, suggesting that "Of Queen's Gardens" and other texts provide a "honey-tongued defense of the subjection of women" (Sawyer 1990:130, 134).

15. The text is quoted as it appears in *Modern Painters.*

16. "Ruskin's social criticism, which exemplifies sage-writing . . . employs all the genre's chief devices . . . [including] a characteristic alternation of satire and positive, even visionary statement, accompanied by a parallel alternation of attacks upon the audience and attempts to reassure or inspire it" (Landow 1993:55–56).

17. See Weltman's discussion of myth and gender in JR's "feminized" science.

18. JR's note, added to the Re-Arranged 1883 edition: "The whole of this chapter is extremely well reasoned and clearly put; nor can I in any necessary point better it. The importance of its contents for future analysis may justify my requesting the reader's fixed attention to its distinctions and definitions" (*WJR* 4:66). Overall, the volume testifies to JR's increasingly "charnel interests" (Rogal 10, 11). Nothing, JR notes, "causes so intense and tormenting a sense of ugliness as any scar, wound, monstrosity, or imperfection" (*WJR* 4:154).

19. Notes were neither secondary nor minor paratextual details for JR. As Hunt states, JR's "exploitation of the footnote is thoroughly creative" (1982a:4); in addition to constant cross-referencing, "there is also a hidden, implicit structure of glossing that is also crucial to his imagination. . . . [His career] may be seen as a constant effort to establish some liaison between two competing modes of existence: on the one hand, the world of myriad facts, . . . on the

other, the need to organise coherent, general principles" (1982a:7). Fellows concurs (1981:xv).

20. "For now we see through a glass, darkly; but then face to face: now I know in part; but then shall I know even as also I am known" (I Corinthians 13:12).

21. *The Seven Lamps of Architecture,* 2nd edition, was published in 1855; as Cook and Wedderburn summarize, it made "'a great sensation' in literary circles. Reviews in the daily and weekly press were prompt and numerous, and for the most part long and complimentary" (*WJR* 8:xxxvii).

22. For a discussion of Lyotard's contention, in *The Postmodern Condition,* that modernism is "an aesthetic of the sublime, though a nostalgic one" (81), see Bedient (108). The sublime in relation to modern women's poetry is discussed in Chapter 4.

23. The two lectures that became *Sesame and Lilies,* "Of King's Treasuries" and "Of Queen's Gardens," were delivered at Rusholme Town Hall, near Manchester, in December 1864. JR published them under the title *Sesame and Lilies* in June 1865; the book did not have a preface. The second edition, complete with preface, appeared in 1866. When revising in the early 1870s, JR added a third lecture, "The Mystery of Life and its Art," which he delivered in Dublin on May 13, 1868. The refashioned *Sesame and Lilies* was published in 1871. Eleven years later, JR wrote yet another preface, and eliminated "The Mystery of Life" (see *WJR* 18:liv-lviii).

24. Ophelia is blamed for "all the bitter catastrophe" in Elsinore "because she fails Hamlet at the critical moment, and is not, and cannot in her nature be, a guide to him when he needs her most" (*WJR* 18:114). A general argument concerning women's responsibility for the world's evils resumes in Letter 80 of *Fors* (*WJR* 29:176).

25. Two and half decades later, however, JR spoke highly of "that great and pure society of the Dead." In a passage that recalls the *nekyia* ritual in Homer's *Iliad* (and thus anticipates Joyce's *Ulysses* and Pound's first Canto), JR states: "We come then to the great concourse of the Dead, not merely to know from them what is True, but chiefly to feel with them what is just" (*WJR* 18:79, 80).

26. In *The Seven Lamps* JR observes, "I know not how we can blame our architects for their feebleness in more important work; their eyes are inured to narrowness and slightness. . . . They ought not to live in our cities; there is that in their miserable walls which bricks up to death men's imaginations" (*WJR* 8:136).

27. JW bragged to dinner guests, among them William and Dante Gabriel Rossetti, that he (a Confederate sympathizer) once traded "fisticuffs" with a Yankee. DGR responded by penning the limerick (Seitz ed. 8).

28. One was later retitled *Nocturne: Blue and Gold—Old Battersea Bridge;* the second features Battersea Reach.

29. Later retitled *Nocturne: Grey and Gold—Westminster Bridge.*

30. Then-contemporary American and British journals preferred Anglicized terms such as "Japanism" and "Japanolatry" (Chisholm 89).

31. JW should be distinguished from the nineteenth-century phenomenon of the Tourist-as-Painter (Gérôme is one example) who documented European imperialist and colonialist expansionism in a highly mimetic mode.

32. Western historians typically call this the "opening" up of Japan; Japanese commentators refer to it as the great "intrusion" (see Storry 70–93).

33. JW's exercises in *Japonisme* also had a pragmatic benefit: they provided "a way of keeping his name before the critics in Paris while he was living in London" (Spencer 1980:62).

34. According to Bénédite, JW first encountered Hokusai's works in 1856 (1905:142). Sandberg disagrees: "Though his discovery of Ukiyo-e prints cannot be determined with absolute precision, documentary and visual evidence point to late 1862 or early 1863. By the next year Whistler was a regular customer at the Port Chinoise in Paris" (1964:500, 503).

35. I am distinguishing between the thoroughly realized *Japonisme* of the 1860s and the mere accessorizing in later works such as *Milly Finch* (ca. 1884), who holds aloft a brilliant red fan. JW's paintings should be compared with the cheerfully Eurocentric ethos of Claude Monet's *La Japonaise* (*Camille Monet in Japanese Costume,* 1876) or the Orientalist "decorations" enhancing the submissiveness of a nude in Ernst Ludwig Kirchner's *Girl Under a Japanese Umbrella* (ca. 1909).

36. Spencer notes "this desire to become an original Japonist rather than a mere *pasticheur* of the art of Japan which . . . occupied Whistler from about 1864 onwards" (1980:64). Sandberg claims JW "suddenly and traumatically discovered the art of Japan. Within two years he had fused Japanese principles of composition with related characteristics of his previous manner until the two were often indistinguishable in his work" (1968:59).

37. JW referred to nudes as "pot-boilers": "'it is better to live on bread and cheese and paint beautiful things, than to live like Dives and paint pot-boilers'" (qtd Starr 531). *Symphony in White: No. 1* debuted at the same Salon des Refusés as Manet's *Déjeuner sur l'herbe;* both occasioned outraged response. Perhaps JW learned that controversial nude figures would generate more critical discussion and public curiosity than the painting itself; erotic engagement compromised the aesthetic experience. JW may have been avoiding the "shocking" revelation of Manet's *Olympia* (1863), which "put the client of art and the client of sex in exactly the same place" (Scholes 2:6). Not until the later years of his career did JW turn to traditional ways of commodifying women's naked bodies—but the paintings, such as *The Little Red Cap, Nude Girl with a Bowl* (ca. 1892), and *Rose and Brown: La Cigale* (ca. 1898), lack energy and artistic engagement. The impetus, I would speculate, was the chief patron of JW's final decade, Charles Lang Freer, who began collecting JW's etchings and prints in the 1880s. The two met in March 1890. Freer was eager to buy *Harmony in Blue and Gold: The Little Blue Girl* (1894- 1903), *Writing on the Wall* (1894–1902), *A Violet Note—Spring* (1894–1899), and *Harmony in Blue and Violet* (1890); JW was willing, if not always able, to accommodate these interests (see Merrill's informative

edition of their letters). A reluctance to complete and then part with *Purple and Gold: Phryne the Superb!* (ca. 1898) had much to do with the death of JW's wife, Beatrice Godwin Whistler, in May 1896.

38. Foot binding is "a prime exemplar of fetishism, where the foot is bound to signify women's . . . submission, but it is then idealised as if the women with bound feet were being praised for having accepted their castration and punishment, deflecting the threat from the male subject" (Pollock 1999:93).

39. The model for both was Joanna ["Jo"] Hiffernan, Whistler's lover. The paintings subtly pander to some male erotic fantasies: although the subtitles (*No.1: The White Girl, No. 2: The Little White Girl*), white dresses, and unbound hair suggest youthful, virginal subjects, the figure in each painting is clearly older.

40. "It must be admitted," Sickert says, "that the listlessness that adds such charm to the *Little White Girl* just borders on lifelessness" (1908:14).

41. JW contemporary Arthur Eddy praises *Symphony in Purple and Rose: Lange Leizen* as "a study primarily in colour, secondarily in line, and not at all in character" (58). Harrison's work on the "represented self-consciousness" of women in Cézanne's paintings is informative.

42. The preparatory pastel, a study in drapery and color effects, features a full frontal view of Frances Leyland (the face is blank). An additional charcoal sketch of the left arm focuses on the movement of fabric. Three etchings are also relevant: *Speke Hall* (1870), *The Velvet Dress* (1873), and *The Silk Dress* (1873). For a very different representation of Frances Leyland, see Dante Gabriel Rossetti's *Mona Rosa* (1867). Frances Leyland's portrait was completed in 1874. In 1881, JW produced a second, strikingly different *Harmony in Flesh Colour and Pink,* a portrait of Lady Meux as a wholly contemporary, occidental figure, featuring a frontal, assertive pose.

43. Female figures are almost always subsumed within the artist's color schema; gown and *Japonisme* elements are carefully orchestrated. In the later portraits of men, however, we find that the colors are more varied; subjects are represented *en face,* their gazes direct and unflinching. Furthermore, the works feature emblems of involvement in public life: Eddy carries a document (1893–1894); Signor Pablo de Sarasate, his violin (1884). In addition to the Leyland portraits, JW produced several visual "pairs," the gendered distinctions of which are striking. *Arrangement in Black No. 3: Sir Henry Irving* (1877) represents the actor in costume as Spanish king Philip II; *Arrangement in Black and Brown: The Fur Jacket* (ca. 1870s), a portrait of JW's lover Maud Franklin, focuses the viewer's gaze on the costume. *Arrangement in Grey and Black No. 1: The Artist's Mother* provides a fascinating counterpoint to *Arrangement in Grey and Black No.2: Thomas Carlyle.* In both, the seated figure faces left; stark rectangles of art work to the left of the heads (and to the right of Mrs Whistler) frame the figures. Pictorial elements are organized against the prominent plane of the baseboards. The apparent immobility of the sitters signfies their advanced age. Yet the draperies featured to the left of Mrs Whistler render the entire spatial field of the painting more domestic,

and enclosed; indoor attire also speaks to a limited, "queenly" sphere. Carlyle, on the other hand, resting either before or after a journey, is wearing his coat and one glove, hat and cloak across his knees (he is gripping his walking stick, another emblem of mobility).

44. "Lange Lijzens" (or "Leizens") or "long Elizas" is the Delft terminology "for the decorative figures on the jar in the picture" (Young 39); the "six marks" refers to the potter's seals (Spaulding 34–35).

45. Spaulding concurs that the figure "is shown, rather unconvincingly, in the act of painting a pot" (34). Merrill is more pragmatic: "she cannot possibly be painting a pot that has obviously been finished and fired" (1998:54).

46. The print, featured in Fenollosa's 1912 study (see below), is identified as part of the "Modern Plebian Art in Yedo" (2:205). The print's pictorial space is sharply divided by a prominent door frame; JW's *Harmony in Grey and Green: Miss Cecily Alexander* (1872–74) is similarly organized.

47. Sickert pronounced the *Japonaiserie* of this painting "even more frankly fantastic" because "the girls who are leaning over [the balcony] are Japanese in costume, but the scene on which they are looking is the grey Thames at Chelsea with its wharves and wharvehouses" (1908:17).

48. As Nochlin, Pollock, and others suggest, the Orientalist painting "absents history and makes time stand still" (Pollock 1992:77). Initially an ardent supporter of JW, Swinburne later criticized the "fairyland" aspect of *Japonisme* (*GA* 256).

49. First delivered in London on the evening of February 20, 1885; subsequently presented at Cambridge (March 24) and Oxford (April 30). A limited edition of the *Lecture* was published in London later that year; an American edition appeared in Boston and New York in 1888. WHP may have attended the Oxford event; JR, who returned as Slade professor from March 1883 to March 1885, was living at Brantwood to recover from a breakdown.

50. Published in December 1878, it was JW's first post-trial riposte against his "enemies." In February 1879, James observed that the pamphlet, "now in its sixth edition, . . . sells for a shilling, and is to be seen in most of the shop-windows" (1914:175).

51. Subsequently, EP would decry civilization as "an old bitch gone in the teeth" (*P/SPo*:64); WL, as Whore of Babylon: "'Civilization' having become brazen in her new rôle as Whore of Babylon has a malignant squint for her traditional retainers and wears her high-brow ornaments with an unconcealed impatience. When she was a Madonna . . . she was the friend of every art. But as a tart she has her living to make" (*DPDS*:163).

52. His inaugural lectures at Oxford in 1870 also stress the importance of line. In November and December 1872, lectures on engraving (subsequently published as *Ariadne Florentina*) define three different schools: the Delineators, the Chiaroscurists, and the Colorists (*WJR* 22:311).

53. These comments by a former student are verified by the actual palette, on display in the Whistler Collection at the Hunterian Museum and Art Gallery, University of Glasgow.

54. Wilde's review, "*Rengaines!,*" appeared in the *Pall Mall Gazette* 21 February 1885; it is quoted *GA* 161.

55. See Materer 1979:99–100. Of the moment during the trial when JW explains that the painting's price reflects "'the knowledge I have gained in the work of a lifetime,'" Dorment says, "It could be argued that with these words, modernism was born" (1992:16).

56. Sponsored by the International Society of Sculptors, Painters, and Gravers; JW had been the first president. Featured were more than 400 etchings, 150 lithographs, 50 drawings, illustrations and pastels, and 50 oil paintings. *Symphony in White, No.1* was exhibited in England for the first time.

57. John Lane and The Bodley Head placed several advertisements in the first issue of *BLAST* (1914); books listed included Gallatin's *Whistler's Pastels and Other Modern Profiles* and *The Portraits and Caricatures of James McNeill Whistler,* and Way's *Memories of James McNeill Whistler.* Symons includes a chapter on JW in *Studies in Seven Arts,* which begins: "Whistler is dead, and there goes with him one of the greatest painters and one of the most original personalities of our time" (1906:121). Readers are reminded that "one of the first to recognise the genius of Whistler" was Baudelaire, an endorsement that would also please the Men of 1914. Symons's earlier book, *The Symbolist Movement in Poetry* (the production of which was assisted and orchestrated by Yeats, who believed the book would champion his own aesthetic projects), had a profound impact on poets such as TSE and EP (see Chapter 3).

58. Wedmore praises Duret's s work as "the only serious, single-minded contribution to men's knowledge of the master that has been received in book form since his death" (16–17). Gallatin published industriously: *Whistler's Art Dicta and Other Essays* (1904), *Whistler's Notes and Footnotes and Other Memoranda* (1907), *Whistler's Pastels and Other Modern Profiles* (1912; enlarged 1913), *The Portraits and Caricatures of James McNeill Whistler: An Iconography* (1913), and *Notes on Some Rare Portraits of Whistler* (1916).

59. JW's portrait of Mallarmé provided the frontispiece for *Vers et Prose* (1893); the two men became good friends. Given the French poet's reputation among the Men of 1914, his endorsement of JW's work functioned as a special imprimatur. To quote EP's 1938 "National Culture: A Manifesto," "I suppose in the long run Jimmy Whistler was not so good a painter as Manet but he had a damn good run for his money. I don't recall any British painter of his time cropping up in a poem by Mallarmé" (1960:7).

60. Only JW, according to Holmes, would dare to leave a seascape "unprettified" (205).

61. The Freer Gallery of Art, which features Asian art and the works of JW, opened in Washington in 1923. Freer not only owned the largest single collection of JW paintings, etchings, and drawings, he purchased "the Peacock Room" from the Leyland house before the building was demolished, and had the entire room—including *La Princesse du Pays de la Porcelaine* and rare ceramics—reassembled in the gallery. (See C. J. H., *The Peacock Room,* and Merrill 1998). As early as 1907, Fenellosa praised the Freer collection because it

"strikingly illustrates the most conspicuous fact in the history of art, that the two great streams of European and Asiatic practice, held apart for so many thousand years, have, at the close of the nineteenth century, been brought together in a fertile and final union" (Fenellosa 1907:365). See also Merrill, ed.

62. EP echoes these remarks in his *Polite Essays* (1937): "There are two kinds of beautiful painting, as one may perhaps illustrate by the works of Burne-Jones and Whistler; one looks at the first kind of painting and is immediately delighted by its beauty; the second kind of painting, when first seen, puzzles one, but on leaving it, and going from the gallery one finds new beauty in natural things—a Thames fog, to use the hackneyed example. Thus there are works of art which are beautiful objects, and works of art which are keys or passwords admitting one to a deeper knowledge, to a finer perception of beauty" (Zinnes ed. 271; see also 287).

63. For the 72nd Annual Exhibition of the Pennsylvania Academy of the Fine Arts (Philadelphia, 19 January to 28 February 1903), Freer lent five Whistler works: *Blue and Gold—The Rose Azalea, Rose and Red: The Little Pink Cap, Rose and Brown: La Cigale, Rose and Gold: The Little Lady Sophie of Soho,* and *Violet and Silver: The Great Sea* (Merrill ed. 185–186 n.4).

64. In an October 1913 letter to Harriet Monroe, EP observed "it is almost impossible for America to understand WHY Whistler and Henry James and Sargent, and every good artist flee her borders" (Zinnes ed. 288).

65. "That Pound was conscious of the affinity," WL recalled, "is suggested by the frontispiece to *Pavannes and Divisions,* in which he is posed in raking silhouette, his overcoat trailing in reminiscence of the Carlyle [Whistler's *Portrait of Thomas Carlyle*]" (Russell ed. 263). WL also insists that "Pound's nearest American analogue in the past is not Whitman . . . or Mark Twain," but JW; both were "interloping American[s] . . . aggressing among the sleepy islanders, ramming novelties down their expostulating throats" (Russell ed. 263).

66. During the three years devoted to Fenellosa's manuscripts, EP produced *Cathay;* a study of Japanese theatre entitled *"Noh" or Accomplishment;* and "The Chinese Written Character as a Medium for Poetry."

67. The subtitle, "On the loan exhibit of his paintings at the Tate Gallery," reminds readers that this "great" *American* artist has been recognized by a major British art institution. First published in *Poetry,* 1912; subsequently included in *Personae.*

68. Whereas Irving and Hawthorne are the product of "our purely colonial conditions," EP observed, "in our own time the country has given to the world two men, Whistler, of the school of masterwork . . . and Mr Henry James" (1912:367). Kenner tries to distance EP and "the Pound era" from JW by situating the latter among predecessors such as Symons (1971:180–181).

69. In his memorial essay for Remy de Gourmont, EP comments, "Just as there is more wisdom, perhaps more 'revolution,' in Whistler's portrait of young Miss Alexander than in all the Judaic drawings of the 'prophetic' Blake, so there is more life in Remy than in all the reformers" (*P/SP* 388).

70. JW's importance was still being cited in the 1920s by EP's contemporaries. The same 1920 issue (1.2) of *The Apple (Of Beauty and Discord)* that featured WL's pen and ink portrait of Pound (97) and a pen drawing by Henri Gaudier-Brzeska (123) also included Jan Gordon's favorable comments about JW. EP contributed to the third issue of *The Apple*.

71. "It is our strength as Americans," EP said in 1936, "that those of us who are any good at all start out to make a record. Whistler set out to beat every European painter" (rpt. 1960:75). In December 1938, trying to persuade WL not to over-work the portrait of him then underway, EP observed, "My instink IZ/ you let that portraT ALONE. Az Jim Whistler said abaht shootink the artist" (*P/L* 203). In what turned out to be EP's last letter to WL, on 3 February 1957 (WL died March 7), EP compares Lewis's canvas to a Whistler (*P/L* 304n).

72. In this broadcast EP repeats the same story about JW (his insistence that he was not *arguing* with someone, but *telling* him) that John Quinn mentioned to Yeats in a letter of August 23, 1907. See Himber 84; Doob 187.

73. As Beerbohm states, enemies "were a necessity" to JW's "nature" (108). Beerbohm praises *The Gentle Art* and JW's "extraordinary talent for writing. He was a born writer" (108–109).

74. JW's book is actually a bricolage of materials: an account of Sheridan Ford's attempts to produce a pirated edition of *The Gentle Art;* excerpted reviews from various London papers; letters from JW to critics and newspapers, and an exchange between JW and Oscar Wilde; highlights of the November 1878 libel trial (the contents modified to enhance JW's performance); and the text of the *Lecture.* The playful wit and malice of JW's marginalia punctuates the whole; quotations are orchestrated to embarrass enemies (especially JR) and flatter JW. His signature butterfly appears in many poses and positions to highlight caustic comments and remonstrate against critics.

75. The Whistler exhibition opened at the École de Beaux Arts on May 10, 1905.

76. Wagner notes an "association between" WL's aesthetics and "much nineteenth-century aesthetics (especially those of Whistler or Baudelaire)," but does not substantiate his remarks (106–107).

77. In *Art,* Bell installs JW as the best example of a combative, self-styled avant-garde artist and rebel from the recent past. (Although Bell refers to JW as a figure from "another age," the painter had only been dead eleven years when *Art* was published.) Bell cannot concede greatness to JW because the cornerstone of the latter's aesthetic discourse—the production of beauty—is that which Bell dismantles in order to promulgate the doctrine of "significant form."

78. From Horace's reference to "'stern Necessity' carrying nails, hooks, and molten lead" (*Odes* 1:35) and the punning implications of force, fortitude, fortune (*fors*) together with key, nail, or rudder (*clava*) Ruskin fashioned his title (Birch 1999b:176–177; *WJR* 27:27–28).

79. A reporter for *The Critic* noted in 1894 that JW had "'mastered'" a new art: "'The Gentle Art of Advertising Oneself'" (qtd Burns 36). In 1898, "with

the idea of being his own dealer, [JW] formed in London an agency he called
the Company of the Butterfly; it got as far as having offices . . . and then
gradually expired from neglect by himself and by patrons who preferred to
buy pictures in a more traditional way" (McMullen 264; see Merrill ed.
125). Freer was an exception to this rule; he worked directly with JW to pre-
view, order, and purchase works.

80. My understanding of JW's exhibition practices is indebted to Bendix, Curry
1987, Jensen, and Koval.

81. Edwards's monumental *Wyndham Lewis: Painter and Writer* includes only
one substantive reference to JW, but it verifies my argument. WL submitted
his *Portrait of T. S. Eliot* "to the Royal Academy's annual exhibition in the
spring of 1938. It was rejected and, thanks to Augustus John's resignation in
protest, Lewis garnered . . . publicity that he exploited through a series of
virulent attacks on the Academy and its values. Emulating Whistler, he attended the press view and published a review damning the majority of ex-
hibits and suggesting that most of the . . . rooms would be more usefully
employed as dance halls and skating rinks" (Edwards 2000:466).

Chapter 2

1. Home Office records indicate that *The Renaissance* was one of the first books
Reading Gaol prisoner C/3/3was given; in September 1895, he received
Greek Studies, Appreciations, and *Imaginary Portraits;* in December 1896, *Gas-
ton de Latour* and *Miscellaneous Studies* (Hart-Davis ed. 399 n.4, 416 n.5).

2. Elements of WHP's writings revisited by many modernists include the development of "imaginary portraits" and fictive voices; "moments" of heightened
awareness and insight; the rewriting of ancient myths; the insistence that, in
a successful work of art, the "transmutation of ideas into images" must take
place (*TR* 88); and a privileging of the "concrete" over the abstract. The list
of critics who have identified Paterian intertextualities in Joyce's writings
(from the 1904 essay "A Portrait of the Artist" and chapter 5 of *A Portrait of
the Artist as a Young Man* to the parodic "Oxen of the Sun" in *Ulysses* and
Anna Livia Plurabelle's musings in *Finnegans Wake*) includes Richard Kain,
Robert Scotto, Harry Levin, Don Gifford, John McGowan, and Frank Moliterno. George Russell (AE) commented on the indebtedness to Yeats in
1902, disapprovingly; in 1922, TSE told Woolf that Joyce was "founded
upon Walter Pater" (Woolf 1978 2:202). EP was more than ready to ridicule
a "Paterine sentimentalesque Hellenism" in a 1914 issue of the *Egoist* (Zinnes
ed. 186), or to declare that WHP "is not dull in the least. He is adolescent
reading, and very excellent bait" (*GK* 160), yet he was also the least reluctant
to acknowledge the importance of WHP's insight, in the "School of Giorgione," that "*All art constantly aspires towards the condition of music*" (*TR* 106).
The latter is cited (slightly misquoted) along with EP's definition of the
"Image" and Whistler's remark, "You are interested in a certain painting because it is an arrangement of lines and colours" in "VORTEX. POUND"

(*BLAST* 1:154); it is repeated in a September 1914 essay on Vorticism (later reprinted in *Gaudier-Brzeska,* 81–94). Letters exchanged with Dorothy Shakespear 1911 to 1913 indicate EP's familiarity with *Plato and Platonism* and *Marius;* EP playfully warns his future wife, "'all the disciples of Pater come to a bad end'. gee!!!" (O. Pound and Litz eds. 260). The poetry from this era indicates a more profound intertextual awareness. Among the poems in *Canzoni* (1911) three focus on writers featured in *The Renaissance* ("The Golden Sestina," a transmutation "from the Italian of Pico della Mirandola"; "Rome," reworked "from the French of Joachim du Bellay"; "Abelard," Part III of "Victorian Eclogues"; 1976:152–153, 154, 158–159); the "Speech for Psyche in The Golden Book of Apuleius" is indebted to Pater's version of the Cupid and Psyche story in *Marius.* "Pater and Co." are kept at arm's length from "us moderns" in an April 1930 essay contributed to TSE's *Criterion* (Zinnes ed. 164); reviewing Adrian Stokes's *The Quattro Cento* for *Symposium* in October 1932, EP criticized WHP's "floribund vocabulary" (Zinnes ed. 222). (See also Monsman 1977:176–177.) "In his early polemics," Mao allows, EP "retained a number of Paterian and Wildean premises" (140). See also Christ 71–73, Bush 26–29. WHP is an unacknowledged interlocutor for TEH. TEH's dismissal of humanism necessitates a Ruskin-like critique of the Renaissance, a stance that ensures antipathy to WHP's works. In early essays, TEH argues against any (Paterian) suggestion that "ethical values" are "relative" (1936:47); "Bergson's Theory of Art" explores the concept of "flux" but never mentions WHP's contributions to the debate. Yet a final comment in "Notes on Language and Style"—"Life is composed of exquisite moments and the rest is shadows of them"—remarkably echoes the "Conclusion" to *The Renaissance* (Hulme 1925:497). A crucial passage in *Cinders*—"All is flux. The moralists, the capital letterists, attempt to find a framework outside the flux, a solid bank for the river, a pier rather than a raft. Truth is what helps a particular sect in the general flow" (Hulme 1936:222)—metaphorically responds to WHP's suggestions that, within the "perpetual flux" of existence (*ME* 1:155), the "elements" of life are "driven in many currents" (*TR* 187). Monsman surveyed WHP "and the Modern Temper" in 1977 (160–186); McGrath's study is excellent.

3. Although "the cult of aestheticism challenges repressive norms of bourgeois masculinity," Felski argues, "it contains a misogynistic dimension that is closely related to, rather than dissolved by, an antirepresentationalism and antinaturalism" (1104). Felski's provocative study of the male aesthete suggests that his "playful subversion of gender norms, his adoption of feminine traits, paradoxically reinforces his distance from and elevation above women" (1100).

4. Anti-Semitism is briefly discussed in Ricks's *T. S. Eliot and Prejudice;* homophobia is not considered.

5. Lentricchia, for example, disparaging the "onanism of Paterian aestheticism" (6), disavows WHP's writings in *Modernist Quartet.*

6. See also Moliterno 71 and Meisel.

7. "The Critic as Artist" advocates the necessity of sin: "it saves us from monotony of type" (*CWW* 4:134). In his 1910 "Futurist Speech to the English," Filippo Marinetti chastises his London audience for "the dismal, ridiculous condemnation of Oscar Wilde. Intellectual Europe will never forgive you for it. . . . As for your twenty-year-old young men, almost all of them are homosexual for a time. . . . [then] they show their heels to Sodom in order to marry a shamelessly licentious young lady" (60).

8. "England emerged from Lupanars and Satanics about 1900, the Bourgeoisie having thoughtfully put Wilde in prison" (*BLAST* 1:133).

9. Homophobia is only mentioned in passing, but Boone's provocative book probes the intersections of "libidinal and textual emanations that look 'perverse'" (14), and compels one to reexamine "the literary and sexual politics of modernism" (4).

10. Chapter 7 of Showalter's *The Female Malady* examines "men's war neurosis" and its "effects on English psychiatric practice." WL faulted the art scene of 1919 for lacking manly strength and purpose: "An effete and hysterical automatism certainly threatens every art; . . . a showy and dessicated scepticism, wedded to a tearful sentimentality, as sweet and heavy as molasses" (*HC* 290–291).

11. "Usury and sodomy, the Church condemned as a pair, to one hell. . . . Dante knew this and said it" (EP 1960:144).

12. EP's preference for these terms can be traced in all of his writings—in a November 1920 letter to New York lawyer and patron John Quinn, he observes that "I don't want to go soft, or get to producing merely 'objets d'art' instead of 'oeuvres'" (*P/Q* 202). McDonald is one of the few critics who acknowledges that "those things [EP] considers non-generative—homosexuality, usury, philology, celibacy—are condemned" in the *Cantos* "in some of the most vitriolic language in American poetry" (24).

13. The raison d'être for *The Jews, Are They Human?*, but individual readers must decide if WL succeeds.

14. Hewitt's essay also cites "the interpretive exclusions practiced by Jameson's analysis [in *Fables of Aggression*] when confronted with the libidinal structure of Lewis's protofascism" (528). Quéma suggests that "a link exists between Lewis's own difficult rite of passage to manhood and his obsessional concern with homosexuality," a "theme" that "recurs like a demonic possession" (98) in his writings. The phrasing demonizes homosexuality, and suggests that it is to blame for homophobia. Quéma wants to psychoanalyze why WL wrote as he did, why his antifeminism should be understood in terms of "Herculean efforts to set himself free from the maternal influence" (91). I am more interested in the cultural and literary effects produced by the homophobia expressed in his texts. Quéma seems impatient that "feminist criticism responds to the undeniable misogyny of some of Lewis's writings" (95); completely unsatisfactory are comments, delayed until the book's final paragraph, on the cleansing of "sexual inversion" suggested in *Hitler*.

15. WL's analysis borrows extensively from the "Homosexual Love" chapter (2: 456–514) of Westermarck's *The Origin and Development of Moral Ideas* (London: Macmillan, 1908).

16. For WL's indebtedness to Marinetti when "blasting" suffragettes, see Chapter 3. As Hewitt explains, WL isolates three main factors "in his genealogy of modern sexuality: the disintegration of the family, the war-experience, and the emergence of the petty bourgeoisie"(539); see WL 1926:239. Dasenbrook acknowledges WL's "opposition to—even hatred of—homosexuality" but also insists that WL "throws out a statement now and then indicating that . . . the explosion of homosexuality in the 1920s is not at all a bad thing" (436).

17. *Childermass* (1928), Book One in WL's four-novel project *The Human Age*, culminates in an interrogation of Alectryon by the Bailiff. The latter understands homosexuality only as a "filthy" and outrageous "vice." Alectryon tries to explain that an "indifferent" but also "highly disinfectant" attitude is best (*ChM* 385). In fact, Alectryon is rehearsing arguments about "the nan-man" taken from *The Art of Being Ruled* and elsewhere (*ChM* 389, 391).

18. Wilde is the "nancy-boy" scapegoat of WL's canon. In *The Diabolical Principle* (1931), he asserts that the "new romanticism" is not, in fact, "new; it is a return to the feverish 'diabolism' that flourished in the middle of the last century in France, and which reached England in the 'nineties,' with Oscar Wilde and Beardsley as its principal exponents" (*DPDS* 42), a point reiterated in *The Hitler Cult*.

19. Having absorbed WL's account, one can never read Barnes's *Nightwood* (1936) or Isherwood's *Goodbye to Berlin* (1939) in quite the same way. Almost as a response to WL's homophobic *flânerie,* Isherwood's text culminates in a visit to the Salomé club, during which an American youth, "very drunk," demands of Fritz and Christopher, "'What's going on here?' . . . Men dressed as *women*? As *women,* hey? Do you mean they're *queer?*' 'Eventually we're all queer,' drawled Fritz solemnly, in lugubrious tones" (238).

20. *Motze* is derived from the slangy German verb *motzen,* to grouse or to complain; WL has arrived at "Grouse-Street." My thanks to Dr. Marietta Messmer for clarification.

21. "Restless analyst" is a phrase borrowed from Henry James, *The American Scene;* see Chapter 4.

22. Prior to this book, WL's texts featured brief anti-Paterian squibs that were important components of his developing aesthetic program. Tarr declares (1918) that "'the lines and masses of the statue are its soul. No restless, quick flame-like ego is imagined for the *inside* of it. It has no inside. This is another condition of art; *to have no inside,* nothing you cannot *see*'" (*Tarr* 354). In *The Caliph's Design* (1919) WL derides Cubism as "purely art-for-art's sake dilettantism" (*HC* 209) and declares the contemporary, "English variety of art- man" the "heir" to WHP and "the aesthete of the Wilde period," someone given to "ecstatic contemplation," purring, gushing, and always drawing attention to himself as a "queerly seductive object" (*HC* 304–305).

Attacks on art-for-art's sake resume in *The Dithyrambic Spectator* (an important catalyst for *MWA*).

23. In the same text that ridicules WHP at least once in almost every chapter, JR is hailed as one of the "most clear-sighted people of the nineteenth-century," someone who also tried to keep "a limited area clear for the operations of the 'impartial truth' of art and of science" (*MWA* 213).

24. Several pages later, however, WL does not hesitate to crib from WHP's non-aesthetic writings: the translation of Prosper Mérimée's text is borrowed from the first essay in *Miscellaneous Studies* (1895).

25. Subsequently WL quotes "Arnold and Pater" to slam the Oxford don's credentials: these "statements of Mr. Eliot's," readers are enjoined, "should satisfy us as to the bona fides of Walter Pater as a moralist. Actually it was this exaggerated development of his ethical will that provided the impulse for his particular contribution to the diabolics of his time" (*MWA* 144).

26. Pawlowski's brief essay on the Woolf-WL relationship is insightful.

27. Buchanan's review, "The Fleshly School of Poetry: Mr. D.G. Rossetti," published under the name of "Thomas Maitland," appeared in the *Contemporary Review,* October 1871.

28. The book was glowingly reviewed for TSE's *Criterion* by the editor's friend (and later, flat-mate) John Hayward, in October 1933 (*CC* 13:158–160). Ironically, Praz became one of the major promoters of WHP's writings in Italy (Ascari 18–19): in 1939, he wrote the preface for Mazzaloni's translation of *Marius,* then edited a major collection of selected works in translation (*Walter Pater,* 1944) as well as translated *Imaginary Portraits.* His translation of *The Renaissance* was published in 1946 (reprinted 1965). WHP was often cited in Praz's criticism.

29. "Romanticism," first published in *Macmillan's Magazine,* November 1876, was reprinted in *Appreciations* (1889) as a "Postscript." WHP defines romanticism as "the addition of strangeness to beauty" (*Ap* 258).

30. Conlon reminds us of WHP's "manifold efforts to introduce the complex culture of France to his own generation and the generation he tutored" (1982b:136). Before TSE read Symons on Laforgue, for example, he read WHP on Flaubert and Baudelaire.

31. An edited, somewhat muted version of the essay appears in *Appreciations* (1889) as "Coleridge."

32. Published in 1873 as *Studies in the History of the Renaissance.* Harsh criticism of its historical merits prompted WHP to rename and reissue it as *The Renaissance: Studies in Art and Poetry.*

33. Contrarily, Yeats noted in 1922: "Three or four years ago I re-read *Marius the Epicurean,* expecting to find I cared for it no longer, but it still seemed to me, as I think it seemed to us all, the only great prose in modern English" (1970:302).

34. "Temperamentally, T. S. Eliot is as *close* as Ezra is exuberant. He is as arrogant as Ezra is modest—as sly as Ezra is open" (*EnS* 187).

35. TSE once said of Paul Elmer More, whom he greatly admired, that he "is primarily a moralist, which is a worthy and serious thing to be" (*SW* 41).

36. More compares the "deadly and deliberate languor that trails through the lines of Pater" with "the virile art of Leonardo"; Paterism, he warns, "leads one inevitably to weariness, and satiety, and impotence" (Seiler ed. 420, 425). Apparently, WHP was seduced by "the call of Oxford," a sirenlike she-place of "fascinating danger" responsible for engendering "a worship of beauty isolated from, and in the end despised by, the real interests of life" (Seiler ed. 421–422). Further reason to despise WHP: the "fruit of his teaching in such men as Oscar Wilde" (Seiler ed. 423). Babbitt compares WHP "to that arch-impressionist, Anatole France" (Child 130). In "Imperfect Critics," TSE comments that Babbitt "shares so many of the ideals and opinions of Mr. More that their names must be coupled" (*SW* 41). Both men are lauded in "To Criticize the Critic" (1961).

37. According to TSE's obituary notice in *The Criterion,* when More composed the early Shelburne pieces, "Walter Pater ruled from the grave, and his living representative was Arthur Symons. I should say myself that More was a better critic than Pater; and I do not think it can be denied that he was of very much larger size than Arthur Symons" (*CC* 16:667). Perhaps he is echoing WHP's description of *La Gioconda:* "like the vampire, she has been dead many times" (*TR* 99).

38. So familiar was TSE with *The Renaissance* and its publication history that he compared the different versions of the "Conclusion" featured in the 1873 and 1888 editions.

39. TSE's note on the inside front cover—"The notes in pencil, on the margin of the *Conclusion,* were made by me, comparing the text with the later edition. T. S. Eliot"—seems to disavow any other markings in the former library book (Mercantile Library, St. Louis). Yet some of the underscorings and marginal braces are wholly consistent with notations found in other books owned solely by Eliot.

40. The Harvard notes are now part of the Hayward Bequest at King's College (P3 / Vol. 19). The course began with studies of Uccello, del Castagno, and Veneziano; comments on the anatomical fineness of Castagno's paintings, the bones and muscles to be discerned underneath the skin, parallel the "skull beneath the skin" observation of "Whispers of Immortality" (*CPP* 52). TSE's Ruskinian "Notes on Italy" are now housed in the Houghton Library, Harvard. An explanation is provided by his brother, Henry Ware Eliot Jr.: "Notes made on a 2 week trip to Italy Summer of 1911 by TSE who was a graduate student at the Sorbonne. Oct. 1910–1911." TSE's copy of Baedecker's *London and its Environs* (Leipzig, 1908) is inscribed "Thomas S. Eliot, October the 14th, 1910" in his mother's handwriting (Hayward Bequest).

41. While extension lecturer in Victorian and Modern English literature for the University of London (1916- 1919), TSE did not include a WHP text on any syllabus (see Schuchard). Arnold and Ruskin were discussed.

42. Analyzing "primarily the essays Eliot wrote between 1916 and 1926," Diepeveen contends that "Eliot clears a space for his own poetry" with "statements that utilize the language of elitism and exclusion to reform the expectations of and attract readers most useful to the success of his poetry" (40).

43. "Observations," a May 1918 review article by "T. S. Apertyx," concludes, "Coleridge occasionally wrote good criticism; and Walter Pater, if he had had a better English style, and been more interested in what he wrote about, might have done something in the same way" (1918c:71).

44. In 1908, "art for art's sake was not an admission of irresponsibility, but a means of self-realization as an artist. Pater's creed, preached by Arthur Symons, gave Eliot the recipe he needed to make an entirely new liquor from Emerson's watered port and Arnold's decaffeinated coffee" (Brooker 905).

45. TSE's "Wordsworth and Coleridge" (*UPUC*) should be compared with WHP's essays on the same subjects in *Appreciations*.

46. "Eliot was one of the chief contributors to the decline of Pater's critical reputation," Conlon observes, "a decline that began about the time 'Hamlet and His Problems' appeared (1919)" (1982a:169). Diepeveen acknowledges that TSE's "often-remarked Olympian tone has a coercive function" (53).

47. The method of *The Sacred Wood*, McDonald observes, is "a process of elimination rather than . . . a construction of a critical theory, the work more frequently insisting on what criticism should not be than elaborating what it should be" (58); it was a crucial step in TSE's desire, shared by EP, "to professionalize literary criticism" (57). Sharpe comments on the "kind of managerial control" TSE exerted on his poetic canon once installed at Faber; organizing the "appearances of his work," he could "manipulate public perception," which "depended in part on what was withheld, as it did on what was revealed" (152).

48. In the sixth Clark Lecture, TSE judges Crashaw's life and "fervent temperament": "He was a born convert. He was Marius the Epicurean" (*VMP* 162, 165).

49. Between 1920 and 1930 there are two published references to WHP in TSE's critical writings: a 1925 note in *The Criterion* that WHP's "thought lacks the logical rigour of his master[,] Newman" (*CC* 3:162), and a more revealing mention in F. H. Bradley's obituary: "Those who belittle the importance of Oxford in the modern world should hesitate over the names of Arnold, Newman, Pater, and Bradley. None of these writers has had, or could have, the prodigious popularity and apparent influence" of Carlyle, Wells, and Shaw; they worked "in comparative obscurity, or in the deceptive certainty of moderate success. But their intentions were not squandered upon their generation; and, in *the gradual dissolution of nineteenth-century idea and ideals,* theirs are amongst the names which carry the most promise of future power" (1924b:1; the italicized phrase is repeated in the final paragraph of "Arnold and Pater," *SE* 442). Arnold and WHP are also briefly juxtaposed in 1944 to argue for the greater merits of "Johnson as Critic and Poet" (*OPP* 191).

50. JR, on the other hand, is praised for his "genuine sensibility for certain types of art and architecture," and his "sharper, more literate social fury" (*SE* 438).

51. TSE's comments on Spinoza should be compared to WHP's in "Sebastian Van Storck"; juxtaposing Giordano Bruno and Montaigne echoes *Gaston de Latour;* the suggestion that "the humanist's personality throws out the idea,

centrifugal, without so much entering into it" (Eliot 1919c:1015) is a travesty of the centripetal/centrifugal paradigm developed in *Plato and Platonism.*

52. The original title of TSE's dissertation; published in 1964 as *Knowledge and Experience in the Philosophy of F. H. Bradley.* See Shusterman 32–33, and Bolgan.

53. The quotation is taken from "Imperfect Critics," but the first part of the essay is derived from "Swinburne and the Elizabethans" (*Athenaeum*, September 1919). The latter was "reprinted, with the addition of a final paragraph, as 'Swinburne as Critic'" (Gallup 204). "Tradition and the Individual Talent" appeared in the November/December 1919 issue of the *Egoist.*

54. TSE revisits his laudatory opinion of Donne in the Clark Lectures, worrying that Donne, like Crashaw, was a "voluptuary of thought" and "religious emotion" (*VMP* 168–169).

55. Letter to Forster 10 August 1929; Forster Letter-Book, vol. 1, number 33, King's College, Cambridge. Praise for *Tarr* is undercut by TSE's assessment of the author: "Mr. Lewis is a magician who compels our interest in himself: he is the most fascinating personality in our time rather than a novelist" (1918e:106). WL responded: "The personality is not, I think, quite the pariah it becomes in the pages of Mr. Eliot: I do not believe in the anonymous, 'impersonal,' catalytic, for the very good reason that I am sure the personality is in that as much as in the other part of this double-headed oddity, however thoroughly disguised" (*MWA* 91).

56. Stein also suggests that *The Renaissance* "anticipates the argument of T. S. Eliot," but adds that "Pater is primarily interested in the capacity of a masterpiece to coalesce tradition and history in the eyes of the observer" (230–231); McGrath concurs (176).

57. WHP compares Pascal's "irony" with that of Socrates in the *Apology;* Pascal's "style," he suggests, "reminds us of the 'Apologia' of Newman" (*MS* 66–67). TSE concludes "The 'Pensées' of Pascal" with a Pascal / Newman comparison (*SE* 416).

58. Bolgan regrets that "none of the three major Anglo-American idealists has actually used the phrase 'objective correlative'" (116); TSE suggested in 1956 that the phrase was coined by Washington Allston.

59. Perhaps TSE was also stung by the denunciation of "metaphysical enquiry" in *Marius* (1:140–141).

60. "Eliot's image of the prison, though adapted from Dante, and Bradley's closed circle both recall, more than Eliot or Bradley might have wished, Pater's 'Conclusion'" (Buckley 168 n.16).

61. TSE's notes admit only one intertextual gesture: Bradley's *Appearance and Reality.* McGrath concurs that Eliot "manages to camouflage Pater's presence" in these lines (43).

62. The speaker of "Bacchus and Ariadne [or] 2nd Debate between the Body and Soul" imagines that "A Ring of silence closes round me and annuls / These sudden insights that have marched across / Like railway-engines over desert plains" (*IMH* 68). As Janowitz suggests, a catalyst for "Animula" (1929) is Chapter 8 of *Marius,* which is prefaced with Hadrian's poem "to

his soul," "Animula, vagula, blandula, / Hospes comesque corporis" (*ME* 1:123). EP's "Blandula, Tenulla, Vagula" comes immediately after "Speech for Psyche" in TSE's edition of the *Selected Poems* (1928). In *Marius,* Chapter 8 follows the full-length version of "The Story of Cupid and Psyche," which Pater "translates" from Apuleius's *The Golden Ass.*

63. See Dijkstra, and Higgins 1997b.

64. Smith identified a Pater-*Gioconda-Waste Land* connection more than 50 years ago.

65. WHP's positive review of Symonds's *Age of the Despots* underscores his endorsement of patriarchy's sphere ideology (see Inman 1990:160–164).

66. See *Facs* for evidence of EP's decisive, substantial editorial work. Koestenbaum offers a provocative reading of their collaboration. Essays by Kenner and Ellmann (in Litz, ed.) elucidate TSE's attempts to craft a city poem in the tradition of Dryden's *Annus Mirabilis.*

67. In "Gerontion," Fresca is one of those "whirled/ Beyond the circuit of the shuddering Bear" (*CPP* 39). The speaker's realization, "I that was near your heart was removed therefrom / To lose beauty in terror, terror in inquisition" (*CPP* 38), is expressed in terms borrowed from WHP's "Leonardo da Vinci" essay, which cites "the extremes of beauty and terror" the painter experienced (*TR* 110).

68. Originally, "Disguise the good old female stench" (*Facs* 39). The lines owe more to Swift ("The Lady's Dressing Room") than Pope; TSE describes Swift as "the great master of disgust" (*SE* 293).

69. "Afternoon," the manuscript poem TSE sent to Conrad Aiken in 1915, mocks "ladies who are interested in Assyrian art" at the British Museum, which is permeated by the "faint perfume of last year's tailor suits" (*LE* 89). In the same letter, "Suppressed Complex" describes a female figure "still in bed with stubborn eyes / Holding her breath lest she begin to think" (*LE* 88).

70. For a summary of translations available in the early 1900s, see *IMH* 177. EP features W. H. Porter's version in *The Spirit of Romance* (19–21).

71. Among conventional paeans to spring subverted by the opening of *The Waste Land* is Remy Belleau's lyric "Avril, la grace, et le ris / De Cypris," quoted by WHP (*TR* 126). Typically, WHP notices the terrors of springtime. Regarding Dionysian rites dramatized in Euripedes's *Bacchanals,* he suggests that one must "catch, in its fulness, that deep undercurrent of horror which runs below, all through this masque of spring" (*GS* 76). Gaston cannot appreciate the "sudden gaieties of Easter" because of a lingering "Lenten pre-occupation with Christ's death" (*GDL* 134); he recalls Ronsard's poems featuring "lines to April" that are like the jonquil: "sweet, but with something of the sickliness of all spring flowers" (*GDL* 51). *Greek Studies* links the annual, temporary return of Persephone with the story "of Linus, a fair child . . . torn to pieces by hounds every spring-time" (*GS* 110); *Plato and Platonism* studies the Spartan *Hyacinthia,* a religious festival in late spring characterized by joyous celebration and "two days of significant mourning after the manner of All Souls' Day" (*PP* 230). TSE's mock "masque of spring" is responding to these

arresting Paterian formulations; they constitute important links in "a chain of secret influences" (*TR* 91).

72. In the "Animula Vagula" chapter, Marius learns from "the thunder and lightning of Lucretius—like thunder and lightning some distance off, one might recline to enjoy, in a garden of roses" (*ME* 1:127).

73. Scott comments on the "discomfiting sense of sexual disorder that motivate[s]" (1:127) segments of TSE's poetry and criticism.

74. The narrative pattern is repeated in "A Child in the House," "Emerald Uthwart," and *Gaston de Latour.*

75. The journal is a textual place for "'conversations with himself' . . . one of his modernisms" (*ME* 2:172).

76. This image, which revisits the pool "filled with water out of sunlight" in "Burnt Norton" (*CPP* 172), recalls the "momentary conjunction of mirrors and . . . still water" in paintings of Giorgione and followers, "by which all the sides of a solid image are exhibited at once. . . . Such ideal instants the school of Giorgione selects . . . exquisite pauses in time, in which, arrested thus, we seem to be spectators of all the fulness of existence, and which are like some consummate extract or quintessence of life" (*TR* 118).

77. After a series of "uncivil clawings," Durét states, "with attacks and recriminations [JW and Wilde] broke with one another completely" (75). In 1906, 500 copies of *Wilde v Whistler* were issued; the text includes Wilde's "Mr. Whistler's Ten O'Clock" and JW's "Tenderness in Tite Street."

78. Reginald Bunthorne, the protagonist of Gilbert and Sullivan's *Patience* (first produced in London, April 1888; revived November 1900), was "a combination of Oscar Wilde and [JW]. The actor George Grossmith played Bunthorne largely as Whistler, wearing his hair in black curls with the famous white lock, an eyeglass and dancing shoes, and included James's deadly 'Haha' as part of the script" (Anderson and Koval 246). WL quotes from *Patience* in *The Art of Being Ruled* to parody male-male "love."

79. According to his biographers, "Jealousy of Wilde's lecturing success [in Canada and the U.S.] was also a motive" for JW's vituperative comments, but "at the heart of the matter lay James's concern that the prevalent image [association with Wilde's "theatrical aestheticism" and their joint "comic" pairing] was failing to impress patrons and collectors" (Anderson and Koval 268).

80. The exhibition "attracted considerable attention"; works displayed included the "'Portrait of the Painter's Mother,' . . . and the portraits of Thomas Carlyle, Miss Alexander, and Mr. and Mrs. Leyland, which were now seen for the first time" (Way and Dennis 7–8).

81. Comments made in a letter to John Miller Gray (art critic, first curator of the Scottish National Portrait Gallery) ca. 1878; Gray had sent WHP a copy of his 1874 review of JMW's exhibition. In August 1878, Gray published a favorable notice of WHP's "The Child in the House." As Conlon notes, WHP would have been familiar with Baudelaire's accolades for JW in *L'Art romantique* (94).

82. Wilde sent WHP a copy of his review, "The Grosvenor Gallery" (*Dublin University Magazine* 90:118- 26) in July 1877 (acknowledged by WHP July 14; *LWP* 24); the comments about Whistler are barbed. Inman suggests that WHP "was prompted by Ruskin's attack on Whistler to write his essay on Giorgione" (90; see also 384–385). While JW was being directly maligned by JR, WHP was being side-swiped by W. H. Mallock's *The New Republic*, first serialized in *Belgravia* from July to December 1876 then published in revised book form in 1877. WHP is parodied as Mr. Rose. A "thinly disguised caricature of Whistler" as Joe Sibley, the "idle apprentice," was featured in du Maurier's *Trilby* in 1894.

83. Birch analyzes the first "Election" of 1869 in 1988b:132–137. The Slade professorship was a three-year appointment; Ruskin held the post from 1870–1878 (when he resigned, after the trial), and 1882–1885.

84. The lecture was delivered in Oxford on April 30, 1885; WHP may have attended (extant letters from 31 March and 2 June indicate that he was in residence at 2 Bradmore Road all that spring).

85. In the spring of 1889, JW was elected honorary member of the Bavarian Royal Academy, and awarded both the Cross of St Michael and a first-class medal. To celebrate, friends in London organized a dinner on May 1(the date was chosen to nettle the British Royal Academy, whose annual exhibition was opening that week; see Weintraub 359–360, Anderson and Koval, 305–306). In addition to members of the organizing committee (among them Albert Moore, Alfred Stevens, Theodore Roussel, and John Singer Sargent), more than "sixty chosen guests paid the one guinea charge to render homage" to JW (Anderson and Koval 306). The dinner is described in the *Sunday Times* as "the heartfelt tribute of true English artists to a master whose work and worth are justly rated by all whose opinion is authority" ("The Dinner" 36). According to Conlon's research, guests included André Raffalovich, Sidney Colvin, Simeon Solomon, and WHP. An excerpt from JW's toast was later published in *The Gentle Art* (285–286). My thanks to Conlon for sharing work carried out in the Whistler Collection, University of Glasgow.

86. In June 1893, WHP reviewed George Moore's *Modern Painting,* praising his "impressionistic" approach to JW (*The Daily Chronicle,* June 10, 1893; rpt 1906:135–142; see Inman 384–385). The painter also receives honorable mention in WHP's unpublished essay "The Aesthetic Life." Did JW read anything by WHP? One can imagine Wilde insisting that he do so; there are Paterian gestures in the "Ten O'Clock Lecture," as Prettejohn suggests (1999b:53). In "Winckelmann" WHP quotes and later paraphrases Hegel's praise for the "'consummate modelling of divine and human forms'" in Greek art, including the famous statue of "'Phryne, who, as the most beautiful of women, ascended naked out of the water, in the presence of assembled Greece'" (*TR* 175; see also 182). Among the nudes JW sold to Freer was *Purple and Gold: Phryne the Superb!—Builder of Temples.* In his study of Swinburne and JW, Spencer suggests that the poet may have "brought to Whistler's attention" the "Winckelmann" essay (1999:71). The only work by

WHP included in JW's library at the time it was bequeathed to the University of Glasgow was a special edition of an excerpt from *Marius the Epicurean: The story of Cupid and Psyche, done into English from the Latin of Lucius Apuleius by Walter Pater* (New York: Russell, 1901).

87. In late fall 1878, WHP canceled plans for a volume to be entitled '*The School of Giorgione' and other Studies*. "[O]ne factor in his decision may have been the vituperative and widely reported debate about aestheticism and criticism at the libel trial of *Whistler v. Ruskin* which took place on 25 and 26 November, just before WHP withdrew the book on 30 November" (Brake 38–39).

88. In 1927, Rawlinson produced the *Selected Essays of Walter Horatio Pater* ("Style," "Wordsworth," "Charles Lamb," "Shakespeare's English Kings," "Leonardo da Vinci," "The Child in the House," Romanticism," and the "Conclusion" to *The Renaissance*).

89. "He was the high priest of the artistic world of his day," Bailey concluded in his unsigned review, "but he was also a Puritan, an ascetic of the asceticism which, as he liked to relate, was practised in Sparta and took its place in the ideal of the . . . immortal pages of Plato" (Seiler ed. 412).

90. Yeats was never persuaded to despise or villify WHP or Wilde; he did not participate in the same public homophobic discourse as his near-contemporaries. Privately he observed that "the ideal of culture expressed by Pater can only create feminine souls" (1972:159). Regarding Wilde's homosexuality, Yeats simply stated that "historical knowledge had lessened or taken away the horror or disgust at his form of vice" (1972:79). Similarly, he was indignant about the smear campaign launched against Roger Casement: "If Casement were a homo-sexual," he exclaimed to Dorothy Wellesley, "what matter!" (1964: 128). Gender is invoked to define stylistic changes in Yeats's poetry; after 1901, he praises his ability to expunge anything "unmanly," any sign of "effeminacy" from his texts (1954:434; 1961:519). The latter express a culturally-sanctioned misogyny, not homophobia. Indebtedness to Wilde and WHP is cited throughout Yeats's prose; he insists upon the continuing relevance of their work. Long after the Men of 1914 established campaigns to damn "the diabolics" with silence or expressive derision, Yeats did otherwise. In major works such as "Certain Noble Plays of Japan," *Per Amica Silentia Lunae, The Trembling of the Veil*, the "Introduction" to the *Oxford Book of Modern Verse*, and "A General Introduction to My Work," he continued to remind readers that the writings of WHP and Wilde are "permanent in our literature" (1936:vi). *The Oxford Book of Modern Poetry* was reviewed in the *TLS* by Hayward, who declared that the "first modernists" who were "still under the spell of Pater's doctrine . . . seem hardly modern to-day" (3); Yeats is faulted for placing WHP "on the threshold of this anthology" (3). Yeats once praised Wilde because he showed "so much courage and was so loyal to the intellect" (1972:22); Yeats's loyalty to his predecessors is commendable, and rare. Whereas beauty is significantly and repeatedly "betrayed" in his writings, the chief apostles of the beautiful are not.

91. Dale cites Hough's *The Last Romantics* (1947) as one of the first major reassessments of WHP's merits (319); reclaiming WHP then became the mission of Bloom and Miller. See Court's discussion of WHP's "early critics." Among the works reasserting the importance of WHP's writings within modernist literary culture are those by Conlon, Christ, and Carolyn Williams (whose book is crucial to an understanding of WHP's historicizing discourse).

Chapter 3

1. In a 1917 letter to WL, then at the Front as part of the Canadian War Memorials Scheme (previously, he had served as a second lieutenant, Royal Garrison Artillery, near Ypres), EP talks of providing "Aunt Sallys," which are "puppet-heads set up, as at a fair, to be knocked down with sticks or balls" (*P/L* 93). WL repeats the Punch and Judy analogy in *Hitler* (194). Holloway discusses the puppet motif in WL's writings and drawings (1980:10).

2. Marinetti also preferred medical discourse, defining war in 1909 as "the world's only hygiene" (42). He was borrowing metaphors from Christabel Pankhurst's Suffragist writings (Lyon 1992:106).

3. "Modernity is not a phenomenon of sensitivity to the fleeting present," Foucault suggests, "it is the will to 'heroize' the present" (1984:40).

4. Julius briefly discusses "the aesthetics of ugliness" in Chapter 4 of *T. S. Eliot, Anti-Semitism, and Literary Form,* but only to advance his argument's moral imperative: to expose the "ugly scenes" and "ugly" poems in Eliot's canon that are disfigured by anti-Semitic remarks (113). See also Sander Gilman, *The Jew's Body* (London: Routledge, 1991).

5. EP informed Dora Marsden of the *New Freewoman* (soon to be renamed, at EP's urging, the *Egoist*) that Rebecca West had "'inspected the data of our peculiar sect, and has not been alarmed unduly'" (qtd B. Scott 1:87).

6. Despite the work of Levenson's introductory essay to analyze the "microsociology of modernist innovation, within which small" and competing groups "were able to create small flourishing communities based on the powers of reciprocal acknowledgment" (1999:6), the *Cambridge Companion* does little to extend exposure to the various "circles" flourishing in America, the U.K., or expatriate Paris.

7. McDonald's informative book is well-researched, but sporadic feminist comments are incidental to the main argument. The "contempt and disgust" toward women expressed by EP and TSE is noted, but McDonald excuses their "apparent misogyny" (83, 79). Similarly "accusations of Fascism and anti-Semitism in the political arena" against TSE and EP are only mentioned (179).

8. WL then observes, "It was scarcely our fault that we were a youth racket. It was Ezra who in the first place organized us willy nilly into that. For he was never satisfied until everything was *organized.* And it was he who made us into a youth racket—that was his method of organization. He had a streak of Baden Powell in him. . . .[W]e were not the most promising material for

Ezra's boyscoutery. But he did succeed in giving a handful of disparate and unassimilable people the appearance of a *Bewegung*" (*BB* 254).

9. "[E]ach generation, like each individual, brings to the contemplation of art its own categories of appreciation, makes its own demands upon art, and has its own uses for art" (*UPUC* 109). WL's anecdote is telling: "In New York City, I met a man who, when elated with 'hooch,' would . . . unburden himself boastfully[:] . . . 'IT WAS *I* WHO MADE AMERICA—YOUNGER-GENERATION-CONSCIOUS!' *Youngergenerationconscious* was of course one flamboyantly sung winged-word" (*DY* 98).

10. EP to John Quinn, November 1920: "So long as America really excludes me, so long as I am to all intents exiled my position has some reality" (*P/Q* 202).

11. Harrison and her work are derided in WL's *The Dithyrambic Spectator* (1931); for Woolf's admiring comments, see *A Room of One's Own* (1929).

12. See Longenbach's excellent analysis in *Stone Cottage* (1988); see also Surette, and Materer, *Modernist Alchemy: Poetry and the Occult* (Ithaca: Cornell University Press, 1995).

13. Ironically, WHP's studies of Demeter and Persephone in the late 1870s (*GS* 79–155) helped to revive interest in what EP termed "the mysteries. Eleusis" (*GK* 144).

14. EP playfully expresses his cult mentality to Marianne Moore. In December 1918 he declares her part of a close "circle": "(you are in it willy-nilly, by the mere fact of writing verse for the members of the reading public capable of understanding)" (*LEP* 142). Six weeks later he recants: because of her "Hawthorne frigidities" she cannot "stand for my temple to Pallas Athene and for my cult of other ancient and less prohibitive deities" (Scott ed. 363–364). Paige omits the long, racially inflected middle section of the "doggerel" that EP wrote to Moore on 1 February 1919; Bush provides a complete transcript (*LEP* 146–147; Scott ed. 362–365).

15. Two other negative references to the modernists' "cult"-mindedness deserve mention. In "The End of the Line," Randall Jarrell suggests that due to TSE and EP, "derogation" of Romanticism became common and "there grew up a rather blank cult of the 'classical'" (76). Robert Hillyer (1895–1961), an established American academic and poet whose *Collected Verse* won the Pulitzer Prize in 1934, vehemently denounced the decision to award EP the 1949 Bollingen Prize for the *Pisan Cantos* in two articles for the *Saturday Review of Literature:* "Treason's Strange Fruit" and "Poetry's New Priesthood" (11 June 1949, 9–11, 28; 18 June 1949, 7–9, 38). In the first he accuses EP and TSE of being the fountainhead for "many outpourings of the new estheticism, the literary cult to whom T. S. Eliot and Ezra Pound are gods" (11 June 1919:10); in the second, he bemoans the "inglorious Age of Eliot with all its coteries and pressure groups" (18 June 1949:38).

16. Remembering Harold Monro's life in London, EP remarked that although the editor and publisher lived in Bloomsbury for "a score of years," he "belonged to no gang" (*BB* 7).

17. The "very concept of alienation," Eagleton suggests, "must secretly posit a dream of authenticity" (1988:132).

18. Huyssen's analysis of modernism and mass culture has had a tremendous impact. Insisting that "mass culture has always been the hidden subtext of the modernist project," and citing the latter's "powerful masculinist mystique," Huyssen concludes: "In the age of nascent socialism *and* the first major women's movement in Europe, the masses knocking at the gate were also women, knocking at the gate of a male-dominated culture. It is indeed striking to observe how the political, psychological, and aesthetic discourse around the turn of the century consistently and obsessively genders mass culture and the masses as feminine, while high culture, whether traditional or modern, clearly remains the privileged realm of male activities" (47, 55, 47). He also suggests that "modernism and mass culture" are "imaginary adversaries" (57), an argument furthered by Chinitz (1995), and Gendron (5).

19. "Pound arrived as an inassimilable and aggressive stranger," WL recalls; "with his Imagism he became aesthetically a troublesome rebel" (Russell ed. 259).

20. See Krauss, and Elliott and Wallace, for informative reconsiderations of the "originality / repetition binary," the "ways in which the second term of that binary has been feminized, and the ways in which the avant-garde . . . has been consistently constructed in the masculine" (Elliott and Wallace 35).

21. Writing to WL in January 1915 from Stone Cottage, Sussex (where he worked as Yeats's secretary), EP offers "Salutations to the brethren" (*P/L* 9). Materer admonishes that "Pound jokingly alludes to the Pre-Raphaelite Brotherhood of the 1850's, with whom the Vorticists should not be confused" (*P/L* 9n).

22. The "youth racket" is *not* to be confused with the "cult of the child" which Lewis lambastes in the 1930s. See the next note, and Chapter 2.

23. WL was always ready to accuse others of having established cults or clubs that worked against the interests of the genuine avant-garde. *Apes of God,* first serialized in *The Criterion,* rails against the "well-to-do" and "their organised hatred of *living* 'genius.' They have even made a sort of cult of the *amateur,* the child artist, and in short any imperfectly equipped person" (1924a:308). This "cult of the child" is analyzed in detail in *Doom of Youth* (1932). Throughout the 1930s, Lewis became increasingly obsessed with the "Hitler cult"—first as a proponent, then as a detractor (see *Hitler,* 1931, and *The Hitler Cult and How It Will End,* 1939); he always admired the Germans as "those past-masters in the cult of sheer stark 'masculinity,' of keeping women women and men men" (*DY* 214).

24. Often silenced in the cultists' accounts of their efflorescence are the names of female sponsors, patrons, and editors who worked assiduously, and spent generously, to make "the new" happen. Quinn was lauded, but Lady Rothermere's financial support for the fledgling *Criterion* was overlooked or derided. Omar Pound and Litz observe that the "late Victorian structure of clubs, societies, literary hostesses, country houses, bookshops, and serious

journals was still in place" when EP arrived in London in 1908, "offering many opportunities to an ambitious young writer" (viii).

25. For an argument against literary historians' "overestimation of Hulme," see Hansen.

26. First published as an appendix to Michael Roberts's *T. E. Hulme* (1938).

27. In private letters and public essays alike, WL was the most candid concerning his "(alas!) undeniable political activity" (*LWL* 61).

28. Exploring the desire for "professionalization" expressed by EP and TSE, McDonald suggests that "excluding women and amateurs drew the boundary lines—a *cordon sanitaire*—around serious artists and serious scholars of the arts" (87).

29. "Manifestoes aim to strengthen a group's position within dominant power relations," Lyon argues, "in part by a characteristic use of the pronoun 'we' (which is always dominated by 'I,' as Émile Benveniste demonstrates). The manifesto uses 'we' to animate a polemical voice of hortatory urgency.... When a nascent group coheres around this 'we,' it in effect claims for itself all good things, including moral infallibility" (113).

30. Original title: "Dante as a Spiritual Leader."

31. This "heroism" is first mentioned in the concluding paragraph of the *Salon de 1845;* a special section is devoted to it in *Salon de 1846.*

32. In "December 1908, Eliot went into the library of the Harvard Union and picked up the newly published second edition of . . . *The Symbolist Movement in Literature.* He was immediately struck by Symons's call for a spiritual vision to eclipse the realistic tradition. . . . [Q]uotations from late nineteenth-century French poets had the effect of a mirror that flashed back to Eliot an image clearer, larger, and more dramatic than anything he had imagined" (Lyndall Gordon 28–29; see also Howarth 103–105).

33. "Let's break out of the horrible shell of wisdom," Marinetti's "Founding" text advises; "Let's give ourselves utterly to the Unknown, not in desperation but only to replenish the deep wells of the Absurd" (40).

34. Lessons in satire and "hate" from EP and WL enabled Yeats to judge the insufficiencies of individual figures more emphatically, to distinguish more bitingly between "the merely clever and pretty" (1959:139) and the authentically beautiful. From the *Responsibilities* volume until *Last Poems,* a number of Yeats's speakers occupy the kind of "outlaw" (1963:308, 1972:90) subject position perfected in EP and WL's texts—self-marginalized figures who reject the shallowness of contemporary life and (most) artistic production, and expose, with no small degree of satisfaction, aesthetic, moral, and social inadequacies and transgressions. To justify this discursive enterprise in historical or "traditional" terms Yeats invokes Jonathan Swift as the patron saint of satire (especially Irish irony and invective), but his immediate tutor was WL. By the mid 1920s Yeats was reading *The Art of Being Ruled, Time and Western Man,* and then *Apes of God.* As he explained to T. Sturge Moore, WL "mixes metaphors in the most preposterous way but he can write; he has intellectual passion. . . . I do not always hate what he hates and yet I am always glad that he hates"

(Bridge ed. 117). In a December 1927 letter, Yeats asked Olivia Shakespear to "tell Wyndham Lewis . . . that I am in all essentials his most humble and admiring disciple. I like some people he dislikes but I accept all the dogma of the faith" (1954:733–734). One month later, he informed Shakespear that WL's book "still fills my imagination. I have a curiously personal feeling of gratitude. He has found an expression for my hatred—a hatred that being half dumb has half poisoned me. I read the last chapter again and again" (1954:734). All readers of Yeats are indebted to Hassett's study of the "poetics of hate" in the canon. See Materer 1980 for a brief discussion of the WL/Yeats connection.

35. The "Technical Manifesto of Futurist Literature" (May 1912) explains the creation of compound words: "The adjective, tending of itself toward the shadows, is incompatible with our dynamic vision. . . . Every noun should have its double; that is, the noun should be followed, with no conjunction, by the noun to which it is related by analogy. Example: man-torpedo-boat, woman-gulf" (Marinetti 84–85).

36. According to Normand, Lewis's satire, however vitriolic, "was never wholly destructive" (2). Powe claims that "Lewis's satire (hyperbole and ridicule) is a therapeutic enema for social poison" (32). Edwards's exhaustive 2000 study carefully considers WL as visual artist *and* writer.

37. In *The Caliph's Design* (1919), a Simmel-like WL argues that the ugly city literally and figuratively sickens its inhabitants: "The life of the crowd, of the Plain Man, is external: he can only live through others and outside himself. Then he, in a sense, *is* the houses, the railings, the statues, the churches, the road houses. . . . He dwindles, grows restless and sick, when not given the opportunities to live and enjoy in the simple, communal manner" (*WLA* 226).

38. TEH reiterates this point in "Bergson's Theory of Art": "Words like creative, expressive, vital . . . are so vague that you can never be sure when you use them that you are conveying . . . all the meaning you intended to" (1924:143). TSE articulates a similar uncertainty in "Swinburne as Poet" (1920): "the language which is more important to us is that which is struggling to digest and express new objects, new groups of objects, new feelings, new aspects" (*SW* 150).

39. EP recalls these sentiments in his last words for and on WL: "Self Condemned, one remembers / somewhere a bulldog, as a sample of beauty as defined St Thomas Aquin[as] / in his Summa 'si perfecta representat rem, 'if it perfectly represent / the thing quamvis turpem? / not that one thought of W. L. as neoThomist" (*P/L* 305- 306). The Aquinas quotation, taken from the *Summa Theologiae,* translates, "An image is said to be beautiful if it perfectly represents the object, however ugly the object itself may be" (*P/L* 306).

40. In TEH's rewriting of history, the humanism of the Renaissance became, in the late eighteenth and nineteenth centuries, "sentimental, utilitarian romanticism" (1936:62). WL accuses homosexuals of sentimentality in *Childermass* (*ChM* 387, 391).

41. TSE informs readers of *The Criterion* that the posthumous publication of TEH's *Speculations* proves him "the forerunner of a new attitude of mind,

which should be the twentieth-century mind, if the twentieth century is to have a mind of its own. Hulme is classical, reactionary, and revolutionary; he is the antipodes of the eclectic, tolerant, and democratic mind of the last century" (1924a:231).

42. The phrase is featured in Bunthorne's Act II duet with Grosvenor in *Patience:* "Ultra-poetical, super- aesthetical" Bunthorne takes pride in being "A Japanese young man, / A blue-and-white young man, /.... A greenery-yallery, Grosvenor Gallery, / Foot-in-the-grave young man!" (Gilbert 41–42). Much of the satiric humor in *Patience* is aimed at exposing Bunthorne and his aesthete-minded followers as frauds. Both Bunthorne and Grosvenor are represented as heterosexual dandies.

43. When Milton Brown wanted to criticize Georgia O'Keefe's paintings from the late 1920s, he suggested that her images of buildings featured a detrimental "prettiness of color" (127); her talents, he argued, were better suited to natural elements such as flowers. In the mid 1920s, when O'Keefe "began to consider using the city as subject matter," she encountered unanticipated resistance: "as she put it, 'the men decided they didn't want me to paint New York.' It was suggested that painting the city was not in the best interest of her career: 'I was told that it was an impossible idea.... ' Unconvinced, she completed *New York with Moon* (1925) and asked that it be included with her other work in the group exhibition 'Seven Americans' staged by Stiegltiz in March 1925. But her fellow exhibitors ... refused to allow the painting to be hung. As she commented in 1965, 'the painters and the art patrons figured it was strictly a man's world,' and apparently, by appropriating the subject of the city ... O'Keefe had invaded that world" (Lynes 442–443).

44. Despite being married to painter Vanessa Bell, Clive Bell used such sexist distinctions throughout his art criticism. Reviewing the Post-Impressionist and Futurist Exhibition in October 1913, he observed that "the painter's job is to create significant form, and not to bother about whether it will please people or shock them. Ugliness is just as irrelevant as prettiness" (1918:185; see also 1918:205–206).

45. Marinetti makes a similar statement in *War, The World's Only Hygiene* (74–75). See Lyon's excellent analysis of the "interaction among oppositional groups" in pre–World War I England (1992).

46. For a discussion of women as "the enemy of the absolute" in WL's writings, see Valerie Parker.

47. EP condemns the forces of "obstructivity" that actively support an artistic status quo: "Inventors are a disturbance, and as such, exceedingly disliked.... It is not the philistine who hates artistic invention with bitterest hatred, it is the derivative and 'established' second rate artist" (1920b:168). He emphasizes the point with a "fable": "The peach leaves observing the peach-stone cried out: 'it is neither leaf nor fruit, away with it! It is ugly, it is hard, it is covered with hideous wrinkles and ridges, away with it! It will probably explode and destroy us'" (Pound 1920b:172).

48. Marinetti declares that "poetry must be conceived as a violent attack on un-known forces," arguing for artists who prefer "violent spasms of action and creation" (41, 42). R. W. Flint prefers to think of this as a "'synthetic' verbal violence" (7) with no appreciable links to human behavior; Marinetti's pro-war comments are excused as "the appalling innocence about war as it seems now" (7). Chase believes that Lewis's "genius . . . prevented him from ever having a politics . . . while Lewis himself did not encourage violence, his thinking and style express affinities with violence" (163–164, 156). Marinetti's 1909 riposte that art "can be nothing but violence, cruelty, and injustice" (42) is rehearsed in EP's 1914 assertion that the artist "must live by craft and violence . . . [his] gods are violent gods" (1914b:68).

49. WL's admirers insist that his "energetic" writing is "alive with violence, comic, and contemptuous imagery—yet delineates subtle arguments . . . that more respectable thinkers ignore" (Edwards 1986:147).

50. Vomitory metaphors also inform EP's praise for WL's *The Caliph's Design,* which he declares "a fine curative and purgative against all the titter of Frys, Bells . . . etc. and as such it should be taken and administered in the cause of public health and morality" (Zinnes ed. 128).

51. This demonstrates further intertexual links with Symons, who remarks that the vers libre of Rimbaud is "alert, troubled, swaying, deliberately uncertain, hating rhetoric. . . . Verse, always elegant, is broken up into a kind of mock-ery of prose" (1898:56–57).

52. My discussion of prosody and hegemony is indebted to Easthope, *Poetry as Discourse.*

53. Jameson suggests that "the prodigious force with which Wyndham Lewis propagates his bristling mechanical sentences and hammers the reified world into a forbiddingly cubist surface may be thought of as a virtual cooptation of the machine" (1979:81–82). According to Blair, Jameson tends "to min-imize the problem posed for latter-day readers by Modernism's vigorous flir-tations with Fascism" (1999:162).

54. Quéma's approach is to mention the rape only in the context of a "body re-bellious to dandyist self-creation. Tarr's philosophy of the 'lonely phallus' stems directly from the dandy's discourse" (134).

55. TEH identifies the romantics as the source of this "bad metaphysic": "You are unable to admit the existence of beauty without the infinite being in some way or another dragged in" (1924:128).

56. For another overview, see Martha Woodmansee, *The Author, Art, and the Market;* for specific modernist studies, see Gendron, Hansen, Rainey, and Wicke.

57. See Koval for an analysis of JW's subversive activities while president of the SBA.

58. JW believed that his rights as creator far outweighed those of the people who happened to purchase his works. Hence his habit of delaying the delivery of works (Freer alone was patient in this regard; see Merrill ed.), taking paint-ings back to "finish" or correct them and then refusing to part with them

again, or expecting owners to part with their works, whenever he demanded, for exhibitions. For the complete story of his battle with Frederick Leyland over the "Peacock Room," see Merrill 1998. The case of Lady Sybil Eden's portrait, 1894–1895, was especially vexed. Her husband dared to question the price; Whistler refused to surrender the painting and return the money already paid; Eden sued; JW then "painted out the face of Lady Eden from the contested portrait and substituted for it that of another lady" (Anderson and Koval 385). Initially, the courts found in favor of Eden, but JW appealed—twice. Finally, in April 1900, "he was given the judgment that he had wanted all along: full costs against Eden" (Anderson and Koval 387). The original court case made headlines in London and Paris; JW stirred the pot by sending a letter to the *Pall Mall Gazette* explaining his right to decide the fate of the canvas. For JW's one-sided account of the *contretemps* see *Eden Versus Whistler. The Baronet & The Butterfly. A Valentine with a Verdict.*

Chapter 4

1. See, for example, Marx, *The Machine in the Garden: Technology and the Pastoral Ideal in America* (1964); Spears, *Dionysus and the City: Modernism in Twentieth-Century Poetry* (1970); Williams, *The Country and the City* (1973); Pike, *The Image of the City in Modern Literature* (1981); Johnston, *The Poet and the City: A Study of Urban Perspectives.* Blanchard defines three kinds of urban literary studies. The first "strives to determine the object relation that exists between literary representations and the reality behind those representations. Such are the works by Dunlap and Weimer on the American novel or by Marx on the Paris of Zola" (Blanchard 22). The second "seeks to derive from the study of literature, and especially prose fiction, a composite notion of the city as repository for most of the ideology of the period. . . . The authors of these syntheses seek a psychological definition of the city" (Blanchard 23–24). The third type, exemplified by the work of Raymond Williams, "seeks to integrate a reading of the city with an overall historical and, in the end, metacritical perspective" (Blanchard 26).

   As Sennett observes, current urban experiences are not the same as those which existed, in North America and Europe, in the first three decades of the twentieth century. At that time, one lived amid a "dense overlay of manufacturing, consumption, politics, housing, and pleasure"; today, within "an ever more marginalized and fragmented geography, . . . each fragment is like a homogenous ghetto: the mall, the housing estate, the industrial park are isolated, self-contained spaces. . . . [The] city has ceased to be a place where social differences interact. . . . It lacks the power to stimulate people" (Sennett 3).

2. WL constructs a dystopic Third City in *Monstre Gai,* which follows *The Childermass* in his post–World War II omnibus *The Human Age.* "Reversing the order of the *Divina Commedia,*" as Bridson suggests, "it is a sort of Purgatorio before we enter the Inferno" (244). Cultists were definitely influenced by the Futurist's contempt for urban commonplaces. "Let's Murder

the Moonshine" (1909) includes an allegory in which Pilgrim Marinetti leads the faithful out of the City of Paralysis in order to "construct the great Futurist Railroad" (47). Their quest takes them to Gout, with its "phthisic vegetation," madmen, and madwomen. The Aeropoet imagines a final immolation of the city to ensure death to all "insipidities" and "Nostalgia"; from his biplane he initiates the attack on the "great swarming populace of Paralysis and Gout, disgusting leprosy devouring the mountainsides. . . . Swiftly we fly against you. . . . Let me direct the fire! . . . Up 800 meters! Ready . . . Fire! . . . Oh! The joy of playing billiard with Death!" (Marinetti 52–53). The description of the massacre seems deliberately to invert the famous aerial passage of Ruskin's *Modern Painters*. Was Marinetti familiar with it? At the end of "Futurist Speech to the English," he observes, "Ruskin would certainly have applauded those passéist Venetians who wanted to rebuild the absurd Bell Tower of San Marco" (Marinetti 64–65). On April 27, 1910, Marinetti published his creative harangue "Against Past-Loving Venice," 800,000 copies of which were launched by Futurist poets, painters, and agitators from the clock tower of St Mark's Square on July 8, 1910.

3. Book 7 of Wordsworth's *The Prelude* summarizes and extends the city's symbolic role as theater and market. In addition to thinking of the "city as a stage," Molesworth argues, it should be recognized as the place "where a distinct sense of self undergoes a staging. We might even begin with a preliminary definition: the city is the stage where staging itself occurs. If . . . the city is the place where everything is both available and vanishing, then we can also see it as the stage in which all prosceniums are unfolding and disappearing" (13–14). The theatrical metaphor is also used in Blanchard's analysis, and Caws's.

4. Green identifies Alexandria as the "modern and rational city"; Jerusalem, "the city of faith"; and Athens, "the city of culture" (277–278). Pike remarks that "the image of the city [has] served as the nexus of many things, all characterized by strongly ambivalent feelings: presumption (Babel), corruption (Babylon), perversion (Sodom and Gomorrah), power (Rome), destruction (Troy, Carthage), death, the plague (the City of Dis), and revelation (the heavenly Jerusalem)" (6–7). Boone, writing about the "alternative systems of experiencing, living in, manipulating, and creating social space" flourishing in queer culture, suggests that one consider "urban space in all of its liberating anonymity, mobility, and diversity" (211).

5. Schorske's thorough study of Vienna's Ringstrasse project is very informative. "Taken as a whole," he observes, "the monumental buildings of the Ringstrasse expressed well the highest values of regnant liberal culture. On the remnants of the *champs de Mars* its votaries had reared the political institutions of a constitutional state, the school to educate the elite . . . and the museums and theaters to bring to all the culture that would redeem the *novi homines* from their lowly origins. . . . Nineteenth-century urban life gradually separated living and labor, residence from shop or office; the apartment building reflected the change" (Schorske 47). For discussions of Hauss-

mann's "redevelopment" of Paris at the behest of Napoleon III, see Collier and Benjamin 1974.

6. In 1901, "more than one-third of families in many of London's inner boroughs were living in one or two rooms; in Finsbury the proportion rose to over 45 per cent" (Hall 20); as of 1925, "almost half the houses in Paris were not connected to a sewer; cholera attacked in 1892, typhoid in 1882 and 1894; deaths from tuberculosis rose during the 1880s and 1890s and again after World War One; bubonic plague attacked one slum during the 1920s" (Hall 22).

7. This was the era of Sant'Elia's design for a *Città Nuova* (1913–1914), Tony Garnier's *Une Cité Industrielle* (1918), Bruno Taut's *Der Stadkröne* (1919), and Le Corbusier's plans for rebuilding Paris, including *Une Ville Contemporaine* (1921–1922). In England, the *Town Planning Review* was launched in the spring of 1910. See also WL, *The Caliph's Design. Architects! Where is Your Vortex?* (1919).

8. Mencken alludes to Sandburg's work in "Metropolis": "I can imagine . . . a New Englander loving the wreck of Boston, or even a Chicagoan loving Chicago, poets, Loop, stockyards and all" (215).

9. EP's recognition of James as "the master" was a crucial element in his construction of a transnational modernism; as Scott observes, "Ezra Pound's account of modernism was recentered in the 1970s by Hugh Kenner in his highly influential work *The Pound Era*" (1:81). For a summary of the ways in which Kenner, Espey, and Bush have discussed EP's "Jamesian aesthetic mode," see Miller.

10. *The American Scene* praises "modern 'impressionistic' pictures, mainly French," by Manet, Degas, Monet, and Whistler (*TAS* 393).

11. Henry's brother, philosopher and psychologist William James, had a very different response to New York, pronouncing it "simply magnificent" in 1907. See Douglas 115–119.

12. *The American Scene* was not a random collection of travel pieces; James planned the book in advance (Howard 808–811). Of the fourteen chapters, ten were initially published in periodicals between April 1905 and November 1906. Further revisions took place between the publication of the English edition on 20 January 1907, and the American, one week later. Running titles composed by James for the English edition were omitted in the American text.

13. *English Hours* is a compilation of essays published variously in Britain and America between 1877 and 1901. "London" first appeared in *Century Magazine* (December 1888).

14. Blair's study is insightful, but she does not consider the formative role of *English Hours*. Furthermore, she prefers to think about "racial theater" as James observed it, and the indices of "whiteness" that he helped to create, without analyzing his racist conclusions. Blair's reconstituted James is a dispassionate observer removed from any visceral race feelings who fully understands and appreciates "ethnographic tenets of race and nation, so as to test and volatilize their limits" (1996:17). I am arguing that *The American*

Scene captures and projects racialized anxiety, anger, and antipathy—negative responses absorbed by a volatile EP, an uneasy TSE, and numerous other readers. See also Ross Posnock, *The Trial of Curiosity: Henry James, William James, and the Challenge of Modernity* (New York: Oxford University Press, 1991). Hutchinson's discussion of James's city texts is absent any awareness of gender, race, and class issues.

15. The representation of Boston and New York in *The Bostonians* is discussed by Hutchinson 204–208.

16. James's experience of Philadelphia as a tourist is thus very different from EP's formative years there. See H. Carpenter 19–25 for a discussion of the city's ethnic and racial complexity in the 1890s and 1900s.

17. As Crapanzano states, "From 1880 to 1920, roughly a million and a half immigrants, mostly Russian Jews and southern Italians, arrived in New York via the infamous Ellis Island, where they were scrubbed, registered, and often assigned new 'American' names. The majority of these immigrants remained in the city. By 1910, 41 per cent of all New Yorkers were foreign-born" (11). See Nancy Foner, *From Ellis Island to JFK: New York's two great waves of immigration.* New Haven: Yale University Press, 2001.

18. The trope is repeated when James visits the "dense Yiddish quarter" of the New York ghetto: the sheer number of people, in close proximity, "was a matter that made the 'ethnic' apparition again sit like a skeleton at the feast. It was fairly as if I could see the specter grin while the talk of the hour gave me, across the board, facts and figures, chapter and verse, for the extent of the Hebrew conquest of New York" (*TAS* 465).

19. In the Jewish ghetto of New York "'architecture' goes by the board . . . the appearance to which ["the frontal ladders and platforms"] most often conduce is that of the spaciously organized cage for the nimbler class of animals in some great zoological garden. This general analogy is irresistible—it seems to offer . . . a little world of bars and perches and swings for human squirrels and monkeys" (*TAS* 466–467).

20. Blair has not considered the structure of James's text: by discussing James's observations of Richmond first, she overlooks the North vs. South plot. James is distanced from "the culture of racist gentility" too thoroughly (Blair 1996:161).

21. Blair contends that "for James the image is resonantly documentary," and encodes "James's own racial uncertainties" (1996:161). Some of the best work in her book focuses on the "representational protocols that will most sensitively register and redact" race in America in the photography of Lewis Hines and Jacob Riis.

22. James imagines cities as chatterboxes: "Washington talks about herself, and about almost nothing else; falling . . . into line with other capitals. London, Paris, Berlin, Rome, goodness knows, talk about themselves: that is each member of this sisterhood talks, sufficiently or inordinately, of the great number of divided and differing selves that form together her controlling identity" (*TAS* 635–636).

23. As de Certeau suggests, the "analytical, coherent, proper meanings of urbanism" are displaced by mobile subjects; the "'wandering of the semantic' produced by the masses . . . [makes] some parts of the city disappear and exaggerate[s] others, distorting it, fragmenting it, and diverting it" (102). For a more thorough reading of de Certeau's "pedestrian rhetorics" see Boone (214).

24. See also Grace, 194–195. Interestingly, only in the final pages of Pike and Johnston's studies are connections made between the city and female signifiers. Pike merely observes that "the typing of cities as female recalls on the one hand Mumford's depiction of early settlements as containers, symbolizing the female principle, and on the other hand Balzac's Paris and Angoulême, cities also under the sign and domination of women" (127). Johnston confines his remarks to an analysis of W. H. Auden's "Memorial for the City," observing that in the final lines of the poem the metropolis "assumes a feminine identity, with some suggestion of the pampered, spoiled, over-publicized American beauty queen" (237).

25. In *Antheil* (1927), EP identifies a "city intuition" that should enable "modern man" to live beneficially in his "cities and in his machine shops with the same kind of swing and exuberance that the savage is supposed to have in his forest. . . . [There is no] reason why the city intuition should be any deader than that of the savage" (1927:137).

26. The scope of the collection is informative; antiurban tropes are pervasive. For a negative assessment of the anthology, see Johnston 156–157.

27. This is the same Don Marquis whose comic verse featured the irrepressible Archy and Mehitabel.

28. TSE's most American city texts are found in the "Inventions of the March Hare" notebook now housed in the Berg Collection (published 1996). In several instances Boston or American place names and titles have been cancelled, replaced by British or European names: "Fourth Caprice in North Cambridge," for example, becomes "Fourth Caprice in Montparnasse" (*IMH* 14).

29. Book III cites Santayana: "'cities are a second body for the human mind, a second organism, more rational, permanent, and decorative than the animal organism of flesh and bone: a work of natural yet moral art'" (*Pat* 116).

30. In his letters, Williams refers to TSE and EP as the "gang" leaders of a "camp," the "pimps of literature" who are "actively the enemies of the highest reaches of the artist's imagination" (Witemeyer ed. 44). In the last decade, critics such as Daniel Morris have begun to speak more frankly about Williams's "paranoid version of international modernist literary culture as a hostile underworld in which Eliot and Pound were the primary conspirators in a plot to sabotage his bid for literary renown" (166).

31. Bremer discusses the American tradition of "civic communities in harmony with nature" (1981:47).

32. To ensure that masculinist privilege extends to cultural production, the lines immediately following "only one man—like a city" signal the first shift to prose in the hybrid text, the separate discursive sphere in which a female

"voice" is to be heard. The individual in question is penning letters to Paterson / "Doctor" Williams, performing in a genre rarely associated with
"high art" because typically identified with the private, personal writings of
women. Her first thought is to apologize for the poems she has sent, to declare: "I know myself to be more the woman than the poet" (*Pat* 15).

33. Although an astute interpreter of the "unreal city" motif in works by several
male poets, Sharpe reduces all women to the status of Woman, and states
that "woman and nature" are "the very entities, that should give . . . meaning" to man and the city (134).

34. In his introduction to the *Caroling Dusk* anthology, Countee Cullen advises
that any "attempt to corral the outbursts of the ebony muse into some defi-
nite mold to which all poetry by Negroes will conform seems altogether futile and aside from the facts" (1927:xi).

35. This analysis of James's and TSE's texts is the result of collaborative work
with Marie-Christine Leps. See Higgins and Leps 1998.

36. For a discussion of the "influence of black speech" (1992:57) on TSE's poetry and EP's, and the argument that the "preemptive mimicry of blacks" enabled these poets to "rebel against English culture and simultaneously . . . to
solidify their domination at home" (1992:61), see North 1992 and 1996.
Other works to be consulted include Baker and Nielsen. TSE's sequence of
verses for "King Bolo and his Big Black Kween" are found in the *Letters*—
1:42, 86, 125–126, 206, 455, 568. Paige's edition of EP's correspondence
omits the portion of a letter to Marianne Moore (*LEP* 146–148) in which
EP muses whether he could have "got[ten] over the Jim Crow law; / could
have bridged the gap" between them if she were "woolled, dark, ethiopian"
rather than "red-headed"; perhaps, he says, he could have "asserted the milk-
whiteness of souls / laved in a Mithraic liquid, / or disinfected with laneline"
(Scott ed. 362–365).

37. For a discussion of racialized discourse in EP's poetry and World War II radio
broadcasts, see Blair 1999. In *Hitler,* WL demands, "When do you think we
may expect you . . . to give your best attention to the safeguarding of your famous White Skin, and as a consequence cease sentimentalizing with regard
to the Non-White World, of what ever hue or kind?" (*Hit* 121). Lewis's
racism "was founded," Mao argues, "not on a conviction that whites were inherently superior, but, on the contrary, on a belief that they put themselves
in danger by surrendering any power whatever to non-whites" (102).

38. Douglas's cultural history of "mongrel Manhattan" is excellent. Among the
facts and statistics that convey a sense of New York's population boom from
1900s to the 1930s are the following: "Between 1918 and 1931 the number
of cars in New York jumped from a modest 125,101 to 790,123, a gain of
roughly 600 percent; by the late 1920s, there were more cars in New York
than in all of Europe. In 1929 and 1930 alone, five major skyscrapers—the
Bank of Manhattan Trust, the Chrysler Building, the Chanin Building, the
Daily News Building, and the Empire State Building—were finished or in
process" (Douglas 17).

39. Harlem, an "entire world bracketed away on the far side of Central Park," was fetishized "as a symbolic site of otherness for the white thrill-seeker"; it was "a social and psychological threshold into the unknown. At such a distance Harlem became a safe place where the dominant culture could indulge its fantasies and fears of the forbidden, marginalized" (Boone 270). Wall compares Harlem and Paris in terms of opportunities for black artists, and comments on white expatriates' lack of "interest in their country's racial situation" (68).

40. *Passing* is a fascinating text in its own right, and important for the way in which it problematizes desire, subjectivity, and racial essentialism. Also crucial are the representation and analysis of the sociocultural presence of whites in Harlem and middle-class African American circles. I mention Larsen's novel deliberately because of a tendency in African American studies to exclude women's texts from the literary canon and to segregate or overlook the authors' cultural contributions. Commentators are taking their cue from many of the male leaders of the New Negro Movement. "The sexist preoccupation of the New Negro idea," its resolutely "masculine" focus, was, as Early suggests, "particularly problematic during the Renaissance as men tended to control the movement and to promote male writers over women writers" (29).

41. James Weldon Johnson, on the other hand, feminizes "My City" for a sonnet salute to Manhattan's "throbbing force": "Her shining towers, her avenues" and even "her slums" are hailed (Cullen ed. 25).

42. In his February 1926 review of *The Weary Blues* for *Opportunity*, Cullen suggests that the "jazz poems" are "interlopers": with all of their "frenzy and electric heat," they do not belong "to that dignified company, that select and austere circle of high literary expression which we call poetry" (Gates and Appiah eds. 3, 4). Implicitly, the "dignified company" also applies to poets such as Cullen. In effect, Cullen is suggesting that the poems lack "finish," Ruskin's term for the faults of Whistler's innovative canvases. In both critiques, references to class are barely voiced yet resounding.

43. James Weldon Johnson discusses "Harlem: The Cultural Capital" in *Black Manhattan*. Although I am economizing by focusing on Hughes's New York poems, his works canvas various African American communities. Typically, the names of famous streets identify places (Beale Street functions metonymically for Memphis, for example), yet the lack of a specific city reference opens up the poem to many readers.

44. "The Negro Speaks of Rivers," the first poem to feature what I have termed his "familiar" yet reflective voice, was composed when Hughes was 17.

45. Chinitz is instructive regarding TSE and the "cultural divide" (1995) and the "gendering" of jazz (1997). "Thus yoked with mass culture, the feminine, the African-American, and the primitive," he observes, "jazz functioned as a central metaphor for the Other. Recent criticism . . . has highlighted the ways in which literary modernism developed in response to the ascendency of the Other. This response, taken collectively, is a powerfully ambivalent

one, incorporating degrees of distrust, welcome, mourning, and emulation" (Chinitz 1997:321).

46. Entitled "Poem" in *Caroling Dusk,* "My People" in Hughes's later collections.

47. The speaker of "I, Too" answers Whitman in the opening line—"I, too, sing America"—then imagines a "tomorrow" when blacks and white will be "at the table together": "They'll see how beautiful I am / And be ashamed—I, too, am America" (Hughes 1994:46). "Note on Commercial Theatre" admonishes those who have stolen or profiteered from black culture, whether on Broadway, in recordings, or other venues of popular culture. "But someday," the speaker predicts, "somebody'll / Stand up and talk about me, / And write about me—Black and beautiful—/ And sing about me . . . / I reckon it'll be / Me myself!" (Hughes 1994:216). Book Five of *Paterson* features a quote from *Really the Blues* by Mezz Mezzrow and Bernard Wolfe; one of Paterson's correspondents argues against any charges of cultural (mis)appropriation and pilfering: "You didn't have to take the finest and most original and honest music in America and mess it up because you were a white man; you could dig the colored man's real message and get in there with him, like Rapp. . . . Man, I was gone with it—inspiration's mammy was with me" (*Pat* 257–258).

48. In 1883 the American Supreme Court declared the Civil Rights Act of 1875 unconstitutional, a judgment that subsequently legitimated the dismantling of post–Civil War initiatives for racial equality. The Plessy *v* Ferguson ruling of 1896 sanctioned the "separate but equal" principle that encouraged Southern states to enact the "Jim Crow" laws that made segregation possible ("Jump Jim Crow" was the name of a minstrel routine devised by Thomas Dartmouth in the late 1820s and popularized thereafter). By 1914, all Southern states had Jim Crow laws in place. The Ku Klux Klan experienced a "resurgence" in membership and antiethnic and antiblack violence in the 1920s (Douglas 315); as Douglas emphasizes, Klan activities were not limited to the South. New York City purportedly had 21 "Klaverns" by 1922 but a state anti-Klan bill passed in 1923 "effectively outlawed it" (Douglas 316). Hughes's "Not a Movie" documents one man's narrow escape from the South, across "that Dixie line" to Harlem: "He didn't stop in Washington / and he didn't stop in Baltimore. . . . / Six knots was on his head / but, thank God, he wasn't dead! / And there ain't no Ku Klux / on a 133rd" (1994:396). See also "One-Way Ticket" (Hughes 1994:361).

49. Compare Sandburg's representation of a white Chicago with Hughes's poems, especially "The Migrant," which follows an African American laborer as he joins with "Polish, Bohunk, Irish" workers on the job. "Iron lifting iron / Makes iron of chocolate muscles" and does not corrode the spirit, like the "cotton field . . . / A thousand miles away" (Hughes 1994:370). Rampersad has established that the intertextual presences of Whitman and Sandburg loom largest in Hughes's early poetry (54–55). Raymond Smith, however, offers this qualification: "Like Walt Whitman, Hughes began his career as a poet confident of his power. Unlike Whitman, however, who cel-

ebrated the particular self ("Walt Whitman, the Cosmos"), Hughes celebrated racial, rather than individual, self" (123).

50. The subtle text features four stanzas with lines of alternating lengths: the
comparatively short, terse lines of stanzas one and three focus on the
speaker's present state during a New York's sunrise; the long, luxurious lines
of stanzas two and four celebrate, retrospectively, dawn "on the island of the
sea" (McKay 1953:63). Like Thomas Hardy, McKay often experiments
within the established parameters of poetic discourse, varying metrics to suit
his subject matter and capture the reader's attention.

51. Atypically in the literature of "Uncle Sam," McKay continues his love-hate
relationship with his adopted country by addressing "her vigor" and "her
hate" in "America" (1973:126). For wholly positive textual cities in McKay's
canon, one has to travel to "Moscow" or "Barcelona."

52. W. E. B. Du Bois's "A Litany of Atlanta" commemorating the "Day of
Death, 1906" is featured in *Caroling Dusk*. Biblical in tone, style, and alle-
gorizing, the text all too typically feminizes racist urban evil: "A city lay in
travail, God our Lord, and from her loins sprang twin Murder and Black
Hate" (Cullen ed. 27- 28). Biblical allegory is also the preferred approach in
Blanche Taylor Dickinson's "The Walls of Jericho," which presents a city of
whites that will not let the "dark ones" in; "Jericho still has *her* high wall,"
the speaker observes, but it is ultimately a "futile barrier of power" (Cullen
ed. 106; italics added).

53. In "Pastoral," the "little sparrows / [that] hop ingenuously / about the pave-
ment" are among the "things" that "astonish" the speaker (Williams 1991
1:70–71).

54. TSE's texts also rewrite the "unreal cities" of Conrad (the "sepulchral" Brus-
sels of *Heart of Darkness,* London in *The Secret Agent*) and Charles-Louis
Philippe's *Bubu de Montparnasse.*

55. Wilde playfully queries in "The Decay of Lying": "Where, if not from the
Impressionists, do we get those wonderful brown fogs that come creeping
down our streets, blurring the gas-lamps and changing houses into monstrous shadows? . . . The extraordinary change that has taken place in the climate of London during the last ten years is entirely due to a particular school
of Art" (*CWW* 4:41).

56. The unfamiliar Letts text is "The Town," with its "people swarming there
like bees" (*SofC* 134–135). TSE may also be echoing James's representation
of "the dense Yiddish quarter" in lower east side New York: "There is no
swarming like that of Israel when once Israel has got a start, and the scene
here bristled, at every step, with the signs and sounds, immitigable, unmistakable, of a Jewry that had burst all bounds. . . . The children swarmed
above all—here was multiplication with a vengeance" (*TAS* 464).

57. Both Howe (51–53) and Johnston (106) identify the importance of Baudelaire and Whitman. "[T]hese two writers produced two of the most original
and influential volumes of nineteenth-century verse . . . our contemporary
literary heritage might be seen as a division between the powerful currents

and undercurrents generated by *Leaves of Grass* (1855) and *Les Fleurs du Mal* (1857)" (Johnston 106).

58. For a summary of the ways in which Baudelaire articulates the "fear, revulsion, and horror" evoked by the "big-city crowd," see Benjamin, "On Some Motifs in Baudelaire," in *Illuminations*, 155–200.

59. Benjamin studies are burgeoning. The "figure of the *flâneur* first appears in Benjamin's writing in 1929" (Rignall 112); in 1935, Benjamin published "Paris—the Capitol of the Nineteenth Century." Three years later, "The Paris of the Second Empire in Baudelaire" was published; in 1939, "Some Motifs in Baudelaire." All appear under the umbrella title of *Charles Baudelaire: A Lyric Poet in the Era of High Capitalism.* One should not assume "anything like a coherent single theory in the various ideas that cluster around that composite and overdetermined figure [of the *flâneur*]," Rignall suggests; "[c]onstituted intertextually from Baudelaire's essays and poetry, from Poe's fiction and Balzac's, from Dickens's letters about his own creative practice, from Marx's theory of commodity fetishism, and from documentary and historical writings about Paris, the *flâneur* is at once an observed historical phenomenon, a type among the inhabitants of nineteenth-century Paris, the representation of a way of experiencing metropolitan life, a literary motif, and an image of the commodity in its relation to the crowd" (113).

60. "When the urban spectacle dazes more than it dazzles," observes Ferguson, "the *flâneur* comes to resemble an exiled figure who has not chosen to ramble about the city but is compelled to do so. Originally a stroller able to quit the city and return home, he becomes over the course of the nineteenth century a drifter without a home" (111).

61. Tester concurs: "Baudelaire is quite explicit about the gender identity of the poet"; his texts "presuppose a masculine narrator or observer. . . . For him, the private world of domestic life is dull and possibly even a cause for the feelings of crisis which Sartre was later to call nausea" (2). Buck-Morss adroitly suggests that, "It was not Benjamin's politics to employ feminism as an analytical frame" (1986:119).

62. For a reexamination of Baudelaire's relationship with Jeanne Duval, its impact on his writings, and the so-called "Black Venus" figure in his poems, see Pollock 1999:261–287; Pollock agrees that "the representation of an exotic, sensual and vicious woman is a trope of Western racism to which Baudelaire's modernist poetry gave renewed currency" (1999:263).

63. "Supplement—Belly Music" was written for the final issue of *Others* 5, 6 (July 1919): 31.

64. EP makes a similar connection between locus and modes of representation in 1921: "'The life of the village is narrative. . . . In a city the visual impressions . . . are cinematographic'" (qtd Howarth 236).

65. TSE parodies such Whitmanesque enthusiasm in Section III of "Suite Clownesque" (ca. 1910, *IMH* 35). Ricks suggests several intertextual gestures at work in this early poem: James's *The American Scene* and Adams's *The Education of Henry Adams* (*IMH* 170).

66. "In bourgeois culture," Pollock observes, "the body operated as a privileged metaphor for social meanings by 'transcoding.' The European bourgeois is the head, his wife is the heart, the working classes of all peoples are the hands, and, in general, they are associated with the lower body—and thus with what is expunged from the bourgeois's cerebral definition of himself: dirt, sexuality, animality. Bourgeois culture has dramatised the anxieties resulting from this metaphoric social body through an obsession with both the city and its key tropic figure: the prostitute, who embodied a fascinating but abject darkness, lowness and sexual mystery that was both a sexual channel and a sewer" (1999:50).

67. The "prostitute has fascinated numerous male writers," Felski notes, "because as a blatant embodiment of the commercialization of sexuality she can symbolize the commodification of the artist in the marketplace. . . . [I]n her dual role as seller and commodity she is seen to expose and subvert the hypocrisy of the bourgeois ideology of romantic love" (1103).

68. Scholes's provocative essay focuses on Picasso and Joyce as figures "central" to masculinist modernism, demonstrating the "astonishing number of formal and thematic features" shared by *Demoiselles d'Avignon* and "Circe," and asking why "each of them chose to embody his most striking formal innovations, aesthetic breakthroughs that changed the face of modern art and literature altogether," in brothel scenes (1:4).

69. For a discussion of the "lack of prurience or moral condemnation" and detachment in Toulouse-Lautrec's brothel work, and a comparison of Lautrec and Degas, see Bernheimer 196–199. Pollock offers a very different reading (1999:75–91).

70. Joyce is the only modernist named in the text; in Part II of Book V, a letter from EP is quoted (*Pat* 254- 255) but the source is not identified.

71. In December 1914, TSE described for Conrad Aiken his need for "female society": "in the city it is more lively and acute. One walks about the street with one's desires, and one's refinement rises up like a wall whenever opportunity approaches" (*LE* 1:118).

72. George Bernard Shaw raises similar issues, but sympathetically, in *Mrs Warren's Profession* (published 1898, first performed in 1902).

73. The first female voice heard in *The Waste Land* belongs to the Sibyl of Cumae. Physically, however, she is reduced to a wizened specter hanging upside down in a cave; her predictions are relegated to scraps in the wind. Structurally, her voice (which can only utter "I want to die" in a language [Greek] that few can understand) is encountered outside the text proper, a further gesture of marginalization. TSE may have absorbed this device from Joyce: Molly Bloom is only given full voice in *Ulysses* after the main (male) narrative has ended.

74. Discussed further by Scholes (1:6–7) and Buck-Morss (1986:120, 1991:184–185). Williams condemns "Our (American) Ragademicians" (1933) as "panders" and "pimps, unsound, / Strictured" (1991 1:364). Although Benjamin cites Karl Marx in his *Passagen-Werk* to the effect that

"'Prostitution is only a *specific* expression of the *general* prostitution of the labourer,'" he does not pursue the analogy; for Benjamin, "while the figure of the flaneur embodies the transformation of perception characteristic of modern subjectivity, the figure of the whore is the allegory for the transformation of objects, the world of things" (Buck-Morss 1986:121). As Shields observes, "Benjamin could have argued that the *flâneur* is closely related to the prostitute, who he characterizes as a person-become-commodity. Seeing only the agency of the masculine figure and only the superficiality of the feminine leads Benjamin to miss the opportunity to [connect these] archetypical responses to the commodification of social relations" (66).

75. They share this characteristic with Joyce's *A Portrait of the Artist as a Young Man* and *Ulysses*. All may have been inspired by the pervasiveness of odors in Baudelaire's *Les Fleurs du Mal:* in poems such as *"Correspondences"* and *"Parfum exotique"* the smells of women's bodies both "intoxicate" and nauseate. In *The American Scene,* the refined nose of James's narrator is all too aware of the "scent, literally, nor further to be followed" of Jews in the Bowery and immigrants in Boston (*TAS* 524).

76. TSE's poetry is well-known for this textual strategy. Prufrock's wishful dismemberment ("I should have been a pair of ragged claws/ Scuttling across the floors of silent seas") is as striking as his castration-anxiety ("I have seen my head [grown slightly bald]/ brought in upon a platter") (*CPP* 15).

77. Nonetheless, "it is by no means possible to assert that modernity may *only* be associated with . . . a metaphoric or actual fragmentation. . . . [Some] modern artists have moved towards its opposite, with a will to totalization" (Nochlin 1994a:53).

78. A car crash also emphatically begins Marinetti's 1909 "Founding and Futurist Manifesto."

79. The women, in contrast, are often "Bare-shouldered, smiling" ("Choices"), figures of dangerous leisure who are always ready to ensnare men "in plots of love."

80. In *Paterson,* the speaker may be "a poet (ridded) from Paradise" (*Pat* 132), but he too can imagine "break[ing] / through the skull of custom / to a place hidden from / affection, women and offspring" (*Pat* 139), another space of homosocial freedom.

81. In the early twentieth century, women writers and painters were "interested in radically redefining" urban and domestic spaces; "the crowds of the metropolis . . . provided for many women an anonymity and indifference that enabled the establishment of alternative domestic relations and communities" (Elliott and Wallace 162). Marcus, among others, has outlined "the feminist realist appropriation of public space in the city in the hopeful novels of the first two decades of the twentieth century" (136). See Squier, ed., *Women Writers and the City,* and the Spring 1980 issue of *Signs.*

82. Mae Cowdery tackles this subject in "A Brown Aesthete Speaks": having "met Keats and Poe," the speaker says, "Beauty is religion in my soul!" (Honey ed. 88). The argument also applies to African American men de-

termined to prove their artistic merits and explore positive subject positions. As Nellie McKay suggests, this "mastering [of] the poetic forms . . . was a political act, . . . [and] viewing those forms as timeless and universal invested the act with even greater power" (6). Cullen is an excellent example of this conundrum. Adopting what many deemed "a highly artificial or conventional mask or persona" (Elliott and Wallace 48) was his way of appropriating a poetic discourse presumed to be the preserve of white males only. Hughes looked within the African American community for legitimation and aesthetic forms; Cullen looked without, refusing to write what he deemed to be "'one note . . . 'propaganda.'" As he explained to the readers of the *Brooklyn Daily Eagle* in February 1924: "'If I am going to be a poet at all, I am going to be POET and not NEGRO POET'" (qtd Early 23). (Hughes responded to this claim in "The Negro Artist and the Racial Mountain," which begins by skewering Cullen: "One of the promising of the young Negro poets said to me once, 'I want to be a poet—not a Negro poet,' meaning, I believe, 'I want to write like a white poet'; meaning subconsciously, 'I would like to be a white poet'; meaning behind that, 'I would like to be white'" [1926: 305].) If identity politics can be reduced, for the sake of argument, to two approaches, sameness and difference, then Cullen's pursuit of sameness should be appreciated. One could think of this as a poetics of proficiency: his goal was not to be an innovator, but to demonstrate that he, a black man whose immediate ancestors were forbidden to read and write, was just as much at home in the high art milieu as anyone else. Occasionally his poems express contemporary concerns—"The Black Christ" is memorable; "Scottsboro, Too, Is Worth its Song" is one of his few texts written in free verse—but Cullen's favorite subject position is racially neutral, ahistorical, and gender nonspecific (comparisons with Moore in that regard would be more instructive than with Hughes). Like Millay, Cullen exploited the possibilities of the sonnet; unlike Millay, he did not attempt to subvert the genre from within or transgress its thematic conventions. By 1927, Early notes, only "Millay surpassed him in American poetry circles in critical and press attention" (7). The careers of both were eclipsed by the late 1940s.

83. The speaker of Effie Lee Newsome's "The Bird in the Cage" (1927) reasons that she is "not better than my brother over the way," yet she refuses to imprison a bird or assume the right to keep anything or anyone "prisoner" (Honey ed. 67). Two years earlier, Newsome applied a wasteland trope to the South with interesting results: "Rank fennel and broom / Grow wanly beside / The cottage and room. . . . / The dahoon berry weeps in blood. . . . / Watched by the crow—I've seen both grow / In those weird wastes of Dixie!" (Honey ed. 69). The title of the poem, "Exodus," lends biblical sanction to African Americans' out-migration to the North.

84. Baudelaire's sonnets "are energized," Clive Scott observes, "by expressive structural imperfections, by exacerbations of the form's unpredictability of rhyme-scheme, of its asymmetry, by discrepancies between prosodic and

syntactic segmentations. Baudelaire's sonnets are the battleground of the sonnet, the most systematic exploration of variation and irregularity" (270).

85. The now-classic discussion of *descriptio locii* conventions is found in Curtius.

86. In "Borderline," H. D. observes that words are too "weathered"—they are "all alike now, the words even one feels sometimes of a foreign language have lost 'virtue'" (1930:114).

87. Readers are indebted to literary historians and critics such as Friedman, Blau DuPlessis, King, and Ostriker. Rainey, on the other hand, provides an ill-tempered account of H. D.'s career in *Institutions of Modernism.* He reserves the final chapter for H. D.'s poetry, only to deny its literary worth and dismiss its importance in modernist scholarship. The "patronage" and financial support that H. D. received from Bryher (Winifred Ellerman) is scorned; any creative development H. D. might have experienced was apparently stymied by the sycophantic "coterie" that supported her. Safe within her lesbian (a word implied, never uttered) "cocoon," H. D. apparently "neither needed nor pursued the give-and-take of exchange with others" (1998:155). Rainey's particular, antifeminist purpose is to prove that H. D.'s writings do not belong in the same books, essays, or classrooms as those of TSE, EP, or Joyce. She is admired, he contends, because she was "a victim of ugly social prejudice," not because of artistic merit (1998:148), because her oeuvre suits the needs of academics with an antimasculine agenda. Rainey will not utter the accursed word *feminist;* instead, he hides behind circumlocutions such as "a far more recent array of agents, among them literary scholars, acting at a conjuncture of cultural, ideological, and institutional interests" or allusions to the "opprobrious label of 'political correctness'" (1998:151, 165). Gradually, however, his mission becomes clear: to lambaste both the "vacuity" of the poetry and the "provincial excess" of its critical champions (1998:164). H. D. is also faulted for not producing a sufficient number or range of critical writings; unlike the prolific TSE and Yeats, H. D. published only "forty-three articles" (1998:155). Rainey omits any reference to Joyce, who also forgot to devote himself to criticism; also unmentioned are the different opportunities that an established publisher such as TSE or a public figure such as Yeats would have had for broadcasting their views, or that James Laughlin provided for EP and many others at New Directions.

88. Her review of *Responsibilities,* Yeats's 1914 volume, is reprinted in Scott ed. 127–129. "The Second Coming" was published in *Dial,* November 1920, and *Michael Robartes and the Dancer,* 1921.

89. Both may be echoing Baudelaire's "Spleen (II)," which tries to remedy Ennui, now the "the size of immortality," with these prescriptive words: "Henceforth, o living flesh, you are no more! / You are of granite, wrapped in a vague dread, / Slumbering in some Sahara's hazy sands, / An ancient sphinx lost to a careless world, / Forgotten on the map" (1993:147).

90. Grimké combines sensuous natural imagery ("the long brown grasses/ That are your lashes") and art to express lesbian desire in "A Mona Lisa." When juxtaposed with WHP's famous exercise in *ekphrasis* (*TR* 98–99), Grimké's

positive eroticism highlights the antifeminist traditions (a woman as strangeness, vampire, whore) to which WHP is limited; his statement that "Lady Lisa might stand as the embodiment of the old fancy, the symbol of the modern idea" (*TR* 99) takes on new resonances. Hull argues that the overt lesbianism of Grimké's work prevented publication in many instances (22, 139–141); much of Grimké's work remains in manuscript. "A Mona Lisa" was published by Cullen in *Caroling Dusk*.

91. Among the male poets, Jean Toomer and Hughes write most evocatively about the South and the discrepancy between the beauty of its landscape and the horror of human activity there; Hughes's poetry of the South is more overtly politicized. In both canons, the deliberate use of traditionally pastoral elements to heighten stories of slavery, forced labor, and lynching is similar to the angry antipastoralism of World War I poets such as Isaac Rosenberg and Wilfrid Owen. Toomer's use of a "field rat" in "Reapers" is very similar to the "droll rat" featured in Rosenberg's "Break of Day in the Trenches."

92. The story of "Strange Fruit," the extraordinary song about lynching that became one of Billie Holiday's signature pieces, was recently retraced by David Margolick. The words and lyrics were composed by Abel Meeropol, an English teacher in the Bronx, New York and a political activist. Holiday debuted the song in 1939; when Columbia, her regular label, refused to let her record the song, Commodore Records stepped in. "Strange Fruit" has "been voted 'best [song] of the century' in *Time,* and named by *Q* magazine as one of the 'ten songs that actually changed the world'" (Carol Birch 20).

93. Nellie McKay suggests that only the poetry of "movement" is positive; "the use of trees" represents the "stationary" lives of women, "immobilized by confining roles" (14).

94. Richard Bruce's poem "Shadow" appeared two years later, in 1927: "Silhouette / On the face of the moon / Am I. . . . Because / I am dark, / Black on the face of the moon" (Cullen ed. 206–207).

95. Raymond Williams refers to their work as "this other elegiac, neo-pastoral mode" (1973:256). He dismisses the Georgian texts because they denied rural Britain's "crisis of wages, conditions, prices; of the use of land" (Williams 1973:257), and instead offered an "extraordinary collocation" of natural observations, classical tradition, and sentimental escapism (1973:257–258).

96. See Yaeger, "Toward a Female Sublime"; Joanne Diehl, *Women Poets and the American Sublime* (1990); Gary Lee Stonum, *The Dickinson Sublime* (1991); Shawn Alfrey's work on Dickinson and *The Sublime of Intense Sociability: Emily Dickinson, H. D., and Gertrude Stein* (2000). My thanks to Dr. Nancy Johnston for bringing this work to my attention.

97. Douglas defines *The Waste Land* is a "meditation on the modern metropolis as 'Nekropolis'" (114).

98. In the final edition of her *Collected Poems,* Moore limited the poem to three lines: "I, too, dislike it./ Reading it, however, with a perfect contempt for it,

one discovers in / it, after all, a place for the genuine" (1981:36). Ellmann and O'Clair reprint the 1921 version.

99. Among the final heap of textual fragments that ends *The Waste Land,* one finds a carefully-placed quote from Gerard de Nerval's "*El Desdichado,*" the disinherited (*CPP* 75).

Works Cited

Alfrey, Shawn. "Against Calvary: Emily Dickinson and the Sublime." *The Emily Dickinson Journal* 7.2 (1998): 48–64.

Anderson, Ronald and Anne Koval. *James McNeill Whistler: Beyond the Myth.* London: John Murray, 1994.

Arnold, Matthew. *Poetical Works.* Eds. C. B. Tinker and H.F. Lowry. London: Oxford University Press, 1950.

Arrowsmith, William. "Ruskin's Fireflies." Bloom, ed., 1986a: 69–103.

Ascari, Maurizio. "Walter Pater in Italy at the Postmodern *Fin de Siècle.*" *Pater Newsletter* 42 (Spring 2001): 18–23.

Babbitt, Irving. 1908. *Literature and the American College: Essays in Defense of the Humanities.* Ed. Russell Kirk. Washington, D.C.: National Humanities Institute, 1986.

———. 1912. *The Masters of Modern French Criticism.* Boston: Houghton Mifflin.

Baker, Houston A., Jr. *Modernism and the Harlem Renaissance.* Chicago: University of Chicago Press, 1987.

Barthes, Roland. "Semiology and the Urban." In *The City and the Sign: An Introduction to Urban Semiotics.* Eds. M. Gottdiener and Alexandros Lagopoulou. Trans. Karen Boklund-Lagopoulou. New York: Columbia University Press, 1986. 87–98.

Baudelaire, Charles. 1918. *Oeuvres Complètes.* 14 Vols. Paris: Nouvelle Revue Française.

———. 1965. *Art in Paris 1845–1862.* Trans. and ed. Jonathan Mayne. London: Phaidon.

———. 1993. *Les Fleurs du Mal/The Flowers of Evil.* Trans. James McGowan. Oxford: Oxford University Press.

———. 1995. *The Painter of Modern Life and Other Essays.* Trans. and ed. Jonathan Mayne. 2nd ed. London: Phaidon.

Bauer, Helen Pike. "Ruskin and the Education of Women." *Studies in the Humanities* 12.2 (December 1985): 79–89.

Baumgarten, Alexander. *Aesthetica.* 2 Vols. Barii: J. Laterza and Sons, 1936.

Bedient, Calvin. "Modernism and the End of Beauty." In *Rereading the New: A Backward Glance at Modernism.* Ed. Kevin Dettmar. Ann Arbor: University of Michigan Press, 1992. 99–116.

Beerbohm, Max. *Yet Again.* London: William Heinemann, 1951.

Bell, Clive. *Art.* 1914. London: Phoenix Library, 1928.

———. 1918. *Pot-Boilers*. London: Chatto & Windus.

Bell, Michael. "The Metaphysics of Modernism." Levenson, ed. 9–32.

Bendix, Deanna. *Diabolical Designs: Paintings, Interiors, and Exhibitions of James Mc-Neill Whistler*. Washington: Smithsonian Institution Press, 1995.

Benjamin, Walter. 1974. *Charles Baudelaire: A Lyric Poet in the Era of High Capitalism*. Trans. Jean Lacoste. Paris: Petite Bibliotheque Payot.

———. 1978. *Reflections*. New York: Harcourt Brace Jovanovich.

Benson, A. C. *Walter Pater*. London: Macmillan, 1906.

Benstock, Shari. *Women of the Left Bank: Paris, 1900–1940*. Austin: University of Texas Press, 1986.

Berger, John. *Ways of Seeing*. London: BBC and Penguin, 1972.

Berger, Klaus. *Japonisme in Western Painting from Whistler to Matisse*. Trans. David Britt. Cambridge: Cambridge University Press, 1992.

Bermingham, Ann. "Reading Constable." Pugh, ed. 97–120.

Bernheimer, Charles. *Figures of Ill Repute: Representing Prostitution in Nineteenth-Century France*. Durham: Duke University Press, 1997.

Bernstein, Gail Lee, ed. *Recreating Japanese Women, 1600–1945*. Berkeley: University of California Press, 1991.

Binyon, Laurence. "A Postscript to *The Renaissance*." *Saturday Review* CX.481 (15 October 1910). Rpt. in Seiler, ed. 412–415.

Birch, Carol. "A song that changed the world." *Times Literary Supplement* 5122 (1 June 2001): 20.

Birch, Dina. 1988a. "Ruskin's 'Womanly Mind.'" *Essays in Criticism* 38.4 (October 1988): 308–324.

———. 1988b. *Ruskin's Myths*. Oxford: Clarendon Press.

———. 1999a. Introduction. Birch, ed. 1–5.

———. 1999b. "Ruskin's Multiple Writing: *Fors Clavigera*." Birch, ed. 175–187.

Birch, Dina, ed. *Ruskin and the Dawn of the Modern*. Oxford: Oxford University Press, 1999.

Blanchard, Marc Eli. *In Search of the City: Engels, Baudelaire, Rimbaud*. Saratoga: Anma Libri, 1985.

Blair, Sara. 1996. *Henry James and the Writing of Race and Nation*. Cambridge: Cambridge University Press.

———. 1999. "Modernism and the politics of culture." Levenson, ed. 157–173.

BLAST 1 (June 1914). London: John Lane, 1914.

BLAST 2 (July 1915). London: John Lane, 1915.

BLAST 3. Eds. Seamus Cooney et al. Santa Barbara: Black Sparrow Press, 1984.

Blisset, William. "Pater and Eliot." *University of Toronto Quarterly* 22.3 (April 1953): 261–268.

Bloom, Harold. 1974. "The Crystal Man." *Selected Writings of Walter Pater*. Ed. Bloom. New York: Columbia University Press. vii–xxxi.

———. 1986. Introduction. Bloom, ed. *John Ruskin*. 1–14.

Bloom, Harold, ed. 1986. *John Ruskin*. Modern Critical Views. New York: Chelsea House.

Board, Marilynn Lincoln. "Constructing Myths and Ideologies in Matisse's Odalisques." Broude and Garrard, eds. 358–379.

Bogan, Louise. 1951. *Achievement in American Poetry, 1900–1950*. Chicago: Gateway Editions.

———. 1954. *Collected Poems, 1923–1953*. New York: Noonday Press.

Bolgan, Anne. *What the Thunder Really Said: A Retrospective Essay on the Making of "The Waste Land."* Montreal: McGill-Queen's Press, 1973.

Boone, Joseph Allen. *Libidinal Currents: Sexuality and the Shaping of Modernism*. Chicago: University of Chicago Press, 1998.

Boscagli, Maurizia and Enda Duffy. "Joyce's Face." Dettmar and Watts, eds. 133–159.

Bourdieu, Pierre. 1980. "The aristocracy of culture." *Media, Culture, and Society* 2.3 (1980): 225–254.

———. 1986. "The production of belief: contribution to an economy of symbolic goods." In *Media, Culture, and Society: A Critical Reader*. Eds. Richard Collins et al. Trans. Richard Nice. London: SAGE Publications. 131–163.

Bowie, Andrew. *Aesthetics and Subjectivity: from Kant to Nietzsche*. Manchester: Manchester University Press, 1990.

Bradley, J. L., ed. *Ruskin: The Critical Heritage*. London: Routledge & Kegan Paul, 1984.

Brake, Laurel. *Walter Pater*. Plymouth: Northcote House, 1994.

Bremer, Sidney. 1981. "Lost Continuities: Alternative Urban Visions in Chicago Novels, 1890–1915." *Soundings* 64.1 (1981): 29–51.

———. 1990. "Home in Harlem, New York: Lessons from the Harlem Renaissance Writers." *PMLA* 105.1 (January 1990): 47–56.

Bridge, Ursula, ed. *W. B. Yeats and T. Sturge Moore: Their Correspondence, 1901–1937*. London: Routledge & Kegan Paul, 1953.

Bridson, D. G. "*The Human Age* in Retrospect." Meyers, ed. 238–251.

Bronfen, Elisabeth. *Over Her Dead Body: Death, Femininity, and the Aesthetic*. Manchester: Manchester University Press, 1992.

Brooker, Jewel Spears. "Substitutes for Christianity in the Poetry of T. S. Eliot." *Southern Review* 21.4 (Autumn 1985): 899–913.

Broude, Norma and Mary D. Garrard, eds. *The Expanding Discourse: Feminism and Art History*. New York: HarperCollins, 1992.

Brown, Milton W. *American Painting from the Armory Show to the Depression*. Princeton: Princeton University Press, 1955.

Buckley, Jerome Hamilton. *The Turning Key: Autobiography and the Subjective Impulse Since 1800*. Cambridge, Mass.: Harvard University Press, 1984.

Buck-Morss, Susan. 1986. "The Flaneur, the Sandwichman and the Whore: The Politics of Loitering." *New German Critique* 39 (Fall 1986): 99–141.

———. 1991. *The Dialectics of Seeing: Walter Benjamin and the Arcades Project*. Cambridge, Mass.: MIT Press.

Bucknell, Brad. "Re-reading Pater: The Musical Aesthetics of Temporality." *Modern Fiction Studies* 38.3 (Autumn 1992): 597–614.

Bürger, Peter. *Theory of the Avant-Garde*. Trans. Michael Shaw. Minneapolis: University of Minnesota Press, 1984.

Burns, Sarah. "Old Maverick to Old Master: Whistler in the Public Eye in Turn-of-the-Century America." *The American Art Journal* 22.1 (1990): 28–49.

Bush, Ronald. *The Genesis of Ezra Pound's Cantos.* Princeton: Princeton University Press, 1976.

Carpenter, Edward. *Love's Coming of Age.* New York: Mitchell Kennerley, 1911.

Carpenter, Humphrey. *A Serious Character: The Life of Ezra Pound.* London: Faber, 1988.

Carroll, Margaret. "The Erotics of Absolutism: Rubens and the Mystification of Sexual Violence." Broude and Garrard, eds. 138–159.

Cary, Elisabeth Luther. *The Works of James McNeill Whistler.* New York and London: Moffat, Yard and Company, 1907.

Cassirer, Ernst. *The Platonic Renaissance in England.* Trans. James Pettegrove. Edinburgh: Nelson, 1953.

Casteras, Susan. "Excluding women: the cult of the male genius in Victorian painting." Shires, ed. 116–146.

Cate, Phillip Dennis. Introduction. Cate, ed. 7–14.

Cate, Phillip Dennis, Julia Meech and Gabriel P. Wesburg, eds. *Japonisme Comes to America: the Japanese impact on the graphic arts, 1876–1925.* New York: H.N. Abrams, 1990.

———, ed. *Perspectives on Japonisme: The Japanese Influence on America.* New Brunswick: Jane Voorhees Zimmerli Art Museum, 1989.

Caws, Mary Ann. "The City on Our Mind." Caws, ed. 1–11.

Caws, Mary Ann, ed. *City Images: Perspectives from Literature, Philosophy, and Film.* New York: Gordon and Breach, 1991.

Chase, Richard. *Walt Whitman Reconsidered.* London: Victor Gollancz, 1955.

Child, Ruth C. *The Aesthetic of Walter Pater.* New York: Macmillan, 1940.

Chinitz, David. 1995. "T. S. Eliot and the Cultural Divide." *PMLA* 110.2 (1995): 236–247.

———. 1997. "'Dance, Little Lady': Poets, Flappers, and the Gendering of Jazz." Rado, ed. 319–335.

Chisholm, Lawrence. *Fenollosa: The Far East and American Culture.* Westport: Greenwood, 1963.

Christ, Carol. *Victorian and Modern Poetics.* Chicago: University of Chicago Press, 1984.

Clark, Suzanne. *Sentimental Modernism: Women Writers and the Revolution of the Word.* Bloomington: Indiana University Press, 1991.

Cohen, Ed. *Talk on the Wilde Side: Toward a Genealogy of a Discourse on Male Sexualities.* New York: Routledge, 1993.

Collier, Peter. "Nineteenth-Century Paris: vision and nightmare." In *Unreal City: Urban Experience in Modern European Literature and Art.* Eds. Edward Timms and David Kelley. Manchester: Manchester University Press, 1985. 25–44.

Colomina, Beatriz. Introduction. Colomina, ed. vii–ix.

Colomina, Beatriz, ed. *Sexuality and Space.* Princeton Papers on Architecture. New York: Princeton Architectural Press, 1992.

Conlon, John. 1982a. "Eliot and Pater: Criticism in Transition." *English Literature in Transition* 25 (1982): 169–177.

———. 1982b. *Walter Pater and the French Tradition.* Lewisburg: Bucknell University Press.

Conner, Patrick. *Savage Ruskin.* London: Macmillan, 1979.

Conrad, Joseph. *Heart of Darkness.* Ed. Robert Kimbrough. 3rd ed. New York: Norton, 1988.

Cookson, William, ed. *Ezra Pound: Selected Prose 1909–1965.* London: Faber, 1973. Abbreviated as *P/SP.*

Cork, Richard. *Wyndham Lewis: The Twenties.* London: Anthony d'Offay, 1985.

Corn, Wanda. "The New New York." *Art in America* (July-August 1973): 59–65.

Court, Franklin. *Pater and his Early Critics.* Victoria: English Literary Studies, 1980.

Cox, F. Brett. "'What Need, Then, for Poetry?': The Genteel Tradition and the Continuity of American Literature." *New England Quarterly* 67.2 (1994): 212–233.

Craige, Betty Jean. "What is Relativism in the Arts?" Craige ed. 1–20.

Craige, Betty Jean, ed. *Relativism in the Arts.* Athens, GA: University of Georgia Press, 1983.

Crane, Walter. *William Morris to Whistler: Papers and Addresses on Art and Craft and the Commonweal.* London: G. Bell & Sons, 1911.

Crapanzano, Vincent. "A cab ride to Paradise." *Times Literary Supplement* (15 June 2001): 11.

Cullen, Countee. 1927. Foreword. Cullen, ed. vii-xii.

———. 1991. *My Soul's High Song: The Collected Writings of Countee Cullen.* Ed. Gerald Early. New York: Anchor Books, 1991.

Cullen, Countee, ed. *Caroling Dusk: An Anthology of Verse by Negro Poets.* New York: Harper and Row, 1974.

Cullingford, Elizabeth. *Gender and History in Yeats's Love Poetry.* Cambridge: Cambridge University Press, 1993.

Cummings, E. E. *Complete Poems.* New York: Harcourt Brace Jovanovich, 1963.

Curry, David Park. 1984. *James McNeill Whistler at the Freer Gallery of Art.* Smithsonian Institution. New York: Norton.

———. 1987. "Total Control: Whistler at an Exhibition." Fine, ed. 67–100.

Curtius, Ernst Robert. *European Literature and the Latin Middle Ages.* Trans. Willard Trask. New York: Harper and Row, 1953.

Dale, Peter Allan. "'Distractions of Spirit': Walter Pater and Modernity." *Papers on Language and Literature* 28.3 (1992): 319–349.

Dasenbrook, Reed W. Afterward. *The Art of Being Ruled.* By Wyndham Lewis. Santa Barbara: Black Sparrow Press, 1989. 432–445.

Davidson, Donald. "The Rise of the American City." Rev. of *The Rise of the City, 1878–1898.* By Arthur Schlesinger. *The American Review* (1933): 100–104.

Deane, Seamus. Introduction. Deane, ed. 3–19.

Deane, Seamus, ed. *Nationalism, Colonialism, and Literature.* Minneapolis: University of Minnesota Press, 1990.

de Certeau, Michel. *The Practice of Everyday Life.* Berkeley: University of California Press, 1984.

DeKoven, Marianne. 1991. *Rich and Strange: Gender, History, Modernism.* Princeton: Princeton University Press.

———. 1999. "Moderism and gender." Levenson, ed. 174–193.

De Laura, David. "Pater and Eliot: The Origin of the Objective Correlative." *Modern Language Quarterly* 26 (Summer 1965): 426–431.

Dettmar, Kevin and Stephen Watt. Introduction: Marketing Modernisms. Dettmar and Watts, eds. 1–13.

Dettmar, Kevin and Stephen Watt, eds. *Marketing Modernisms: Self-Promotion, Canonization, and Re-Reading.* Ann Arbor: University of Michigan Press, 1996.

Diepeveen, Leonard. "'I Can Have More Than Enough Power to Satisfy Me': T. S. Eliot's Construction of His Audience." Dettmar and Watt, eds. 37–60.

Dijkstra, Bram. *Idols of Perversity: Fantasies of Feminine Evil in Fin-de-Siècle Culture.* Oxford: Oxford University Press, 1986.

"The Dinner to Mr. Whistler." *Sunday London Times* 5 May 1889: 6.

Donohue, Joseph. "Oscar Wilde Refashioned: A Review of Recent Scholarship." *Nineteenth-Century Theatre* 21.2 (1993): 117–132.

Doob, Leonard, ed. *"Ezra Pound Speaking." Radio Speeches of World War II.* London: Greenwood, 1978.

Dorment, Richard. 1992. "Paint in the public's face. The absurd Whistler v Ruskin affair." *Times Literary Supplement* (26 June 1992): 16–17.

———. 1998. "We marvel and are aghast." *Times Literary Supplement* (27 March 1998): 18–19.

Douglas, Ann. *Terrible Honesty: Mongrel Manhattan in the 1920s.* New York: Noonday Press, 1996.

Duncan, Carol. *The Aesthetics of Power: Essays in Critical Art History.* Cambridge: Cambridge University Press, 1993.

Durét, Théodore. *Whistler.* Trans. Frank Rutter. London: Grant Richards, 1917.

Eagleton, Terry. 1988. "Capitalism, Modernism, and Postmodernism." *Against the Grain: Selected Essays.* London: Verso. 131–147.

———. 1990a. *The Ideology of the Aesthetic.* Oxford: Basil Blackwell.

———. 1990b. "Nationalism: Irony and Commitment." Deane, ed. 23–42.

Early, Gerald. Introduction. Cullen 1991: 3–73.

Easthope, Antony. *Poetry as Discourse.* London: Methuen, 1983.

Eddy, Arthur Jerome. *Recollections and Impressions of James A. McNeill Whistler.* Philadelphia and London: J.B. Lippincott, 1903.

Eden Versus Whistler. The Baronet & The Butterfly. A Valentine with a Verdict. Paris: Louis-Henry May, 1899.

Edwards, Paul. 1986. Afterword. *The Caliph's Design.* By Wyndham Lewis. Santa Barbara: Black Sparrow Press. 145–163.

———. 2000. *Wyndham Lewis: Painter and Writer.* New Haven: Yale University Press.

Eliot, T. S. 1916. "An American Critic." *New Statesman* (24 June 1916): 284.

———. 1917. "The Borderline of Prose." *New Statesman* (19 May 1917): 157–159.

———. 1918a. "Recent British Periodical Literature in Ethics." *International Journal of Ethics* 28.2 (January 1918): 270–277.

———. 1918b. "Style and Thought." *Nation* 22.25 (23 March 1918): 768–769.

———. 1918c. "Observations." *The Egoist* 5.5 (May 1918): 69–71.

———. 1918d. "Contemporanea." *The Egoist* 5.6 (June/July 1918): 84.

———. 1918e. "Shorter Notices." *The Egoist* 5.6 (June/July 1918): 87.

————. 1919a. "A Foreign Mind." *Athenaeum* 4653 (4 July 1919): 552–553.

————. 1919b. "Swinburne and the Elizabethans." *Athenaeum* 4664 (19 September 1919): 909–910.

————. 1919c. "Humanist, Artist, and Scientist." *Athenaeum* 4667 (10 October 1919): 1014–1015.

————. 1920a. "Dante." *Athenaeum* 4692 (2 April 1920): 441–442.

————. 1920b. *The Sacred Wood.* London: Methuen, 1960. Abbreviated as *SW.*

————. 1920c. "The Poetic Drama." *Athenaeum* 4968 (14 May 1920): 635–636.

————. 1921a. "Prose and Verse." *Chapbook* 22 (1921): 3–10.

————. 1921b. "London Letter." *Dial* 71.2 (August 1921): 213–217.

————. 1924a. "A Commentary." *The Criterion* 2.7 (April 1924): 231–235.

————. 1924b. "A Commentary." *The Criterion* 3.9 (October 1924): 1–5.

————. 1927. "The Silurist." *Dial* 83.3 (September 1927): 259–263.

————. 1933a. *The Use of Poetry and the Use of Criticism.* London: Faber, 1964. Abbreviated as *UPUC.*

————. 1933b. *After Strange Gods.* New York: Harcourt, Brace & World.

————. 1935. "A Commentary." *The Criterion* 14.57 (July 1935): 610–613.

————. 1950. *Selected Essays.* New York: Harcourt, Brace & World. Abbreviated as *SE.*

————. 1957. *On Poetry and Poets.* London: Faber. Abbreviated as *OPP.*

————. 1965. *To Criticize the Critic and Other Writings.* London: Faber, 1978. Abbreviated as *TCC.*

————. 1969. *The Complete Poems and Plays.* London: Faber. Abbreviated as *CPP.*

————. 1993. *The Varieties of Metaphysical Poetry.* Ed. Ronald Schuchard. New York: Harcourt Brace. Abbreviated as *VMP.*

————. 1996. *Inventions of the March Hare: Poems 1909–1917.* Ed. Christopher Ricks. London: Faber. Abbreviated as *IMH.*

Eliot, T. S., ed. *The Criterion, 1922–1939.* 18 Vols. London: Faber, 1967. Abbreviated as *CC.*

Eliot, Valerie, ed. 1971. *"The Waste Land": a facsimile and transcript.* London: Faber. Abbreviated as *Facs.*

————. 1988. *The Letters of T. S. Eliot.* Vol. 1: 1898–1922. London: Faber. Abbreviated as *LE.*

Elliott, Bridget and Jo-Ann Wallace. *Women Artists and Writers: Modernist (im)positionings.* London: Routledge, 1994.

Ellmann, Richard, ed. *The Artist as Critic: Critical Writings of Oscar Wilde.* New York: Random House, 1968.

Ellmann, Richard and Robert O'Clair, eds. *The Norton Anthology of Modern Poetry.* 2nd ed. New York: Norton, 1988.

Evans, Lawrence, ed. *Letters of Walter Pater.* Oxford: Clarendon Press, 1970.

Fabricant, Carole. "Binding and Dressing Nature's Loose Tresses: The Ideology of Augustan Landscape Design." *Studies in Eighteenth Century Culture* 8 (1979): 109–135.

Falkenheim, Jacqueline. *Roger Fry and the beginnings of formalist art criticism.* Ann Arbor: UMI Research Press, 1980.

Feldman, Jessica. *Gender on the Divide: The Dandy in Modernist Literature.* Ithaca: Cornell University Press, 1993.

Fellows, Jay. 1975. *The Failing Distance: The Autobiographical Impulse in John Ruskin.* Baltimore: Johns Hopkins University Press.

———. 1981. *Ruskin's Maze: Mastery and Madness in His Art.* Princeton: Princeton University Press.

Felman, Shoshana. "Rereading Femininity." *Yale French Studies* 62 (1981): 19–44.

Felski, Rita. "The Counterdiscourse of the Feminine in Three Texts by Wilde, Huysmans, and Sacher-Masoch." *PMLA* 106.5 (1991): 1094–1105.

Fenellosa, Ernest F. 1903. "The Place in History of Mr. Whistler's Art." *Lotus: In Memoriam—James A. McNeill Whistler.* (Special Holiday Number, December 1903): 14–17.

———. 1907. "The Collection of Mr Charles L. Freer." Rpt. Spencer, ed. 365–367.

———. 1912. *Epochs of Chinese and Japanese Art.* 2 Vols. London: William Heinemann.

Ferguson, Priscilla Parkhurst. 1993. "The *Flâneur* and the Production of Culture." In *Cultural Participation: Trends Since the Middle Ages.* Eds. Ann Rigney and Douwe Fokkema. Philadelphia: John Benjamins Publishing. 109–124.

———. 1994. "The *flâneur* on and off the streets of Paris." Tester, ed. 22–42.

Fine, Ruth E., ed. *James McNeill Whistler: A Reexamination.* Studies in the History of Art, 19. Washington, D.C.: National Gallery of Art, 1987.

Finneran, Richard J., ed. *Critical Essays on W.B. Yeats.* Boston: G.K. Hall, 1986.

Fleissner, Robert. "'Prufrock,' Pater, and *Richard II:* Retracing a Denial of Princeship." *American Literature* 38 (1966): 120–123.

Flint, R. W. Introduction. Marinetti, 3–36.

Foucault, Michel. 1972. *The Archaeology of Knowledge.* Trans. A.M. Sheridan Smith. London: Tavistock Publications.

———. 1973. *The Order of Things: An Archaeology of the Human Sciences.* New York: Vintage Books.

———. 1978. *The History of Sexuality.* Vol. 1. Trans. Robert Hurley. New York: Vintage Books, 1990.

———. 1979a. *Discipline and Punish: The Birth of the Prison.* 1975. Trans. Alan Sheridan. New York: Vintage Books.

———. 1979b. "Truth and Power." In *Michel Foucault: Power, Truth, Strategy.* Eds. Meaghan Morris and Paul Patton. Sydney: Feral.

———. 1984. *The Foucault Reader.* Ed. Paul Rabinow. New York: Pantheon Books.

Frisby, David. "The *flâneur* in social theory." Tester, ed. 81–110.

Fry, Roger. 1903. "Mr Whistler." *Athenaeum* 25 July 1903. Rpt. Spencer, ed. 345–347.

———. 1905. Introduction to the Third Discourse. *Discourses.* By Sir Joshua Reynolds. London: Seeley & Co., 1905. 39–47.

———. 1908a. "Letter to the Editor." *Burlington Magazine* 12.60 (March 1908): 374–375.

———. 1908b. "Art Books." *Burlington Magazine* 12.60 (March 1908): 172.

Gallatin, A. E. 1904. *Whistler's Art Dicta and Other Essays.* Boston: Charles E. Goodspeed; London: Elkin Mathews.

————. 1907. *Whistler: Notes and Footnotes.* New York: The Collector and Art Critic; London: Elkin Mathews.

————. 1913a. *The Portraits and Caricatures of James McNeill Whistler.* London: John Lane.

————. 1913b. *Whistler's Pastels and Other Modern Profiles.* 2nd ed. New York: John Lane.

————. 1918. *Portraits of Whistler: A Critical Study and an Iconography.* London: John Lane, The Bodley Head.

Gallup, Donald. *T. S. Eliot: A Bibliography.* London: Faber, 1969.

Gates, Henry Louis Jr. and K. A. Appiah, eds. *Langston Hughes: Critical Perspectives Past and Present.* New York: Amistad Press, 1993.

Gaudier-Brzeska, Henri. "VORTEX. GAUDIER BRZESKA." *BLAST* 1 (June 1914): 158.

Gendron, Bernard. "Jamming at Le Boeuf: Jazz and the Paris Avant-Garde." *Discourse* 12.1 (Fall-Winter 1989–1990): 3–27.

Gilbert, Sandra and Susan Gubar. *No Man's Land: The Place of the Woman Writer in the Twentieth Century.* 3 Vols. New Haven: Yale University Press, 1989.

Gilbert, W. S. *Patience: or Bunthorne's Bride.* London: G. Bell and Sons, Ltd., 1911.

Gilman, Sander. *The Jew's Body.* London: Routledge, 1991.

Gordon, Lyndall. *Eliot's Early Years.* Oxford: Oxford University Press, 1977.

Gordon, Susan Phelps. 1993a. "Heartsight Deep as Eyesight: Ruskin's Aspirations for Modern Art." Whelchel, ed. 116–157.

Gordon, Susan Phelps and Anthony Lacy Gully. 1993b. "Introduction." Whelchel, ed. 10–51.

Grace, Sherill. "Quest for the Peaceable Kingdom: Urban / Rural Codes in Roy, Laurence, Atwood." In *Women Writers and the City: Essays in Feminist Literary Criticism.* Ed. Susan Merrill Squier. Knoxville: University of Tennessee Press, 1984. 193–209.

Gray, Basil. "'Japonisme' and Whistler." *Burlington Magazine* CVII (1965): 324.

Green, Martin. *Cities of Light and Sons of Morning: A Cultural Psychology for an Age of Revolution.* Boston: Little, Brown and Company, 1972.

Greever, Garland and Joseph Bachelor, eds. *The Soul of the City: An Urban Anthology.* Boston: Houghton Mifflin, 1923. Abbreviated as *SofC.*

Gross, John, ed. *The Modern Movement.* A *TLS* Companion. Chicago: University of Chicago Press, 1992.

Grosz, Elizabeth. "Bodies-Cities." Colomina, ed. 253.

Guiati, Andrea. "Filippo Tommaso Marinetti." In *Dictionary of Literary Biography.* Detroit: Bruccoli Clark Layman, 1992. 114:122–134.

H., C. J. [? C. J. Holmes] *The Peacock Room: Painted for Mr. F.R. Leyland by James McNeill Whistler. Removed in its Entirety from the Late Owner's Residence and Exhibited at Messrs. Obach's Galleries at 168 New Bond Street, London.* London: n.p., 1904.

Hall, Peter. "Metropolis 1890–1940: Challenges and Responses." Sutcliffe, ed. 19–66.

Halter, Peter. "'How Shall I Be a Mirror to this Modernity?': William Carlos Williams, Alfred Stieglitz, and the Artists of the Stieglitz Circle." In *Poetry and the Fine Arts: Papers from the Poetry Sessions of the European Association for American Studies Biennial Conference, Rome 1984.* Eds. Roland Hagenbüche and Jacqueline Ollier. Regensburg: F. Pustet, 1989. 72–101.

Hansen, Miriam. "T. E. Hulme, Mercenary of Modernism, Or, Fragments of an Avantgarde Sensibility in Pre–World War I Britain." *ELH* 47.2 (Summer 1980): 355–385.

Harpham, Geoffrey Galt. *On the Grotesque: Strategies of Contradiction in Art and Literature.* Princeton: Princeton University Press, 1982.

Harrison, Charles. 1994. "The Effects of Landscape." Mitchell, ed. 203–239.

———. 1997. "Cézanne: Fantasy and Imagination." *Modernism/ Modernity* 4.3 (September 1997): 1–18.

Harrison, Jane. *Ancient Art and Ritual.* 1913. Bradford-on-Avon: Moonraker Press, 1978.

———. *Prolegomena to the Study of Greek Religion.* Cambridge: Cambridge University Press, 1903.

Hart-Davis, Rupert, ed. *The Letters of Oscar Wilde.* London: Rupert Hart-Davis, 1962.

Hassett, Joseph M. *Yeats and the Poetics of Hate.* New York: St. Martin's Press, 1986.

Hauser, Arnold. 1974. *The Sociology of Art.* Trans. Kenneth Northcott. Chicago: University of Chicago Press, 1982.

———. 1986. *Mannerism: The Crisis of the Renaissance and the Origin of Modern Art.* Trans. Eric Mosbacher and Arnold Hauser. Cambridge, Mass.: Belknap P.

Hayward, John. "Mr Yeats Selects the Modern Poets: A Time of Literary Confusion." *Times Literary Supplement* (21 November 1936): 3.

H. D. [Hilda Doolittle]. 1914. "Responsibilities." Scott, ed. 127–129.

———. 1930. "The Borderline Pamphlet." Scott, ed. 110–125.

———. 1979. *End to Torment.* Eds. Norman Pearson and Michael King. New York: New Directions.

———. 1983. *Collected Poems 1912–1944.* Ed. Louis Martz. New York: New Directions.

Hegel, G. W. F. *The Phenomenology of Spirit.* Trans. J. B. Baillie. London: Allen and Unwin, 1910.

Heller, Michael. "The Cosmopolis of Poetics: Urban World, Uncertain Poetry." Caws, ed. 87–96.

Helsinger, Elizabeth. "The Ruskinian Sublime." Bloom, ed., 1986a. 117–132.

Herbert, Alice. *Heaven and Charing Cross.* London: John Lane, 1922.

Herbert, Robert. Introduction. In *Georges Seurat, 1859–1891.* Ed. Robert Herbert. New York: Metropolitan Museum of Art, 1991. 3–10.

Herr, Cheryl. "The Erotics of Irishness." *Critical Inquiry* 17.1 (Autumn 1990): 1–34.

Hewitt, Andrew. "Wyndham Lewis: Fascism, Modernism, and the Politics of Homosexuality." *ELH* 60.2 (1993): 527–544.

Higgins, Lesley. 1993. "Jowett and Pater: Trafficking in Platonic Wares." *Victorian Studies* 37.1 (Autumn 1993): 43–72.

———. 1997b. "'Lovely seaside girls' or 'Sweet murderers of men'? Fatal women in *Ulysses.*" In *Gender in Joyce.* Eds. Marlene Corcoran and Jolanta Wawrzycka. Gainesville: University Press of Florida, 1997. 47–61.

Higgins, Lesley and Marie-Christine Leps. "Passport, please: legal, literary, and critical fictions of identity." *College Literature* 25.1 (Winter 1998): 94–138.

Hillyer, Robert. "Treason's Strange Fruit: The Case of Ezra Pound and the Bollingen Award." *Saturday Review of Literature* (11 June 1949): 9–11, 28.

———. "Poetry's New Priesthood." *Saturday Review of Literature* (18 June 1949): 7–9, 38.

Hilton, Tim. *John Ruskin: The Later Years.* New Haven: Yale University Press, 2000.

Himber, Allan, ed. *The Letters of John Quinn to William Butler Yeats.* Ann Arbor: UMI Research Press, 1983.

Holloway, John. *The Victorian Sage: Studies in Argument.* London: Macmillan, 1953.

———. 1980. "Machine and Puppet: A Comparative View." Meyers, ed. 3–14.

Holmes, C. J. "Whistler and Modern Painting." *Burlington Magazine* 14.70 (January 1909): 204–206.

Honey, Maureen, ed. *Shadowed Dreams: Women's Poetry of the Harlem Renaissance.* New Brunswick, NJ: Rutgers University Press, 1989.

Houghton, Walter. *The Victorian Frame of Mind.* New Haven: Yale University Press, 1957.

Houghton, Walter and G. Robert Stange, eds. *Victorian Poetry and Poetics.* 2nd ed. Boston: Houghton Mifflin, 1968.

Howard, Richard. Notes. James, *The American Scene.* 808–833.

Howarth, Herbert. *Notes on Some Figures Behind T. S. Eliot.* Boston: Houghton Mifflin, 1964.

Howe, Irving. "The City in Literature." *The Critical Point.* New York: Horizon Press, 1973.

Hughes, Langston. 1926. "The Negro Artist and the Racial Mountain." In *Voices from the Harlem Renaissance.* Ed. Nathan Huggins. New York: Oxford University Press, 1976. 304–309.

———. 1994. *The Collected Poems of Langston Hughes.* Eds. Arnold Rampersad and David Roessel. New York: Knopf.

———. 1999. *Poems.* Ed. David Roessel. New York: Knopf.

Hull, Gloria T. *Color, Sex, and Poetry: Three Women Writers of the Harlem Renaissance.* Bloomington: Indiana University Press, 1987.

Hulme, T. E. 1925. "Notes on Language and Style." *The Criterion* 3.12 (July 1925): 485–497.

———. 1936. *Speculations: Essays on Humanism and the Philosophy of Art.* Ed. Herbert Read. London: Routledge & Kegan Paul.

———. 1955. *Further Speculations.* Ed. Samuel Hynes. Minneapolis: University of Minnesota Press.

Hunt, John Dixon. 1982a. "Oeuvre and footnote." Hunt and Holland, eds. 1–20.

———. 1982b. *The Wider Sea: A Life of John Ruskin.* New York: Viking Press.

———. 1986. "*Ut pictura poesis,* the Picturesque, and John Ruskin." Bloom, ed., 1986a. 51–68.

Hunt, John Dixon and Faith M. Holland, eds. *The Ruskin Polygon: Essays on the Imagination of John Ruskin.* Manchester: Manchester University Press, 1982.

Hutchinson, Stuart. "Henry James: The American City and the Structure of Experience." In *The American City: Literary and Cultural Experiences.* Ed. Graham Clark. New York: St. Martin's Press, 1988.

Huyssen, Andreas. *After the Great Divide: Modernism, Mass Culture, Post-Modernism.* Bloomington: Indiana University Press, 1986.

Inman, Billie Andrew. *Walter Pater and his Reading, 1874–1877, With a Bibliography of his Library Borrowings, 1878–1894.* New York: Garland, 1977.

Isherwood, Christopher. *Goodbye to Berlin.* 1939. London: Methuen, 1987.

James, Henry. 1905. *English Hours. Collected Travel Writings: Great Britain and America.* The Library of America 64. New York: Literary Classics of the United States, Inc., 1993. 1–263.

———. 1907. *The American Scene. Collected Travel Writings: Great Britain and America.* Library of America 64. New York: Literary Classics of the United States, Inc., 1993. 351–736. Abbreviated as *TAS*.

———. 1914. *Notes on Novelists, with Some Other Notes.* London: J.M. Dent.

Jameson, Fredric. 1979. *Fables of Aggression: Wyndham Lewis, the Modernist as Fascist.* Berkeley: University of California Press.

———. 1981. *The Political Unconscious: Narrative as a Socially Symbolic Act.* London: Methuen.

Janowitz, H. D. "*Marius the Epicurean* in T. S. Eliot's Poetry." *Journal of Modern Literature* 15.4 (1989): 589–592.

Jardine, Alice. *Gynesis: Configurations of Woman and Modernity.* Ithaca: Cornell University Press, 1985.

Jarrell, Randall. "The End of the Line." *Kipling, Auden, and Co.: Essays and Reviews, 1935–1964.* New York: Farrar, Straus and Giroux, 1980. 76–83.

Jensen, Robert. *Marketing Modernism in Fin-de-Siècle Europe.* Princeton: Princeton University Press, 1994.

Johnson, James Weldon. "The Dilemma of the Negro Author." *The American Mercury* 15 (1928): 477–481.

Johnson, Lionel. *Post Liminium: Essays and Critical Papers.* Ed. Thomas Whittemore. London: Elkin Mathews, 1911.

Johnston, John H. *The Poet and the City: A Study in Urban Perspectives.* Athens, GA: University of Georgia Press, 1984.

Jowett, Benjamin, ed. and trans. *The Dialogues of Plato.* 4 Vols. New York: Charles Scribner's Sons, 1911.

Julius, Anthony. *T. S. Eliot, Anti-Semitism, and Literary Form.* Cambridge: Cambridge University Press, 1995.

Jung, C. G. *Symbols of Transformation.* Trans. R. F. C. Hull. Princeton: Princeton University Press, 1956.

Kalaidjian, Walter. "Marketing Modern Poetry and the Southern Public Sphere." Dettmar and Watt, eds. 297–319.

Katz, Tamar. "'In the House and Garden of His Dream': Pater's Domestic Subject." *Modern Language Quarterly* 56.2 (June 1995): 167–188.

Keane, Patrick. *Terrible Beauty: Yeats, Joyce, Ireland, and the Myth of the Devouring Female.* Columbia: University of Missouri Press, 1988.

Keating, Peter. "The Metropolis in Literature." Sutcliffe, ed. 129–146.

Kemp, Wolfgang. *The Desire of My Eyes: The Life and Work of John Ruskin.* Trans. Jan van Heurck. New York: Farrar, Straus and Giroux, 1990.

Kenner, Hugh. 1971. *The Pound Era.* Berkeley: University of California Press.

———. 1983. *A Colder Eye: The Modern Irish Writers.* New York: Knopf.

———. 1986. "The Sacred Book of the Arts." Finneran, ed. 9–20.

Kent, Susan Kingsley. *Sex and Suffrage in Britain: 1860–1914.* Princeton: Princeton University Press, 1987.

King, Deborah. "Multiple Jeopardy, Multiple Consciousness: The Context of a Black Feminist Ideology." In *Feminist Social Thought: A Reader.* Ed. Diana Meyers. New York: Routledge, 1997. 220–242.

Koestenbaum, Wayne. *Double Talk: The Erotics of Male Literary Collaboration.* London: Routledge, 1989.

Koval, Anne. "The 'Artists' have come out and the 'British' remain: the Whistler faction at the Society of British Artists." Prettejohn, ed. 90–111.

Krauss, Rosalind E. "Poststructuralism and the Paraliterary." In *The Originality of the Avant-Garde and Other Modernist Myths.* Cambridge, Mass.: Harvard University Press, 1985. 291–295.

Kurrik, Marie Jaanus. *Literature and Negation.* New York: Columbia University Press, 1979.

Kuspit, Donald. "Individual and Mass Identity in Urban Art: The New York Case." *Art in America* 65 (September-October 1977): 67–77.

Lambourne, Lionel. *The Aesthetic Movement.* London: Phaidon, 1996.

Landow, George P. 1971. *The Aesthetic and Critical Theories of John Ruskin.* Princeton: Princeton University Press.

———. 1993. "How to Read Ruskin: the Art Critic as Victorian Sage." Whelchel, ed. 52–79.

Lang, Andrew. Review of *Greek Studies,* March 1895, *Illustrated London News.* Rpt. Seiler, ed. 331–335.

Lehan, Richard. "Cities of the Living/ Cities of the Dead: Joyce, Eliot, and the Origins of Myth in Modernism." In *The Modernists: Studies in a Literary Phenomenon.* Eds. Lawrence Gamache and Ian MacNiven. London: Associated University Press. 61–74.

Lentricchia, Frank. *Modernist Quartet.* Cambridge: Cambridge University Press, 1994.

Leps, Marie-Christine. *Apprehending the Criminal: The production of deviance in nineteenth-century discourse.* Durham: Duke University Press, 1992.

Levenson, Michael. 1984. *A Genealogy of Modernism: A Study of English Literary Doctrine 1908–1922.* Cambridge: Cambridge University Press, 1986.

———. 1999. Introduction. Levenson, ed. 1–8.

Levenson, Michael, ed. *The Cambridge Companion to Modernism.* Cambridge: Cambridge University Press, 1999.

Lewis, Wyndham. 1917. *The Code of a Herdsman.* Rpt. ed. Alan Munton. Glasgow: The Wyndham Lewis Society, 1977.

———. 1918. *Tarr.* Rev. ed. London: Calder and Boyars, 1928. Abbreviated as *Tarr.*

———. 1919. *The Caliph's Design: Architects! Where is Your Vortex?* Ed. Paul Edwards. Santa Barbara: Black Sparrow Press, 1986.

———. 1924a. "The Apes of God." *The Criterion* 2.7 (April 1924): 300–310.

———. 1924b. "Art Chronicle." *The Criterion* 3.9 (October 1924): 107–113.

———. 1926. *The Art of Being Ruled.* Ed. Reed Way Dasenbrock. Santa Barbara: Black Sparrow Press, 1989. Abbreviated as *Art.*

———. 1928. *Childermass.* Book One, *The Human Age.* London: Methuen, 1956. Abbreviated as *ChM.*

———. 1931a. *The Diabolical Principle and The Dithyrambic Spectator.* London: Chatto & Windus. Abbreviated as *DPDS.*

———. 1931b. *Hitler.* London: Chatto & Windus. Abbreviated as *Hit.*

———. 1932. *Doom of Youth.* London: Chatto & Windus. Abbreviated as *DY.*

———. 1934. *Men Without Art.* Ed. Seamus Cooney. Santa Rosa: Black Sparrow Press, 1987. Abbreviated as *MWA.*

———. 1935. "The Skeleton in the Cupboard Speaks." *A Short Survey of Surrealism.* Ed. David Gascoyne. London: Cass, 1970.

———. 1937. *Blasting and Bombardiering.* London: Eyre & Spottiswoode. Abbreviated as *BB.*

———. 1939a. *The Hitler Cult.* London: Dent. Abbreviated as *HC.*

———. 1939b. *Wyndham Lewis the Artist: From "Blast" to Burlington House.* London: Laidlaw & Laidlaw. Abbreviated as *WLA.*

———. 1969. *Wyndham Lewis on Art.* Eds. Walter Michel and C. J. Fox. New York: Funk & Wagnalls.

———. 1975. *Enemy Salvoes: Selected Literary Criticism.* Ed. C. J. Fox. London: Vision. Abbreviated as *EnS.*

———. 1989. *Creatures of Habit and Creatures of Change: Essays on Art, Literature, and Society 1914–1956.* Ed. Paul Edwards. Santa Rosa: Black Sparrow Press. Abbreviated as *CH.*

Litz, A. Walton, ed. *Eliot in His Time: Essays on the Occasion of the Fiftieth Anniversary of "The Waste Land."* Princeton: Princeton University Press, 1973.

Lochnan, Katherine. *The Etchings of James McNeill Whistler.* New Haven: Yale University Press, 1984.

Longenbach, James. 1987. *Modernist Poetics of History: Pound, Eliot, and the Sense of the Past.* Princeton: Princeton University Press.

———. 1988. *Stone Cottage: Pound, Yeats, and Modernism.* New York: Oxford University Press.

———. 1999. "Modern poetry." Levenson, ed. 100–129.

"Long Live the Vortex!" *BLAST* 1 (June 1914): 7.

Lowell, Amy. *The Complete Poetical Works of Amy Lowell.* Boston: Houghton Mifflin, 1955.

Lynes, Barbara Buhler. "Georgia O'Keefe and Feminism: A Problem of Position." Broude and Garrard, eds. 436–449.

Lyon, Janet. 1991. "Transforming Manifestoes: A Second-Wave Problematic." *Yale Journal of Criticism* 5.1 (1991): 101–127.

———. 1992. "Militant Discourse, Strange Bedfellows: Suffragettes and Vorticists before the War." *differences* 4.2 (1992): 100–132.

Lyotard, Jean-François. *The Postmodern Condition: A Report on Knowledge.* Trans. Geoff Bennington and Brian Massumi. Minneapolis: University of Minnesota Press, 1984.

MacDonald, Margaret. "Maud Franklin." Fine, ed. 13–26.

Macfall, Haldane. *Whistler: Butterfly, Wasp, Wit, Master of the Arts, Enigma.* Edinburgh: T. N. Foulis, 1905.

Maidment, Brian. "Interpreting Ruskin 1870–1914." Hunt and Holland, eds. 159–171.

"Manifesto." *BLAST* 1 (June 1914): 11.

Mann, Patricia. "Recognizing Men: A Feminist Vision." *Social Text* 16 (Winter 1986 / 87): 17–37.

Mannheim, Karl. "The problem of generations." *Essays on the Sociology of Knowledge.* London: Routledge and Kegan Paul, 1952.

Mao, Douglas. *Solid Objects: Modernism and the Test of Production.* Princeton: Princeton University Press, 1998.

Marcus, Jane. "A Wilderness of One's Own: Feminist Fantasy Novels of the Twenties." Squier, ed. 134–160.

Margolick, David. "Strange Fruit." *Vanity Fair* (September 1998): 310–320.

Marinetti, F. T. *Marinetti: Selected Writings.* Ed. R. W. Flint. Trans. Flint and Arthur Coppotelli. New York: Farrar, 1972.

Marx, Leo. "The Puzzle of Anti-Urbanism in Classic American Literature." In *Literature and the Urban Experience: Essays on the City and Literature.* Eds. Michael Jaye and Ann Chalmers Watts. New Brunswick: Rutgers University Press, 1981. 63–80.

Masterman, C. F. G. "Realities at home." In *The Heart of the Empire: Discussions of Problems of Modern City Life in England.* Ed. Masterman. London: T. Fisher Unwin, 1901.

Materer, Timothy. 1979. *Vortex: Pound, Eliot, and Lewis.* Ithaca: Cornell University Press, 1979.

———. 1980. "Lewis and the Patriarchs: Augustus John, W. B. Yeats, and T. Sturge Moore." Meyers, ed. 47–63.

Materer, Timothy, ed. 1985. *Pound / Lewis: The Letters of Ezra Pound and Wyndham Lewis.* New York: New Directions. Abbreviated *P/L.*

———, ed. 1991. *The Selected Letters of Ezra Pound to John Quinn, 1915–1924.* Durham: Duke University Press. Abbreviated *P/Q.*

McDonald, Gail. *Learning to be Modern: Pound, Eliot, and the American University.* Oxford: Clarendon Press, 1993.

McGrath, F. C. *The Sensible Spirit: Walter Pater and the Modernist Paradigm.* Tampa: University of South Florida Press, 1986.

McKay, Claude. 1953. *Selected Poems of Claude McKay.* Intro. John Dewey. New York: Bookman Associates.

———. 1973. *The Passion of Claude McKay: Selected Poetry and Prose, 1912–1948.* Ed. Wayne F. Cooper. New York: Schocken Books.

McKay, Nellie. Introduction. Honey, ed. 1–41.

McLuhan, Marshall. "Lewis's Prose Style." Meyers, ed. 64–67.

McMullen, Roy. *Victorian Outsider: A Biography of J. A. M. Whistler.* New York: E. P. Dutton, 1973.

Meech, Julia. "Collecting Japanese Art in America." Cate, ed. 41–56.

Meisel, Perry. *The Myth of the Modern.* New Haven: Yale University Press, 1987.

Menand, Louis. *Discovering Modernism.* New York: Oxford University Press, 1987.

Mencken, H. L. *Prejudices: Sixth Series.* New York: Knopf, 1927.

Merrill, Linda. 1992. *A Pot of Paint: Aesthetics on trial in "Whistler v Ruskin."* Washington, D.C.: Smithsonian Institution Press.

———. 1998. *The Peacock Room: A Cultural Biography.* Washington, D.C.: Smithsonian Institution Press; New Haven: Yale University Press.

Merrill, Linda, ed. *With Kindest Regards: The Correspondence of Charles Lang Freer and James McNeill Whistler, 1890–1903.* Washington, D.C.: Smithsonian Institution Press, 1995.

Meyers, Jeffrey, ed. *Wyndham Lewis: A Revaluation.* Montreal: McGill-Queen's Press, 1980.

Millay, Edna St. Vincent. *Complete Poems.* New York: Harper & Row, 1956.

Miller, Vincent. "Mauberley and his Critics." *ELH* 57.4 (1990): 961–976.

Millet, Kate. *Sexual Politics.* Garden City: Doubleday & Company, 1970.

Mitchell, W. J. T. 1992. "Ekphrasis and the Other." *South Atlantic Quarterly* 91.3 (1992): 695–719.

———. 1994a. Introduction. Mitchell, ed. 1–4.

———. 1994b. "Imperial Landscape." Mitchell, ed. 5–34.

Mitchell, W. J. T., ed. *Landscape and Power.* Chicago: University of Chicago Press, 1994.

Moers, Ellen. *The Dandy: Brummel to Beerbohm.* London: Secker and Warburg, 1960.

Molesworth, Charles. "The City: Some Classical Moments." Caws, ed. 13–23.

Moliterno, Frank. *The Dialectics of Sense and Spirit in Pater and Joyce.* Greensboro: ELT Press, 1998.

Monsman, Gerald. *Walter Pater.* Boston: Twayne, 1977.

Moon, Brian. "Theorising Violence in the Discourse of Masculinities." *Southern Review* 25.2 (1992): 194–204.

Moore, George. *Modern Painting.* Rev. ed. London: Walter Scott Publishing Co., 1893.

Moore, Marianne. 1981. *The Complete Poems of Marianne Moore.* New York: Viking Press.

———. 1986. *Complete Prose.* Ed. Patricia Willis. New York: Viking Press.

Morris, Daniel. "A Taste of Fortune: *In the Money* and Williams's New Directions Phase." Dettmar and Watt, eds. 161–187.

Morris, Meaghan. "Great Moments in Social Climbing: King Kong and the Human Fly." Colomina, ed. 1–51.

Mott, Christopher. "The Art of Self-Promotion; or, Which Self to Sell? The Proliferation and Disintegration of the Harlem Renaissance." Dettmar and Watt, eds. 253–274.

Mulliken, Mary Augusta. "Reminiscences of the Whistler Academy. By an American Student." *The Studio* 34 (1905): 237–241.

Mulvey, Laura. "Pandora: Topographies of the Mask and Curiosity." Colomina, ed. 53–71.

Mumford, Lewis. 1938. *The City in History: Its Origins, Its Transformations, Its Prospects.* New York: Harcourt, Brace, Jovanovich, 1970.

———. 1940. *The Culture of Cities.* Rev. ed. London: Secker and Warburg.

———. 1969. "Utopia, The City and the Machine." *Daedalus* 94 (1969): 251–271.

Nelson, Cary. "The Fate of Gender in Modern American Poetry." Dettmar and Watt, eds. 321–360.

Newall, Christopher. "Ruskin and the Art of Drawing." Whelchel, ed. 81–115.

Nielsen, Aldon. *Reading Race: White American Poets and Racial Discourse in the Twentieth Century.* Athens, GA: University of Georgia Press, 1988.

Nochlin, Linda. 1988. *Women, Art, and Power and Other Essays.* New York: Harper & Row.

———. 1991. *The Politics of Vision: Essays on Nineteenth-Century Art and Society.* 1989. London: Thames and Hudson.

———. 1992. "Morisot's *Wet Nurse:* The Construction of Work and Leisure in Impressionist Painting." Broude and Garrard, eds. 230–243.

———. 1994a. *The Body in Pieces: The Fragment as a Metaphor of Modernity.* 1994 Walter Neurath Memorial Lecture. London: Thames and Hudson, 1994.

———. 1994b. "Body Politics: Seurat's *Poseuses.*" *Art in America* 82.3 (March 1994): 70–77, 121, 123.

Nord, Deborah Epstein. "The Urban Peripatetic: Spectator, Streetwalker, Woman Writer." *Nineteenth Century Literature* 46.3 (1991): 351–375.

Normand, Tom. *Wyndham Lewis the Artist: Holding the Mirror Up to Politics.* Cambridge: Cambridge University Press, 1992.

North, Michael. 1992. "The Dialect in/of Modernism: Pound and Eliot's Racial Masquerade." *American Literary History* 4 (1992): 56–76.

———. 1996. *The Dialect of Modernism: Race, Language, and Twentieth-Century Literature.* Oxford: Oxford University Press.

Olmsted, John Charles, ed. *Victorian Painting: Essays and Reviews.* 3 Vols. New York: Garland, 1980–1985.

Ortner, Sherry B. "Is Female to Male as Nature Is to Culture?" In *Woman, Culture, and Society.* Eds. Michelle Rosaldo and Louise Lamphere. Stanford: Stanford University Press, 1974. 67–87.

Ostriker, Alicia Suskin. *Stealing the Language: The Emergence of Women's Poetry in America.* Boston: Beacon Press, 1986.

Paige, D. D., ed. *The Letters of Ezra Pound, 1907–1941.* London: Faber, 1961. Abbreviated as *LEP.*

Parker, Rozsika and Griselda Pollock. *Old Mistresses: Women, Art, and Ideology.* London: Pandora, 1981.

Parker, Valerie. "Enemies of the Absolute: Lewis, Art and Women." Meyers, ed. 211–225.

Parkinson, Thomas. "The Passionate Syntax." Finneran, ed. 20–38.

Partee, Morriss H. *Plato's Poetics: The Authority of Beauty.* Salt Lake City: University of Utah Press, 1981.

Pater, Walter. "Coleridge's Writings." *Westminster Review* 85 (January 1866): 48–60. Abbreviated as *CW.*

————. 1873. *The Renaissance: Studies in Art and Poetry.* The 1893 text. Ed. Donald L. Hill. Berkeley: University of California Press, 1980. Abbreviated as *TR.*

————. 1885. *Marius the Epicurean.* 2 Vols. London: Macmillan, 1910. Abbreviated as *ME.*

————. 1887. *Imaginary Portraits.* London: Macmillan, 1910. Abbreviated as *IP.*

————. 1889. *Appreciations.* London: Macmillan, 1910. Abbreviated as *Ap.*

————. 1892. Introduction. *The Purgatory of Dante Alighieri.* Trans. Charles Shadwell. London: Macmillan. xiii-xxviii.

————. 1893. *Plato and Platonism.* London: Macmillan, 1910. Abbreviated as *PP.*

————. 1895. *Greek Studies.* London: Macmillan, 1910. Abbreviated as *GS.*

————. 1895. *Miscellaneous Studies.* London: Macmillan, 1910. Abbreviated as *MS.*

————. 1896. *Gaston de Latour.* London: Macmillan, 1910. Abbreviated as *GDL.*

Pawlowski, Merry. "On Feminine Subjectivity and Fascist Ideology: The 'Sex-War' Between Virginia Woolf and Wyndham Lewis." In *Virginia Woolf and the Arts.* Eds. Diane Gillespie and Leslie K. Hankins. New York: Pace University Press, 1996. 243–251.

Pennell, E. R. and J. 1908. *The Life of James McNeill Whistler.* 2 Vols. London: William Heinemann.

————. 1941. *The Whistler Journal.* Philadelphia: Lippincott.

Pike, Burton. *The Image of the City in Modern Literature.* Princeton: Princeton University Press, 1981.

Poe, Edgar Allan. *The Complete Works of Edgar Allan Poe.* 4 Vols. Ed. A. Harrison Jones. New York: AMS Press, 1965.

Poirier, Richard. "The Pater of Joyce and Eliot." In *Addressing Frank Kermode: Essays in Criticism and Interpretation.* Eds. Margaret Tudeau-Clayton and Martin Warner. Urbana: University of Illinois Press, 1991. 169–188.

Pollock, Griselda. 1988. *Vision and Difference: Femininity, Feminism, and the Histories of Art.* London: Routledge.

————. 1992. *Avant-Garde Gambits 1888–1893: Gender and the Colour of Art History.* London: Thames and Hudson.

————. 1999. *Differencing the Canon: Feminist Desire and the Writing of Art's Histories.* London: Routledge.

Pound, Ezra. 1912. "Patria Mia." *New Age* (October 24, 1912). Rpt. Spencer, ed. 367–368.

————. [writing as Bastien von Helmholtz]. 1914a. "Suffragettes." *Egoist* 1.13 (July 1914): 254–256.

————. 1914b. "The New Sculpture." *Egoist* 1. 8 (16 February 1914): 67–68.

————. 1915a. *Cathay.* London: Elkin Mathews.

————. 1915b. "Affirmations. II. Vorticism." *New Age* 16 (January 14, 1915): 277–278.

————. 1916. *Gaudier-Brzeska: A Memoir.* Rev. ed. New York: New Directions, 1974.

————. 1919. "'Ésope,' France and the Trade Union." *New Age* 25/26 (October 23, 1919): 424.

————. 1920a. "The Curse." *The Apple (Of Beauty and Discord)* 1.1 (1920): 22, 24.

——. 1920b. "Obstructivity." *The Apple (Of Beauty and Discord)* 1.3 (1920): 168, 170, 172.

——. 1923. "On Criticism in General. Et qu'on me laisse tranquille." *The Criterion* 1.2 (January 1923): 143–156.

——. 1924. "George Antheil." *The Criterion* 2.7 (April 1924): 321–331.

——. 1926. *Personae: The Collected Poems of Ezra Pound.* New York: Liveright. Abbreviated as *Per.*

——. 1927. *Antheil and The Treatise on Harmony.* Chicago: Pascal Covici.

——. 1928. *Selected Poems.* Ed. T. S. Eliot. London: Faber & Gwyer. Abbreviated as *P/SPo.*

——. 1937. *Polite Essays.* London: Faber and Faber.

——. 1938. *Guide to Kulchur.* New York: New Directions, 1970. Abbreviated as *GK.*

——. 1958. *Pavannes and Divagations.* New York: New Directions.

——. 1960. *Impact: Essays on Ignorance and the Decline of American Civilization.* Ed. Noel Stock. Chicago: Henry Regnery.

——. 1968. *Literary Essays of Ezra Pound.* Ed. T. S. Eliot. 1954. New York: New Directions. Abbreviated as *LEEP.*

——. 1970. *Cantos.* New York: New Directions. Abbreviated as *Can.*

——. 1976. *Collected Early Poems of Ezra Pound.* Ed. Michael John King. New York: New Directions. Abbreviated as *P/EP.*

Pound, Omar and A. Walton Litz. Preface. Pound and Litz, eds. vii-ix.

Pound, Omar and A. Walton Litz, eds. *Ezra Pound and Dorothy Shakespear: Their Letters 1909–1914.* New York: New Directions, 1984.

Powe, B. W. *The Solitary Outlaw.* Toronto: Lester & Orpen Dennys, 1987.

Preston, Peter and Paul Simpson-Housley. Introduction. In *Writing the City: Eden, Babylon, and the New Jerusalem.* Eds. Preston and Simpson-Housley. London: Routledge, 1994. 1–16.

Prettejohn, Elizabeth, ed. *After the Pre-Raphaelites: Art and Aestheticism in Victorian England.* New Brunswick: Rutgers University Press, 1999.

Prideaux, Tom. *The World of Whistler, 1834–1903.* New York: Time-Life Books, 1970.

Pugh, Simon. 1990a. Introduction: Stepping out into the open. Pugh, ed. 1–6.

——. 1990b. "Loitering with intent: from Arcadia to the arcades." Pugh, ed. 145–160.

Pugh, Simon, ed. *Reading Landscape: country–city–capital.* Manchester: Manchester University Press, 1990.

Quéma, Anne. *The Agon of Modernism: Wyndham Lewis's Allegories, Aesthetics, and Politics.* Lewisburg: Bucknell University Press, 1999.

Rado, Lisa. "Primitivism, Modernism, and Matriarchy." Rado, ed. 283–300.

Rado, Lisa, ed. *Modernism, Gender, and Culture: A Cultural Studies Approach.* New York: Garland, 1997.

Rainey, Lawrence. 1998. *Institutions of Modernism: Literary Elites and Public Culture.* New Haven: Yale University Press.

——. 1999. "The cultural economy of Modernism." Levenson, ed. 33–69.

Raleigh, Sir Walter. *In Memoriam. James McNeill Whistler.* London: William Heinemann, 1905.

Ramazani, Jahan. *Yeats and the Poetry of Death: Elegy, Self-Elegy, and the Sublime.* New Haven: Yale University Press, 1990.

Rampersad, Arnold. "Hughes's *Fine Clothes to the Jew.*" Gates and Appiah, eds. 53–68.

Raser, Timothy. "The Fate of Beauty in Romantic Criticism." *Nineteenth-Century French Studies* 14.3–4 (Spring-Summer 1986): 251–259.

Rawlinson, H. G. Introduction. *Selected Essays of Walter H. Pater.* London: Macmillan, 1927. vii–xviii.

Reilly, Patricia. "The Taming of the Blue: Writing Out Color in Italian Renaissance Theory." Broude and Garrard, eds. 86–99.

Richter, Simon. *Laocoon's Body and the Aesthetics of Pain: Winckelmann, Lessing, Herder, Moritz, Goethe.* Detroit: Wayne State University Press, 1992.

Ricks, Christopher. *T. S. Eliot and Prejudice.* London: Faber, 1988.

Rignall, John. "Benjamin's *flâneur* and the problem of realism." In *The Problems of Modernity: Adorno and Benjamin.* Ed. Andrew Benjamin. London: Routledge, 1989. 112–121.

Roberts, Michael. *T. E. Hulme.* London: Faber, 1938.

Rodgers, Audrey. *Virgin and Whore: The Image of Women in the Poetry of William Carlos Williams.* Jefferson: McFarland, 1987.

Rogal, Owen. "'Morbid and Fearful Conditions of Mind' in Ruskin's *Modern Painters II.*" *The Victorian Newsletter* 85 (Spring 1994): 9–13.

Rose, W. K., ed. *The Letters of Wyndham Lewis.* Norfolk: New Directions, 1963. Abbreviated as *LWL.*

Rubin, Gayle. "Thinking Sex: Notes for a Radical Theory of the Politics of Sexuality." In *Pleasure and Danger: Exploring Female Sexuality.* Ed. Carole Vance. Boston: Routledge and Kegan Paul, 1985. 267–319.

Ruskin, John. *The Works of John Ruskin.* Library Edition. Eds. E. T. Cook and Alexander Wedderburn. 39 Vols. London: George Allen, 1903–1912. Abbreviated as *WJR.*

Russell, Peter, ed. *Ezra Pound: A collection of essays . . . to be presented to Ezra Pound on his sixty-fifth birthday.* London: Peter Nevil, 1950.

Said, Edward. 1978. *Orientalism.* New York: Vintage Books.

———. 1990. "Yeats and Decolonization." Deane, ed. 69–95.

Sandberg, John. 1964. "Japonisme and Whistler." *Burlington Magazine* 106.740 (1964): 500–507.

———. 1968. "Whistler Studies." *Art Bulletin* 50 (1968): 59–64.

Sandburg, Carl. *Complete Poems.* New York: Harcourt, Brace and World, 1950.

Sanders, Leslie. "'I've wrestled with them all my life': Langston Hughes's *Tambourines to Glory.*" Gates and Appiah, eds. 197–204.

Sawyer, Paul. 1985. *Ruskin's Poetic Argument: The Design of the Major Works.* Ithaca: Cornell University Press.

———. 1990. "Ruskin and the Matriarchal Logos." In *Victorian Sages and Cultural Discourses.* Ed. Thaïs Morgan. London: Rutgers University Press, 1990. 129–141.

Schenck, Celeste. "Exiled by genre: modernism, canonicity, and the politics of exclusion." In *Women's Writing in Exile*. Eds. Mary Lynn Broe and Angela Ingram. Chapel Hill: University of North Carolina Press, 1989. 226–250.

Schmidt, Peter. "Some Versions of Modernist Pastoral: Williams and the Precisionists." *Contemporary Literature* 21.3 (1980): 383–406.

Scholes, Robert. "In the Brothel of Modernism: Picasso and Joyce." October 1995. 3 pts: 1–8, 1–9, 1–5 pp. http://www.modcult.brown.edu/people/scholes/Pic_Joy/Part_1_340.html

Schorske, Carl. *Fin-de-Siècle Vienna: Politics and Culture*. New York: Alfred A. Knopf, 1980.

Schuchard, Ronald. "T. S. Eliot as Extension Lecturer." *Review of English Studies* n.s. 25.98 (1974): 163–173, 292–304.

Scott, Bonnie Kime. *Refiguring Modernism*. 2 Vols. Bloomington: Indiana University Press, 1995.

Scott, Bonnie Kime, ed. *The Gender of Modernism: A Critical Anthology*. Bloomington: Indiana University Press, 1990.

Scott, Clive. "Baudelaire Among the English." *Comparative Criticism* 10 (1988): 267–285.

Scotto, Robert. "'Visions' and 'Epiphanies': Fictional Technique in Pater's *Marius* and Joyce's *Portrait*." *James Joyce Quarterly* 11 (1974): 41–50.

Sedgwick, Eve Kosofsky. 1985. *Between Men: English Literature and Male Homosocial Desire*. New York: Columbia University Press.

———. 1990. *Epistemology of the Closet*. Berkeley: University of California Press.

Seiler, R. M., ed. *Walter Pater: The Critical Heritage*. London: Routledge & Kegan Paul, 1980.

Seitz, Don C. *Writings by and about James Abbott McNeill Whistler: A Bibliography*. Edinburgh: Otto Schulz & Company, 1910.

Seitz, Don C., ed. *Whistler Stories*. New York: Harper & Brothers, 1913.

Sennett, Richard. "The body and the city." *Times Literary Supplement* No. 4668 (18 September 1992): 3–4.

Sennett, Richard, ed. *Classic Essays on the Culture of Cities*. New York: Meredith Corporation, 1969.

Shakespeare, William. *The Riverside Shakespeare*. Ed. G. Blakemore Evans et al. Boston: Houghton Mifflin, 1974.

Sharpe, William C. *Unreal Cities: Urban Figuration in Wordsworth, Baudelaire, Whitman, Eliot, and Williams*. Baltimore: Johns Hopkins University Press, 1990.

Sharpe, William and Leonard Wallock, eds. *Visions of the Modern City: Essays in History, Art, and Literature*. Baltimore: Johns Hopkins University Press, 1987.

Shields, Rob. "Fancy footwork: Walter Benjamin's notes on *flânerie*." Tester, ed. 61–80.

Shires, Linda, ed. *Rewriting the Victorians: Theory, History, and the Politics of Gender*. London: Routledge, 1992. 18–30.

Shor, Naomi. *Reading in Detail*. London: Methuen, 1987.

Showalter, Elaine. *The Female Malady: Women, Madness, and English Culture, 1830–1980*. Harmondsworth: Penguin, 1987.

Shrimpton, Nicholas. "Ruskin and the Aesthetes." Birch, ed. 131–151.

Shusterman, Richard. "Eliot as Philosopher." In *The Cambridge Companion to T. S. Eliot.* Ed. A. David Moody. Cambridge: Cambridge University Press, 1994. 31–47.

Sickert, Bernhardt. *Whistler.* London: Duckworth and Co., 1908.

Sigg, Eric. *The American T. S. Eliot.* Cambridge: Cambridge University Press, 1989.

Signs. Special Issue: *Women and the American City.* Ed. Catherine Stimpson. 5.3 (Spring 1980).

Simmel, Georg. "The Metropolis and Mental Life." Sennett, ed. 47–60.

Simons, Patricia. "Women in Frames: The Gaze, the Eye, the Profile in Renaissance Portraiture." Broude and Garrard, eds. 39–57.

Sinfield, Alan. "'Effeminancy' and 'Femininity': Sexual Politics in Wilde's Comedies." *Modern Drama* 37.1 (1994): 34–52.

Smith, Grover. "T. S. Eliot's Lady of the Rocks." *Notes and Queries* 194 (19 March 1949): 123–125.

Smith, Raymond. "Langston Hughes: Evolution of the Poetic Persona." Gates and Appiah, eds. 120–134.

Sonstroem, David. "Millet Versus Ruskin: 'Of Queens' Gardens'." *Victorian Studies* 20 (1977): 283–297.

Soucy, Anne-Marie. "Identification with Urban Marginals: the representation of the subject in Baudelaire's late poetry." *University of Dayton Review* 18.3 (Summer 1987): 67–74.

Spaulding, Frances. *Whistler.* Oxford: Phaidon, 1979.

Spears, Monroe. *Dionysus and the City: Modernism in Twentieth-Century Poetry.* New York: Oxford University Press, 1970.

Spencer, Robin. 1980. "Whistler and Japan: Work in Progress." *Japonisme In Art: An International Symposium.* Society for the Study of Japonisme. Tokyo: Kodansha International, 1980. 57–81.

——. 1989. Introduction. Spencer, ed. 25–32.

——. 1999. "Whistler, Swinburne, and art for art's sake." Prettejohn, ed. 59–89.

Spencer, Robin, ed. *Whistler: A Retrospective.* New York: Wings Books, 1989.

Spengler, Oswald. "The Soul of the City." Sennett, ed. 61–88.

Squier, Susan Merrill. "Virginia Woolf's London and the Feminist Revision of Modernism." Caws, ed. 99–119.

Squier, Susan Merrill, ed. *Women Writers and the City: Essays in Feminist Literary Criticism.* Knoxville: University of Tennessee Press, 1984.

Squire, J. C. "Pater and Marius." *Marius the Epicurean.* By Walter Pater. 2 Vols. London: Macmillan, 1929. vii–xxiii.

Starr, Sidney. "Personal Recollections of Whistler." *Atlantic Monthly* 101.4 (April 1908): 528–537.

Stead, C. K. *Pound, Yeats, Eliot, and the Modernist Movement.* Hong Kong: Macmillan, 1986.

Stein, Richard. *The Ritual of Interpretation: The Fine Arts as Literature in Ruskin, Rossetti, and Pater.* Cambridge, Mass.: Harvard University Press, 1975.

Stetson, Erlene, ed. *Black Sister: Poetry by Black American Women, 1746–1980.* Bloomington: Indiana University Press, 1981.

Stevens, Wallace. *The Palm at the End of the Mind.* Ed. Holly Stevens. New York: Vintage Books, 1972.

Storry, Richard. *A History of Modern Japan.* Harmondsworth: Penguin, 1960.

Summers, David. "'Form,' Nineteenth-Century Metaphysics, and the Problem of Art Historical Description." *Critical Inquiry* 15.2 (Winter 1989): 372–406.

Surette, Leon. *The Birth of Modernism: Ezra Pound, T. S. Eliot, W. B. Yeats, and the Occult.* Montreal and Kingston: McGill-Queen's Press, 1993.

Surtees, Virginia. *The Paintings and Drawings of Dante Gabriel Rossetti (1828–1882): A Catalogue Raisonné.* Oxford: Clarendon Press, 1971.

Sutcliffe, Anthony. "Introduction: Urbanization, Planning, and the Giant City." Sutcliffe, ed. 1–18.

Sutcliffe, Anthony, ed. *Metropolis 1890–1940.* London: Mansell, 1984.

Svarny, Erik. *"The Men of 1914": T. S. Eliot and early Modernism.* Milton Keynes: Open University Press, 1988.

Swasey, Robert. "The City in Summer." *Others* 2.1 (1916): 134.

Swinburne, Algernon. "Mr Whistler's Lecture on Art." *Fortnightly Review* (June 1888). Rpt. Spencer, ed. 252–254.

Sword, Helen. "Leda and the Modernists." *PMLA* 107.2 (1992): 305–318.

Symons, Arthur. 1898. *The Symbolist Movement in Literature.* New York: E. P. Dutton, 1958.

———. 1906. *Studies in Seven Arts.* London: T. and A. Constable and Company.

———. 1932. *A Study of Walter Pater.* London: Charles J. Sawyer.

Symons, Julian. *Makers of the New: The Revolution in Literature, 1912–1939.* London: Andre Deutsch, 1987.

Tester, Keith. Introduction. Tester, ed. 1–21.

Tester, Keith, ed. *The Flâneur.* London: Routledge, 1994.

Timms, Edward and David Kelley, eds. *Unreal City: Urban Experience in Modern European Literature and Art.* Manchester: Manchester University Press, 1985.

Underhill, Evelyn. *Mysticism: A Study in the Nature and Development of Man's Spiritual Consciousness.* 1911. Rpt. New York: Meridian Books, 1960.

Urch, Kakie. "The [Em] Space of Modernism and the Possibility of *Flâneuserie.*" Rado, ed. 17–46.

Varnadoe, Kirk. Introduction. *Modern Portraits: The Self and Others.* Department of Art History and Archaeology, Columbia University. New York: Wildenstein, 1976.

Wade, Allan, ed. *The Letters of W. B. Yeats.* London: Rupert Hart-Davis, 1954.

Wagner, Geoffrey. *Wyndham Lewis: A Portrait of the Artist as the Enemy.* New Haven: Yale University Press, 1957.

Walden, Sarah. "Reviving Whistler's mother: A voyage around the painting, by its restorer." *Times Literary Supplement* (14 October 1994): 20–21.

Wall, Cheryl. "Paris and Harlem: Two Culture Capitals." *Phylon* 35 (March 1974): 64–73.

Walsh, Susan A. "Darling Mothers, Devilish Queens: The Divided Woman in Victorian Fantasy." *The Victorian Newsletter* 72 (Fall 1987): 32–36.

Way, T. R. and G. R. Dennis. *The Art of James McNeill Whistler: An Appreciation.* London: George Bell and Sons, 1903.

Wedmore, Frederick. *Whistler and Others.* London: Sir Isaac Pitman and Sons, 1906.

Weintraub, Stanley. *Whistler: A Biography.* New York: Truman Talley Books / E. P. Dutton, 1988.

Weltman, Sharon Aronofsky. "Myth and Gender in Ruskin's Science." Birch, ed. 153–173.

Werner, Alfred. Introduction. Whistler, *The Gentle Art of Making Enemies.* v-xxii.

Whelchel, Harriet, ed. *John Ruskin and the Victorian Eye.* New York: Harry N. Abrams, 1993.

Whistler, James A. McNeill. 1888. *Mr. Whistler's "Ten O'Clock."* London: Chatto & Windus.

———. 1892. *The Gentle Art of Making Enemies.* 2nd ed. New York: Dover, 1967. Abbreviated as *GA.*

White, Hayden. "The Limits of Relativism in the Arts." Craige, ed. 45–74.

White, Morton and Lucia White. *The Intellectual versus the City: From Thomas Jefferson to Frank Lloyd Wright.* Cambridge, Mass.: Harvard University Press and MIT Press, 1962.

Whitman, Walt. *The Complete Poetry and Prose of Walt Whitman.* 2 Vols. Garden City: Garden City Books, 1948.

Wicke, Jennifer. "Coterie Consumption: Bloomsbury, Keynes, and Modernism as Marketing." Dettmar and Watts, eds. 109–132.

Wigley, Mark. "Untitled: The Housing of Gender." Colomina, ed. 327–389.

Wihl, Gary. *Ruskin and the Rhetoric of Infallibility.* New Haven: Yale University Press, 1985.

Wilde, Oscar. "Mr Whistler's Ten O'Clock." *The Pall Mall Gazette.* Rpt. Spencer, ed. 228–229.

———. 1910. *Complete Works of Oscar Wilde.* 10 Vols. Ed. Robert Ross. New York: Bigelow, Brown & Co. Abbreviated as *CWW.*

Wilde v Whistler. Being an Acrimonious Correspondence on Art between Oscar Wilde and James A. McNeill Whistler. London: Privately printed, 1906.

Williams, Carolyn. *Transfigured World: Pater's Aesthetic Historicism.* Ithaca: Cornell University Press, 1989.

Williams, Raymond. *The Country and the City.* New York: Oxford University Press, 1973.

Williams, William Carlos. 1919. "Supplement—Belly Music." *Others* 5.6 (July 1919): 30–31.

———. 1963. *Paterson.* New York: New Directions. Abbreviated as *Pat.*

———. 1991. *The Collected Poems of William Carlos Williams.* 2 Vols. Eds. A. Walton Litz and Christopher MacGowan. New York: New Directions.

Williamson, George. *A Reader's Guide to T. S. Eliot.* New York: Noonday Press, 1961.

Witemeyer, Hugh, ed. *William Carlos Williams and James Laughlin: Selected Letters.* New York: Norton, 1989.

Wolff, Janet. 1981. *The Social Production of Art.* New York: St. Martin's Press.

———. 1983. *Aesthetics and the Sociology of Art.* London: George Allen & Unwin.

———. 1990. *Feminine Sentences: Essays on Women and Culture.* Berkeley: University of California Press.

Woodmansee, Martha. *The Author, Art, and the Market.* New York: Columbia University Press, 1994.

Woolf, Virginia. 1978. *A Writer's Diary.* Ed. Leonard Woolf. London: Triad Grafton, 1978.

———. 1990. *The Essays of Virginia Woolf. Volume 2: 1912–1918.* Ed. Andrew McNeillie. New York: Harvest/HBJ.

Wordsworth, William. *The Poetical Works.* Eds. Edward de Selincourt and Helen Darbishire. Oxford: Clarendon Press, 1949.

Wylie, Elinor. *Collected Poems.* New York: Alfred Knopf, 1932.

Yaeger, Patricia. "Toward a Female Sublime." In *Gender and Theory: Dialogues on Feminist Criticism.* Ed. Linda Kauffman. New York: Basil Blackwell, 1989. 191–212.

Yeats, John B. *Letters to his Son W. B. Yeats and Others, 1869–1922.* Ed. Joseph Hone. London: Secker & Warburg, 1983.

Yeats, W. B. 1936. Introduction. *The Oxford Book of Modern Verse.* Ed. W. B. Yeats. Oxford: Clarendon Press. v-xlii.

———. 1954. *The Letters of W. B. Yeats.* Ed. Allan Wade. London: Rupert Hart-Davis.

———. 1959. *Mythologies.* New York: Macmillan.

———. 1961. *Essays and Introductions.* New York: Macmillan.

———. 1963. *Explorations.* Ed. Mrs. W. B. Yeats. London: Macmillan.

———. 1964. *Letters on Poetry from W. B. Yeats to Dorothy Wellesley.* London: Oxford University Press.

———. 1966. *The Variorum Edition of the Poems of W. B. Yeats.* Eds. Peter Allt and Russell K. Alspach. Corrected ed. New York: Macmillan.

———. 1970. *Autobiographies.* London: Macmillan.

———. 1972. *Memoirs: Autobiography—First Draft and Journal.* Ed. Denis Donoghue. London: Macmillan.

Young, Andrew McLaren. Introduction and Chronology. *James McNeill Whistler: An Exhibition of Paintings and Other Works.* London: Arts Council of Great Britain, 1960: 7–30.

Young, Andrew McLaren, et al., eds. *The Paintings of James McNeill Whistler.* 2 Vols. New Haven: Yale University Press, 1980.

Zinnes, Harriet, ed. *Ezra Pound and the Visual Arts.* New York: New Directions, 1980.

Index